Explaining Yugoslavia

by

John B. Allcock

Columbia University Press New York

D0905861

I do not believe that history has to be a series of swindles (although it usually has been) foisted on a brainless mob whose destiny is always to be led or driven, as one gets a pig back to the sty by kicking it on the bottom or rattling a stick inside a swill bucket. I think we human beings can choose our own fate. To some extent, anyway.

David Caute, *Dr. Orwell and Mr. Blair*, London: Phoenix, 1994, p. 188.

ACKNOWLEDGEMENTS

Since in one way or another this book has been in the making for at least a decade the task of acknowledging my gratitude to numerous institutions and individuals is immense. A comprehensive and conscientious undertaking of that duty would occupy several pages, and still run the risk of omission. There are, nevertheless, several persons and organisations whose assistance and support has been exceptional, and to whom I am happy to extend my gratitude here.

My work on Yugoslav affairs would possibly have petered out long ago had it not been for the fact that I have been privileged to work within a group at Bradford who have shared a commitment to and interest in the study of the region. The membership of the Postgraduate School of Yugoslav Studies, and subsequently the Research Unit in South East European Studies, has changed over the years. I have learned from all of the colleagues and students with whom I have worked. Three individuals stand out, however, for the consistency and weight of their support. My debt of gratitude to the late Fred Singleton has been considerable, not in the least because it was through Fred's enthusiasm that I became implicated in the study of Yugoslavia. John Horton, the Deputy Librarian of the J.B. Priestley Library, has been an enthusiastic and inexhaustable source of bibliographical guidance over many years. I am constantly astonished by the depth and breadth of Bradford's holdings of Yugoslav materials, and in very substantial measure that is due to John's efforts. Marko Milivojevic has been with us for many years, and I cannot enumerate the cups of coffee, glasses of beer, or curries we have shared in the course of swapping ideas and experiences about Yugoslavia. This book would have been the poorer without his friendship.

Other Bradford colleagues and friends who have offered particularly helpful comments either on my ideas or on all or part of the script are Alan Carling, Bob Jiggins and Antonia Young. I have appreciated feedback on various aspects of the project from Leslie Benson, Branka Magas, Hugh Poulton and Phil Wright.

No project of this kind would be possible without the aid of libraries. I have recorded my gratitude to the library of my own University, but in addition I want to thank the staff of the Serbian Academy Library and the National Library of Croatia, for assistance given during various scholarships. The Warden and Fellows of St. Antony's College, Oxford, kindly granted me a term as a Senior Associate Member in 1993, during which time I was able to complete a good deal of the reading on Ottoman economic history. I have also appreciated the grant of access to the collection of the Keston Institute.

Over the years I have received a great deal of assistance and encouragement from colleagues in several Yugoslav academic institutions. Particularly important in that respect have been the *Institut drustvenih nauka* in Belgrade; the *Institut za socioloski i politicko-pravni istrazuvanja* in Skopje; the *Fakultet za sociologijo politicne vede in novinarstvo* in Ljubjana; the *Fakultet za turizam i vanjsku trgovinu* in Dubrovnik; and the *Filozofski fakultet* at the University of Zagreb. On several occasions the Inter-University Centre in Dubrovnik has brought together distinguished and stimulating intellectual company, acquaintance with which is surely reflected at many points in this book.

Scholarships from the following institutions have contributed significantly to the ease and fruitfulness of several visits to Yugoslavia: the Academies of the several republics of Yugoslavia, via the inter-Academy agreement with the British Academy; the British-Yugoslav cultural exchange agreement, via the British Council; the Ford Foundation, via the NASEES/BUAS Joint Committee on Research Development; and the University of Bradford.

It is particularly difficult to single out for public thanks the numerous friends who have sustained, guided and lodged me in Yugoslavia. Some do stand out for the durability of our friendship, the openness of their hospitality and the richness of their intellectual support: Ivan Bernik; Simo and Zorana Elakovic; Zagorka Golubovic; Marija and Miro Jilek; Dimitar and Aneta Mircev; Milan and the late Djurdja Mesic. Above all, I want to remember with fondness and gratitude my late friend Vuki Popovic.

My Department, Interdisciplinary Human Studies, has provided a congenial, flexible, good humoured, stable and tolerant context for the eccentricities of my work, for which I am very grateful.

The debt which I owe to my family, and especially to my former wife Sheila, can never be fully measured nor adequately recompensed. The earliest recorded phrase of one of my sons was, "Daddy in Yugoslavia". I hope that this book will give them some idea of what it was all about, and why their patient bearing of my frequent and sustained absences might have been worthwhile.

John Allcock

TABLE OF CONTENTS

x

1

BALKAN SOCIETIES IN THE MODERN WORLD

It has been said that one of the principle educational purposes of sociology is to "make the familiar strange", enabling students to see the taken-for-granted world of everyday existence as something that is contingent and marvellous. It could be said, however, that in this book I set out to make that which is strange (ie. the Balkans) familiar to readers from other parts of the world. The Balkan countries have for a long time served as a symbol of otherness against which it is possible to measure European normality. Surveying the development of the image of the Balkans, Maria Todorova quotes the remark of Baron d'Estournelle de Constant, introducing the report of the Carnegie Commission on the Balkan Wars of 1912-13, in which he poses the question: "What then is the duty of the civilized world in the Balkans?". The plain implication of his question is that "the civilized world" stands outside and apart from "the Balkans" (Todorova 1997:4). In much the same way the press and politicians agonised over the outbreak of war in the region in 1992, often using the revealing description of the conflict as located in "Europe's back yard". The oddity of excluding Yugoslavia from the "common European home" in which Mihail Gorbachev claimed domicile for Russia, relegating it to the "back yard", generally passed without notice.

In reply to such images of Balkan strangeness, I insist upon the need to place the region within a wider European context, so that it is necessary to understand *their* history as a component of *our* history. Both are rendered intelligible only within a shared frame of reference which can be summed up under the heading of "modernisation". Where do the Balkan countries stand in relation to the main changes which have encompassed Europe as a whole over the past three centuries? I argue that the entire region is embarked upon exactly the same sociological process, namely *modernisation*, and that it shares this experience with the rest of Europe—indeed, modernity is global in its scope.

The concept of modernisation as it has emerged from the classical texts of sociology, especially the work of Max Weber, is summarised concisely by Jürgen Habermas.

> The concept of modernization refers to a bundle of processes that are cumulative and mutually reinforcing: to the formation of capital and the mobilization of resources; to the development of the forces of production and the increase in the productivity of labor; to the establishment of centralized political power and the formation of national identities; to the proliferation of rights of political participation, of urban forms of life, and of formal schooling; to the secularization of values and norms. (Habermas 1987:2)

The concept reaches beyond the related but narrower notion of "industrialisation". The term "industrialisation" refers to the process by which human communities have come to address ever larger and more organisationally and technically complex economic tasks, co-ordinating their actions over longer periods of time and within a wider space. "Modernisation" goes beyond this emphasis upon a complex of economic and technical relations, to convey the sense that concomitant political and cultural changes have also come to be bound together historically with these in a more or less coherent configuration. Anthony Giddens, who has emerged as one of the most influential sociological interpreters of modernity, defines it in terms of "a single overriding dynamic of transformation" along the lines summarised in the above passage (Giddens 1990:11).

The very term "Balkan", however, tends to suggest an exclusion from Europe, and hence from modernity. Before getting down to the task of analysing historical developments and specific issues in the region, therefore, it is important to pause and explore briefly these key ideas of "modernity" and "modernisation", which appear to sit so uneasily with our habitual images of Balkan society.

Modernity: modernisation

For those reared in the British educational system in particular, but probably much more generally, there is a tendency to assume that the "modern" world is more or less the same as "industrial society", and that the "modernisation process" refers to the experience of "industrial revolution". It is important to grasp, however, that the changes which I discuss here are much more general than this, in four particular respects. They can be traced over a much longer historical period. They involve change in many more dimensions than the technical and organisational factors suggested by "industry". They demand recognition of the *active* importance of local cultures as components of the modernisation process. They require a reappraisal of the nature and importance of "tradition" in relation to modernity.

Historical duration

The period which we know as the "industrial revolution" dates only from the last quarter of the eighteenth century: but the modernisation process has been afoot for a much longer period than this. The emergence of the industrial phase of capitalism had its origins in what Fernand Braudel has called the "long sixteenth century" (Braudel 1972). Max Weber's studies of the cultural impetus towards rationalisation, which he sees as central to the modern age, he also traced back to the period of the Reformation (Weber [1904-5] 1930). Immanual Wallerstein has analysed in some detail the extension of market relations which followed in the wake of the great wave of European exploration of this same period (Wallerstein 1974, 1980 and 1983). Recognising that the formation of states has been both one of the most characteristic institutional developments of the modern world, and one of the most important preconditions for other aspects of change, Norbert Elias and Charles Tilly (in rather different ways) have followed the protracted story of the European state from its origins in the late middle ages (Elias [1939] 1994; Tilly 1990).

Although industrial production and organisation only arrived relatively late in the Balkans (generally towards the end of the nineteenth century, but in some areas not until after World War II) the region can be seen to have been implicated over a much longer period in these wider developments. If we are to understand the region in relation to modernity, therefore, it will be necessary for us at the very least to adopt a broad historical vision, and on occasions to sketch historical changes of some considerable duration.

The modernisation process in the Balkans does not begin only with the decay of the two great multinational empires which dominated the region until the First World War (Habsburg and Ottoman). They should certainly not be regarded simply as *obstacles* to the modernisation process either, but as the media through which modernity acquired specific form, pace and direction

Multidimensionality

As I have already suggested in the quotation from Habermas above, the sociological idea of modernisation reaches well beyond the related but narrower notions of industrialisation and the development of capitalism, with their emphases upon complexes of technical and economic relations. Certainly modernity encompasses industrialisation, and the movement towards a "created environment", and the process of capital accumulation, with its attendant developments of markets for the factors of production. As Giddens has insisted, however, to these more familiar processes should be added other points of emphasis which may be said to have featured less prominently within the classic tradition of sociology. The modern world is also characterised by the extension of "surveillance", involving the spread of greater control of information and social supervision, and greater control of the means of violence. Of equal importance is the transformation of *symbolic* resources within modern society and the extension in range and complexity of processes of communication.

Under conditions of modernity many types of social relations become "disembedded" from their former immediate contextual frameworks (especially kinship and locality) and set free to recombine in novel forms across space and time. This process of disembedding is exemplified by mechanisms such as monetary exchange and expert knowledge, which become detached from any specific context in which they may have been generated, and are available as resources for deployment in a wide variety of social settings which are distant in space or time from their original setting.

In modern societies, these processes of distanciation and disembedding require new assessments of social risk. New structures and criteria for mutual trust must be established in order to make possible the continuation of sustained and concerted action where space/time constraints are extended well beyond those typical of pre-modern communities. Finally, although Giddens recognises that all social life is to some extent characterised by the capacity of social actors to reflect self-consciously upon their situation and their own action within it, the extent and systematic significance of reflexivity is greatly enhanced under conditions of modernity.[1] This reflection takes a wide variety of forms, ranging from the growth of scientific and expert knowledge to the spread of the media of mass communication. These cultural changes should be regarded as significant on a par with more familiar changes of a material kind.

Modernisation, then, is a complex process which takes place along many different dimensions—economic, political and symbolic (or "cultural"). There is more than one respect in which society may be said to be becoming more modern; and there is more than one way in which development along these separate dimensions might be combined. The key issues therefore relate to the diversity of ways in which the modern world is mediated to the pre-modern world, and the multiplicity of possible modes of insertion of the pre-modern into the modern. The Balkan region as a whole has indeed been characterised by its backwardness, measured by the speed and extent of industrialisation. Along other dimensions, however, it is necessary to recognise the relative thoroughness of its engagement with, and penetration by, modernity.

An earlier tradition of the study of modernisation came to be rejected in sociology because it was believed to be ethnocentric. Modernisation, seen as no more than the cultural reflection of industrialisation, was taken to be a synonym of *westernisation*. A basically diffusionist account of the process described a single model of social and technical organisation, spreading from its point of origin in western Europe, and imposing itself gradually throughout the world.[2] This approach was regarded as inadequate for two reasons: it tended to overemphasise the uniformity of that process; and it was insufficiently sensitive to the endogenous, local forces making for change.

The undue attention to the single dimension of industrialisation made for a representation of the modernisation process as essentially *uniform*. It led to the representation of non-industrial areas primarily in terms of their presumed deficiencies--their lack of industry. Devoid of the appropriate material and cultural resources, their fate was to await passively the arrival of modernity from the West. Frequently the pre-modern world was portrayed even more starkly in terms of its *resistance* to modernisation. Pre-modern cultures were characterised by patterns of behaviour or values which had to be actively discarded if "development" was to take place.[3]

The discovery of the importance of the dimension of *symbolic resources* to the modernisation process, however, runs counter to both of these impulses. Pre-modern societies can not be conceptualised as societies without culture (without symbolic resources) even if the characteristics of these cultures are not readily compatible with the technical rationality of industrialism. The modernisation process therefore cannot be depicted solely in terms of the imposition of western culture upon a cultural *tabula rasa*, or the filling of a vacuum. Neither can it be represented as the deletion of cultures which are either deficient (lacking the basis for "achievement orientation", as an earlier generation of theorists expressed it) or even recalcitrant. Modernisation should no longer be conceptualised in terms of the *replacement* of pre-modern by modern culture, but rather in terms of an *encounter* with modernity, in which the symbolic resources of pre-modern societies are deployed in order to mediate and even to appropriate elements of modernity.

Putting the matter another way: modernising Balkan societies do not cease, by virtue of the modernisation process, to be Balkan: *they are modernising specifically as Balkan societies*. That process may at present be incomplete: but we are not justified in concluding from that fact that the incompleteness of their modernisation is a consequence of the retention of their "Balkanness", and that modernity can only be attained once they have been purged of that distinctive inheritance.

Tradition and Modernity

Of key interest in the Balkans is the manner in which the past actively interacts with the present. Although Giddens makes a great deal of the importance of time throughout his work, paradoxically he does not take a very *historical* view of the process of modernisation. Time is viewed from the point of view of distanciation, and perhaps as a resource: but it is less centrally considered from the point of view of its relevance to social causation, which I take to be the primary preoccupation of the historian, and of historical sociology. Whereas in this account I do not need to address the question of how modernisation got under way in the first place, I do need to explain how the South Slav lands came to be implicated in that process; and this can only be attempted through a method of presentation which is thoroughly historical. For this reason a good part of my analysis will revolve around the notion of "tradition" and its continuing liveliness in framing and ordering the present.

In contrast to the somewhat reverential approach to these concepts which characterised earlier generations of social thought, there has been a tendency in recent social science to dismiss "tradition" and "heritage" as artificial and manipulative. Hobsbawm and Ranger have drawn attention to the importance of the "invention of tradition" (Hobsbawm and Ranger 1983). Whereas this is understandable as a reaction to the somewhat static and uncritical appreciation of tradition which at one time certainly featured in large areas of anthropology, in many respects the balance now needs to be redressed. "Tradition" is by no means only ideological and manipulative. Without presupposing the existence of the past as a "primordial" given factor of culture, it is necessary to recognise that the process of reflexively representing identity in the present necessarily involves work upon the past. The past provides the materials, the symbolic resources, with which peoples conceptualise themselves in relation to their present (and their imagined future). The acquisition of modern identities, therefore, does not consist in the simple abandonment of traditional identities, but in their reconstitution. As John Thompson puts it, traditional identities come to be "remoored" in modernity (Thompson 1995: Chap. 6). Tradition is not displaced by modernity, but subsumed within and articulated in relation to it.

To the extent that the concept of modernisation is to provide one of the primary points of reference for this book, it is necessary to acknowledge that it must be written historically. The Balkan region has been humorously characterised as having too much history. (No doubt the reasons for this belief will become apparent in the rest of this book, if they are not already known to the reader.) Nevertheless, it is primarily in relation to this past that Balkan identities are defined and deployed. This means that it will not be acceptable for me to provide a brief historical "background" before getting to the meat of the matter. It will be necessary to provide an essentially historical account, in order to do justice to the character of the relationship between the South Slav lands and the more completely modernised core countries of Europe. An approach which is thoroughly historical will also be required if justice is to be done to the relationship in which the peoples of the region stand to their own past, and the subjective dimension of the modern identities which are being created.

Globalisation

"Modernity (Giddens tells us) is inherently globalising" (Giddens 1990:61). His modern world is a single world: it is no longer a world which is polarised between the modern and the pre-modern, or the industrialised and the pre-industrial. The once popular frame of reference which divided the world into a "First" (developed, capitalist) World, a "Second" (state socialist) World, and a "Third" (poor and underdeveloped) World no longer has any place here. The processes to which he draws attention are partially dependent upon industrialisation, but also are capable of running ahead of it to the extent that the entire world is now touched by modernisation. Consequently, the "modern world" should now be understood as a global system. It is only possible to understand the South Slav lands by paying attention to the context within which they are situated. The trajectory of their development needs to be explained in relation to wider processes, involving neighbouring states, the Mediterranean region, the continent of Europe as a whole and indeed the world.

Until fairly recently the social sciences were not very helpful in providing tools which serve the kind of contextual discussion which I have in mind. After the exuberant attempts of the "founding fathers" to tackle issues relating to the explanation of capitalism, the discipline settled into a level of discourse which attended almost exclusively to the affairs of the individual nation state.[4] It could be taken for granted, for the most part, that when a social scientist used the word "society" the term was being used as a synonym for the nation state. More recently, however, a variety of theoretical tools have become available within the social sciences which have been addressed in one way or another to these wider issues, and which thereby command our interest.[5]

The project of constructing theories which escape from the limitations of modelling specific nation-states or economies (and which address those processes which

27

combine, relate or organise these entities) goes back at least to the early 1970s (Sklair 1991:2; Shannon 1989). The result has certainly not been theoretical consensus: in fact in his excellent and concise review of the development of theories of "the global system" Sklair distinguishes as many as five quite different ways of classifying such systems (Sklair 1991:10-11).[6] The theoretical projects of this kind which have emerged within the past two decades have approached the problem from a wide variety of quite different angles, extending from a concern with the general characteristics of capitalism; through attempts to explain the nature of "under-development" and the prospects for its amelioration; via the study of the system of nation-states, the superpower balance and the prospects for international governance; to general expositions of the properties of "modernity" or "post-modernity".

Probably the most influential conceptual framework of this kind to have been developed has grown out of the work of Immanuel Wallerstein (see esp. Wallerstein 1974 and 1980). His seminal approach has been described by Sklair as "the most systematic available for the analysis of the global system" (Sklair 1991:33). That Wallerstein's work is of undoubted interest and value as a frame within which the development of the South Slav lands can be oriented has been recognised by Berend and Ranki in their economic history of "the European periphery" (Berend and Ranki 1982); by Nicos Mouzelis in his widely-cited contribution to the sociology of Balkan politics (Mouzelis 1986); by John Lampe in his review of the nature or Balkan "backwardness" (Lampe 1989); and by Mojca Novak in her study of Slovene industrialisation (Novak 1991).

Wallerstein's framework has undoubtedly been surpassed in many respects as a vehicle for conceptualising the issues surrounding the theory of globalisation. Nevertheless, it seems to me that he can still serve as a valuable corrective to some of the looser usages of globalisation theory. In its flexibility of articulation between elements of multidimensionality, there is a danger that discussion of globalisation might fail to rise above the banal generality that "everything is connected to everything else". No sociology which remained at this level of operation, however, would be worth taking seriously. At least Wallerstein's "world-system" approach has the advantage of a clear insistence upon the logical and empirical priority of certain kinds of structural linkages. Elements in the system (whether or not we elect to characterise these as "core" and "periphery") do stand in an essentially hierarchical relationship to each other. I am clear that (for example) Giddens is clear on these points: but since discourse about globalisation has become a self-sustaining project we find that their importance is often lost—especially in the wilder recesses of the "post-modernism" debate! Consequently, because of the general impact of Wallerstein's work, and the seriousness with which it has been taken by a succession of major interpreters of Balkan society, his conceptualisation of problems will be seen to shape in significant measure the presentation of the following chapters.

Above all, I derive one important insight from his work, which infuses this book. He is insistent upon the fact that there is only one "world-system". His approach runs directly counter to the image of three "Worlds", with its presumption that western capitalism and state socialism stood on more or less equal footing as alternative

29

trajectories of modernisation. As Orlando Lentini remarks, however, summarising Wallerstein:

> A corollary of the vision of capitalism as a historical system, born in Europe and developed as a world-system, is that it is not possible to "modernize" and to "develop" out of this system or to leave out of consideration its internal dynamics. (Lentini 1998:137)

The story of the collapse of Yugoslavia belongs within a wider narrative of the failure of "really existing socialism" to live up to its own claims to represent a superior route to modernity. The theorisation of this set of problems has yet to be undertaken seriously; and I hope that if nothing else this book might make a small contribution to that enterprise, at least by placing the matter on the agenda of sociology.[7]

The Balkans, Europe and the World

It may indeed be useful to describe the Balkans (in Wallerstein's terms) as standing in a "semi-peripheral" relationship to a capitalist world-system: but that description does not exhaust the account. It leaves room for the fact that marginality or dependency in one form or another has been a more durable feature of the situation of this part of the world than its relationship to a specifically capitalist socio-economic system, especially if the terms of discussion are construed in a sufficiently generous manner to cover the crucial dimension of cultural dependency.

Above all, it is their simultaneous and multiple subordination with respect to different types of "centre", within an accelerating process of globalisation, which has given to the South Slav lands in particular the extreme complexity which renders contemporary analysis so difficult. One primary task of this book is to address the dimensions and levels of that problem, and to examine the ways in which these dimensions cut across or reinforce each other.

These observations, although they are of a very general kind, are not intended solely as high-level historical generalisations. They have a direct contemporary relevance, and impart a particular direction to our understanding of the fall of Yugoslavia. In particular, they have two concrete consequences which are sufficiently important to demand attention before I turn to the specific issues which form the subject-matter of the following chapters.

A popular ideological misrepresentation of the independence process in Croatia and Slovenia depicts them as regaining their "rightful" place in the West, as opposed to the "oriental" (i.e. ex-Ottoman) societies to which they have hitherto been unequally yoked. The achievement of independent statehood is interpreted as a part of the process of their re-incorporation into "Europe", and the resumption of their former relative "advancement".

The implication of the argument which I develop here is that (certainly with respect to Croatia) this is a false hope, and a misperception of their situation. The judgement of multiple marginality applies permanently and chronically to the whole region, and is deeply rooted in the past. It is not a temporary mishap which has befallen one part of the former Yugoslavia, which can now be simply remedied by a little constitutional surgery. There are several reasons why this notion of re-incorporation into "Europe" is unhelpful.

In the first instance, the republics of former Yugoslavia, separately as together, still stand at the confluence of important geopolitical and economic spheres of influence. Even if one confines ones attention to the relationship between Yugoslavia and western Europe, the efforts of different western states to engage with the Balkans has had a very diverse character, and their separate efforts have typically cut across each other, frequently replicating long-established patterns of continental conflict. The similarities are striking, for example, between the competition among different European states to shape the process of railway construction in the region during the nineteenth century, and the conflict within the European Community over their response to the disintegration of the Yugoslav federation. If "the Balkans" have come to signify conflict and fragmentation this is because the region has been the arena in which the larger conflicts of European powers have been concentrated, and to some extent conducted by proxy. The Balkans can not escape their condition, therefore, by becoming more "European", as their defining condition as "Balkan" itself derives from that "European" context. Their becoming more "European" can only be expected to make them more "Balkan".

A third and frequently overlooked reason has to do also with the differential responses of local elites and peoples to "Europe", and their perception of their own relationship to "Europe". This too has differed markedly, and the pursuit of quite diverse images of their own "Europeanness" has had its own consequences, especially in ensuring the lack of easy co-operation between the several Balkan peoples. The conflict between Serbs and Croats over the meaning of the Yugoslav idea, and the nature of any unified South Slav state, can be seen as only one expression of this wider and deeper split in their understanding of their place in Europe, and the nature of European civilisation.

It is necessary to avoid entrapment in local definitions of these differences in this area of problems. Croats and Slovenes haughtily dismiss "southerners" as not really European, but as repositories of a residual Asiatic culture derived from the Ottoman Empire. Serbs represent Croats and Slovenes as agents of the subordination of the region to germanisation. These must be recognised by outsiders, however, as purely prejudicial images which may well be rooted as much in the sense of inferiority of the peoples of the region *vis-à-vis* Europe as in any objective facts of the situation. We decry the muddle and ineffectiveness of European Community and UN intervention in the collapse of Yugoslavia, shaking our heads and saying how complex it all is. We are tempted to explain the intractability of the Yugoslav question by reference to the essential characteristics of Balkan societies themselves. These are somehow inherently beyond comprehension within the presumed terms of a common European culture. There is a grain of truth in this, in that there are clearly problems of mutual intelligibility. Nevertheless, it is important to recognise that the principal root of the problem does not lie in any essential unintelligibility on the part of the Balkans, but in the structural relationship between the Balkans and the rest of Europe (and indeed the world): and in particular in our response to them and in theirs to us.[8]

The implication of my argument is that whether we like it or not, the Balkan region is still is involved in the same modernisation process which includes ourselves. It is the enduring character of this structural relationship which must be addressed. The intractability of the problems lies not so much in the imponderable and probably irrational attributes of Balkan peoples, expressed in such phrases as "age-old hatreds", but in the nature of their situation of multiple marginality. This tends to subvert any simple attempt on the part of observers from western Europe to make intelligible the Balkans.

One of the most important of the roots of Wallerstein's theory was the analysis of world poverty provided by theorists of "dependency". The focal point of this approach was the insistence that poverty or "under-development" were not to be explained solely by reference to the presumed characteristics of poor countries. They were underdeveloped precisely because we were developed: the developed and under-developed worlds belonged together as elements of a common "figuration", and could not be comprehended separately.[9] An analogous point must be made in relation to our understanding of the Balkans. To insist upon their marginality with respect to the European centre does not place them in a world apart from or beyond us. If they are marginal, it should not be forgotten that it is within *our* margin that they are to be found. They will remain unintelligible, therefore, only for as long as we persist in the attempt to define "them" in opposition to "us", avoid the imperative of encompassing both "them" *and* "us" within a common figuration, and neglect to include them within our understanding of the global character of the world in which we are all situated.

Notes

1. In this respect, "modernity is itself deeply and intrinsically sociological" (Giddens 1990:43).

2. Probably the primary and most influential exponent of this phase of modernisation theory was Marion J. Levy. (See Levy 1966.) If not a "technological determinist" he certainly takes technology (power, tools) as the primary yardsticks of modernity. The issue is considered usefully in Robertson and Khondker 1998:31-2.

3. I have in mind the kind of view popularised by Rostow's influential treatment of the "stages of economic growth" (Rostow 1960). "The value system of these societies was generally geared to what might be called a long-run fatalism" (p.5). The process of demolishing this view of modernisation was begun my Myrdall (1968), but has never been completely eradicated from development studies.

4. Perhaps the problem was there from the outset: after all, Adam Smith did address himself to the study of the "wealth of nations". Robertson (1993) argues that in its early development sociology was better at conceptualising such questions than has often been recognised.

5. The development of theories of globalisation I take to be one of the most important conceptual contributions of contemporary sociology. For recent reviews of the field see Albrow 1996; Axford 1995.

6. Waterman (1993:2) refers to a "veritable explosion of interest in globalisation and related problems". His paper contains a useful bibliography on the topic. Robertson and Khondker draw our attention to the variety of "discourses of globalization" (Robertson and Khondker 1998:26).

7. This important topic is adumbrated in Lavigne ed. 1992, but discussion remains at a disappointingly atheoretical level.

8. Stoianovich makes the following interesting observation:

> This book depicts the Balkans as an integral part of the first Europe. Their exclusion from the new Europe and the organization of the new Europe on the basis of money and power rather than culture may result, in fact, in the suicide of Europe itself. (Stoianovich 1994:3)

9. The concept of "figuration" I take from Elias 1978. This approach to development/underdevelopment is classically formulated by André Gunder Frank (Frank 1971).

2

MARKETS, INDUSTRY AND TRADE BEFORE 1945

Some preliminary framing generalisations

There has been no period in world history during which the South Slav lands have found themselves close to the centre of a "world-economy". Although the mediaeval history of the region featured the rise of numerous indigenous states, they were typically short-lived, and usually tributaries of larger neighbouring powers. They were finally eliminated or reduced to peripheral significance during the fifteenth century, after which the shape of events was determined in many respects by the incorporation of the region into the two great world empires, the Austro-Hungarian and Ottoman, until their final collapse between 1912 and 1918.

Although these empires were large and populous states, and among the largest economies of the world at the time, they shared certain significant features in common. It has become a commonplace of historical writing about the region to compare and contrast Ottoman backwardness with Austro-Hungarian advance. A consequence of the approach which I take here, however, is that I present the economic and social history of those parts of the South Slav lands which were incorporated in *both* of these former empires, within a *common* framework. I seek to understand their relative backwardness in terms of their shared plight as occupants of what Wallerstein terms the "semi-periphery" of the primary centres of capitalist development in Europe.[1] It is these *common* features of experience which interest me rather than the more conventional attempts to explain the greater advancement or backwardness of one or the other.

The formation of a united South Slav state after 1918 brought together regions which were indeed economically disparate: but description of these differences is not exhausted by the Habsburg/Ottoman divide. The internal economic diversity of these Empires was at least as noteworthy as the contrasts between them. It is more important to note the differential access of particular regions to wider patterns of trade which did not correspond simply to state boundaries.

Furthermore, the differences in level of development which have plagued the recent history of Yugoslavia can be presented as to a significant extent artefacts of their subsequent enfranchisement from imperial control, and especially the period of their later unification. It is only then that the industrialisation process really gets under way, and the process of differentiation is intensified after 1945 under the Communist regime.[2] The unevenness of the process of economic modernisation, and the differential insertion of the country's regions into process of globalisation (which to some extent can be considered to have laid the economic basis for the break-up of Yugoslavia), should therefore be considered in important respects as features of more recent history, rather than as the more or less inevitable outcome of archaic historical patterns.

In this chapter I treat the very uneven process of the economic modernisation of the region through the transformation of trade, commerce and manufacturing to the end of the Second World War. In the next I address the specific configuration of problems which has afflicted socialist Yugoslavia, and which might be said to stem from the tension between socialism and economic modernisation.

The Ottoman Empire and the explanation of backwardness

One of the commonplace generalisations of Balkan studies has to do with the slow economic development, and in particular the lack of industrialisation, of the former Ottoman areas. While this is in part well founded, the explanatory frameworks within which the problem is posed are often misleading. Two broad and parallel avenues of explanation are typically followed in the search for an account of Ottoman backwardness. The first dwells upon the presumed characteristics of Islam itself as a source of an economic ethic. The second looks for reasons in the social and economic structure of the Ottoman Empire

i) Islam and the roots of backwardness

Frequently the economic backwardness of the Ottoman lands in comparison with "the West" is traced to Islam itself, and in particular to its supposed scriptural antipathy to usury. The argument often takes the form of a banal version of the Weberian emphasis on the cultural factors which have been relevant to the rise of modern capitalism in western Europe, and to some extent can be traced to Max Weber's own remarks about the economic characteristics of Islam (Weber 1963:262-66; 1968:576-90, esp. p.583).[3]

As Ernest Gellner has pointed out, however, it is possible to conduct a mental experiment in European history which considers the possible consequences of the success of Muslim expansion into Europe, had the Ottoman armies not been turned back at the gates of Vienna (Gellner 1981). We might just as well under these circumstances be asking ourselves, he argues, what the inner connections were between Islam and economic modernisation. Gellner's question is not absurd.[4] As he has observed, Orthodoxy in eastern Europe can be characterised as engaged in a thoroughly problematic confrontation with modernity, so that perhaps it is Stoianovich's "conquering Orthodox merchant" which requires explanation just as much as the economic characteristics of Islam (Stoianovich 1960). Gellner goes so far as to insist that in many respects "Islam is, of the great monotheisms, the one closest to modernity", although with respect to economic modernisation his discussion does not go beyond the statement of this broad speculative hypothesis (Gellner 1981:7).

The argument more typically follows a course with which we are familiar through an earlier social scientific debate about modernisation, which, developing out of the Weber thesis, sought the roots of backwardness in the lack of suitable "achievement orientation" on the part of people in backward economies. There are some important conceptual distinctions to be drawn in this area. Whereas it may be true that Islam was spread initially in Europe by a warrior caste who despised the calling of trade and turned their backs upon peaceful and productive accumulation, this does not mean that *Islam in general* can be written off as an economic dead letter and as inevitably antipathetic to economic modernisation. In any case, as Inalçik has insisted, the Ottoman Empire was a multi-ethnic and multi-confessional state. Although its ruling stratum ensured the social and political dominance of Muslims, a high proportion of its population, certainly in the Balkans, were Christians (Inalçik, in Inalçik and Quataert 1994:19: also Todorov 1991). Can it be assumed unproblematically that their economic orientations were typically favourable to modernisation? Resort to *Islam* (without further qualification) as an explanatory factor is at best weak, and at worst smacks of racism.[5]

ii) Backwardness and the structure of Ottoman society

The second avenue of enquiry which we are offered follows the characteristics of Ottoman social organisation. Until recently accounts of Ottoman economic life tended to confine themselves to discussion of the fiscal organisation of the Empire (for example, Gibb and Bowen 1950, esp. 235-58; Lybyer 1966, esp. 167-82.) " shorthand notation for the Ottoman state may be 'the fiscal state'"(Serif Mardin, cited in Issawi 1996:237). Analysis of the economic structure of the Empire therefore consisted until recently largely of an account of the organisation of the Sultan's treasury. Historians generally confined themselves to a discussion of these issues, not only because that was the only aspect of economic life which interested the Ottomans themselves, but because they believed that there was very little else to talk about.

Various reasons have been advanced in support of this belief in the truncated character of the Ottoman economy: the power of the guilds; the backwardness of Ottoman technology; the underdevelopment of the transport system; the lack of appropriate systems of financial accounting and institutions of credit. Following Weber, a great deal of the weight of explanation has fallen upon the excessive burden of state regulation, and the nature of Ottoman jurisprudence (Weber 1968:1095). Whereas there may well be substance in all of these points, they should be subjected to critical examination for two reasons.

In the first place, many of these points are factually incorrect if taken to apply equally across the five centuries of Ottoman presence in the Balkans. If true in comparison with western Europe in the late nineteenth century, they do not appear to have been true of the sixteenth century. The Ottoman economy·was not static, and consequently we should be wary of generalisations about it which are not qualified with respect to time. What is more, if the primary cause of backwardness in these regions was their subordination to an Islamic empire, as Michael Palairet has recently argued with great cogency, it is remarkable that their retardation seems to have been intensified rather than reversed following their liberation from "the Turkish yoke" (Palairet 1997). In the second place, it is necessary to distinguish between the forms of economic life in different parts of the Ottoman Empire. It is not possible to read off an account of *Balkan* conditions from a generalised notion of an "Ottoman Economy".[6]

The development of Ottoman under-development

One key to the understanding of the idea of Ottoman backwardness is *time*. As in several other parts of the world. it is possible to argue with respect to the Ottoman Empire that a period of development (including to some extent "proto-industrialisation") was followed by a phase of "de-development".[7]

i) The Ottoman Empire as an economic power

The ideal-typical form of the Ottoman system of military landholding (discussed briefly in Chapter 4) coincided with the expansionist phase of the Empire, and can be considered to have come to an end after the death of Suleiman, in 1566 (Lampe and Jackson 1982:21, 23 and 26). This change precipitated important shifts in social and political relations within the Ottoman ruling stratum. The end of the expanding frontier moved the burden of military expenditure from booty to taxation (Lampe and Jackson 1982:26 and 30). It is this period of Ottoman history which probably best fits the characterisation of the Empire as a kind of "command economy" or a "fiscal state".

Nevertheless, standing on the periphery of Europe, the Ottoman lands were positioned to meet important economic needs elsewhere in the continent, so that the "Levant trade" with the Empire emerged as a major feature of the European economy.

> Founded on wheat and silk in the sixteenth century, it (i.e. the "Levant trade") grew to include cattle, wool, mohair, hides and finally cotton and tobacco in copious quantities. .... Though subject to fluctuation in volume and content, the Levantine exports reached new levels in the seventeenth and eighteenth centuries, steadily feeding Western markets with commodities which, generally speaking, required extensive use of the land, thereby freeing land in the vicinity of the ports of destination for more capital-intensive and labour-intensive uses. (McGowan 1981:3)

Although primary products certainly made up the greater part of this external trade, manufactured goods also featured significantly, particularly textiles and leatherwork. Attention to the significance of the Ottoman lands as a European trading partner, therefore, should act as a caution to over-generalisation about the inevitability of their economic inertia. Scholarly concentration upon trade with the West at the expense of other important areas of the Empire has also contributed to a "Eurocentric perspective" on the Ottoman economy (Quataert, in Inalçik and Quataert eds. 1994: 824).

The tendency of western scholars to write off the Ottoman economy has also stemmed in large measure from the direct comparison which has been made with models of "industrial revolution", in which British experience has predominated. Discussion has been distorted by the relative lack of large factories in the Ottoman lands; by excess attention given to certain features of the guild system; and by a failure to note the importance of some very expansive sectors of manufacturing (for example, tobacco) (Quataert, in Inalçik and Quataert eds. 1994:889).

Equally significant has been the lack of serious interest in luxury goods, for which the Porte created a very considerable demand. To western scholars preoccupied with the rise of iron and cotton during the "industrial revolution" the trade in silks and spices, high quality glassware and ceramics may seem to be beside the point. Their actual economic effect should not be overlooked, our gaze diverted by a Non-Conformist contempt for "luxury"!

> In 1690 the *seraglio* employed some 15,000 persons directly in the Sultan's service: "to which one must add the "houses" of the Grand Vizier and other high officials: a population for whom luxury was the mandatory expression of power and whose level of consumption was very much higher than their average contemporaries. (Castellan 1992:134)

Economic historians of France are capable of attributing to the propensity to consume of the Absolutist court at Versailles a dynamic power: but oddly the same causal mechanism has been overlooked in relation to the Porte.

Nor was the impact of the state confined to the demand for luxuries. As Todorov has insisted, the importance of the Imperial armies as a market for textiles and leather goods as well as armaments and munitions should not be underestimated (Todorov

1991:383 and 385-6). During the seventeenth, and even the eighteenth centuries, the Ottoman economy remained one of the largest and most dynamic in the world. Preoccupied with industrial manufacture, however (and especially with the production of capital goods) western European historians have tended to underestimate its significance.

ii) Ottoman economic subordination to the West

A declining trend in Ottoman military power became detectable during the late seventeenth and eighteenth centuries.[8] Of the 109 years from the siege of Vienna to the Treaty of Jassy (1792) the Ottomans were at war for 41 years, during which time they lost land steadily in the face of both Habsburg and Russian expansion (Barraclough ed. 1978:196). McGowan detects a turning point after about 1760, whereas Keyder believes that the real reversal of Ottoman economic fortunes does not come about until after the Napoleonic Wars (McGowan, in Inalçik and Quataert eds. 1994:639; Keyder 1991:161). Whatever the dating ascribed by scholars to the gradual economic eclipse of the Empire, there is general unanimity that the causes are to be sought in the failure of Ottoman competitiveness in relation to the newly industrialising economies of western Europe.

One of the events of greatest significance here was the signature of the Anglo-Ottoman Commercial Convention of 1838. Faced with the growing military threat from Russia in Central Asia, and from Mohammed Ali in Egypt, British diplomatic support was secured at a high price, namely, through a convention which imposed an levy of 5% on the goods of foreign importers and exempted them from internal duties, while exacting 8% from domestic exporters--a condition of negative protection

45

(Issawi 1966:38-40). It is from this time that Ottoman manufactured goods, and especially the substantial Ottoman textile production, began to be undermined by the import of cheaper industrially mass-produced goods from western Europe.

Nevertheless, the overall volume of Ottoman trade with the industrialising countries continued to grow throughout the nineteenth century, although there was a continuing movement away from the export of manufactured goods towards the export of agricultural produce and raw materials. Textiles and leather goods were replaced by raw cotton and hides. A particular impetus in this direction was given by the American civil war, stimulating European demand for Turkish grains, cotton and tobacco (Issawi 1966:60-64).

During the nineteenth century also the competition between the major European powers began to act as a brake on development by creating in effect a mutual veto on Balkan railway investment. Austrian and German transcontinental projects competed with each other not only for the co-operation of the Porte, but also the compliance of the other powers. The main North-South continental rail link, which would have been of great importance to Ottoman trade, was not completed until the 1880s (Turnock 1989:143-162).

The process of de-development which can be identified during the nineteenth century is not attributable solely to the negative impact of economic and military competition with the West. There is also a place for the consideration of institutional factors, and the failure of organisational structures to adapt to changing circumstances.

The new course of Ottoman openness to external trade was signalled also by the administrative reform programme (the *Tanzimat*) initiated by the *Hatti-sharif* of Gulhane of 1839, which sought to lay the foundations of a modern salaried administration. Even so, the institutional conservatism of the state continued to act as an inhibiting factor on economic change. This was important especially in relation to the free movement of capital, and was expressed in the hostility of the Porte to admitting foreigners to take a direct role in internal economic activity. This resulted in the creation of distinctive organisational forms, designed to place "trustworthy" intermediaries between the Islamic state and the *giaour* outsider. The institutions of *berat* (licensing) and the *dragoman* (originally an interpreter, but subsequently a factor with much wider powers and responsibilities) gave a particular complexity and inertia to commercial life in Istanbul (Lampe and Jackson 1982: 31-32; Quataert, in Inalçik and Quataert eds. 1994: 837-41).

This same suspicion prevented direct outside investment in the Empire until the mid-nineteenth century, and provided a brake upon the import of foreign technology. Hence tentative attempts at industrialisation from the 1840s withered. The main area of foreign capital import was in railway building, which tended to confirm Ottoman dependency upon western Europe, supplying it with primary products, rather than establishing it as an industrial producer in its own right.

These points by no means amount to a systematic treatment of Ottoman economic history. They ought to suffice to make the point, however, that one should refrain from over-generalisation about the necessary or inevitable character of "Ottoman backwardness", recognising not only that the backwardness of the Empire relative to western Europe has varied over time, but also that this process has been shaped at many points precisely by the nature of the relationship between the two. In the Ottoman Empire it seems that we have a classic case of the "development of underdevelopment" to which André Gunder Frank drew attention in his studies of

47

Latin America (Frank 1969 and 1971). The backwardness of the Ottoman economy is not to be explained primarily in terms of an "Islamic" legacy which placed it *outside of Europe*, but in significant measure by reference to the changing character of its *permanent involvement in Europe*.

Regional diversity in the Ottoman economy in the Balkans

If it is unwise to generalise about the Ottoman economy without qualifying that picture with respect to time, it is even more risky to attempt to generalise without acknowledging its enormous regional diversity. In this respect there were significant differences between the patterns of economic organisation and integration found in Bosnia and Serbia, and those of the other parts of the South Slav region under Ottoman rule.[9]

i) Bosnian "proto-industrialisation"

In relation to the model of development followed by de-development, Bosnia presents an interesting case of "proto-industrialisation". Mining constituted a significant sector of the Bosnian economy ever since Roman times. Tuzla was an important centre for the extraction of salt (Skene 1854, Vol. II: 128 and 209; Samic 1960: 215). Arsenic and lead were mined at Olovo, copper and quicksilver at Kresevo, and silver at Srebrenica. Bosnia was noted for the high quality of its iron ore, and substantial forges operated during the late eighteenth century at Zvornik, Vares, Fojnica and Sutjeska. The French traveller Chaumette de Fosses (visiting in 1807-8) records that upwards of 2,000 people were employed in ironwork here (Samic 1960: 211-12).

A good deal of the product of this industry was utilised in the manufacture of weapons, especially knives and swords, which were taken to Sarajevo for finishing (see also Skene 1854: 209). Leather manufacture was important at Visoko, as was the fur trade. Felix de Beaujour estimated in the late eighteenth century that whereas the annual revenue from agriculture in Bosnia was 15 million francs, that from manufacture and mining was 30 millions (Samic 1960: 212). The importance of this has been underestimated perhaps because the textile production of the region was generally confined to lower-quality cloths, and therefore tended not to figure significantly in the external trade of the Empire (Samic 1960: 214). Similarly, a good deal of the product of metallurgical industry went to Egypt.[10]

Sarajevo was exceptional among Balkan cities, and experienced something of a "take-off" in the late eighteenth and early nineteenth centuries (McCarthy, in Pinson ed. 1994:61). Many Balkan towns remained mere centres of the artisanate: but Sarajevo became an internationally significant commercial centre, with French and Austrian merchant houses adding their offices to the much older representation of Ragusans. This distinctive economic profile was reflected also in the social structure of the area.

Although scholarly tradition has given pride of place to the role of non-Muslim groups in trade (Vlahs--or *Cincari*—Ragusans and Jews) in Sarajevo (and also to some extent in Mostar) there was a Muslim mercantile class of considerable significance from the sixteenth century onwards (Heywood, in Pinson ed. 1994: 31-2). It was common to find Muslim merchants, sometimes wealthy and powerful ones. Indeed, such figures held an established place within civic organisation, known as *tüccars* or *bezivgans* (Sugar 1977: 82). Examining the ethnic affiliation of the population of ten Balkan cities in the mid-nineteenth century, in relation to their occupational structure, Todorov reports that 52.6% of those engaged in "commerce" were Muslims (Todorov 1983:403). The composition of the mercantile and manufacturing groups differed between the principal Balkan cities. Salonika, for example, supported an extremely large Jewish community. In other urban settlements of Macedonia and Serbia the *Cincar* influence was strong. Sarajevo seems to have been distinctive in the strength of Muslim representation among its commercial elite at a level above the artisanate (Lampe and Jackson 1982:27).[12]

The process of "proto-industrialisation" which I have suggested here was gradually curtailed during the nineteenth century, as its products came into competition with those of the more advanced manufacturing regions of western Europe. Sarajevo's under-development was also furthered by its administrative and commercial "demotion" under Austrian occupation after 1878 (Pinson, in Pinson ed. 1994: 121; Palairet 1997).

The economic distinctiveness of Bosnia is underlined by its historical pattern of trade. In spite of its administrative status within the Ottoman order, Sarajevo's trade was never directed primarily towards Istanbul, but always looked towards the Dalmatian ports (especially Ragusa and Split) (McCarthy, in Pinson ed. 1994: 67-8). Until the end of the seventeenth century Venice was a significant trading partner.

The attractive power of the Habsburg lands began to increase, however, during the late eighteenth century, partly as a result of the eclipse of the Venetian Republic. The Treaties of Karlowitz (1699) and Passarowitz (1718), which stabilised the northern frontier of the empire, led to the opening of new trading opportunities (McGowan 1981: 23). It becomes necessary to speak increasingly from this point of a "bifurcation" of commercial networks in the Ottoman lands (Lampe and Jackson 1982:39 and 42). Even before the Austrian occupation, a growing part of Bosnian trade flowed northwards, encouraged by resettlement of lands previously devastated and depopulated by war. Railway construction enabled Banja Luka to emerge as a logging centre after 1872 (McCarthy, in Pinson ed. 1994: 69-70).

In spite of the title of Peter Sugar's respected study of *The Industrialization of Bosnia-Hercegovina: 1878-1918*, the economic impact of Austrian occupation and the incorporation of the provinces into the Habsburg state was ambiguous (Sugar 1963). Austrian annexation of Bosnia has been looked at as a stimulus to economic development in that area; but well before the protectorate was established in 1878 a substantial part of Bosnia's trade had already come to be oriented northwards and westwards. The occupation itself resulted in the confirmation of patterns which were already largely in place.

The Austro-Hungarian Common Ministry of Finance, under the aegis of which Bosnian affairs were placed, operated with an explicit and clear policy in relation to the province, certainly under the administration of Benjamin Kallay (1882-1903). "The main aims were financial self-sufficiency for the *Ländesregierung* and a higher standard of living for the population." (Sugar 1963:101) The first aim was clearly dictated by the desire not to burden the exchequer as a result of this new and internally rather controversial responsibility. The second was prompted by the wish not to be saddled with a rebellious and dissatisfied population which boosted further the Slav element of the Empire's population.

The religious mixture of the region, and its sensitivity in terms of future relations with Croatia and Serbia (not to mention neighbouring European powers and Russia) inclined the administration towards a pragmatic political alliance with the Muslim landlords (Sugar 1963:33). This dictated a policy of avoiding interference with the pattern of landholding in the search for economic modernisation. Any augmentation of the income of either the state or the population, therefore, had to be secured by other means. Consequently, when economic change did come it took two forms: the expansion of the communications network, and the promotion of primary activities-- food, minerals and to a limited extent, energy.[13]

The production and processing of agricultural produce, including leather goods, forest products, and mineral extraction constituted the backbone of this structure. Richer in natural (especially mineral) resources than the Croatian lands or Slovenia, the province did experience the limited creation of manufacturing industry, primarily basic chemical products, after 1895 (Sugar 1963: Chaps. 5-7). Important features of many of these industries were their tendency to dispersion in a predominantly rural setting, and their largely seasonal character. Such industrialisation as there was therefore created little by way on a dynamic of urbanisation and promoted a labour force which was composed to some extent of peasant-workers (Berend and Ranki 1977:39-40).

Under Kallay's administration commercial banking began to be established, almost entirely serviced by Austrian capital. After 1903, however, financial institutions in Bosnia-Hercegovina joined the movement evidenced elsewhere in the Slav parts of the Empire, of attempting to serve an explicitly nationalistic programme, opening (primarily) as "Serbian" or "Muslim" banks (Sugar 1963:242-43).

In spite of the fact that Bosnia-Hercegovina is often characterised as typical of Ottoman backwardness, by the outbreak of war in 1914 parts of it displayed a degree of industrial development not significantly behind that of Croatia. There was, however, "little by way of an industrial base or adequate financial services, and the legacy of a customs duty policy that had been inappropriate for fostering economic growth" (Pinson, in Pinson ed. 1994: 118). In many respects, therefore, Bosnia-Hercegovina may be said to represent in its uneven development and ambiguous orientation the distinctive characteristics of John Lampe's "imperial borderlands" (Lampe 1989). It is interesting to note that many of the respects in which economic activity remained "embedded" in pre-modern structures can be seen as the results of Austrian administration as much as they are the legacy of Ottoman rule.

ii) Serbian commercial reorientation

Incorporated into the Ottoman Empire in the late fourteenth and early fifteenth centuries, the Serb lands led the way in the establishment of independent Balkan states, following the second and successful revolt of 1813-15. Among the primary causes of the Serb uprisings was the dissatisfaction of the Serb *knezovi* (local magnates) with the deteriorating security of the Ottoman northern frontier region, and the threat which this posed to their growing trade in livestock. Following the abolition of the Serbian Patriarchate in 1766 the cultural centre of Serb life came to be established in the monasteries of the Fruska Gora, and the town of Karlowitz (Sremski Karlovci) within the Habsburg Military Frontier. Many Serbs were employed in the military service of the Emperor; and not unnaturally economic links also began to expand across the Danube and Sava. The seeds of this uprising can be traced to the process of economic reorientation which took place in the regions of the Sumadija and lower Morava valley, in the latter part of the eighteenth century, and especially after the Treaty of Passarowitz.

After the principality had secured a measure of autonomy, trade with Austria-Hungary gathered pace in the hands of a group of indigenous merchants. Commerce had been historically in the hands of *Cincari*. These outsiders were at first expelled by Prince Milos, and moved from Serbian towns to Zemun. Subsequently they were tolerated, and developed a symbiotic relationship with Serb merchants by specialising in imports, leaving the clique surrounding Milos to monopolise the export trade in livestock. Their Orthodox faith inclined them to pro-Hellenic sympathies, although it also facilitated eventually their more or less complete assimilation with Serbs (Popovic 1937: esp. 277-90). Consequently, there emerged a small but wealthy and highly cohesive indigenous bourgeoisie engaged in trade, and also in money-lending with fortunes made from the sale of Turkish estates expropriated after 1830. From the mid-nineteenth century, therefore, the Serbian merchant class acquired a very different character from that in Croatia and Slovenia, dominated by Austrians and Hungarians.

Serbia rapidly developed an extraordinary degree of dependency upon the Austro-Hungarian market for its livestock. "More than any other Balkan state during the pre-1914 period, Serbia found the pattern of its export growth shaped by dependence upon a single foreign market." (Lampe and Jackson 1982:173. See also tables on pp. 174 and 181.) "Between 1881 and 1893 Serbia obtained from Austria-Hungary 60 percent of all its imports and sold to that country 93 percent of its exports. In the period 1894-1905 these shares were 66 and 83.5 percent, respectively." (Tomasevich 1955:149)

This pattern was disrupted by the rise of commercialised agriculture on the Hungarian latifundia, which at first compelled a move to other crops (especially grain and prunes). The gradual replacement of the export of livestock by processed food products can be regarded as the first stimulus in Serbia towards the development of large-scale manufacturing. The wave of protectionism which affected the European states in the 1890s tended to exclude goods from the Balkans just at a time when the region was trying to gain a greater involvement in international markets (Berend and Ranki 1980:105-115.). The protectionist "Pig War" with Austria of 1906-10 saw a decline in the proportion of its exports going to the Dual Monarchy, to little over a quarter.

The pace of Serbian development throughout the nineteenth century was severely limited by the slowness with which its communications links were modernised, because of the competition between the major states for control over trans-continental rail links through the Balkans (Berend and Ranki 1980:96-98; Turnock 1989:Chap. 4)). Few rail projects did not have potential international consequences, and hence were never entirely free from foreign interference or even veto (Milward and Saul 1977:440). In 1868 the Ottoman government was persuaded to grant concessions for the building of a Vienna to Istanbul link, via Belgrade, Nis, Sofia and Plovdiv, which was finally opened only in 1888.[14]

The relative isolation of Serbia is reflected in the lateness and low level of the involvement of foreign investment capital. Only Bulgaria in 1911 had a lower *per capita* foreign national debt than Serbia. (Berend and Ranki 1980:83). French capital was deployed in the development of copper mining around Bor in north-eastern Serbia. Throughout the later part of the nineteenth century, however, various and contradictory attempts were made by the Serbian government to promote industrial development. The state exempted new factories from import duties and direct taxation in 1873, and subsequently introduced preferential rail freight rates (Milward and Saul 1977:438-39).

As elsewhere in the Balkans, the inflow of foreign investment should not be directly equated with economic modernisation. Often rail development was underwritten specifically because of its perceived military significance; and around 1911 "of the capital raised in foreign loans by Serbia 41 per cent went to finance military expenditure" (Milward and Saul 1977:443-44, and 441). International involvement in Serbian finances from the very beginning was directed as much to the needs of the state as to the modernisation of production or commerce. "In Serbia a government credit institution, *Uprava fondova*, was reorganised in 1898 into a land mortgage bank, *Hipotekarna banka*, but half its credits were made available for buildings in Belgrade." (Milward and Saul 1977:456)

As in other Balkan countries, international involvement was typically through the ownership and control of banks, such as the *Banque Franco-Serbe*, or the *Srpska kreditna banka* (in spite of its name, owned jointly by the *Comptoir d'Escompte* and the *Länderbank*). Whereas the state tended to direct resources under its control into debt service, railways or military expenditure, the commercial banks were involved directly with productive activity, particularly mining and power generation.

Although the Serbian economy became gradually more involved with wider patterns of economic activity, especially with the Dual Monarchy, this took the form overwhelmingly of the export of Serbian primary produce in return for cheap European manufactured goods. Domestic industrialisation never achieved more than a token development. The first Serbian factory was only opened in 1880 (Berend and Ranki 1977:27). By 1905 there were 58 enterprises in the whole of Serbia which could be called "factories", the majority of these engaged in textile manufacture or food processing (Milward and Saul 1977:439).

It would be a mistake, however, to ascribe this degree of backwardness solely to the legacy of the Ottoman Empire. Serbia was among the first to rid itself of "the Ottoman yoke". Even before its "emancipation", however, Serbia had begun a process of incorporation into the Austro-Hungarian sphere of economic interest. It is more fruitful to look for an explanation of Serbian backwardness in terms of the position of Serbia in a contested space at the centre of the Balkan Peninsula, and the early commitment of its ruling class to a specific and narrowly-based commercial niche, defined by a particular kind of economic subordination in Europe.

iii) The southern provinces

The transformation of Ottoman agriculture (discussed in the next chapter) which led to the creation of larger and sometimes more commercialised estates, was inhibited in Serbia by the extent of afforestation, and in any case ceased after the revolution. For other reasons, it made little headway in Bosnia-Hercegovina. This was, nevertheless, a significant feature in Macedonia. The railway from Salonika reached Skopje in 1873, after which commercial production got under way of new cash crops, especially rice, tobacco, cotton and opium poppies (Naval Intelligence Division 1944: Vol. III, 35). From 1878 onwards Macedonia's chances of economic development were constantly subverted by the endemic insecurity in the region engendered by the action of terrorist bands, and by the Ilinden uprising of 1903 and its aftermath.

Kosovo and the Sandzak were even slower to be drawn into economic modernity. Caravan routes from the Adriatic had passed through Pec, Prizren and Pristina before the abolition of the Serbian Patriarchate in 1766. From the end of the eighteenth century, however, the Slav population of the area declined steadily, and its principal commercial activity was dominated by a relatively local livestock trade with northern Albania. Economic revival began with the expansion of the Trepca mines, serviced by the railhead at Kosovska Mitrovica, opened in 1874. The opening of this opportunity stimulated some reorientation of agricultural exports towards Salonika.

Russian sponsorship of Montenegro, and the fear of the western European powers of a Tsarist fleet based in the Bay of Kotor, ensured that the tiny principality remained cut off from the Adriatic coast and limited in its trade. Wilkinson observed in 1848 that "Montenegro contains few towns. It may indeed be doubted whether any deserve that name" (cited in Warriner ed. 1965:367). Referring to the "utter poverty" of the region, Tomasevich tells us that: "it was estimated that around 1912 approximately one third or more of all able-bodied men had permanently or temporarily emigrated" (Tomasevich 1955:129). Its small trade in smoked meat and fish, and other agricultural goods such as tallow and honey, found its way to Italian markets, but largely went to the cities of the Albanian coast.

The roots of backwardness in the Habsburg lands

I have already alluded to the need to avoid over-generalisation about the characteristics of an "Ottoman economy"; and this caution is at least as necessary in relation to its northern neighbour. Any attempt to characterise the Habsburg Empire as a whole must result in a regression to some meaningless mean. The spectrum ranged from the relatively advanced industrialisation of the Czech lands to the extreme retardation of Galicia. This diversity also extended to the South Slav regions, which on the whole fell among the more backward regions of the Empire in spite of the "industrial stirrings" experienced in Slovenia or Croatia-Slavonia (Good 1984:146).

From its early beginnings in the thirteenth century the Habsburg state expanded, reaching its maximum extent and power during the late seventeenth century. Having established the *antemuralis christianitatis* on the Sava, however, the story of the Empire becomes one of slow decline. After Passarowitz (1718) Austria never won another major military conflict with a rival state (Anderson 1974:309). This military weakness was further revealed by the Napoleonic experience, but became clearly evident during the nineteenth century, when following the loss of Lombardy at Solferino (1859) and the defeat at Sadowa (1866) the House of Habsburg was gradually stripped of its northern Italian possessions (Anderson 1974:324). The significance of these events went largely unrecognised, however, so that the collapse of the Habsburg Empire under the impact of World War I came as a general surprise.

It is a paradox of Austro-Hungarian history that at one level it might appear that the political preconditions for economic modernisation were well advanced. In matters of personal freedom and equality before the law the revolutions of 1848 set standards which were in many respects unrivalled elsewhere in Europe, creating at least the potential for innovative entrepreneurial action and the free movement of labour. The historian is therefore presented with a problem in explaining why, in the event, capitalism should have made such slow headway.

i. Military insecurity and the disruption of war

During the gradual recovery of Habsburg control over the Hungarian lands a Military

Frontier region was established, extending eventually along the entire northern border

with the Ottoman Empire. This territory, which came to occupy around half of

Croatia-Slavonia, was given special constitutional status in 1578, and expanded

especially after the Turkish defeat at Mohacs in 1687 (Rothenberg 1960 and 1966).

The tenure of land was granted to settlers in return for the constant availability of

trained manpower to fight in the Habsburg armies. This area developed its own

distinctive economic regime, with land owned and cultivated in large extended family

holdings (the *zadruga*). Throughout the eighteenth century the Ottoman frontier was

repeatedly disrupted by war.[13] Even in years of peace the institutional structure of the

Military Frontier did not make for economic progress, retaining the most effective of

the labour force for non-productive activity, and isolating producers in *zadruga*

holdings.

Above all the Frontier remained seriously under-populated, in spite of the fact that

colonisation of the region was a constant concern of the imperial authorities. "By the

census of 1786-87, the total population of Backa and Srem each exceeded 20,000 and

that of the larger Banat approached 300,000" (Lampe and Jackson 1982:65). These

relatively slight figures represented a ten-fold increase since the start of the century:

and as late as 1805 it was estimated that the entire population of Slavonia, civil and

military, was only 458,044 (Demian, cited in Warriner ed. 1965:325, also 328-9). The

Frontier was capable of providing neither a buoyant market nor a basis for expanding

production. As the institutions of the Military Frontier were only gradually abolished between 1869 and 1886, this region did not really begin the process development until the end of the century.

ii) The role of the state

As in the Ottoman lands, the state can also be said to have been partly responsible for the comparative retardation of economic modernity also in the Habsburg areas of south-eastern Europe (Berend and Ranki 1980:esp.59-60; see also Allcock 1977). The reforms of Joseph II (1780-90) conveyed the impression of economic dynamism and commitment to economic modernisation, attacking vigorously the legacy of feudalism. Nevertheless, it seems that *Josephinismus* was primarily motivated by an awareness of the political and especially the military deficiencies of the Empire, and by a concern to make the economy support the state. (The Josephine reforms did not apply in the Hungarian lands, including civil Croatia and Slavonia.) Trade was viewed from the point of view of its potential for enhancing imperial revenues. (One is almost inevitably reminded of the conventional descriptions of the Ottoman Empire as a "fiscal state"!) Following the *Ausgleich* of 1867, which created the constitutional settlement of the "Dual Monarchy", and its reflection in the *Nagodba* (agreement) which regulated relations between Croatia and the Hungarian crown in 1868, there was a perceptible change of pace in economic development, although this was a consequence in part of the competition generated by economic nationalism rather than the direct result of any administrative streamlining.

A further significant factor which contributes to the explanation of this pattern was the extent to which technical and economic development was led by military concerns. This is illustrated vividly by the peculiarities of railway construction in

Dalmatia, where Austrian military interest effectively over-ruled the concerns of local mercantile ambitions (Peric 1983:44-50). The Slovene iron and steel industry seems to have retained its tenuous hold in large measure because of its proximity to the Imperial naval dockyards of Pola (Pula) and Fiume (Rijeka).

iii) Problems of communication

The railway age dawned slowly and late in this part of Europe,.as is suggested by the fact that the first line built on Habsburg land remained horse-drawn until 1860 (Gross 1976:253-4; Turnock 1989:147). Poor overland communications delayed the emergence of the Habsburg Adriatic ports as significant outlets for the trade of central Europe, until the consolidation of rail travel after 1860. The access to the Adriatic through Trieste and Fiume, which might have facilitated the rise of the Empire as a primary trading nation, never realised its potential.

As the South Slav lands were divided between Austrian and Hungarian jurisdictions they remained relatively isolated from each other as well as marginalised in relation to the main economic centres of the Empire. Early development concentrated on the *Nordbahn* linking Vienna with the German system to the north (in which direction the Czech lands developed a strong economic orientation). This was not integrated with the *Sudbahn*, however, which linked Budapest to Trieste via Marburg (Maribor) and Laibach (Ljubljana), completing the connection in 1860. Further lines connected Zágráb (Zagreb) to Laibach in 1862, and to Fiume only in 1875 (Turnock 1989:148-49).

Development was hampered by local rivalries among Slav interests. As early as 1862 a "railway conference" was held in Croatia under the sponsorship of Ban Sokcevic, intended to promote a Zemun-Rijeka line which would provide a communications spine for Croatia-Slavonia. The project was damaged not only by the action of Hungarian magnates, who saw in this a threat to the centrality of Budapest as the hub of the Hungarian economic sphere, but also by the rivalry between representatives of different towns through which alternative lines would have passed (Karaman 1991:93).[14]

Economic activity was weighted strongly in the direction of the export of agricultural produce. From the point of view of the South Slav lands, this tended to promote a pattern of communication links which fed particular export markets rather than constituted a part of an integral domestic economy. This was strongly illustrated in the grain-growing areas of Hungary, including the Vojvodina, where railway development and the growth of modern steam-powered flour milling reflected Hungary's emerging status as the breadbasket of the Empire (Milward and Saul 1977:290; Magosci 1993:90-92).

Dalmatia followed a somewhat different trajectory from the rest of the Croat lands. The decline of its shipping and the ruin of its viticulture by phylloxera left a depressed and increasingly depopulated backwater until the rise of tourism in the last two decades of the nineteenth century. The uncooperative nature of the Austrian authorities in Bosnia-Hercegovina also left the region without effective rail contact to the rest of the Empire, and dependent upon marine communication.

The distinctive character of tourism is that it was developed largely with domestic capital (although the major shipping line upon which it depended was Austria-Lloyd), organised in the main upon the civic-nationalistic principle. The local basis of its finance, however, contrasted sharply with its necessarily international orientation in the market. By the turn of the century Dalmatia had developed a contradictory and contrasting combination of the extreme backwardness of its agriculture, still tied to the *kolonat* system of landholding, and a buoyant and outward looking tourist trade, which, reliant upon marine communication, turned its back upon a poverty-stricken Croatian hinterland (Allcock 1989).

iv) Problems of the supply of capital and credit

Until the 1860s and the penetration of outside financial institutions, the major sources of credit were local, relatively wealthy peasants or small merchants, who lacked the technical and cultural means to put to really effective use their resources. As in the Ottoman lands, in Croatia-Slavonia financial services were also often in the hands of ethnic outsiders--Armenians, *Cincari*, Jews and Greeks as well as Austrians and Hungarians.[15] Their social exclusion made for poor integration of their resources towards the end of economic modernisation, as they were socially cut off from other groups (richer peasants or minor gentry, or local Slav and Magyar professionals) with whom they might have formed a dynamic alliance (Berend and Ranki 1977:31-35). What emerged as a characteristic of the culture of the middle strata, particularly in the Hungarian lands, was therefore a "conservative, romantic anti-capitalism" (Berend and Ranki 1977:33).

An early stimulus to the development of financial institutions was given by the various stages in the reform of feudal land holding relations, particularly as labour dues were commuted to rents or mortgages, and the peasantry were drawn into the market for credit (Hocevar 1965:60). The reform of land tenure began in the Austrian lands in 1857, and lasted about 15 years. In this process the Rothschild house began to play an important role, with the foundation of its *Creditanstalt* in Vienna in 1855

(Berend and Ranki 1977:22; Hocevar 1965:62). A Hungarian Land Credit Institute

was founded in 1863, and a National Small Holdings Land Mortgage Institute in 1879

(Milward and Saul 1977:294). These were state sponsored institutions, and they

played a significant role in the mechanisation of agriculture and the related

industrialisation of food processing.

Savings banks began to be founded in the late 1860s: but the Raiffeisen movement

only took off in the South Slav regions after 1885. This was closely associated with

the movement to establish chambers of trade, and emerged typically on the initiative

of local magnates (Karaman 1991:Chap.4; Hocevar 1965:Chap.3). Following the Slav

Congress in 1868, attempts were made to popularise the idea of co-operative savings

institutions, following Czech models. These caught on only slowly, however,

inhibited by the Austrian banking crisis of 1873. Indeed, the movement only acquired

significant momentum in the 1880s, particularly in Slovenia, where co-operation came

to be linked closely to the Slovene People's Party. Aggregating local resources and the

small savings of the peasantry and craftsmen, the financial potential of the savings

movement was strictly limited.

Writers from the Yugoslav region generally tend to speak of "foreign capital" when

what they mean is *Austrian or Hungarian* capital. This is tendentious to say the least,

and certainly misleading, as the region was still at the time a part of Austria-Hungary.

Furthermore, the necessity of framing their work (until recently) within a Marxist

perspective has led Yugoslav economic historians to create a history of capitalism as a

theoretically necessary antecedent to socialist revolution. Consequently there has been

a tendency to exaggerate the rapidity and extent to which the Habsburg regions of the

South Slav lands were effectively incorporated into international flows of capital in the nineteenth century. In fact international finance was slow to find its way into the South Slav lands. When it did it only acted to reinforce the patterns already established--supporting food processing and the extractive industries (especially timber products) and the infrastructure necessary to move their output. "The major European importers saw the whole area merely as a source of raw material supply and they intended to keep it that way" (Milward and Saul 1977:430; see also Berend and Ranki 1980:122).

Moreover, the penetration of such external finance as did find its way into the region should not be viewed as an independent factor. The role of the state in this respect was vital "in providing a satisfactory framework for foreign capital investment, ... the state was in numerous ways, sometimes subtle and indefinable, performing a range of functions beyond the scope of even the most international of the investment banks". (Milward and Saul 1977:319) Investment often moved in the first instance, into local government (Berend and Ranki 1980:81). British and French investors were heavily committed in railway development, as this often served the development of their own industries.[17]

v) The failure of industrialisation

A feature of early nineteenth century society in the Habsburg-ruled South Slav areas was the lack of urbanisation. In 1869, for example, Zagreb had only 20,402 inhabitants: by 1910 this had risen to just under 75,000. Only five other settlements in Croatia-Slavonia in 1910 had populations of more than 10,000 (Vuco 1948:323). The lack of vigorous mercantile centres and the small numbers of the population facilitated reliance upon craft production. Across Croatia-Slavonia noble estate-holders made some attempts to establish modern manufacture throughout the first half of the nineteenth century. An attempt was made to establish a silk mill in Osijek, and sugar refining, saw and flour mills, iron and glass-ware all made their appearance (Karaman 1991; Good 1984:145-6). In spite of the efforts of Croatian economic historians to identify an "age of manufacture" in Croatia, and to demonstrate the vigour of Croatian entrepreneurs, the majority of these endeavours deployed relatively small amounts of investment, engaged a relatively limited labour force and often were short-lived (Bicanic 1951: cf. Lampe and Jackson 1982:71-72). The mechanisation of Croatian textile production did not get under way until well into the 1850s, and handicraft production continued to play an important role.

The branches of activity which did develop were primarily concerned with consumption goods rather than capital goods, and often craft based rather than industrial. Thus the manufacture of paper, and the milling of flour, brewing and tobacco production were the main success stories. Ship-building on the Adriatic largely failed to make the transition to the new iron construction, and declined only to be revived after 1945.[18] Saw mills made up two thirds of Croatia's industrial capacity as late as 1910 (Karaman 1991:83).

The notable exception to this picture was the creation of an iron and steel manufacturing capacity in Slovenia, which after 1869 was linked to the extraction of coal in the Zagorje, stimulated by the construction of railways (Good 1984:156; Lampe and Jackson 1982:66 and 73-74). In this case the impact of rail communication was markedly different from other branches of industry, in that one of the most common causes of the failure of infant industries to consolidate themselves was their inability to cope with the flood of cheaper competition from the stronger industrial centres elsewhere in Europe. Slovene glass manufacture is a case in point. The manufacture of cotton textiles (initiated in Slovenia in 1828, with a modern mill constructed in 1837 with English backing) only survived by concentrating upon the coarsest and cheapest fabrics (Arnez 1983:200).

Arnez has noted that between 1869 and 1880 the proportion of the economically active labour force in industry in Slovenia remained roughly constant at around 12%, indicating "a stagnant economy" (Arnez 1983:170). There were centres of economic dynamism: but these were disparate, and linked often to outside rather than inside developments.

In spite of the undoubted advancement of some areas, the overall relative position of Austria-Hungary in relation to western Europe was one of backwardness. Although the Empire was Europe's second most-populous country by 1914, it produced only 6% of the continent's industrial output. "Industrial" employment amounted to 19.7% of total employment in 1890, and 22.6% in 1910. Even in textiles, among the region's most advanced "industrial" sectors, as late as 1902 Austria was "one of the countries in which the battle between hand looms and power looms still continues" (Gross 1976:265). "In 1883, when *circa* 90 per cent of world iron production was smelted with mineral fuel, more than half the output of the Monarchy was still charcoal smelted." (Gross 1976:271)

Export sectors formed "modernizing enclaves" within the economy as a whole, in a manner reminiscent of the wider debate in development economics about "dual economies" (Lampe and Jackson 1982:78). As the nineteenth century advanced, the South Slav areas of the Monarchy were flooded with cheap imported manufactures from the more developed regions, as well as from western Europe, at the expense of domestic handicraft production and infant industries. In spite of the undoubted existence of pockets of relative economic advancement, the balance of the evidence suggests that the South Slav lands were among the most backward of the Habsburg regions. Income per capita in 1911-13, for example, stood at 850 crowns in Lower Austria, and 761 crowns in Bohemia. In Styria and Carinthia, however, the figures were 519 and 556 crowns respectively: in the Littoral and Dalmatia (the Empire's poorest province) the figures were 522 and 264 crowns (Good 1984:150). Broader indicators of social development produce similar results. Literacy rates in 1910 for Trieste and Dalmatia stood at 73% of the average for the Empire as a whole; and in Croatia-Slavonia, 76%. Savings deposits *per capita* were a mere 27% of the average in the former region, and 35% in the latter (Good 1984:156).[19] The general estimate provided by Milward and Saul could hardly be more stark in its characterisation of the under-development of the Balkan regions of the Dual Monarchy: "it would be pointless and misleading for us to analyse the industrialisation process" (Milward and Saul 1977:431).

The "First Yugoslavia" and the problems of modernisation

i) The problematic consequences of unification

The economic legacy of the lands brought together to form the "Kingdom of the Serbs, Croats and Slovenes" in 1918 was a meagre one.

At the end of the nineteenth century .... the Balkan peninsula lacked some of the most important attributes for a major effort at industrialization. First, the new national states were deficient in many of the raw materials, notably coal and iron, that had provided the basis for the development of heavy industry in countries such as Britain, Germany and the United States. Second, the lack of domestic capital. .... The massive sums necessary could be obtained only by loans from abroad, but the Balkans were not an attractive field for investment at the time. .... A third hindrance to industrial development was the weak internal market. The urban population was less than 20 percent in Romania, Bulgaria and Serbia and 30 percent in Greece. The great peasant majority purchased few manufactured goods; most items could still be produced at home or obtained from the local artisan. Fourth, and perhaps most important, the population lacked skills .... there was still no large sector of the population with the technical training necessary to organize modern enterprises. .... Even more serious was the shortage of trained craftsmen or men who could readily master the technological skills necessary for the new industrial techniques. (Jelavich 1983:19-20)

To this catalogue of general problems afflicting the Balkan region it is necessary to add others which were specifically relevant to the new kingdom. Large parts of the country suffered from serious devastation as a result of the wars, which in the south of Serbia had lasted with little respite from 1912 to 1918.[20] Of the 16 years which elapsed between 1903 and the end of World War I, Macedonia had experienced eight of war.

To the direct losses resulting from the war should be added the indirect losses, such as the disruption of markets. Austria, Hungary and Germany, formerly among the principal trading destinations for goods from the South Slav lands were now defeated countries, themselves struggling with the task of economic reconstruction. Consequently the Vojvodina was separated from its former lucrative Hungarian markets for beer and flour. The security of the state was further put into question by the delay in settling essential border issues. The borders of the new state were regulated by seven agreements reached over several years, sometimes after protracted and acrimonious negotiation and the threat or actual use of force.[21]

The fact that the new state was composed from a union of former states, or fragments of states, posed serious problems of the lack of institutional integration. Serbia and Montenegro had had their own legal and monetary systems. Slovenia, Dalmatia and Bosnia-Hercegovina had been primarily under Austrian influence, whereas Croatia-Slavonia and the Vojvodina had been parts of the Hungarian half of the Monarchy. Macedonia, Kosovo and the Sandzak of Novi Pazar had been incompletely absorbed by Serbia after the Balkan Wars, and still bore the institutional marks of their recent Ottoman past (Beard and Radin 1929: esp. Chaps. I, II, X and XII). Communications within the Dual Monarchy had tended to focus upon either Vienna or Budapest; and the rather localised nature of many railway lines meant that from the Austro-Hungarian Empire alone the new state inherited no fewer than five incompatible rail systems (Mirkovitch 1933:100-11).

The creation of a unified currency system was a process fraught with contention between the interests of holders of the former Austro-Hungarian kronen and the Serbian dinar (Hocevar 1965:122-23; Lampe and Jackson 1982:378-79). The fact that the new currency was not stabilised until 1925 acted as a considerable negative stimulus to new economic initiatives, both domestic and foreign. In short, there was nothing in 1918 which could be said to characterise an economic *system* for the new kingdom.

To this economic disorder was added the problem of constructing an effective state accepted as legitimate by its citizens, on the basis of a complex patchwork of ethnicities, divided by language, religion and historical tradition. The basic issue of the constitution of the state was not settled until 1921, and thereafter remained contested. "Yugoslavia had in some respects the most difficult task of any of the countries of the region in post-war reconstruction." (Kaser and Radice eds.1985:44.)

The modernisation of the economy in the "First Yugoslavia" after 1918 was hampered before 1930 by the exigencies of post-war reconstruction, by the need to get into position the basic framework of institutions and infrastructure, and by the preoccupation of government with issues other than economic development. When it did turn its attention to economic matters, agrarian reform tended to come to the top of the agenda. Yugoslavia was defined by its political leadership in all areas as primarily a "peasant country", which in the shadow of the Russian Revolution, and the Hungarian "Soviet" at the end of the First World War, meant that the foremost political problem was to head-off rural unrest.

The early post-war years did see some industrial advancement in Slovenia, in the development of hydro-electric power, redressing to some extent the relative scarcity of mineral fuels. Here Swiss and Czech capital played an important role, as it did in industrial development based upon this infrastructure, particularly in the expansion of textile manufacture, domestic hardware and glass. British money was also invested in lead mining (Hocevar 1965:163). Generally speaking, however, the lack of a sense of economic direction meant more of the same--an economy based principally upon the extraction and export of primary products.

ii) The impact of the world financial crisis

Directly or indirectly, a change of economic orientation in Yugoslavia (as it was named after 1929) was precipitated by the world economic crisis. To the impact of the American stock market crash of 1929 must be added the ripples created by the Austrian *Creditanstalt* crisis of 1931. At the same time Yugoslavia suffered appreciably from the effects of the "Hoover Moratorium" on the payment of German war reparations in 1931, prompting the imposition of drastic exchange controls (Kaser and Radice eds. 1986:32-33). Emigrant remittances all but dried up, and indeed migrant labour began to return to the country. Export trade was crippled by the system of clearing, until this was circumvented by Germany's active exploitation of the weakness of the Balkan economies in order to boost its own trade and industry after 1934 (Kaser and Radice eds. 1985:57-61 and Chapter 7; Naval Intelligence Division 1944: Vol. III, 168).

The effects of these events were uneven. The impact of depression was catastrophic upon trade, so that between 1928 and 1932 the terms of trade for Yugoslavia deteriorated by some 14% (for its primary markets in agriculture by more than 30%). Nevertheless, one effect of depression was to reduce the burden of external debt, so that the ratio of debt service to exports fell from 23% in 1931 to 9% by 1937 (Kaser and Radice eds. 1985:5 and 18). Slovene textile production and steel making actually grew during the depression, by replicating a pattern familiar to the under-developed world, utilising imported machinery pensioned off from elsewhere (Hocevar 1965:134).

Things began to take a different course after 1931 for several reasons. The gradual emergence of the world from economic crisis had two specific effects in Yugoslavia. There was a relative waning of French economic influence, and in accordance with the policy of *Grossraumswirtschaft* Yugoslavia's trade became more closely integrated with Germany (Kaser and Radice eds. 1985: Vol.I, 59-62, 292-6 and 444-6). The discovery of the Dalmatian coast as a major European tourist destination gave a considerable boost to Yugoslavia's export balance. The flow of foreign visitors passed the quarter of a million mark, spending more than 1.5 million bed-nights in Yugoslav accommodation, in 1935 (Savezni Zavod za Statistiku 1989:339-40; Allcock 1989). By 1936 earnings from tourism represented the second largest non-goods item (after emigrant remittances), with a balance of 179 million dinars (£648,000:Tomasevich 1949:196; Mirkovitch 1933).

Overall economic progress was slow, even in comparison with that of other Balkan countries. Net growth of industrial output 1929-1939 was 32%; but this compared poorly with rates of 43% for Romania, 75% for Greece and 143% for Bulgaria. *Per capita* national income grew in the same period by 2%; but this compared with 8% for Romania, 11% for Greece and 35% for Bulgaria (Spulber 1963:358-59).

iii) The role of the state

A feature of both the Habsburg and Ottoman legacies to the unified South Slav state was the propensity of the state to intervene in the working of economic institutions. The state continued to have a significant influence upon the direction of economic change, although that influence largely tended to embody the inherited traditions of regulatory control rather than any modern concept of the role of government as a catalyst of economic development. Although the Yugoslav government did adopt more or less consistent policies of protection with respect to domestic manufactures, this was not backed by an effective policy of import substitution. Handicraft production continued to decline, to be replaced by mass-produced goods from western Europe. In the period of nationalistic struggle after unification, the Belgrade-based central government sought to weaken the links of the Zagreb banks with Vienna, actually destabilising for some time the country's financial institutions (Spulber 1963: 357).[22]

State-owned enterprises included those dealing with transport, and the exploitation of forests and mines, as well as more common activities such as the postal system. In the period 1926-38 these sources (not including the state monopolies on commodities such as salt, petrol and matches) provided between 28-39% of government revenues (Dimitrijevic1962:14; Naval Intelligence Division 1944: Vol. III, 258).

The level of military expenditure continued to be very high: and this was reflected in patterns of industrial construction. The state arsenals in Kragujevac and Sarajevo emerged as among the largest manufacturing enterprises in the country.[23] The greater part of directly controlled state investment, however, was relatively unproductive, absorbed by expenditure on government buildings and other similar projects (Kaser and Radice eds. 1985:291).

Rudolf Bicanic has summarised the dominating economic role of the state across the inter-war years. "The state is the biggest employer .... the biggest entrepreneur .....the biggest purchaser .... the biggest trader .... the biggest organiser and owner of the means of transport .... the biggest accumulator of capital .... the biggest financier ....

the biggest regulator of exchange and the organiser of both internal and external

trade". (Bicanic 1938:202)

iv) The role of foreign investment

The financial structure of the country retained the characteristic lineaments of

underdevelopment and dependency. The inter-war years have been depicted as the

hey-day of the penetration into the Balkans of foreign capital (Vuco 1948; Kukoleca

1941 and 1956; Bicanic 1951; Dimitrijevic 1962). Tomasevich has noted that the total

foreign investment in private corporations in Yugoslavia at the end of 1937 amounted

to 33 per cent of all corporate financial resources (Tomasevich 1949:188). It is true

that in this period there was an appreciable influx of funds from abroad: but it is

important to note certain limitations which have led to the exaggeration of its

significance.

I have already noted of the pre-unification period that Yugoslav writers have a

tendency to treat Austrian and Hungarian ownership as evidence of "foreign

investment". Although there was some repatriation of capital after 1918, former

proprietors often sustained an interest in Yugoslav holdings after the war. This results

in "foreign investment" by default. Furthermore, it is essential to distinguish foreign

involvement from foreign *investment* in two respects. A good deal of the participation

by foreign companies took the form of the secondment of specialist personnel rather

than the commitment of funds. Finally, it is important to separate productive

investment from the holding of government stock (Kaser and Radice eds.1985:292).

By far the most important destination of overseas investment within Yugoslavia was the government itself, often in association with the armament programme, but also for other purposes such as the stabilisation of the currency, the support of the state's needs for funds in excess of the yield from taxation, or the service of former debts. A very substantial proportion of what has been indiscriminately lumped together as "foreign investment" (particularly by Yugoslav commentators) was no more than international holdings of public debt, 82.5% of which was in foreign hands in 1937 (Kaser and Radice eds. 1985:292).

For these reasons it seems that in place of the predominant Yugoslav emphasis upon the penetration of foreign capital as the primary feature of the economic history of the period, the view of Lampe and Jackson offers an alternative assessment. "The two decades that began with the Depression and ended with the consolidation of Communist power everywhere in Southeastern Europe except Greece served to isolate the area from European trade and finance." (Lampe and Jackson 1982:434)

Unless these qualifying clauses are considered it is possible to gain a somewhat distorted view of the nature of Balkan economic development. Herein lies yet another significant continuity with the pre-1914 situation, in that rudimentary *domestic* accumulation was relatively far more significant than has often been allowed for. The problem was often not that no domestic saving was available, but that given a shortage of investment capital and a diversity of opportunities not all needs could be satisfied. An underestimated factor in this respect has been the impact of the land reform programme, which created a vast market for relatively secure mortgages against which the relatively more risky industrial initiatives found it difficult to compete. As a consequence, a huge volume of potential credit was tied up irrecoverably when the government announced in 1931 a moratorium on peasant debt.

iii) Patterns of regional difference

In spite of the effort made in pursuit of industrialisation between the wars, Yugoslavia remained an overwhelmingly agrarian economy. The census of 1921 reported 78.9% of the working population as engaged in agriculture, fishing and forestry, and by 1931 this figure had fallen only to 76.3%. (Naval Intelligence Division 1944: Vol. III, 2. The figures for industry and mining were 9.9% and 10.8% respectively.) The degree of its dependence upon agriculture is partially concealed by the statistical artificiality of the notion of "industry", as by far the greater part of its manufacturing industry was concerned with the elementary processing of agricultural produce, and this pattern was also reflected in the structure of its exports.

There were areas which had experienced a rudimentary industrialisation. In Slovenia these were localised largely around Ljubljana, Celje and Maribor, and the steel-making capacity of Jesenice. In Croatia-Slavonia, with the exception of timber (dispersed along the Podravina) and flour milling, industrialisation was mainly confined to the region around Zagreb, with subsidiary centres in Osijek and Slavonski Brod.[24] In the Vojvodina and Srijem only Novi Sad, Subotica and Zemun stood out as industrial centres, although milling and sugar manufacture were fairly widely dispersed. In Serbia, in addition to the development of mining in the vicinity of Bor, Majdanpek, Senj and Zajecar, and the state arsenals at Kragujevac, any industrial activity was limited to the area around Belgrade, the development of which was also boosted by its adoption as the new state capital. Mining was fairly widely dispersed in

Bosnia, but in addition to Sarajevo perhaps only Zenica, Vares and Tuzla could be characterised as industrial towns.[25] Elsewhere the industrial presence was at token levels.

The development of a technically and organisationally modernised economy was not limited to "industry" in the narrower sense; and there were also limited areas in which, in spite of the disruption of the Land Reform, there was appreciable *rural* development (see Chap. 4). It is worth noting also the persistence of areas of economic backwardness, which were identifiable even within regions which have been generally characterised as economically more advanced. The upland regions of Slovenia, in the absence of the more recent development of tourism, including the Pohorje and the karst areas, remained persistently depressed, and like their Croatian counterparts suffered a steady drain of population. With the exception of those coastal settlements touched by tourism and commercial viticulture, the Croatian countryside south of Ogulin was characterised by the most desperate poverty (Bicanic 1981 [1936]). Slovenia, southern Croatia and Dalmatia, much of Bosnia-Hercegovina and Montenegro were never able to meet their own requirements for grain. Consequently, there were acute discrepancies of view regarding the likely benefits of tariff protection for different sectors of the economy (Lampe and Jackson 1982:402-415).

In spite of early attempts by Belgrade to inhibit the process, and the extension of the sphere of operations of the Slovene banks into the Croat lands, Zagreb emerged as the primary centre of commercial banking (Hocevar 1965:164-65; Lampe and Jackson 1982:397). An important factor limiting the power of Slovene capital was the division of Slovene financial institutions into commercial banks and savings co-operatives, the latter especially serving an strictly local remit.

Although parts of Slovenia retained their position among the more economically advanced regions of Yugoslavia in the inter-war years, it is important to note that in overall terms Slovenia did not extend its lead in this period: in fact measured by some indices the degree of regional disparity was reduced. (Table 3.1. See also Kukoleca 1941:78-9.)

Table 3.1: Change in the number of workers in Selected Industries: Slovenia and Yugoslavia--1933-1936

	Increase or decrease (-), percent	
	Slovenia*	Yugoslavia
Textiles	42.5	66.6
Clothing	00.0	54.0
Metallurgy and metalworking	12.0	33.0
Lumber and wood products	-3.0	25.0
Shoes	-4.0	12.0
Leather	13.0	42.0
Paper	13.0	28.0
Printing	12.0	15.0

* Dravska banovina

Source: Hocevar 1965:141

Several reasons can be adduced to explain this pattern. The Slovene economy and that of the Vojvodina were disrupted particularly by separation from their former markets in the Dual Monarchy. Yugoslav government policy actively favoured a "Danubian" orientation, which focussed public support for development elsewhere. The effects of this were seen most obviously in the pattern of inter-war railway construction. This pattern of industrial location was modified significantly by the strategic thinking which prompted the shifting of the armaments industry into central Bosnia. Hocevar has drawn attention also to the importance of disparate wage levels, by which Slovene industry found itself undercut by the cheaper labour force available in other areas of the country (Hocevar 1965:140-42). This pattern of events contrasts strongly with that observed in Yugoslavia after 1945.

The economic impact of the Second World War

In treating the economic history of Yugoslavia two tendencies can commonly be observed with respect to the events of 1941-45. Either the period is passed over altogether, as a hiatus in economic activity, or attention centres upon the effects of the war, and in particular upon Yugoslavia's wartime losses.

> .... Some 82.000 buildings had been destroyed, 3.5 million people were homeless, and an estimated 35 per cent of prewar industry .... had been lost or put out of operation. Over 50 per cent of railway trackage, 77 per cent of locomotives and 84 per cent of wagons had been destroyed. (Rusinow 1977:19; cf. Kaser and Radice eds. 1986:509)

Without wishing to minimise the damage and suffering occasioned by war, to confine discussion to this aspect of its importance is to present an unbalanced picture. The consequences were in many respects less disruptive than those of World War I, although with important sectoral and regional differences.[26]

An early consequence of occupation was the German take over of former state industries, the property of foreign nationals (in which they included Jews), and the nationalisation of key industrial sectors (Kaser and Radice eds. 1986:332-6 and 342-3). The key role played in this respect by local *Volksdeutsche* made them particularly exposed targets for expropriation after the war. Increasingly centralised control of aspects of economic life in support of the Axis war effort built upon the foundation of a pre-war state already inclined to active intervention. "The role of the state ministries is the obvious point of continuity" (Lampe and Jackson 1982:530). In diverse ways, therefore, the experience of war prepared the ground for the regime of nationalisation under the Communists after 1945 (Jelavich 1983:384-5).

The dismemberment of Yugoslavia fragmented the country into seven different currency zones, leaving a legacy of acute financial confusion, but drew the major centres of financial activity into closer association with the systems of the Axis powers. The extent of active collaboration by the Zagreb banks resulted in their subsequent discredit, and was a factor in the shift of the financial centre of gravity to Belgrade after 1945 (Lampe and Jackson 1982:551-3).

Production was to be subordinated to the needs of the Axis war machine: and this was particularly effective in the case of mineral extraction. Surprisingly, perhaps, in this respect several sectors of Yugoslav industry actually *increased* their output during the war years. This came about in some cases because of additional investment in new capacities, or in relevant infrastructure, especially where this also served military needs. Modern installations were constructed, for example, to further the extraction of molybdenum near Vranje (Kaser and Radice eds. 1986:355 and 406). Copper became almost the scarcest of minerals, and there was some reconstruction of the copper mining plant at Bor (Lampe and Jackson 1982:569; Kaser and Radice 1986:408). Mineral extractive, metalurgical and engineering industries were expanded in those areas of Slovenia which were incorporated directly into the *Reich*. (The aluminium factory near Ptuj, was constructed specifically to serve the German war effort.) The benefits of increased levels of industrial activity were not reaped by the local population, however, as the costs both of additional investment, and where possible the costs of Axis occupation, were also shifted onto them.[27]

The picture was, of course, uneven. Plants producing consumer goods, especially where they became cut off from former markets by the war, were allowed to atrophy. In the final phases of the war the Germans shipped large quantities of machinery back to the *Reich*, especially from Serbia. Serbia also was made to bear the burden of forced labour in Germany. Bosnian industry was disrupted especially by the *Partizan* war effort. In many cases, however, shortage of fuel was as serious an impediment to continued production as the direct impact of war.

To some extent, therefore, the pattern of nationalisation embarked upon by the post-1945 government may be looked upon as prefigured within the wartime period.[28] Already by December 1945 the sequestration of the property of foreign nationals and collaborators had placed in the hands of the state 53% of all industrial capacity (in Slovenia 69%) (Lampe and Jackson 1982:570-71). A significant proportion of the early economic measures of Tito's regime reflect characteristically nationalist rather than specifically Communist approaches to problems--not only state appropriation of the property of foreign nationals, but also the currency reform and the agrarian reform of 1945.

Conclusion

The part of the Balkan Peninsula upon which Yugoslavia was constructed is very diverse geographically and culturally. The trajectories of historical change through which its several regions have passed have been disparate in many ways. The different levels of this diversity left their mark in terms of contrasting degrees of economic modernisation by the end of the Second World War. In the past these features of the region have been allowed to eclipse other factors which, from a sociological point of view, may be said to be equally important. In this chapter I have drawn attention to their *common heritage* as semi-peripheral areas with respect to the emergence of a dominant European capitalism.

By the time of the formation of the "Second Yugoslavia" in 1945, in spite of the "industrial stirrings" detectable in parts of Slovenia, Croatia and Bosnia, Yugoslavia was still predominantly a peasant society, in which three quarters of its population still obtained their living by working the land. The process of economic modernisation in many respects had barely begun. Nevertheless, as I have endeavoured to demonstrate here, the entire region can already be seen to have become inserted into much wider European and even global processes of production and exchange. In that respect, along with other countries of the Balkan region, Yugoslavia had become established as a supplier of food and industrial raw materials, marketed for processing and consumption in the more developed countries of western Europe. In many areas tentative steps towards the development of indigenous manufacturing industry had been halted, and infant industries overwhelmed by the import of mass-produced articles from the West.

This situation of dependency and under-development contributed directly to the dissatisfaction which enabled the Communist Party of Yugoslavia between 1941 and 1945 to turn a "War of National Liberation" against Axis occupation into a socialist revolution. The story of the attempt to change that state of affairs, and to use socialism as an instrument of modernisation in Yugoslavia, occupies my next chapter.

Notes

1. The utility of this conceptual framework with respect to the Habsburg Empire has been questioned in Balazs 1997. Note, however, that the period covered by her work ends in 1800, and in any case her work is notable for its silence on the South Slav parts of the Hungarian kingdom. Even if her objections hold good for Bohemia they do not challenge my claim with respect to the Balkans.

2. It was only as this work approached completion that I encountered the recent work of Michael Palairet (1997), which provides a magisterial survey of the economic "evolution" of those parts of the Balkan region formerly under Ottoman rule. I would like to have had the opportunity to use it more fully and systematically as a source. His primary thesis can be summed up as follows:

> The Balkan countries were not drawn into the main stream of European economic development before 1914. It is nevertheless common currency that even this most retarded of European regions was slowly modernizing, and that from the end of the nineteenth century, the hitherto infinitesimal tempo of change was speeding up, and resulted in slow, faltering, but still significant economic growth. This book takes a different view. The Balkan countries were subject to a distinct evolutionary dynamic which was not intrinsically developmental, but this dynamic was overlaid in the different territories studied by changing institutional arrangements which temporarily caused performance to deviate from a long-run declining trend. (p.1.)

Three important points can be made in relation to the potential relevance of his thesis for my own work. It is important to be clear about the sense in which one uses the term "modernisation". I believe that the sense in which I have used it, which includes the monetisation and commoditisation of peasant economies, is not inconsistent with Palairet's argument. I want to question the impression that is given by (perhaps one reading of) his thesis, that the Balkan economies somehow stood apart from the wider patterns of European economic change. I am persuaded by his argument that the region was "not drawn into the main stream of European economic development", but I believe that my thesis is still correct, that the Balkan countries bore a considerable impact of that developmental process. I have expressed this in Frank's terms as the "development of under-development". Their backwardness can be regarded as in part a consequence of the nature of their contact with metropolitan Europe. Finally, it is important to note that Palairet's work is tangential to the wider point that I have affirmed at several points in this book, which challenges the view which is also "common currency", that the economic and social history of the region falls neatly into contrasting "Habsburg" and "Ottoman" patterns. I would be interested to see his analysis extended in its application to include the Austro-Hungarian sphere of influence, as I believe that several of the processes to which he has drawn attention could be identified with equal clarity there also.

3. Those familiar with the economic history of the Indian Ocean must be aware of the importance there of the Arab trader. The penetration of capitalism into East Africa was largely carried by the "Levantine", and by Asians, many of whom were Muslims. Weber himself observes that "the Tartars in the Russian Caucasus are often very 'modern' entrepreneurs" (Weber 1968:1095). See Turner 1992: Chap. 3.

4. Gellner does address other issues relating to Islam and modernity, especially the question of the link between Islamic universalism and the development of the modern nation (Gellner 1983).

5. Inalçik also poses the pertinent question that perhaps the notion of backwardness as a specifically Ottoman legacy is questionable because it can have no relevance to the explanation of backwardness in

areas which were never touched by Ottoman rule. (Inalçik and Quataert eds. 1996:19.) It is instructive

to bear in mind the caution expressed by Lewis in relation to Ottoman historiography.

> Western scholars .... Have been influenced by the national historiographical legends of the
>
> liberated former subject peoples of the [Ottoman] Empire in Europe and Asia. They have tended
>
> to blame all the defects and shortcomings of their societies on the misrule of their fallen
>
> imperial masters, and have generalized the admitted failings of Ottoman government in its last
>
> phases into an indictment of Ottoman civilization as a whole. (Lewis 1970:215)

6. Both of these ideas are developed fully and authoritatively in Palairet 1997. It is unfortunate that I

became acquainted with his work too late to take full advantage of it in the preparation of this book.

Nevertheless, I am happy to emphasise its scholarly significance.

7. The problem is discussed by Caglar Keyder, who refers both to the "well-established" nature of the

debate about de-industrialisation, although he concedes that theoretical consensus in this area is backed

by relatively little scholarship (Keyder 1991:162-63).

8. There is a diversity of views among economic historians about the timing and causation of the

reversal of Ottoman economic fortunes. During the sixteenth century, the opening of long distance sea-

going trade routes pulled the rug from under the land-based traditional caravan route as the means of

supplying several highly-priced commodities to European markets (McGowan 1981:19). It has also

been argued that changes in world bullion flows following upon European conquests in the Americas

had a strongly deleterious effect upon the Ottoman monetary system (Lampe and Jackson 1982:29-30).

These factors perhaps should be considered only to have laid the ground-work for de-development,

however, rather than counted among its primary causes. Cf. Palairet 1997.

9. Cf. For further and fuller consideration of these issues, Palairet 1997.

10. The importance of this general issue has been underlined by Donald Quataert. "International

commerce has been the most widely discussed topic in Ottoman social and economic history while trade within the Empire as well as Ottoman commerce with Egypt, Iran and India have been neglected almost totally." He argues that this results in a considerable misrepresentation of the balance of Ottoman economic activity, and an underestimation of its scale. (Inalçik and Quataert eds. 1994:824)

11. There is some obscurity and indeed controversy about who were the *Cincari*—indeed as to whether there was a single ethnic group to which the name *Cincar* should apply (as with the Jews), or whether it was a rather loose and general epithet applied to many foreign mercantile groups. The most systematic and thorough study is Popovic 1937. The difficulty stems in part from the fact that Greek remained even into the nineteenth century as the principal language of commerce in the region, used equally by groups of very different provenance. (Anybody wishing to explore at first hand the ambiguities in this area should spend an afternoon in Krusevo graveyard, in Macedonia.) I tend to favour the view that *Cincari* can be shown to emerge as a fairly coherent group both in terms of their internal and external identification, from the semi-nomadic Vlah drovers and cattle-traders who were widely dispersed in the Balkans.

12. In the absence of further sociological and historical research interpretation of these facts must remain speculative. Nevertheless, what (one might ask) was the essential, sociologically relevant difference between a Muslim *tüccar* and a Christian, Ragusan merchant? Why should the former be regarded as representing economic backwardness and lack of dynamism, and the latter presage the rise of capitalism? Heywood's phrase (applied in another context) seems to be apposite in this case, that "latter-day demonologies and national religious myths .... have done their part in blurring the issue" (Heywood, in Pinson ed. 1993:32).

13. Railway building, although it did have consequences for the civilian economy, was motivated as often as not by military considerations.

14. By the end of the nineteenth century, however, only Finland was lower than Serbian the European league-table of length of line per head of population. Only Norway, Finland and Russia were worse-off

than Serbia in terms of km. of line per sq. km. of land area. (Berend and Ranki 1980: Tables 5.11 and 5.13. Also Lampe and Jackson 1983:211)

15. The Austro-Hungarian Empire was at war with Turkey in 1683-99; 1716-18; 1737-39; and 1788-91.

16. This project was eventually realised in 1891.

17. Around the turn of the century, railways accounted for 40% of all British and 50% of all French capital exports (Berend and Ranki 1980:79-80). This investment was not always directed for the benefit of the locality (Milward and Saul 1977:429). Berend and Ranki comment upon the priority given to international lines and the neglect of local economic needs (1980:126).

18. The backwardness of Croatian industry is suggested by the foundation in Rijeka in the 1850s of a mill for the manufacture of sails!

19. It is interesting that, with respect to these wider indices of economic and social advancement, the Slovene lands were clearly differentiated from Croatia. It is worth noting also that in the period covered by Good's figures (1890-1910) the degree of differentiation between the provinces of the Empire actually increased, with Croatia falling relatively further behind. No figures are provided for Bosnia-Hercegovina, but cf. Palairet 1997. Chap. 8.

20. Serbia alone lost 275,000 men, or almost 40% of those mobilised, a half of its industrial equipment, and a third of its plants (Jelavich 1983:136; Lampe and Jackson 1982:407). For the impact of the Balkan Wars, see Kennan ed. 1993. Some regions actually gained from the war. Mining in Bosnia, for example, using prisoner of war labour, was given an important boost by the Central Powers during the war years (Naval Intelligence Division 1944: Vol. III, 166).

21. For a fuller discussion of these issues, see below Chapter 7.

22. The theory of a Belgrade-based conspiracy against Zagreb (of which the foremost advocate has been Rudolf Bicanic) needs to be treated with caution when it comes to accounting for the difficulties experienced by Croatian firms in raising loans later in the period (Bicanic 1938:28-9 and 41). Croatian banks themselves were by no means averse to weakening their nationalistic principles when better investment opportunities were available in the capital! (Lampe and Jackson 1982:390-91 and 410).

23. The development of Bosnian military industry also illustrates the importance of growing economic ties with Germany during the thirties. The Zenica factory was re-equipped by Krupp in 1938 (Naval Intelligence Division 1944: Vol. III, 169).

24. Karaman provides a valuable map indicating changes in the distribution of industrial plants in Croatia up to 1910 (Karaman 1991:217). There is little reason to believe that the distributional pattern changed significantly in the inter-war years.

25. A methodological difficulty attaches to the task of estimating the scale and significance of "industrialisation" throughout the South Slav lands. It is evident that commentators use diverse criteria as to what constitutes a "factory", or an "industrial" establishment. Mallat remarks that *"le grand atelier n'existe pas encore en Serbie"*, distinguishing *"ouvriers"* from *"magasiniers"* and *"boutiquiers"* (Mallat 1902:205). There is doubt as to whether Karaman's figure for northern Croatia in 1910 is based upon the same assumptions as those used by Olivier in his account of Bosnia-Hercegovina (Karaman 1991:20; Olivier 1911:333). Are their criteria the same as those used in Spulber 1963:352, and in Milward and Saul 1977:439? Given the extremely uneven character of statistics from the region it is actually rather difficult to arrive at meaningful comparative statements about relative levels of industrialisation. On this general point see Kukoleca 1941:2-10.

26. There are considerable deficiencies in the data with respect to several sectors of Yugoslav economic life (and especially the period 1943-45) which make firm or detailed statements about patterns difficult. See esp. Kaser and Radice eds.1986: Chapters 17 and 18.

27. Kaser and Radice eds. (1986:353) inform us that the burden of the costs of occupation may have been exaggerated, and there is some doubt about the significance of this.

28. Nesovic discusses the decentralised character of economic organisation during the period of the "national liberation struggle", under the system of *narodno-oslobodilacki odbori* (Committees of National Liberation). He specifically attacks the notion that the provisioning of the military was "something accidental or usually improvised (from hand to mouth)", arguing that it was "a kind of very interesting economic system" (1964:37).

3

THE "SECOND YUGOSLAVIA" AND

THE CONTRADICTIONS OF MODERNITY

Addressing the subject of economic modernisation in socialist Yugoslavia it is important to note that I am not attempting to write a systematic economic history of the region. Several very useful texts already provide this kind of account.[1] My account emphasises those aspects of economic modernisation which are of particular *sociological* interest, and continues the themes of continuity and discontinuity in the processes of modernisation and globalisation. Its balance is influenced also by the need to suggest the rectification of some gaps in the general picture of economic change in this period, and to take a position on some unresolved or controversial issues. There are three areas to which I give particular attention here: (i) the continuing politicisation of the economy, and the role of the state as an interface with the global economy; (ii) the character and importance of self-management; and (iii) the problem of regional differentiation and its significance.

i) The role of the state as an interface with the global economy
In approaching the characteristics of economic change in post-war Yugoslavia writers characteristically highlight the *discontinuity* of the move from capitalism to Communism, and generally structure their presentation of the "Yugoslav system"

around the features which marked it as distinctive--above all the system of "workers' self-management". If adopted exclusively, however, this focus undervalues some important *continuities* across the wartime experience.

Capitalist structures of ownership and production (as I have suggested in the previous chapter) generally remained under-developed in the South Slav lands before 1945, in spite of the existence of small and isolated pockets of their advance. The centres of capitalist commercial and productive activity were located *outside* the region, giving to the entire Balkan Peninsula at best a "semi-peripheral", or clientship status. Socialism as an ideology affirmed Yugoslavia's independence from world capitalism; and the policy of industrialisation embarked upon by the Communist regime constituted an attempt to escape from semi-peripheral dependence as a supplier of primary produce. In spite of this appearance of difference, however, there is at least one key respect in which it is possible to identify continuity between pre- and post-war economic policies.

During the life-time of the "First Yugoslavia" the state dominated all institutions directly or indirectly, especially after the establishment of the royal dictatorship in 1929. The co-operative movement and the trade unions were co-opted; the banks (especially the mortgage banks) were controlled by state nominees; and the market for key products was subjected to central regulation, especially the market for grains through the marketing monopoly *PRIZAD*. The state emerged as the most active and important interface between local economic activity and the emerging world economy, as the principal broker and recipient of foreign credit; the regulator of the country's participation in international trade; and the major force in structuring the relations between labour and capital. This pattern was reinforced by developments

93

between 1941 and 1945; and the pivotal role of the state was built upon rather than initiated by the Communists.

ii) The character and importance of self-management

One of the difficulties of the economic historiography of Yugoslavia in the post 1945 period has been the tendency of writers to frame the phases of *economic* development primarily in terms of basically *political* criteria. In particular, the several transformations of the system of workers' self-management have been taken as indicating changes in underlying economic realities (Singleton and Carter 1982; Dyker 1990). There are two respects in which a consideration of the system of workers' self management belongs in this chapter. I contend that self-management is to be understood principally as having to do with legitimation (i.e. as a *political* phenomenon) and may be regarded as an "economically relevant" rather than as an "economic" phenomenon (as Max Weber puts it). Having said this, however, self-management does provide the institutional frame within which economic activity has been conducted throughout most of the post-1945 period in Yugoslavia, and merits consideration in that respect.

Self-management viewed from a sociological point of view can also be regarded as a significantly *anti-modern* feature of the Yugoslav economy. The imposition of a structure of vertical segmentation, as much as central planning, as a specifically socialist characteristic of the economy, has militated against the development of markets of the factors of production, especially labour and capital.[2] The interest of this point lies at least in part in that it points to a fundamental contradiction within the Yugoslav economy, between the modernising imperatives which are typical of the

94

industrialisation process itself, and localising, anti-modern tendencies which are implicit within its political framework. In as far as institutional differentiation can be regarded as an essential attribute of modernity, in spite of the shift of policy objectives in the post-war period, the politicisation of the economy expressed largely in the form of self-management continued to be a brake on modernisation, or at least to constrain its forms and direction.

iii) The problem of regional differentiation

One result of pre-1941 development was the modification of regional differences within Yugoslavia. Against the background of the problems of unification, the world financial and trade crisis, and the land reform, manufacturing industry made only limited progress. Mining and the rudimentary processing of metals and chemicals advanced in Bosnia; large-scale commercialised agriculture was stimulated in some of the formerly less-developed areas (especially Macedonia and Bosnia); tourism generated some economic dynamism in parts of Dalmatia. Zagreb and Belgrade grew rather as commercial and administrative centres than as industrial cities. On the other hand some of the former enclaves of economic modernity (such as parts of Slovenia and the Vojvodina) were actually held back by the inter-war situation.

Commentators on the Yugoslav economy tend to take the view that regional economic differences in Yugoslavia can be viewed as a more or less automatic continuation of differences rooted in the Ottoman/Habsburg eras, and confirmed during the inter-war years. By way of contrast, I argue that it is the *post-war* process of state-directed industrialisation that gave the greatest stimulus to the creation of regional disparities, enhancing relatively rudimentary differences of economic development.

Post-war socialist reorganisation

The programme of energetic industrialisation upon which the new regime embarked after 1945 has been depicted as a specifically Communist strategy--the economic dimension of "hard-boiled dictatorship" (Hoffman and Neal 1962: Chap. 6). In many ways, however, this can be seen as no more than a rational response to the situation in which the new Yugoslavia found itself. There was an urgent need for industrial reconstruction and the rehabilitation of infrastructure after the war (Bicanic 1973:78). Yugoslavia was a major beneficiary of the United Nations Relief and Reconstruction Agency (UNRRA), which "from the outset in April, 1945, until their termination in June, 1947 .... totalled $415.6 million, the largest sum dispensed to any of the European economies and fully one fifth of the UNRRA aggregate" (Lampe, Prickett and Adamovic 1990:21). A very large proportion of this aid took the form of food: nevertheless, a significant proportion also was made up of machinery and coal. UNRRA aid was delivered to *governments*, which tended not only to concentrate relief in the state sector but also to subsidise consumption, leaving the government free to put its own efforts at accumulation into industry (Bicanic 1973:27).[3]

It is not so much in the choice of the *goal* of industrialisation that Yugoslavia can be said to have exhibited a specifically Communist orientation as in its choice of *methods*. In this the Yugoslavs opted for open imitation of the Soviet model of central planning. By the end of 1946 large enterprises in industry, mining and quarrying, banking transport and wholesale trading, had been nationalised, as well as agricultural properties designated by the land reform. By the end of 1948 the remaining industrial concerns and retail businesses were nationalised, leaving in private hands only small artisan workshops, small retail outlets and peasant farms, with the stated objective of eliminating the exploitation of labour.

The First Five Year plan was introduced in January 1947, based upon the Soviet model.[4] Whatever the general strengths or weaknesses of central planning, it was scarcely appropriate to apply directly Soviet designs in Yugoslavia, which had no large internal market and was not an energy-rich state (Singleton and Carter 1982:110-11; Waterston 1962:14-16). Nevertheless, the early post-war years for Yugoslavia saw spectacular increases in both output and productivity, with 1938 levels on most indices already surpassed by 1947 (Savezni Zavod za Statistiku 1989). Investment in industry (particularly the capital goods sector) was to be expanded as much as possible. Industrial output was to be raised as quickly as possible. The proportion of the labour force employed in industrial occupations was to be increased as fast as possible. In evaluating these objectives, and translating them into policy, properly economic criteria seem to have played very little part (Sirc 1979:8-9). The measure of success was usually taken to be the level of aggregate output, regardless of the cost of that achievement or the marketability of the product.

Yugoslav aspirations for rapid development were challenged suddenly in June 1948 by the irruption of the dispute with the Cominform, which led the following year to Yugoslavia's expulsion from the socialist bloc. One of the primary causes of the dispute had been Yugoslavia's protests about the adverse and even exploitative nature of the system of bilateral trade agreements which the Soviets were creating. Their protests had been especially vigorous about the terms of their participation in the Danube shipping organisation *JUSPAD* and the joint stock company for air transport, *JUSTA*.

The impact of the break upon trade has been perhaps the most obvious consequence, and the most frequently commented upon feature.

> Yugoslavia was then dependent upon the Eastern bloc for roughly 50 per cent of its imports, but for some items dependency was much greater. All of Yugoslavia's coal and coke imports, 80 per cent of its pig iron needs, 60 per cent of its petroleum products, four-fifths of its fertilizer requirements and virtually all specialized machinery, steel tubes, railway cars and locomotives came from the Soviet Union and its satellites. Now trade from this source dried up completely. (Hoffman and Neal 1962:144)

Although the imposed need to reorient its pattern of trade was clearly an event of prime importance, which imposed all kinds of practical and ideological difficulties upon the Yugoslav regime, the trade effects were possibly less important than some others which have received less attention.[5] The replacement of eastern European trade partners was actually achieved relatively rapidly, and there is no indication that the new terms of trade achieved by the Yugoslavs were worse than those which they were forced to abandon.[6]

One of the main economic consequences of the break of 1948 was an attempt to strengthen the economic independence of the country. This aim was interpreted in terms of industrialisation, moving away from the role which the Yugoslavs believed that the Soviet Union had envisaged for them, perpetuating their pre-war position, as suppliers of primary products.[7] Closely linked to this was the increasing attention paid to military requirements. In part military needs were covered by resort to foreign (especially American) aid (Lampe, Prickett and Adamovic 1990:40, 58, 70-71). Nevertheless, investment was increased also in domestic production. Both of these factors worked together in giving a further stimulus to concentration upon production goods at the expense of consumption goods.

An additional consequence of the dispute was that the Yugoslavs were compelled to re-examine some aspects of the centralised planning model, moving tentatively towards what later became known as "market socialism". This reappraisal was partly motivated by political needs (such as the need to boost morale), and self-management and the rhetoric of decentralisation may well have been directed to these ends.

Not all of the changes introduced in the centralised planning model, however, can be accounted for in these terms. The break with the Soviet bloc coincided with the onset (and period of the deepest freeze) of the Cold War; and American and western European governments were not slow to perceive the political leverage which might be exercised through the subsidisation of Yugoslav independence. In many respects the biggest contrast between pre- and post-war economic policy is between the reliance upon exports before the war versus deficit funding based upon external credit post-war, and in particular the greater reliance of the Yugoslav economy upon western sources (Lampe, Prickett and Adamovic 1990). From the outset, therefore, Yugoslav economic policy can be seen to consist of the resultant of two apparently contradictory demands of the socialist and autonomist aspirations of the Communist Party, and the exigencies of the primarily capitalist system of international exchange.

The re-evaluation of central planning

The move away from the Soviet model of planning actually begins quite early. The Yugoslav government backed away from the regime of compulsory deliveries in agriculture as early as 1951 (Wright 1986). The 1953 constitutional revision replaced the former Federal Planning commission by two new bodies, the Federal Institute for Economic Planning and the Federal Statistical Institute, initiating a decentralisation process which devolved many functions of the old federal bodies to republican levels (Waterston 1962:25-36).

Motivated by excessive and naive enthusiasm, and undertaken against the context of the collapse of both the collectivisation programme in agriculture and its relationship to the other socialist countries of eastern Europe, the first plan failed to achieve its targets. The period of reappraisal resulted in delay in the introduction of a Second Five Year Plan until 1957. During the interval a succession of annual plans was adopted which were more indicative than normative in character. (In Yugoslav terminology they concentrated upon establishing "basic proportions" (Sirc 1979:16-17; Dyker 1990:27-28).

Although some commentators have been rather harsh in their assessment of the first decade of Yugoslav socialism, in many respects progress was impressive.[8]

> From 1948 to 1951, over the period of administrative socialism, there was a very marked relative increase in the production of machinery and equipment, which rose to (an index value of) 153. This increase continued at the same rate from 1952 to 1954, when the index was 157. The greatest jump ahead was from 1956 to 1960, when the index reached 184. (Bicanic 1973:93)

The rate of progress was rather slower in the areas of the production of raw materials and consumer goods (see Kaser and Radice eds. 1986a: Chap. 25). In spite of these achievements it is generally agreed that the period was marked by a number of serious economic weaknesses.

1. Economic planning took place within a frame defined by the aim of economic independence. As a consequence of the above, there was a general neglect of issues of comparative advantage. Self-reliance combined with a more general tendency among socialist thinkers to place excessive importance upon industrial production. (Dyker has termed this "investment good fetishism"--1990:56.)

2. This introverted economic focus resulted in a lack of attention to exports. The later plans often achieved their targets but at a cost of staggering import bills. Over the period 1950-1965, the value of foreign trade *per capita* was lower for Yugoslavia than for any of the other centrally planned economies of Europe with the exception of Romania and Albania (Kaser and Radice eds.1986a:111). The serious disincentives to international trade which were built into the regime of foreign exchange controls were never seriously addressed.

3. In common with socialist central planning elsewhere in this period, levels of aggregate output became the primary emphasis of the plan, and were taken as constituting the principal indicator of economic success. Low per capita productivity and low efficiency of capital were tolerated, or even not considered as problems.[9] Agriculture now served, not as the source of exports to pay for the import of manufactured goods, but as a source of surplus labour to be recruited into industry; as the source of production surpluses to feed the towns; and as the target of an adverse internal balance of trade, the proceeds of which were available to boost industrial

investment. In the "First Yugoslavia" agriculture had absorbed a huge proportion of the available credit in the form of agricultural mortgages, generated by the Land Reform. In the "Second Yugoslavia" resources were pumped systematically from the countryside to generate development in the towns (Dyker 1990:59).

The import of capital, which had come to play an important role in pre-war Yugoslavia, now also changed its function. Instead of serving the development of extractive industries and the infrastructure necessary for the transport of their product, the import of funds now either undergirded basic industrialisation or subsidised consumption, especially that of the state. Expanded production was not used to pay for capital imports, and stored up a variety of problems for the future, including inflationary pressures and a huge balance of payments problem. This went unnoticed, as the institutional form of these payments (designated as "aid" rather than as "investment") led to their misrecognition. The sums involved, however, were considerable. (Lampe, Prickett and Adamovic 1990: Table 3.1; Dyker 1990:45.)

The 1957 Five Year Plan, introduced a framework of new regulations. It is partly the success of this plan which concealed the wider weakness of economic policy and structure, and deferred serious consideration of the underlying problems. The plan achieved its targets within four years--a period which has been characterised as the "great leap forward" (Dyker 1990:Chap. 3). "In comparison with an average annual growth rate of 1.9% for 1948-1952, and of 8.4% for 1953-1956, an annual average rate of 11.8% (13% for industry) was reached during the first four years of implementation of the quinquennial plan 1957-1961." (Meneghello-Dincic 1970:76) Output targets were exceeded across a wide range of sectors, and exports rose. Nevertheless, there were reasons for concern. Domestic investment declined across the plan period; and imports outstripped exports by a considerable margin, resulting in a growing balance of payments deficit--from 13,184 million dinars in 1956 to 59,618 millions in 1960 (Meneghello-Dincic 1970:77-9: Singleton 1976:143-5).

In spite of the successes of the Second Plan, the problems which were foreshadowed in this period soon began to unroll rapidly. The Third Five Year Plan, introduced in 1961, was abandoned after only one year. Problems of the inefficiency of Yugoslav production, and the rate of inflation, reached a level of seriousness which could not be ignored, and placed upon the agenda issues of wider structural reform.

The development of "workers' self-management"

Before turning to a consideration of that reform process, however, it is important to place the account of Yugoslav economic performance within its context of institutional change. From a political and ideological point of view self-management provided the pivot of the distinctive "Yugoslav road" to socialism. It sat increasingly awkwardly, however, with the claim that this road was also defined in terms of "market" socialism, especially in the light of the distortions which it introduced into the market for labour.

The system of self-management was ushered in by the "Basic Law on the Management of State Economic Enterprises and Higher Economic Associations by Work Collectivities", of June 1950.[10] This focussed initially upon the management of "enterprises", as a consequence of which "self-management" has come to be associated even in academic discussion principally with "workers' control", and especially the management of factories; but the system rapidly evolved beyond this base. Under the constitutional reform of 1953, communes (*opstine*) received a considerable augmentation of their powers, including the powers of taxation and participation in the affairs of enterprises within their territory. The interdependence of enterprises and municipalities (particularly the importance of the latter) has often been under-estimated, but the essential characteristics of the system and its economic consequences are only understandable when they are viewed together.[11]

Attempting to make sense of the Yugoslav system within their discipline, western economists have subsequently developed a model of what has come to be known as the "Illyrian firm". The central conceptual feature of the model is management by the working collective.[12] The model of the "Illyrian firm" contains two presuppositions. It postulates a tendency on the part of workers to prioritise security of employment above the profitability of the enterprise. It anticipates that workers will choose to defend their own wage levels without due reference to other economic criteria which might be assumed to be more central in determining "entrepreneurial" behaviour. Studies of the Yugoslav self-managing enterprise have indicated that the model does accurately diagnose these as features of their activity.[13]

"Decentralisation" has increasingly been taken to mean, in relation to Yugoslavia, the *republicanisation* of economic policy. There has also been, nevertheless, an extremely important dimension of economic *parochialism*, centred in the commune and the enterprise, which deserves attention both for its political and its economic significance, which dates from the changes of this period. Taken together, the effects of the weight given to communal government and the introverted behaviour of workers employed in the "Illyrian firm", tended to produce a significant fragmentation and narrowing of perceived economic interest. From the point of view of the theory of modernisation, self-management can be seen as operating not only to inhibit the creation of a meaningful market for labour, but also as continuing to institutionalise the "embeddedness" of labour relations within the locality.

Explanation of the disintegration of Yugoslavia has frequently focussed upon the activity of self-interested republican political elites. In this respect, the search for the causes of the break-up of the federation has focussed n the period following the death of President Tito in 1980. Two observations need to be made in this respect. In the first place, Tito himself was directly involved in the creation of the system, so that he cannot be distanced from its consequences. In the second place, and much more significantly, it is apparent that disintegrative tendencies can be seen to have been built into the Yugoslav economy from the very initiation of the self-management system in the 1950s, can be regarded as an integral feature of that system, and have relatively little to do with the removal of Tito's personal authority.

The reform process and its contradictions

i) Political responses to economic problems

A recurring contradictory feature of post-1945 economic development in Yugoslavia has been the fact that although the country was rapidly becoming *industrialised*, from a sociological point of view its *modernisation* was significantly retarded. The modernisation process entails, firstly, the facility of social agents to enter into more extensive spatio-temporal combinations and, secondly, a differentiation of economic from political institutions as part of a wider process of the functional specialisation of institutional orders. The kind of localisation of economic organisation which I have already diagnosed may be said to indicate a relative failure of the modernisation process in the first of these senses. In spite of the dismantling of much of the central planning apparatus of the period of "administrative socialism", the depoliticisation of the economy was not significantly advanced, which may be taken as suggesting of the retardation of the modernisation process in the second sense.

Whenever the country encountered *economic* problems, including those relating to its *external* economic environment (its insertion into the "world-system"), the response came in the form of a largely *political* reform of its institutional order, which failed to address the specifically economic problem in question. What is more, that political response characteristically took the form of an acceleration of the fragmenting processes of republicanisation and parochialisation.

Of this period of Yugoslav history Joseph Bombelles has remarked that "the Yugoslav case demonstrates that the 'building of socialism' and steady economic development are two separate, and frequently incompatible objectives" (Bombelles 1968:178).[14] Perhaps in the light of his remark my observation might be rephrased as "whenever the country encountered problems of economic development, the response came in the form of a redoubled attempt to build socialism". This is certainly apt as a diagnosis of the reform period of the 1960s.

The failure of the new Five Year Plan in 1961 precipitated a vigorous debate between advocates of a "liberal" movement towards a market economy and those who believed that economic salvation lay in the stricter enforcement of central economic discipline.[15] The response to economic crisis was a curious compromise--a two pronged approach which linked a new constitution to a package of economic reforms.

The constitution promulgated in April 1963 was the fruit of protracted debate within the League of Communists (LC), resulting in a remarkable attempt to break both with models of "bourgeois democracy" and the legacy of the Soviet Union and the "People's Democracies".[16]

A new Federal Assembly consisted of no fewer than five chambers, one of which was elected on the basis of traditional territorial constituencies, but the other four were nominated by and from work organisations and elected by communal assemblies. The structure demonstrated two noteworthy characteristics. Although the process of delegation remained firmly in the hands of the LC, it soon became evident that the new chambers were far more lively and critical than might have been expected. "Yugoslav parliamentary life became .... more exciting and effective than in any other Communist single-party state" (Rusinow 1977:152). The new, more highly educated, "technocratic" assemblies, composed of people with varied and direct experience of economic and other organisations and their problems, tended to interpret issues and the implications of policy directly in terms of the interests of local constituents, and less in relation to the "party line". The consequences of these changes were re-enforced by two subsequent developments.

The timing of the congresses of the Federal and Republican Leagues was reversed, so that republican LC delegations came to the 8th Congress in December 1964 with already consolidated positions on key issues. The Federal Congress therefore became an opportunity for horse-trading on a regional basis rather than the source of authoritative central policies which were then transmitted to the republics for endorsement or implementation.

In July 1966 a further impetus was given to the republicanisation of Yugoslav politics by the disgrace of Aleksandar Rankovic at the Brioni Plenum of the Central Committee. The former head of the security services had been a staunch centraliser and, as a close colleague of Tito, highly influential. His downfall represented much more than his personal elimination from politics. A direct consequence of the affair was a thorough overhaul of the security apparatus, and its placing "under the effective supervision of 'representative bodies and their executive organs', which in due course meant parliamentary commissions overseeing the work of secretariats of internal affairs" (Rusinow 1977:190). Although this period has been depicted as marking the triumph of "liberalism" (and there is undoubtedly some truth in that) possibly of greater importance in the long term was a further decisive shift of political weight towards the republics and communes.

ii) The politicisation of capital and credit

The "liberal" credentials of the Yugoslav system were in evidence in the succession of economic reforms which accompanied these political changes. Among the primary motive forces behind the movement towards "market socialism", lay the weakness of the country's financial system, and the failure to develop an effective means of allocating capital.

The magnitude of the economic problems facing Yugoslavia had already resulted, in 1961, in the revaluation of the dinar, and the securing of a substantial loan ($275 millions) from the IMF. At the end of 1963 the General Investment Fund was abolished (hitherto the major instrument for the centralised allocation of investment) and two instruments then took responsibility for the allocation of capital--the banks, and a Fund for Supporting the Development of the Underdeveloped Regions, created in 1964.

In March 1965, a new Law on Banks and Credit Transactions heralded more than thirty measures reconstructing the financial system and the foreign trade regime. The move away from central government as the primary source of investment finance began in advance of legislation. In 1961 the state had been responsible for more than 60% of investment finance; and by 1964 this proportion had declined to 36.5%. By 1968, however, the figure had fallen to 15.7%. The banks increased their share in provision across the same period from less than 1% to more than 47% (Singleton 1976:154).[17]

At the heart of the country's financial problems lay an institutional contradiction. The rather decentralised banking system which had grown up produced close links between banks and large enterprises at the local level. These collaborated with local political elites in the procurement of investment funds. Instead of providing a check upon economic activity (the voice of economic realism, making for the more effective allocation of investment) the financial system acted as a cushion against reality.

Alongside this decentralised banking structure was placed a nominally centralised structure of monetary control, headed by the National Bank of Yugoslavia. Although on paper this was a powerful institution, it was in practice ineffective as a regulator of monetary supply. Its governing body, composed of nominees of the principal republican banks, was unable to distance itself from the structures of political patronage which they in turn represented. It acted as an independent regulator only to the extent that competing regional interests cancelled each other out, ensuring neutral inactivity in place of policy. The pattern of allocation of credit responded to pressures channelled through the structure of local and regional patronage, and as a consequence the system of credit allocation was being tested constantly by the potential of the self-management system to raise personal income levels at a faster rate than could be justified by the growth of enterprise earnings.

The fact that banks increased significantly their role as the avenues through which credit and investment were distributed certainly did not mean that the widely heralded movement towards "market socialism" included the creation of a genuine market for capital. There was indeed a movement away from the centrally planned, political mechanism for the disbursement of capital, but towards a regionally or even locally controlled and pragmatically co-ordinated (but equally politicised) mechanism. Instead of connecting Yugoslav producers with the "international division of labour" Yugoslav financial institutions served rather to insulate the economy from the demands of that wider world.[18]

The debate about economic reform was phrased in large measure in terms of Yugoslavia's more complete inclusion in "the international division of labour", and "market socialism". To some extent these concerns were reflected in the creation of additional capacities which could respond to world market opportunities. This is the era, for example, of the most rapid creation of the Dalmatian tourist industry (Allcock 1986). From around half a million foreign tourists in 1957 the number soared to 3.6 million by 1967, during which time Yugoslavia's earnings from this source in convertible currencies rose from US$ 4.5 million to 133 millions (Savezni Zavod za Statistiku 1989:342 and 343). Other investments, however, were less obviously suited to taking advantage of Yugoslavia's comparative advantages. .

A good deal of the political difficulty faced by the Yugoslav economy lay in the institutional structures for handling foreign trade and foreign exchange, and the reforms included the elimination of the "dysfunctional complexity" of a system of multiple foreign exchange rates, which had varied with industrial sector (Rusinow 1977:172).[19] The foreign exchange regime was reorganised in a series of measures beginning in 1961, and in 1962 Yugoslavia acceded to GATT (Dyker 1990:64-5). In 1965 a further revaluation (the introduction of the "New Dinar") took the exchange rate from 750 to 1,300 to the dollar, largely with the intention of harmonising Yugoslav monetary policy with world markets. The foreign exchange regime tended to concentrate hard currency earnings in the banks, creating a sense of resentment on the part of the enterprises which actually earned the money.

In some measure the problems associated with the foreign exchange regime have been misrepresented. The controversial "retention quotas" which permitted earners of foreign exchange to retain direct control only over a portion of their earnings, was attacked at the time (especially in Croatia and Slovenia) as a device for ensuring that hard currency reserves remained under the control of Belgrade. As the banking system was substantially federalised, however, the real issue appears to have been that as the banks operated with no obvious economic rationality in the reinvestment of these resources, the system was in general excessively politicised. In this process it is unclear to what extent the direction of resources was determined by "Belgrade", as *republican* political elites were also enmeshed in the network of political intervention in the foreign exchange regime.

iii) The politicisation of regional differences

One of the problems which had already become apparent by the time of the economic reform was the growing disparity between the economic development of different republics. GDP/capita for Yugoslavia as a whole had risen by 1960 by 191.7% (a rate of growth matched by Slovenia and exceeded by Vojvodina). For Bosnia-Hercegovina and Kosovo GDP/capita had risen between 152-154%; for Montenegro by 143.7%; and for Macedonia by only 111.4% (Vojnic, in Akhavan and Howse eds. 1995). Looked at in other terms, in 1952 Slovenia's GDP/capita had been 181.8% of the Yugoslav average: that of Croatia had been 121.4%. The rate for Montenegro had been 87.6% of that average, however, the rate for Macedonia 71.4%, and for Kosovo only 46.5%. By 1960, however, Slovenia and Croatia had sustained their relative advantage, but the figure for Montenegro had fallen to 65.7%, and for Macedonia to 63.9% of the average. More dramatically, in 1952 GDP/capita in Bosnia-Hercegovina had been 95.5% of the average, but by 1960 had declined to 76%.[20] Whereas in 1952 the GDP/capita of the poorest region (Kosovo) had been a quarter of that in the richest region (Slovenia), by 1960 this had fallen to a fifth (although the greatest *relative* decline had been seen in Bosnia-Hercegovina and Montenegro). These figures can be taken as crude indices of growing social and economic differentials along a wide range of other dimensions—educational and cultural provision, unemployment, poverty, and a range of demographic indicators of welfare.[21]

The mechanisms of central planning had evidently done nothing to meet the socialist preference for equity, and indeed by these and other measures inequality had expanded in the decade since the Communist take-over. In February 1965 the growing discontent associated with these widening disparities was answered by the creation of a Federal Fund for Supporting the Development of the Underdeveloped Republics and Regions (*Fond federacije za kreditiranje privrednog razvoja privredno nedovoljno ravijenih republika i krajeva*--the "Development Fund"). The Development Fund replaced for former General Investment Fund, and was specifically intended to address this problem. It was to be financed by a levy of 1.85% of the social product of all federal units, which would then be disbursed to those units which were classed as "underdeveloped".

The mechanisms which were established in order to tackle this problem, while undoubtedly making for the transfer of appreciable sums to the poorer republics, tended to exacerbate the political conflict which surrounded it. The scheme was flawed from the start because its operation was defined in terms of the differences between *republics,* and not *regions*. Discussion of *regional* inequalities in Yugoslavia has almost without exception been couched in terms of *republican* inequalities. Republics should not be considered as the only units which might be relevant to an analysis of regionalisation.[22] Areas of poverty and backwardness extended across republican boundaries. The traditionally "passive" karst region, characterised by post-war depopulation and the abandonment of land, included parts of Bosnia-Hercegovina, Croatia, Montenegro and Slovenia. Similarly the area of backward, traditional agriculture of the upper Morava valley extends into both Serbia and Macedonia.

The Development Fund defined its tasks, however, exclusively in terms of inter-republican differences—not unnaturally in a political system which had already come to be defined in terms of a balance between republics and provinces. While actually masking some of the real problems to be addressed, therefore, the solution was envisaged in terms of the transfer of resources between republics, and the problems and processes making for the differentiation of *natural regions* were never addressed outside this framework.

The problem was aggravated by the Communist propensity to define economic development in terms of *industrialisation*. This resulted in a tendency to locate heavy industry and mineral extraction in the poorer republics, and to allow light industry and commercial activities such as tourism to take the lead in the better-off republics. Ramet notes that:

> between 1956 and 1970, 63.9 percent of all investments in Kosovo went into industry, with only 12.4 percent for agriculture, 8.9 percent for transport development, and 11.1 percent for non-economic projects. …. It emerges that some 85 percent of all industrial projects undertaken in Kosovo were in heavy industry and …. more than half of all investments (about 55 percent) went into heavy industry during this period. (Ramet 1992:146).

This strategy was self-defeating as an address to the problem of inequality, for four reasons.

Rates of return were higher for those activities which were located in regions which were already more developed. In order to make any sense of location decisions, which were often economically dubious, it was necessary to match investment in productive capacity in the poorer areas with complementary investment in infrastructure, which contributed only indirectly to productivity. Taken together, these factors served to underline the politically controversial nature of investment decisions, in that the republics which were on balance donors claimed that the same resources invested in their own areas would have yielded better results.

The activity of the Development Fund was misdirected for another reason, in that it neglected the social foundations of economic activity, apparently in the belief that development would result from the sheer volume of investment. Two important social factors at least, however, began to have an appreciable effect during the 1960s, which undermined the development effort. The republics were characterised by strongly contrasting demographic patterns. In the inter-war years all of Yugoslavia had experienced very high rates of population growth, although these began to decline during the 1930s. In the poorer regions, however, the impact of war itself produced a temporary rise, deferring the decline, and in the poorest regions of all (especially Kosovo) rates of fertility remained very high. Household size across Yugoslavia declined from 5.10 in 1921 to 3.62 in 1981. In Slovenia the figures fell from 4.88 to 3.18, and in Croatia the decline was from 5.09 to 3.23. In Macedonia, however, household size fell from 5.53 in 1921 to only 4.39 in 1981; in Bosnia from 5.62 to 4.00, and in Montenegro from 6.61 to 4.09. By way of contrast, although household size in Kosovo began to decline in the immediate post-war years, the trend was reversed after 1961, with rates rising from 6.32 in that year to 6.92 by 1981 (Vojnic, in Akhavan and Howse eds. 1995:Table 4-3).

A closely related point must be made in relation to the failure of the poorer areas to develop their educational provision, especially in the field of technical education. Consequently, the poorer regions were both fighting against an adverse demographic trend, and failing to match the availability of investment funds with the corresponding provision of a suitably prepared labour force. In spite of the transfer of funds, therefore, unemployment in these regions continued to rise.

Dragomir Vojnic has summed up the problem well.

(L)ow return on investment and …. a large natural increase in population ….

created a sort of vicious circle. All felt that the policy was unjust and

exploitative towards them. The less developed republics did not adequately

appreciate the efforts of the more developed in terms of redistributing assets.

The more developed, on the other hand, in addition to criticising the weak

performance of redistributed assets, did not sufficiently respect the benefits in

terms of the common Yugoslav market. While redistribution on behalf of the

less developed republics could be clearly measured and expressed in terms of

statistics, the benefits of the common market to the more developed could only

be presumed rather than quantified statistically. (Vojnic, in Akhavan and Howse

eds. 1995:104-5. Cf. Hoffman and Hatchett 1977.)

iv) The balance of the reform process

The reform package of 1965 certainly represented a serious attempt to grapple with

the economic issues along a number of dimensions. There were several matters,

however, which were not addressed in that process.

   In looking for sources of strain within the Yugoslav economic system engendered by

the reform process one needs to bear in mind the huge burden of the "socio-political

organisations" (basically political functionaries) which became apparent at this time.

This can not be considered purely as a federally imposed burden on the republics, but

a politically imposed burden endemic in the socialist system. In spite of the fact that

the economic changes introduced during the 1960s have generally been described in

terms of the furtherance of "market socialism", the system continued to bear the

burden of surveillance which was characteristic of all of the states of eastern Europe.

Indeed decentralisation merely generated additional structural ramifications to this problem.

Falling from 8% of total employment immediately after the war, by 1955 employment in the "socio-political organisations" settled between 4-5% (Savezni Zavod za Statistiku 1989:58-9). (The "socio-political organisations" included not only the League of Communists, but also a range of bodies such as the *Socialisticki Savez* (Socialist Alliance) and the official youth and women's organisations.) Throughout the 1970s average earnings for this group of employees were 121% of the average earnings for all workers (Savezni Zavod za Statistiku 1989:76-7). A useful comparative indication of the size of the economic burden imposed by this political apparatus is the fact that after health (but before education) the socio-political organisations constituted the largest budgetary heading for "non-economic activities", consuming throughout the 1970s more than 20% of expenditure in this sector (Savezni Zavod za Statistiku 1989:48).

There were also some persistent major blind-spots with respect to certain sectors, especially agriculture and services, the role of which was never addressed properly in the reform process. A tentative attempt was made at taxation reform: but post-war governments have never really addressed fiscal measures as an instrument of economic policy. It was a persisting problem of the Yugoslav economy (as of the "real socialist" economies more generally) that problems of distribution figured centrally in policy thinking, but problems of *redistribution* were always treated inadequately, and considered at the collective (usually regional) level, rather than the level of individual or family incomes.

Although it emerged subsequently that far too little was done in the sixties to address the central structural problems of the Yugoslav economy, the difficulties faced by the regime should not be underestimated. The fact that the Communist Party of Yugoslavia changed its name in 1954 to the League of Communists of Yugoslavia, was intended to signal a fundamental shift in the relationship between party and society, the continuing weight of commitment to Marxist-Leninist political methods and economic orthodoxies should not be ignored. It is usually argued that the dismissal of Rankovic as head of internal security in 1966 signified the breaking of the back of resistance to the reform process. Even then, however, certain features of Marxist dogmatism remained entrenched within the system, crippling until it was too late any flexible address to some key issues. Obviously the nature of private property in the means of production. and the role of private employment in the economy, were the principal cases in point.[23]

Singleton and Carter give an excellent summary of the contradictions of Yugoslav economic practice in this period (1982:136-37). "Etatism" is denounced in favour of liberalisation and the market: but in fact the response is often to increase state intervention. There is a continuing tendency to produce political answers to economic questions. Hence (as came to be the case on a regular basis) the discovery of structural economic problems was met by the reform of self-management and, constitutional changes.

Successive planning laws adopted a more "indicative" style: but it is important, in looking at Yugoslav economic policy in this period to distinguish between rhetoric and substance. It is wise not to neglect the range of real controls which still were in the hands of government right down to the 1980s, especially with respect to price-formation.

There was growing recognition during this period of the positive importance of the remittances of migrant labour--reluctantly at first, but then the export of labour almost became an instrument of policy. By 1973 over 1 million Yugoslavs and their dependants were working abroad. "In 1975 for every hundred workers employed in Yugoslavia twenty worked outside the country." (Jelavich 1983:392-93) Their regular remittances made an enormous difference to the balance of payments, and their absence offered significant relief to the large problem of unemployment (Mesic 1992). The situation nevertheless only served to conceal real problems in the economy, and to underline the way in which Yugoslavia had become dependent upon the import of funds, which at the private as well as the public level were used disproportionately to subsidise consumption rather than investment.[24]

Economic factors in the break-up of Yugoslavia

In the wake of the disintegration of the Yugoslav federation, and perhaps understandably so in view of the seriousness of the accompanying armed conflict, the attempt to provide an explanation has dwelt quite disproportionately upon the factor of ethnic diversity. Nevertheless, I contend that no explanation which does not place at its heart economic factors deserves to be taken seriously. At the core of that explanation must lie the continuing contradiction between the exigencies of an economy which is modernising with respect to its technical capacities, and which is increasingly integrated into global patterns of exchange, and the deeply-rooted resistances to modernisation which have come to be built into the system.

Although general awareness of the seriousness of Yugoslavia's economic difficulties probably coincides with the death of President Tito, it is evident that these were gestating for a much longer period. Danger signals can be seen in the emerging conflict over regional development, and in the early retreat from the commitment to economic reform, both of which were reflected in the constitutional reconstruction of 1974-6.

The path of industrialisation upon which the Yugoslavs had embarked resulted in a fall in the proportion of the economically active population engaged in agriculture from 53 % at the and of World War II to 48.5% by the census of 1971, and a fall in the rural population from 67% to 38%. The urban population increased by two and a half times in this period. By 1970, 39% of the labour force were employed in the productive social sector (Lydall 1984:160). As I demonstrate in the next chapter, agriculture also had been undergoing an appreciable transformation. During the later 1960s, however, the attempt of the reform programme to match technical modernisation with a corresponding modernisation of economic organisation, in terms of the development of markets, ran into severe political difficulties which effectively put that process into reverse.

One of the areas to benefit most dramatically from the reform process was Croatia, which during the 1960s experienced rapidly growing prosperity on the basis of the expansion of its tourist trade (Allcock 1986). This expansion was made possible in large measure by international aid and investment in projects such as the Adriatic highway (completed partly with American money), the Babin Kuk project near

Dubrovnik, and the Bernardin Project in Slovenia (both financed by the World Bank) as well as by large internal transfers.

One feature of the growing republicanisation of structures, however, was that Croats began to resent the exchange controls which limited their access to the full measure of the resulting hard currency income. Tourism enjoyed among the highest "retention quotas" of any sector of exports. Nevertheless, the foreign exchange regime came to be linked to the redistributive operations of the Development Fund in an argument which depicted Croatia as milked of the fruits of its economic success in order to support either economically dubious projects in the underdeveloped regions, or to subsidise government profligacy in "Belgrade".

In relation to the domestic economic scene "liberal" forces were in the ascendant everywhere--nowhere more so than in Serbia, where the LC was led by Marko Nikezic. The steady republicanisation of the economy, however, meant that the commitment of liberals to widening the scope of market forces came to be given a nationalist expression, and the case for accelerated economic modernisation came increasingly to be posed in terms of a conflict of interests between the Federation and the republics. As *republics* were readily conceptualised in *national* terms, the dispute over economic modernisation came to be represented (certainly in popular and journalistic discourse) as a matter of the adverse effects of the power of "Belgrade" working together with the "backward South" (Bosnia-Hercegovina, Macedonia, Montenegro) upon the economic development of the "advanced" North (Croatia and Slovenia). Economic modernisation thereby came to be linked generally to the forces of nationalism which the Tito regime had worked so hard since 1945 to defeat.

Matters came to a head in the "Croatian Spring" of 1971-72, in which the leadership of the LC in Croatia attempted to use the emotional force of arguments about national interest in order to create a popular mass movement which could become the political vehicle for the advancement of their case. Their creation of an ill-assorted temporary coalition of the cultural conservatives surrounding the cultural organisation *Matica Hrvatska*, student radicalism (still resentful about the repression of the movement of 1968) and market-minded modernisers proved to be too much of a threat to the regime. The spectre of nationalism was just too threatening in the wake of the serious disturbances which had swept Kosovo, also in 1968—doubly so when voices were heard demanding the republicanisation of the armed forces. The "Croatian Spring" was suppressed, and the occasion seized to oust modernisers also in other republics (the Milosavljevski faction in Macedonia, supporters of Kavcic in Slovenia, and of Nikezic in Serbia).

The manifest response to crisis was, as Harold Lydall puts it: "As always when in difficulties, the Party's first though was how to give the conflict a 'class war' flavour" (Lydall 1984:88). In practical terms this meant a movement to "strengthen self-management". This took two concrete forms--the new constitution of 1974 and the "Law on Associated Labour" (*Zakon o udruzenom radu--ZUR*) of two years later. The ideological tie which united them was the decision that the key to the country's problem was the threat of "technocracy" and "managerialism" unleashed by economic reform. It was necessary to put the organised working class back into the saddle.

Society was generally to be made over in the image of "associated labour", so that the "basic organisation of associated labour" (*osnovna organizacija udruzenog rada--OOUR*) became the fundamental unit out of which not only economic enterprises were constructed, but the key to access to rights and participation in general. Together with the neighbourhood community (*mjesna zajednica*) authority was in principle delegated upwards from these basic building blocks. Larger and more complex enterprises consisted of a federal arrangement of these "basic organisations" into a "complex organisation of associated labour" (*slozena organizacija udruzenog rada-- SOUR*).[25] Similarly, in local government, the municipality (or commune—*opstina*) was seen as a federal arrangement of neighbourhood communmities.

The provision of social services and administrative functions, and the undertaking of contractual arrangements between economic and other institutions, were achieved through the formation of a network of "social compacts" (*drustveni dogovor*) and the creation of "self-managing communities of interest" (*samoupravna interesna zajednica*).

> On paper at least, almost all the rules of economic and political behaviour were changed. Almost all the old terminology was also changed, so that nothing was easily recognizable; and everyone was obliged to learn a new vocabulary, which only a few Yugoslavs could properly understand. (Lydall 1984:90)

As a feat of the imagination the process of *oourizacija* and its concomitants was truly formidable: but as a practicable set of institutional arrangements for the conduct of economic and social affairs it was a disaster. With hindsight it appears to have been intended to square the ideological circle. By constructing everything from the ground up on the basis of a system of "delegation" it was intended to strengthen workers' control at the expense of "managerialism", but in a manner which owed nothing to the traditions of "bourgeois democracy". The system depended nominally upon popular consent: but the base of grass roots organisation was easily controlled by the local *kadrovi* of the LC, and the higher in the structure of delegation one went the more thoroughgoing was that control. Just as "liberal" appeals to democratisation could be trumped by reference to the element of unrivalled popular participation in the new system, so appeals to the market could also be countered by the apparently voluntaristic and contractual character of the structure of self-managing agreements. Over large sections of the economy the movement towards market forms which had been under way since the reforms of 1965 was actually reversed, and replaced by networks of locally administered price-fixing.

While superficially giving way to everything demanded by liberal reformers, therefore, both on the economic and political fronts, the new structures can be seen to have represented a significant step backwards into a degree of politicisation of society which it is not unreasonable to describe as "Stalinist". The tone of developments was set at the 10th. Congress of the LCY in May 1974, which actually re-emphasised the importance of the tradition of "democratic centralism" (Jelavich 1983:400). In the years which followed the real nature of these changes was revealed in an appreciable shift in the social composition of Yugoslav elites (Cohen 1989:158). The "technocratic" culture of the 1963 constitution (noted by Rusinow) was replaced by a process in which "political professionals" gave way to "professional politicians" (Cohen 1989: Chap. 4).

Far from contributing to economic modernisation, the entire tendency of these legislative changes was to promote rigidity and stasis by bringing into being a set of organisational forms of truly bewildering complexity. These were placed in the hands of a political class which became their privileged interpreters. It is my belief that,

124

taken together, the Constitution of 1974 and *ZUR* contributed as much as any other feature of Yugoslavia's history to its eventual collapse.

These changes were taking place, however, against the background of world events which was to make the country's context ever more difficult. Whereas the institutional changes to which I have referred can be regarded as self-inflicted injury, the changes in the world economic system which coincided with these domestic events probably could not. One consequence of Yugoslavia's commitment to industrialisation was the creation of a relatively heavy demand for energy. "The problem has been exacerbated by the recent expansion of industrial enterprises that are high-power consumers, including aluminium and copper smelting, steel production in electric furnaces, and plants producing industrial chemicals" (Poulson 1992:55).

Yugoslavia generated an unusually high 50% of its power needs from hydro-electric sources, and had some resources of coal and oil. Nevertheless, 40% of its energy needs had to be imported, a substantial proportion of which was in the form of oil. The sudden rise in world oil prices of 1973-4 had a dramatic impact upon the Yugoslav economy. Yugoslavia was far from being alone in its failure to anticipate this problem. As Marko Milivojevic has pointed out "OPEC from its formation in 1960 took over ten years before it established itself as a credible and effective organisation. It was ignored by the OECD Governments for most of the 1960s" (Milivojevic 1985:127). Some of Yugoslavia's principal investment decisions at this time were based upon the assumption of the availability of cheap energy, particularly the *Naftovod* project, which constructed an oil pipeline from the Omisalj terminal on the island of Krk to Novi-Sad and Pancevo (Dyker 1990:107-8). The rapid expansion of Croatia's tourism was also undergirded by the fact that around 90% of foreign tourists arrived by road.

Although Yugoslavia's first and only nuclear power plant at Krsko, on the Slovene/Croatian border, was projected at this time, the importance of accounting permanently for high energy prices was not assimilated. By the time of the second "oil shock" of 1979 little had been done to adjust the country's economic strategy, and the failure to meet the costs of energy imports was being regularly covered by borrowing rather than by exports or by greater efficiency.

The energy sector was not the only area in which the Yugoslav economy was hit by adverse world movements. The construction of an aluminium smelting industry in Montenegro was projected to rely upon domestically produced hydro-electricity from the Mratinje Dam. Its rationale was undermined by the collapse of world aluminium prices after 1972. The response to the situation was made more difficult by two other features of the economic environment.

The general European and world recession which attended these changes hit Yugoslavia at the level of its balance of payments in other indirect ways. It is worth singling out for comment the importance of emigrant remittances. A period of employment abroad had almost become by the mid-1970s a standard part of the Yugoslav way of life. "In the period between 1964 and 1975 as many as 2.3 million Yugoslav citizens, including dependent family members, might have been living and working for some time as migrants in Western Europe" (Mesic 1992:194-5). Their remittances home, together with those from longer-term émigrés, acquired an extremely important role in helping to compensate for a persisting negative balance of trade. With a negative trade balance of $1,438 in 1971, Yugoslavs abroad had remitted home $852 million (59% of the deficit) (Dyker 1990:94). By 1980, when the deficit on trade had moved to $$6,086 million, the flow of remittances had grown to $1,902 million—but by then a contribution of only 31%. The deteriorating employment situation in other European countries was not only reducing the employment opportunities abroad for Yugoslav citizens, and reducing the disposable income available to them to support families at home, it had even set in motion a movement of return, which also placed a strain upon the market for employment in Yugoslavia itself (Lydall 1984:160-162).[26]

The other contextual feature which bore upon the growing Yugoslav economic crisis was the global character of the debt problem. Yugoslavia was far from being alone in accumulating huge foreign debts in this period, and its burden might be considered to be relatively insignificant in relation to those of Brazil and Mexico. Yugoslavia in the late 1970s found itself in the same boat as other non-oil producing developing countries, facing a serious problem of indebtedness. The external debt of these countries grew overall by an estimated 264% between 1973 and 1980, in which context the expansion of Yugoslavia's indebtedness by 283% is not uniquely high (Milivojevic 1985:2-4). The problem of indebtedness was generated by a reciprocal mechanism involving the availability of huge sums (especially "petrodollars") looking for profitable outlets for investment as well as by the demand for credit on the part of the indebted.

Across the entire post-war period also Yugoslavia had shown itself to be a model creditor, never seeking rescheduling or defaulting on payment. The atmosphere of ready credit on a world scale was challenged by a global anxiety about the security of credit extended to these countries, and not specifically in relation to Yugoslavia.

Indeed, looked a comparatively Yugoslavia might be said to have remained throughout the 1970s a relatively secure investment. Until 1980 its debt/service ratio remained steady, and even declined slightly, whereas this ratio grew alarmingly for some other major debtor states, such as Brazil, Venezuela or Spain. The peak years of Yugoslav indebtedness were 1975-1980 (Lydall 1984:44). Although the ratio between its external debt and the volume of exports rose from 75.6% in 1974 to 133.6% in 1979, the figure actually fell over the following two years, again in a pattern which compared relatively favourably with that of many other debtor states. The action of the international financial community in imposing conditions of increasing stringency upon credit after 1982, and insisting upon certain modifications to internal economic policy, cannot be considered to have been solely triggered by a lack of confidence in Yugoslavia, but by agreement that the global pattern of debt should be brought under increasingly close surveillance and tight control. By 1980 Yugoslavia's foreign debt had climbed to around $15 billion, consuming 25% of all foreign earnings in debt service (Lydall 1989:41 and 44-46; Jelavich 1983:401). Throughout the 1970s, however, the Yugoslav political and economic leadership remained unprepared to address these fundamental problems of debt, inflation and low productivity, and were preoccupied with essentially domestic political issues, especially the inter-republican power struggle.

One of the consequences of workers' self-management was the very high cost of small business entry. The law required a standard administrative and accounting framework for worker-managed enterprises which presented serious disincentives for the small enterprise. A high proportion of the administrative and financial costs of social services were also accounted for, collected and even disbursed at the level of the firm (Bateman 1993). Furthermore, the regime remained hostile to the idea of filling this gap by increased resort to the initiative of individual entrepreneurs outside the social sector. In spite of the insistence of both domestic and foreign economists, the question of property reform was defined as off limits until it was too late, and the Markovic government introduced a new *Zakon o preduzecima* ("Law on Enterprises") in 1989.

In spite of the outward commitment to "market socialism", which might have been expected to alert policy-makers to the problems, in many respects it was a case of "business as usual". New planning laws were enacted in 1970, 1976 and 1979 (Singleton and Carter 1982:Chap. 13. Indeed, a new plan was launched as late as 1981-1985.) The notion of "indicative planning" has been used in relation to Yugoslavia, and comparisons with the French system have often been made. Such comparisons are of dubious validity, however, in that the French system does rest upon a developed set of market mechanisms for all factors of production. Market mechanisms never developed for the factors of production in Yugoslavia, and in relation to goods and services were constantly subject either to political interference, or bound within frameworks of regional autarky.

The system of agreements and compacts made for real rigidities in the flow of investment, and "market socialism" lacked a proper market for capital.[27] There was by this time, however, an urgent need to reequip neglected basic industries, introduced immediately post-war as "political factories". Too much attention was also being paid to "downstream" sectors, such as the effort put into building up the motor manufacturing capacity of *Crvena Zastava* in Kragujevac without proper attention to the nature and efficiency of steel production in Smederevo.

The emphasis upon communal responsibility also made for the retention of labour and the lack of a proper market for labour. Consequently there was a paradoxical combination of over-manning in some areas, and the massive concealment of unemployment, particularly in the villages, which led to serious underestimation of the real levels of unemployment.

The deteriorating economic situation set in motion a spiral of collapsing economic security. From being the envy of other "real socialist" countries, the Yugoslavs suddenly found themselves facing galloping inflation, rising unemployment and lack of institutional direction at the top. Insecurity is a dreadful solvent of order; and served to exacerbate the political dimension of Yugoslavia's problems. In the search for explanations for their own difficulties, republican political elites tended to resort to blaming other republics, creating a culture of paranoia. Everyone was surrounded by enemies, although the "enemies without" of the Cold War period were now replaced by the "enemies within" of other republics and other nations (Cavoski 1992).

The federal regime was quite unable to respond to this situation. It could only have done so by stepping outside the limits of its established ideology and taking a hard and critical look at the need to reform of property relations and reappraise self-management. What is more, it needed to reconstruct the entire Titoist edifice of the balance of federal/republican/local influence. The programme of economic reform, designed by Ante Markovic, and widely believed both domestically and internationally to be credible, turned out to be impossible to introduce in practice. The changes which it envisaged could only be implemented by a government which had legitimacy: and the rapidly escalating political dimension to the crisis (in which the running was effectively made by republican coteries within the LC) effectively ensured that their own relegitimation pre-empted that of the federation. At a time (during 1988-1990) when republican leadership groups within the LC were steadily acceding to the demands for relegitimation through democratically contested elections within their own republics, these same groups were blocking moves to make available the same mechanisms of relegitimation for the federation.

The only alternative remaining was that economic reform might have been brought in by an authoritarian central government, possibly as the result of a military *coup d'état*. Indeed, this eventuality was widely anticipated among foreign observers of the country (Milivojevic 1988). This solution was precluded, it seems, by two factors. The heavily politicised military were the strongest defenders of "*AVNOJ* Yugoslavia", and hence extremely reluctant to undermine the structure by action which challenged the legitimacy of the system to which they were committed. They were also among the most committed of the leadership groups in their opposition to relegitimation through electoral contest, and deeply suspicious of free market institutions. In retrospect, therefore, it was unrealistic to expect, therefore, that they might ever have been the bearers of a modernising revolution, dependent upon the support of the West.

Conclusion

Travelling in Yugoslavia just before its break-up, engaged in a project studying the first cycle of freely-contested elections, in each of the republics I asked a range of professional politicians, senior academics and other influentials, the same question. "Which is the most serious problem facing Yugoslavia today: the economy, the constitution, or Kosovo?" All (except the Kosovars) said, usually without hesitation, "the economy". Yet economic interests were either too politically dependent, or too fragmented, to act independently and enforce any real change until it was too late.

There has to date been no adequate analysis of the economic dimension to the collapse of the Yugoslav state. Certainly ample attention has been paid to the importance of regional economic differences in that process, but generally speaking it has been assumed that the economic aspects of regional conflict were in a sense subordinate to the political aspects, flowing from the conflict between regional elites.[28] A proper appraisal of this process needs to examine fully the interaction not only of domestic factors of economic structure and organisation together with political factors, but to relate these also to consideration of the manner in which the Yugoslav regime mediated the pressures bearing upon Yugoslavia from its international, global, context. A preliminary hypothesis for such an investigation, however, which I have suggested here, is that the Yugoslav system embodied a persistent contradiction between the technical and organisational imperatives of its economic development, partly deriving from its insertion into global processes of economic modernisation, and the anti-modern character of its search for a specifically socialist path to modernity.

Notes

1. A selective review of these includes: Dirlam and Plummer 1973; Sirc 1979; Singleton and Carter 1982; Lydall 1984 and 1989; Prout 1985; Dyker 1990 and Madzar in Allcock, Horton and Milivojevic eds. 1991; Vojnic, in Akhavan and Howse eds. 1995. A proper discussion of the economic roots of the eventual disintegration of Yugoslavia has yet to be undertaken.

2. Further aspects of the sociological significance of self-management are discussed in Chapter 9.

3. To the effects of the international aid programme on Yugoslav development should also be added consideration of the payment of war reparations be Germany, Italy, Hungary and Bulgaria (Kaser and Radice eds. 1986:574). Bulgarian reparations were waived in anticipation of the creation of the Balkan Federation, plans for which were scuppered by the dispute with the Cominform (see below).

4. Singleton and Carter (1982:110) remark that the speech in which Boris Kidric presented the plan to the V Congress of the CPY was based on an article by Stalin. On the objectives of the First Five Year Plan see Waterston 1962: Appendix A; Singleton and Carter 1982:112-13.

5. The impact of the weather was actually measurably more severe (Singleton and Carter 1982:115-6).

6. "It transpires that the value of Yugoslav imports fell from 88.4 billion dinars in 1949 to 69.2 billion in 1950, but rose again in 1951 to 115.1 billion dinars, 30 per cent more than before the blockade, and subsequently remained at that level." (Sirc 1979:2)

7. Astonishingly this is a subject which is not treated at all in either Bicanic 1973 or Kaser and Radice eds. 1986a. Singleton and Carter 1982, Lydall 1984, and Dyker 1990, although purporting to deal primarily with the economy of Yugoslavia, in fact confine their attentions almost exclusively to the

political dimension of the break. Here the foremost concerns have been the impact of the break with the Soviet Union upon the adoption of self-management, although other authors have commented upon the stimulus which was given to the Non-Aligned Movement. For comment on the specific significance of *economic* differences as causal factors in the dispute, see Armstrong 1951:78-81; Newman 1952:104-9; Clissold 1975: 43, 58-9, 167 and 230; Samary 1988:74-77; Crampton 1994:256-8.

8. See, for example, Sirc 1979. Differences in assessment of Yugoslavia's economic performance often reflect a different choice of base-line for comparison. Certainly the First Five Year Plan failed to achieve its targets: but as these are generally agreed to have been totally unrealistic in the first place, they have little value as standards of comparison. Dyker 1990 seems to have a rather more balanced view.

9. For all the irrationalities of the period of "administrative socialism", the strategy adopted by the Yugoslavs was not entirely unreasonable, and cannot be accounted for simply by reference to socialist dogmatism. As Dyker has pointed out:

> whatever imbalances its development in the 1950s engendered, engineering must be allowed pride of place amongst industrial sectors as an engine of extensive development. It is normally fairly highly labour-intensive, but affords considerable scope for the employment of a dual technology approach, as Soviet experience has illustrated. In addition, it provides an excellent training ground for the new proletariat, an ideal context for on-the-job training in basic industrial skills. (Dyker 1990:58)

10. For the text of the law, see Boskovic and Dasic eds. 1980.

11. Fred Singleton has drawn attention to this point, however (1976:128-31). See also Jambrek 1975 and Drulovic 1978 for more sustained treatment of the issues.

12. The *locus classicus* for the formulation of the characteristics of a "labour-managed economy" is Vanek 1970. The concept of the "Illyrian firm" seems to be much older, however, and can be

attributable to Ward 1958. See also Wachtel 1973: esp. Chap. 3. The concept is commented upon regularly in the general texts on the Yugoslav economy.

13. The most thorough discussion of these issues I have encountered is in McFarlane 1988: Chap. 13, "The political economy of self-management".

14. The tensions between economic development and "building socialism" are the central concerns (although handled in strongly contrasting ways) of Milenkovitch 1971 and Samary 1988.

15. The contrasting propositions of the "White Book" and the "Yellow Book" are set out concisely in Singleton and Carter 1982:135-7.

16. A useful account of the link between constitutional and economic reform during this period is Rusinow 1977: Chap. 5.

17. The share of investment coming as self-financing by enterprises rose slightly, from 29.5% to 31.2%. Note that the important distinction between *central* and *local* or *republican* institutional sources in blurred in these figures. My own estimate is that local financing of investment increased its share from around one third to more than two thirds in this interval.

18. The reform programme was incomplete in another important respect, namely, its failure to address the issue of price control. These controls were relaxed in relation to a range of goods, but the movement towards the market mechanism was far from complete. Dyker 1990:32-33 and 63-65; Lydall 1984:256-262.

19. Its purpose had been to support the import of raw materials, which would be transformed by Yugoslav industry, in order to encourage subsequent exports. The actual effect was simply to subsidise imports. See Bombelles 1968:162-65.

135

20. The most remarkable change is to be seen in the Vojvodina, which in 1952 had been one of the more backward areas of the federation, with 89.5%, but by 1960 this had soared to 107.8%.

21. For a fuller discussion of the problem, see Ramet 1992 Chap. 8; Plestina 1992. The difficulties of producing uncontroversial measures of differentiation are not to be underestimated, and the index I have chosen here would be refined considerably in the hands of an econometrician. Harold Lydall has made this point effectively (Lydall 1989:188).

22. This point has been suggested in Ramet 1992:148-150. It is argued systematically in Mihailovic 1980. As Ramet points out, all of the republics (even Slovenia) contained "pockets of underdevelopment", to which the existence of the federal Development Fund was often an irrelevance.

23. Grbic 1984. See for fuller discussion of these issues my essay on tourism and the private sector in Yugoslavia, Allcock, Horton and Milivojevic eds. 1992:387-413.

24. As in the pre-war period private savings tended to be ploughed in very large measure into the support of housing.

25. This process of *oourizacija* turned a large engineering group in Slovenia into 31 semi-independent, self-managing entities.

26. There are serious difficulties in the interpretation of unemployment figures in Yugoslavia, and arguments have been advanced that they both seriously overestimate and underestimate the "true" picture. Advocates of "overestimation" point out that a high proportion of registered "job seekers" were actually in employment. Those who argue of "underestimation" stress the levels of underemployment in all areas of the Yugoslav economy, the time which had to elapse before those without work could actually claim benefit, and the cushioning effect of widespread landholding, which often took potential employees out of the active labour market. The point here rests, however, on relative rather than absolute figures.

27. In this respect the problem of the immobility of capital is a continuity with the pre-war period.

28. A start has been made in this endeavour by Lydall 1989 and Dyker 1990, although they both wrote on the eve of the maturation of the Yugoslav crisis. See also Woodward 1995 and Akhavan and Howse eds. 1995.

4

ECONOMIC MODERNISATION:
THE AGRARIAN ECONOMY

Why agriculture?

Although in the previous two chapters I have addressed the general process of the modernisation of the South Slav lands and their incorporation into global economic processes, I have decided to devote an additional chapter to agrarian affairs, for several reasons.

The subject of rural issues has received far too little attention on the part of those who have addressed the economic history of the region. Tomasevich (1955) stands out among the very few attempts to address these questions centrally, but his monumental work is confined to the pre-Communist period.[1] The modernisation and globalisation processes, however, can not be reduced to *industrialisation*, and developments in the countryside can not be considered as "those parts of the economy which modernity cannot reach", but as the very locus of modernisation.

Under the former Empires, and during the time of the "First Yugoslavia", agriculture rather than industry represented the primary locus of capital accumulation, and the main avenue through which the region was incorporated into nation-wide (and even world-wide) markets. The *urban* economy often remained mired in traditionalism and localism, as a craft-based sector addressing the needs of local markets. The export-based economy which developed was created around the supply of primary products, drawn from the agrarian economy and mining. In substantial measure, therefore, the South Slav lands came to be inserted into the global economy precisely through agriculture.

The lateness and incompleteness of the processes of urbanisation and industrialisation in Yugoslavia has meant that most Yugoslavs have only been one generation from the village. Failure to acknowledge this fact can lead one to overlook or at least underestimate the importance of cultural continuity, and the persistence of patterns of life rooted in the countryside.[2]

After the collapse of the collectivisation programme, and the retreat from the systematic attempt to industrialise the countryside in the early 1950s, the regime largely turned its back upon agriculture. Part of the trouble experienced by the Yugoslav economy under Communism had to do with the failure to modernise agrarian production because of the League of Communists' blinkered view of the institution of private property. Nevertheless, I believe that any attempt to provide an adequate appreciation of the social development of the South Slav lands must give appropriate attention to the modernisation of the countryside.

Modernisation, commoditisation and the development of capitalism

Attempting to summarise the characteristics of agrarian society and economy in the South Slav lands before their unification, it is important to differentiate three dimensions along which their progressive incorporation into wider, modern structures might be measured. These are: the degree of their monetisation; their implication in commodity exchange; and the relative development of capitalistic relationships of production, property and employment.

Writing of the "classic" peasant society, Henri Mendras writes:

> The peasant economy has, in principle, no place for money: it is a non-monetary economy. ....Money is completely external to the system, and penetrates from the outside into the heart of the peasant economy, introduced by the environing economy of which it is the occasion, the agency and the sign. (Mendras 1976:44)

The economy of "self-sufficiency and barter" which Mendras considers to be characteristic of peasantries was eroded rapidly and early in south-eastern Europe. A degree of *monetisation*, which we can take as a kind of base-line for the integration of the peasantry into wider economic processes, is to be found in all areas of the Balkan Peninsula by the outbreak of the First World War, although its relative advancement varied between regions.

The stimulus to monetisation came from three directions which were common to both of the former great empires. The state itself was one of the most powerful influences in this direction, with its demands for taxation. Certain basic demands of the peasant household could only be met by monetary transaction--even if these were reduced to the Montenegrin tribesman's need for gunpowder, weapons and coffee. Probably of greatest significance as time passed was the fact that the growing implication of the local ruling classes within wider and more complex networks of transaction provided a powerful lever upon them to commute traditional feudal dues to money payments in order to meet their own requirements for cash.

Whereas a basic level of *monetisation* might be considered to be relatively universal in this region, however, there does appear to have been a considerable difference in the extent to which different localities became primarily devoted to the regular, matter-of-course, production of agricultural *commodities intended for exchange*. Most of Slovenia, some parts of Slavonia and the Adriatic coast, and above all the Vojvodina were deeply and consistently engaged in the production of commodities for the market; but so too were parts of Bosnia, the Danube-Lower Morava areas of Serbia and parts of Macedonia. Monetisation and the growth of commodity production were intimately linked, of course, especially in those areas where the commutation of feudal dues for rents, or their replacement by a debt of indemnity, drove the peasant's need for a regular cash income. In certain specific areas, such as the Dalmatian coast or Montenegro, the peasant's needs for money were supported as much through the remittances of migrant workers as through changes in the pattern of production. The Sandzak of Novi Pazar, Kosovo and Montenegro, together with large areas of Adriatic Croatia, and even parts of alpine Slovenia, however, remained relatively marginal to systematic commodity exchange.

The spread of socio-economic relations which can be called *"capitalistic"* was a much more circumscribed affair. Forms of accumulation through usury were extremely widespread, and once again were linked intimately to the shift from feudal obligations in kind and labour to the payment of rents or indemnities. Before the Balkan Wars, however, the structure of credit provision was primitive in the extreme, and resided in the hands of local individuals such as wealthy peasants, inn-keepers, merchants or landlords. Where credit was mediated through banks this was extended almost exclusively to the holders of large estates.

Capitalistic *production*, in which the farm was run as a business, especially where this involved the dependency of the enterprise upon the recruitment of wage labour, was very localised indeed. Before their unification, the only part of the South Slav lands which exhibited any appreciable development of capitalism in this sense was the Vojvodina.

The agrarian economy in the Ottoman lands[3]

The conventional discussion of the Ottoman rural economy in the Balkans begins with the *timar* system--the allocation of revocable fiefs to spahis, with the intention that the revenue from the estate should be used to sustain armed knights and their retainers in a state of readiness for the service of the Sultan. Whereas this was the main-stay of the early Ottoman feudal system in the Balkans, this ideal system decayed in important respects over time.

By the middle of the sixteenth century (when the initial expansionist phase of the Empire in Europe was running out of steam) Constantinople had a population of around half a million (Hegyi and Zimanyi 1986:125-6). Although the population of several large towns (such as Belgrade and Skopje) declined significantly during the eighteenth century in the wake of the disruption of the wars against Austria, "the expansion of towns, population and industry in western and central Europe during the eighteenth century created a rising demand for rural Balkan products: grains, hides, cattle, meat, oil, wax, silk, wool, cotton, tobacco and timber". (Carter 1977a:178. See also Hegyi and Zimanyi 1986:134-5; Carter 1977:176-82.) The Balkan regions of the Empire were indispensable as a source of these products, which flowed along the ancient trade routes to the capital, other cities, and even into international trade.

After the middle of the seventeenth, and during the eighteenth centuries, the *timar* holding (the non-hereditable prebend which reverted to the Sultan upon the death of the holder) was increasingly replaced by a hereditable estate, although this process was uneven in its speed and distribution. Several analytically separable processes are potentially confusable here--the move away from the prebendiary system; the commutation of the labour dues of the *reaya* (peasantry) for cash payment; the commercialisation of agricultural production; the consolidation of holdings into "sizeable plantation-like estates"; and the bringing into cultivation land which had been abandoned, or which had previously been uncultivated, under new legal arrangements in response to population pressure (McGowan, in Inalçik and Quataert eds. 1994:870-5; Lampe and Jackson 1982:33-9).

Attempts to see in these processes the general emergence of a primitive capitalist system of production no longer seem to be supportable (Lampe and Jackson 1982:33-4). Particularly in areas such as those close to expanding communication routes, however, along with the concurrent extension of the practice of tax-farming, the emergence of *ciftlik* estates can be taken as an important index of a growing *commercialisation* of the Ottoman rural economy.

Macedonia (together, to a lesser extent, with Kosovo) are the only areas later to be incorporated into Yugoslavia which did experience a substantial development of *ciftlik* estates (McGowan 1981: 56-79, esp. map p. 77). This is associated with the rapid expansion during the second half of the nineteenth century of the areas under crops such as tobacco, opium, rice and cotton, all of which figured significantly in trade serving a wider market.

The suppression of the Ilinden uprising of 1903 had devastating consequences for Macedonia; and this was followed shortly by the Balkan Wars and the Great War. As a consequence of these developments, a noticeably polarised structure of land-holding emerged before 1919. At the beginning of this century 76,920 households subsisted on holdings of less than five hectares, while at the other end of the scale 174 large estates shared between them 56,448 hectares (Bojanovski, Djonov and Pemovska 1955). The latter were typically *cifcije*, cultivated on the basis of traditional labour obligations or share-cropping arrangements rather than by wage labour, although they were mainly oriented towards production for the market.[4]

In the Serbian lands the process of *ciftlik*-building was retarded by the extent of forested land, and in any case interrupted by the expulsion of the Turks. In 1833 the Ottoman system was abolished by a land reform which consolidated ownership in the hands of those who tilled the land. Throughout the nineteenth century the policy of the state was to ensure the creation of a stratum of small peasant proprietors, and its protection through a succession of legislative acts providing for a "protected minimum homestead" from which the peasant could not be alienated as a result of indebtedness (Tomasevich 1955:37-48). While these paternalistic efforts on the part of the state undoubtedly succeeded in their aim of perpetuating peasant cultivation, they also introduced a substantial degree of structural immobility. The irony of the Serbian experience, therefore, is that its legacy of rural backwardness was in part a consequence of the attempts made there to avoid the perceived negative effects of Ottoman "feudalism".

The Serbian countryside was dominated by holdings of 5-20 hectares. Nearly two fifths of all rural households fell into this category before the First World War (Tomasevich 1955:206). There were few of the dwarf holdings which were particularly numerous in those areas which were formerly parts of the Austro-Hungarian Empire. Serbia also differed from several of these regions in that it contained no latifundias: an estate of more than 100 hectares was "large" in the independent kingdom at the turn of the century.[5]

With a largely pastoral economy and an acute scarcity of arable land, Montenegro was characterised by very small holdings. The tiny kingdom escaped the creation of large estates partly through its exclusion from either of the two great empires.

Bosnia and Hercegovina were marked by the extreme diversity of agrarian conditions. Some parts of the provinces remained in near autarkic isolation--the upper Podrina, the highland areas west of the Vrbas, and the greater part of Hercegovina (it is appropriate at this point also to include reference to the Sandzak). Others participated in the pattern of development more typical of northern Serbia, on the basis of the export of specific crops such as plums (especially the Posavina and lower Podrina).

Because the Austrian authorities elected not to antagonise the Muslim landlords after the occupation of 1878, extension of the land reform implemented elsewhere in the Dual Monarchy was never contemplated here. The historical estates of the Muslim agas and begs remained intact until the Reform of the inter-war years. On the whole, the situation appears to have resembled that in Macedonia, with more than 90% of the free peasants and more than three quarters of serfs working farms of less than 10 ha, and a large proportion of the land concentrated in the hands of a relatively small number of noble families.[6]

The agrarian economy in the Habsburg lands

Although some Balkan historians have argued that the formerly Ottoman lands are to be distinguished from the formerly Habsburg lands by the relative "advancement" of the latter, even within the Austro-Hungarian Empire there were regions which in their degree of backwardness compared with the "Asiatic" retardation of the south. Several areas within the Dual Monarchy before 1918, subsequently incorporated into the unified South Slav state, for quite diverse regions were characterised by acute backwardness.

The lands of the Military Frontier were burdened until the end of the eighteenth century by permanent insecurity and proneness to Ottoman raids. Even after the direct threat of Ottoman attack had receded in the nineteenth century the military vocation of the population continued to have a severe impact upon their chances of modernising agriculture. During the Napoleonic Wars the Frontier lost every ninth inhabitant. "As late as 1860, when the Frontier was in its last stages of existence, it gave one soldier for every nine inhabitants while the remainder of the Habsburg Empire gave one soldier for every 142 inhabitants." (Tomasevich 1955:76)

Until the reorganisation of the Frontier after 1850 there were severe restrictions on the disposal and accumulation of land. Although the abolition of serfdom in 1848 speeded up the dissolution of the traditional *zadruga* (extended family community) conditions were placed upon dissolutions within the Frontier areas. Until its demilitarisation in 1873, and its reunification with civil Croatia in 1881, there were significant institutional brakes upon the economic modernisation of the Frontier, and mechanisms which operated to ensure its continuing relative poverty, backwardness and social isolation.

Both under the influence of Venetian law and the local system developed within the formerly independent Ragusan Republic, the Dalmatian peasantry laboured under particularly oppressive forms of feudal obligation. These consisted broadly speaking of forms of share-cropping, the most common of which was known as the *kolonat* (Tomasevich 1955:112-19). Although the region was taken into the Austrian part of the Empire in 1813, and some reform was achieved in 1878, feudal obligations remained in force until the post-unification Land Reform.

In Dalmatia there are certain similarities with the pattern found in Bosnia, in that holdings tended to be fragmented into tiny parcels. More than 60% of farms were no more than 2 ha. in extent. There were no latifundias here, although there were a number of farms of more than 50 ha. each. The apparent disparities in holdings in this region are rather less pronounced, however, when we look at the distribution of arable land only. Only of a fifth of Dalmatia was classed as arable in 1902; and two thirds of the area of the 154 estates of more than 100 ha. was rough pasture or waste, while more than a quarter of it was afforested (Ivsic 1926:283: Tomasevich 1955:207-8).

Dalmatia's history as the locus of several vigorous trading cities (notably Ragusa, Spalato and Zara) ensured a measure of urban prosperity before the mid-nineteenth century. Their rural hinterland was even then noted for its poverty. The shipping interests of the region were slow to take advantage of the transformation wrought by the arrival of steam, and after a brief boom occasioned by the Crimean War, the eastern Adriatic sank into steady decline. A brief revival was experienced in the later 1870s and 1880s, after the French vineyards were devastated by phylloxera--an opportunity to which the Adriatic wine producers were able to respond. They too succumbed to the disease in the following decade, however, crippling this branch of agriculture for several decades. With its extreme shortage of arable land the region suffered the most serious levels of over-population of any in the South Slav lands, and emigration rates were very high whenever this was possible.

The Slovene lands occupied a position midway between Serbia and Dalmatia. As in Serbia nearly 40% of the peasants of Carniola occupied farms in the range 5-20 ha. As in Dalmatia, though, this more mountainous region featured large expanses of afforested and unproductive land, which tended to belong disproportionately to large estates, where it was valued for sporting rather than economic reasons. The 332 farms of over 100 ha. held only 3% of the land, but 25% of the pasture, 33% of the forest and 42% of the marshes.[7] Here too we find a large proportion of tiny holdings in 1902, with more than 20% of the farms owning 2 ha. or less (Ivsic 1926:163). Other areas also remained pockets of real poverty for similar reasons, notably parts of Istria, Gorizia and Gradisca.

The Habsburg landholding system, especially where this was based upon the Hungarian "donational system", permitted the development of large estates. Several, but by no means all of these, moved into commercialised agriculture during the last quarter of the nineteenth century, in the Banat, Backa and Srijem. Otherwise the dismantling of feudalism and the commutation of feudal obligations to rents forced a steady monetisation of the economy, although the patterns of exchange in which peasants were enmeshed remained quite localised. An important feature of this process was the widespread availability of part-time and seasonal employment in activities such as flour and timber milling, laying the basis for the later emergence of the widespread phenomenon of the "peasant worker" (Kostic 1955).

Probably our fullest information about agrarian affairs in pre-unification Yugoslavia comes from Croatia-Slavonia outside the Military Frontier, and located in the Hungarian part of the Dual Monarchy. Here the stratum of "middle-sized" estates (between 5-20 ha.) lay at the upper end of peasant holdings. More than 99% of all farms were of 50 ju. (29.8 ha.) or less, and these contained about 68% of the total farm area. Parcelisation had proceeded at least as far as in Dalmatia, and further than in Macedonia. Furthermore, Croatia-Slavonia contained a relatively large number of latifundias and large farms. Estates of between 100 and 1,000 ha. only accounted for 0.22% of the total number of holdings; but the 930 farms in this category included 5.22% of the land. The 209 latifundias of more than 1,000 ha. each, although only a tiny percentage of the total number of farms, amassed between them more than a fifth of the region's area. The largest of these was that of Count Taxis Thurn, at Gorski

Kotar, with more than 64,000 ju. (36,800 ha.) (Stojsavljevic 1965: 25-6. See also Ivsic

1926:142 ff.). Twelve estates between them comprised roughly 6% of the area of the

region.

Yet another distinctive pattern emerges if we turn to the Vojvodina. Roughly 59% of

the total area of the Banat and Backa in 1910 belonged to 1,569 properties (only 1.4%

of holdings) (Ivsic 1926:158 and 161). The complement of these huge concentrations

of land, however, was not a mass of pocket-handkerchief holdings, as in Croatia.

Instead, the land was worked by an army of landless labourers who, together with

their families, made up more than 40% of the population, and more than a third of

those gainfully employed in agriculture at the time. (Jovanovic 1930:266.)

The most prominent feature to emerge from this brief survey is the variety of

agrarian conditions in the different parts of the South Slav lands before their

unification. These differences in the size of holdings turn out to provide a short-hand

key also to a diversity of types of ecology, technology and socio-legal relations.

Agriculture in the "First Yugoslavia"

i) The Agrarian Reform and its consequences

No small part of the economic difficulties faced by the South Slav peasantry after the

unification is attributable to the effects of war. This is particularly the case in Serbia

and Macedonia, where agriculture entered the 1920s with a considerable need for

credit in order to restock herds and rebuild and equip farms. Hard on the heels of war came the Agricultural Reform, which in spite of being demanded by the peasantry, and generally regarded as for their benefit, brought with it economic problems. Whereas reform freed the peasant from "feudal" burdens, the old order had also carried with it certain privileges for the peasant, so that the balance sheet of reform is by no means as obvious as may at first seem to be the case. The Agrarian Reform was one of the most significant factors which cut across any spontaneous processes of change in agriculture; and no consideration of Yugoslav agriculture would be complete without an assessment of this series of measures and their significance.

Writers during the Communist period tended to concentrate upon its role as a means of temporarily pacifying a potentially revolutionary peasantry in the turbulent period following 1918 (Mirkovic 1952:80; Eric 1958:14; Stojsavljevic 1965:48 ff; Vuco 1968:46). There can be little doubt, however, that both directly and indirectly the attempts at agrarian reform in the inter-war period did have a profound effect on rural social and economic structures. The priority with which the new Kingdom of Serbs, Croats and Slovenes regarded the subject is indicated by the fact that the first pronouncement of the Regent (his Manifesto to the People of 6 January 1919) expressed the wish that a "just solution to the agrarian question" be found, and committed the government to the setting up of a Commission to prepare the ground for legislation. The first legislative steps followed in the "Interim Decree" of 5 February 1919 (Tomasevich 1955:347-9).

The old feudal institutions such as *kmetstvo* or *kolonat* were abolished, and former serfs were declared to be the owners of the land which they tilled. A commitment was made to expropriate all "large estates", but against the payment of indemnity, although the decree left both the definition of a "large" estate and the size and mechanism of indemnification to future legislation (Franges 1934; Ivsic 1926). Estates belonging to certain classes of foreign nationals were to be expropriated without recompense. Larger forest properties were to revert to the state, although peasant rights to cutting and grazing were guaranteed. Certain restrictions were placed upon transactions in land until the final settlement of the Reform. The territories of pre-1912 Serbia and Montenegro were specifically exempted from its provisions as they lacked both large estates and structures of traditional dependency.

The Interim Decree has been heavily criticised for leaving open some of the most important aspects of the reform, giving interested parties ample time to organise their forces in opposition to the detailed legislation. The delay was not necessarily dictated by incompetence or knavery. Seven separate legal systems had to be integrated within the new kingdom. In areas acquired from Turkey after 1912 in particular the records of titles to land were in very bad order. Many of the expropriated foreign estate holders sued the Yugoslav government in the International Court at The Hague, seeking compensation. The process was only finally liquidated when the royal dictatorship took the matter in hand between 1931 and 1936.

"Large estates" were finally defined by law in June 1931. The size of these depended upon soil conditions, land use, and social factors such as the degree of local over-population on the land. In areas such as Dalmatia or Hercegovina, where land was scarce, cultivation dominated by the intensive production of crops such as grapes or olives, and population very dense, the maximum was defined as 50 ha. of cultivated land, or 100 ha. of land in general. In areas such as Srijem or the Vojvodina, where land was plentiful, of a good quality, and largely devoted to the cultivation of cereals, "large estates" were defined as 300 ha. of cultivated land, or 500 ha. of land in general.

In Bosnia and Hercegovina more than a million ha of land was distributed to tenants on lands of the former agas and begs. In Macedonia, Kosovo and the Sandzak the Reform also faced the problem of dismantling the legal framework of the Turkish system of landholding, especially the former *cifcije*. It also had to cope with the colonisation of land abandoned by the former landlords, or depopulated by the ravages of war. The colonisation programme was by no means a purely economic project. It had been initiated by the Serbian government in 1913 with a primary aim of strengthening the Serb or pro-Serbian elements of the population in those areas with large Albanian or Bulgarian elements. Although this project involved relatively small amounts of land (ca. 162,000 ha. by 1936) its political impact was disproportionately large (Malcolm 1998:279-88).

Some of the most complicated problems of the Reform were encountered in the northern areas (Slavonia and the Vojvodina) where the expropriation of "large estates" was rendered politically problematic by the entanglement of the issues with the question of the settlement of reparations between Yugoslavia and Hungary. By the end of 1935, 720 large estates (more than 1.25 million ha.) had been expropriated, the majority of these belonging to foreign nationals. Additional land was purchased from the former owners to aid rationalisation of holdings. As in Macedonia there was a substantial political dimension to the redistribution process. In an attempt to "rectify" the ethnic balance of the region beneficiaries were drawn not only from among the landless or poor local population but also from among volunteers who had fought on the side of the Serbs and their allies in the War, or Slav "optants" who had been left on the wrong side of the border in 1919, but who chose Yugoslav nationality.[8] More than 600,000 peasant families benefited from redistribution (of fewer than 2 million pre-war holdings). Nearly 2.5 million ha were affected--an area totalling nearly a quarter of the country's agricultural land.

Although the owners of large estates were successful in several regions in resisting the egalitarian intentions of the reform (retaining much of their land to be redistributed in a second measure introduced by the Communists after World War II) many of the larger aggregations of land were broken up. Generally speaking the grants of land made under the Reform were in small parcels, and to small-holders, with the average award varying by category between 3 and 8.5 ha. (McGowan 1949:154).

Although the Land Reform was frequently justified by reference to its supposed effect in promoting the security and independence of the small-holder, in many ways it served to render their economic situation more precarious. Under the former traditional systems of landholding often the peasants' obligations to the landlord were reciprocated by the payment of a proportion of the crop from the land on which they laboured, the use of draft animals for their own haulage, and access to the lord's woods for firewood or grazing. The reform did away with many of these arrangements (Franges 1934:132; cf. Jovanovic 1930:253). Before the Reform small farms had in effect been capitalised either by larger estates or through communal resources. Reform meant that these capital goods had to be provided by the private peasant either through direct investment or by renting them from those who already possessed them. Under the stimulus of population pressure there had been for some time a tendency to divide common land between the usufructories, a tendency furthered by the Reform. (Ivsic 1926:146-53, 263 ff. and 293 ff.; Jovanovic 1930:256 ff.; Tomasevich 1955:424; Stojsavljevic 1965:28-9.)

By far the greater repercussions from the Reform, however, originated as a result of the provisions laid down in the Provisional Decree in 1919, to indemnify the expropriated landlords. There were also, generally speaking, two broad classes of problems which needed to be settled separately, namely, the abolition of feudal dependency and the redistribution of large estates.

The overall pattern which emerges from the welter of legislation following 1919 is that the state undertook to pay indemnity to the landlords, where feudal or similar relationships were to be terminated, in the form of government bonds. Thus in Bosnia and Hercegovina and in Dalmatia these obligations of dependency were liquidated between 1921 and 1930. These earlier bond issues did not fare particularly well in the market. The landlords in Macedonia ands the Sandzak therefore sought and obtained the major part of their indemnity in cash. Funds were made available through the *Drzavna hipotekarna banka* (State Mortgage Bank) for these purposes. Indemnity for all other types of beneficiaries, however, had to be paid by the beneficiaries themselves; and mortgages were made available to them through special co-operatives *(agrarne zajednice)*.

The question of the indemnification of landlords in the northern areas was only settled after 1931, following the agreement internationally of resettlement arrangements, reparations, and related matters. Here the central problem of the

Reform was the price to be paid to large estate holders for the land expropriated from them. In this case it was laid down that the cost should be borne by the beneficiaries of the Reform rather than by the state, and the beneficiaries were mortgaged for the amount of the indemnity through the *Privilegovna Agrarna Banka.*

An accurate assessment of the total amount of mortgage debt taken on by the Yugoslav peasantry under the Agrarian Reform is impossible. Franges estimated in 1934 that the total cost of the programme would be 2,075,000,000 dinars (£8 millions), of which the subjects of the Reform (the beneficiaries) would have to pay 913,000,000 dinars (£3.5 million. Franges 1934:321-2). Eric reported that between 1936 and 1940 the courts had reached a decision with respect to 909 of the 1,122 expropriations notified in the northern territories alone, the cost of land redemption in these cases totalling 415,857,720 dinars (£1.6 million), to which should be added conveyancing charges and tax (Eric 1958:437).[9] Sketchy though they are these indications do give us an idea of the size of the financial commitments on the part of the peasantry involved in the scheme.

The other side of the story is, of course, the situation of the landlords. The economic practice of many of the larger farms in the northern areas was little affected by the redistribution of lands, as the more economically progressive of them had been able to retain substantial proportions of their holdings under the provisions for a "supermaximum" in special cases. The most notable results of these changes were seen in the former Ottoman areas. Many of the smaller landlords, particularly in Bosnia-Hercegovina, were themselves reduced by the reform to the status of peasants; but the larger proprietors often did rather well out of the compensation they received.

They did not copy some of their northern counterparts, however, in the conversion of their estates into commercial farming businesses. More typically their compensation was invested in urban real estate, in trade and in usury, so that capitalism in the Yugoslav countryside was generally characterised by capitalistic *finance*, but not by capitalistic *production*. The conversion of their assets resulted, in effect, in the export of capital from agriculture, and not in investment making for its modernisation.[10]

In spite of the changes which were imposed upon peasant society, the peasant tended to remain a peasant. The rich peasant was still no more than a rich peasant, in that he simply owned more land; but he had not made the transition to regarding his holding as a capitalistic business. In Germany and pre-revolutionary Russia land reform involved a deliberate attempt to build up the prosperous, independent peasant proprietor of middle or larger holdings. The main result of the Yugoslav experience, however, was the entrenchment of the small peasant on the land. Here Land Reform was primarily a *political* response to the widespread pressure of over-population, and not directed by any clear concept of modernisation, let alone the development of capitalism.

On the one hand state intervention in the grain market promoted the commercialisation of agriculture and the involvement of cultivators in international commodity exchange. By confining agriculture within a pattern of smallholdings, and because of the burden of debt which it helped to create, however, the Land Reform actually inhibited its technical or organisational modernisation.

ii) Agricultural labour and capital in the "First Yugoslavia"

Most Yugoslav writers working on agriculture since 1945 have assumed that it is possible to identify a period of the "development of capitalism" antecedent to the emergence of a socialist Yugoslavia. This model required that the peasantry should be shown to be experiencing a process of "proletarianisation", and simultaneously that it must be possible to identify a nascent class of indigenous capitalists. It is important to challenge both elements of this presumed structure of relationships.

"Proletarianisation" and "pauperisation" are not synonyms. The proletariat are those who are deprived in the process of the development of capitalism of their ownership of the means of production, so that the only means of obtaining a livelihood open to them is the sale of their labour-power. This fact defines what Max Weber called their common "class situation": or in the terminology of Marxist sociology, the proletariat thus defined is a class "in itself". There is typically an expectation that there will be a correspondence between these initial conditions for the development of a class and the development of class consciousness (I prefer "class culture").

To speak of a "proletariat" it is not sufficient that market relationships must have replaced the "natural economy", and that agricultural production should have become largely commoditised. It is necessary that wage labour should bring with it the seeds of a new identity. Unless these features come to define the economic and social situation of the rural population, it does not matter how poor the peasantry become, they are still a peasantry. The evidence points, however, towards the fact that against very considerable odds the rural population managed to cling on to their identity as peasants.

The evidence points towards the growth of wage labour as an important factor in the rural economy only in a few specific regions in pre-war Yugoslavia. Data for Serbia in 1897 show that at that time 11% of rural households were without land at all (Tomasevich 1955:206). These tended to be concentrated in the valleys of the Sava-Danube, and in the lower Morava. In 1910, 41.55% of the farm population of the Banat, and 4.8% in Backa, were landless employees and their families (Ivsic 1926:159-60). These are, however, exceptions among the Yugoslav regions, and a consequence of the organisation of labour in the Hungarian latifundia which developed during the second half of the nineteenth century. Elsewhere there seems to have been little wage labour before the end of the century, except possibly in parts of Slovenia and the Dalmatian coast where commercial lumbering and the wine trade were established.

The Census of 1931 reckoned there to be 478,527 farm workers of various kinds throughout the whole of Yugoslavia, representing 9.4% of the rural labour force. Excepting the Prefecture of Belgrade only two of the *banovine* (Dravska and Dunavska) had more than a fifth of their agricultural labour force employed as workers, journeymen or apprentices. The Savska *banovina* lags a distant third, with less than 10% of its agricultural labour force in these groups. In Bosnia, Montenegro and southern Serbia fewer than 4% of the rural workforce could be considered "proletarian" by this criterion.

The rate of expansion of wage labour was slower in agriculture than in other sectors of the economy (Vuco 1968:57). The countryside served as a passive reserve of labour which was gradually being absorbed elsewhere, rather than a sector of a modernising economy which had its own dynamic.

"Journeymen" made up more than three quarters of all those employed in agriculture in every region. They were typically employed intermittently as labourers on larger and more prosperous farms in a pattern dictated by the seasonal rhythms of agriculture. These seasonal workers, often recruited from a wide area, might be as little involved in the cash economy as many "subsistence" peasants, since it was not unusual for their remuneration to be in kind (usually grain), or in the grant of small plots of land (Vuco 1968:50-2 and 60-1; Mirkovic 1952:40). Mining and timber processing (more significant than factory work in pre-war Yugoslavia) employed many of these workers on a seasonal basis when they were not engaged in farm work. Thus in Yugoslavia between the wars we find the development of the phenomenon of the "peasant worker" who has continued to form a significant component of post-war rural social structure (Kostic 1955; Bicanic 1981:Chap. 24).

A significant factor in bridging the gap between the yield from dwarf farms and the needs of those dependent upon them was cottage industry. Whereas the annual average income from manufacturing industry for the years 1923-5 was 5,823 million dinars, the value of the product of cottage industry was estimated at 4,837 millions (Tomasevich 1955:174 and 337 ff.). Throughout this period cottage industry was fighting a loosing battle against the factory-made article; but its significance for the situation of the Yugoslav peasant should not be underestimated. Like industrial or agricultural employment of a seasonal nature it enabled the villager to retain a place on the land when there was no longer enough land to meet all the needs of the family.

In a situation in which over-population and under-employment in agriculture could not be remedied either by further emigration or industrialisation, cottage industry helped the rural poor to fend off complete pauperisation and retain a stake in village culture (Bicanic 1981:Chaps. 9 and 10).[11]

Yugoslav writers repeatedly cite the depression following 1929 as one of the most destructive hammer-blows of capitalism, driving the peasant into the proletariat. In fact the reverse may well be argued with equal vigour. Only an expanding urban and industrial economy could have drawn the poor peasantry away from the land and turned them into proletarians. For as long as depression prevented that expansion, no matter how hard the lot of the villagers, they stood more of a chance on the land, where they stayed, often making considerable sacrifices in order to retain even a parcel of it.

At first sight the development of agricultural production for profit might appear to have been of central importance in the economy of inter-war Yugoslavia. Throughout this period, with the exception of the most acute years of the depression, the balance of trade remained in Yugoslavia's favour. Agriculture generally made up over half of the country's exports (Tomasevich 1949: esp. 173 and 204; Naval Intelligence Division 1945: Vol. III, 228 ff; Tomasevich 1955:620 ff.). Livestock products remained the most important group of these items, representing slightly under one fifth of the total value of exports. Although in the early 1920s grains followed closely in second place, these tended to decline in importance during the following two decades, while industrial crops such as hemp, tobacco and hops steadily increased their share of the total. The economic viability of the country depended without question in significant measure upon its ability to sell the surplus product of its farms.

Commercialised farming, however, was very unevenly developed at this time. The Vojvodina was overwhelmingly the primary producer of most of the country's export crops, with some important exceptions. Tobacco and opium were found mainly in Macedonia; Slovenia was important in the export of hops; exportable wine tended to be concentrated in Slovenia and on the Dalmatian coast; plums were produced in Bosnia (Naval Intelligence Division 1949: Vol. III, 80-10.). Nearly a third of the country's area under maize, and nearly half of its yield of this crop, were grown in the Dunavska *banovina* in 1938, and the same situation obtained with respect to wheat. (See Map 2) Other important cash crops, such as sugar beet, oil seeds and hemp, tended to be similarly concentrated in the northern plains. Elsewhere in the country agriculture centred upon the needs of the producers, and on very localised markets.

[Map about here]

If we are looking for the capitalistic farmer, producing cash crops almost exclusively for the market and for profit, only in the larger estates of the Vojvodina, in some areas of Slavonia, a small part of northern Serbia, central Macedonia and parts of Slovenia do we find any number of farms run as businesses. Although they played a disproportionate role in the provision of agricultural exports they are quite untypical of the generality of Yugoslav farming in this period.

iii) Capital and credit in the countryside

Capital tended to accumulate, even in the Danubian plains, not in the hands of the

producers (whether large landowners or peasants) but in the hands of those who

directed *trade, commerce and finance.* The system operated initially to siphon the

surplus out of the productive process, even if it later found its way back in the form of

credit.

The financing of Yugoslav agriculture presents an initially paradoxical picture. There

is, on the one hand, a widely-repeated belief that the countryside was starved of credit

and investment before the Second World War. (See for example, Stavrianos

1958:634.) On the other hand it is recognised that one of the most acute problems

which faced the peasantry during this period was its indebtedness. Komadinic

estimated that in 1932 peasant debts amounted to 6,880 million dinars (£24.86

millions), with more than 32% of rural households being in debt (Komadinic 1934:20-

21).[12]

Differences in regional pattern can be seen with respect to the institutional sources of

credit to agriculture: the banks (which can be divided into state-run and predominantly

commercial undertakings), agricultural co-operatives, and private money lenders.

Banking was generally under-developed in Yugoslavia in the years before the

revolution. The commercial banks were better organised and their services more

widely available in the ex-Habsburg areas. Roughly 40% of all the credit provided to

peasants by the commercial and savings banks in 1932 went to the Dunavska

banovina, which contained the rich lands of the formerly Hungarian Vojvodina.

An equally skewed distribution is revealed if we look at the credit provision through

the state-owned banks established to support the Agrarian Reform programme--the

Drzavna hipotekarna banka and the *Privilegovna agrarna banka*. Here the factors

which shaped the distribution of resources appear to have been the ethnicity of the

recipient of credit rather than any economic criteria. In 1932, 62% of the credit to

peasants from the *DHB*, and 86% from the *PAB*, was with *banovine* in which Serbs

were a majority of the population (Drinska, Dunavska, Moravska, Vrbaska and

Zetska). The presence of Dunavska and Drinska *banovine* in this list is not surprising,

as it is to be expected that these two regions would figure prominently in the work of

banks specifically dedicated to the support of the Agrarian Reform programme.

Moravska was only marginally affected by the Reform programme, however, lying

almost entirely within the former Serbian kingdom. Largely Serb Zetska,

encompassing eastern Hercegovina and the Sandzak, was involved to some extent in

the reform programme, but by far the largest part of its area was made up of

Montenegro, which was not (Bicanic 1981:10; Mirkovic 1952:89; Stojsavljevic

1952:99).[13]

The state banks were overshadowed as providers of credit to the peasantry by the co-

operatives. About 12% of peasant indebtedness was to co-operatives in the early

1930s. Post-war historians have tended to disparage the co-operative movement as an

attempt to deceive the peasantry into thinking that there was an alternative route for

the village economy which did not lie through the valley of capitalism. "Credit co-

operatives were .... a bridge across which capital continued its brisk advance on the village" (Vuckovic 1945). Also they were regarded in communist Yugoslavia as a distraction from the more proper goal of socialism.[14]

The first viable enterprise of this nature in Serbia was set up by Mihailo Avramovic in the tiny village of Vranovo, "one hour's journey by ox-cart from Smederevo", in 1894.[15] The stimulus to the growth of Slovene co-operation came from the Catholic Congress in Ljubljana in 1892. Under the inspiration of the Christian Socialist Dr. Josip Krek a number of societies were founded in the following years, and the first Slovene association of co-operative societies was launched in 1900 (Avramovic 1924:72 ff; Stojsavljevic 1952:126-8). In both the Danubian region of Serbia and in Slovenia the movement spread rapidly before the First World War, although it was not until after the war that much progress was made elsewhere.

Possibly it was the relatively adequate facilities provided by commercial banks which retarded progress in Croatia, where the first association of co-operatives did not develop until 1918. Although attempts were made to found societies in Bosnia and Hercegovina before the Great War these made little headway until the Agrarian Reform gave the peasants an incentive to improve their own land and farming practice, although here, to some extent, the movement became ethnically politicised (Stojsavljevic 1952:128-9). The same seems to have been true of southern Serbia and Macedonia. In general terms, there was a broad correlation between economic development and the growth of co-operatives.

The economic significance of co-operative societies in the First Yugoslavia would seem to have been considerable. In 1930, individual membership of societies passed three quarters of a million, and by 1938 totalled more than 1.4 million. There were more than 11,000 branch societies in 45 organisations: more than 5,000 of these branches were concerned with credit provision. In 1938, the total assets of the Yugoslav co-operatives amounted to around 3,656 million dinars (£13.2 millions), and the volume of credit outstanding to members in that year accounted for between 12 and 15% of all credit provision to agriculture (Cukanovic 1971:19-20). When one takes into consideration the fact that around 56% of the total assets of the co-operatives in 1938 consisted of the savings of their members, it becomes apparent that this must be considered to be one of the most important forms of accumulation in the First Yugoslavia.

One of the major problems associated with credit provision by both the banks and the co-operative societies was their tendency to restrict lending to those clients with better security. The commercial banks tended to lend to the better-off peasants while the co-operatives were mainly patronised by those with a moderate-sized holding (Jovanovic 1930:378 ff; Komadinic 1934:44; Mirkovic 1952:89; Stojsavljevic 1952:99, 107, 116 and 123). The poorest peasants, lacking the security which their better-off colleagues could offer, were forced to look to the private money-lender, who dominated agricultural credit in Yugoslavia between the wars.

In 1932, 45% of peasant debt was to the account of the private money lender, to whom extortionate rates of interest were typically paid. This institution was generally known by the name *zelenastvo*: the peasant borrowed money on the security of the crops in the fields while they were still green, these being his only security (*zelen* = green). The typical *zelenas* might be the village store keeper, a local salaried official or a wealthy peasant. Many of those compensated under the Agrarian Reform scheme made up for the depreciation in the value of their government bonds by securing a more-than-adequate return on the loan of cash to the peasantry.

Although credit was easy in the villages in the boom years of 1919-25 the rapid down-turn in the economy in the crisis years which followed soon meant that many of those who formerly would have been able to secure funds easily were forced to turn to the only source still open to them--the local money-lender. *Zelenastvo* was particularly important as a means of issuing and obtaining credit in the most backward areas of the country, where no other institutions existed, such as Montenegro, Kosovo, the Sandzak, Hercegovina, Lika and areas of the Croatian karst.

The Yugoslav countryside in the inter-war years constituted a vast sponge which retained a huge supply of labour in excess of the needs of agriculture. This was an immense reservoir of *potential* proletarians. Three factors stood between the poor peasant and full proletarianisation.

The wage relationship was insufficiently established in the village. With the exception of certain specific localities wage labour remained marginal to the operation of peasant farming, which typically remained dependent upon the labour of members of the farm family, only supplemented by seasonal assistance from the outside. Landholding remained the sheet anchor of the peasant. Although cultivation of the soil was reinforced by cottage industry and seasonal work elsewhere, the possession of a plot of land was the central fact around which other elements of the basic domestic economy were organised.

A good deal of historical discussion lacks an appreciation of the actual life process of farm families, such as one gleans from anthropological studies, which underline the interdependence of these activities, and their sequential weaving together (Lodge 1941; Trouton 1952; Halpern 1958; Erlich 1966; Stahl 1986). Across the life cycle of the peasant family, changing economic fortunes interacted with the shifts in the structure of the family (especially the balance between its productive and dependent members) to encourage opportunistic switches of strategy. Consequently, for the majority of peasants, rural society was not structured into a range of clearly distinguishable strata ("small", "middle" ore "rich" peasants) each developing their own class consciousness. The peasant community was composed of a variety of families, which were linked to each other by ties of kinship, locality and customary obligation, whose members moved in time along trajectories which might take them (sometimes simultaneously) through several of these purely economic categories (Galeski 1972).

The attitude of the state towards the peasantry in pre-war Yugoslavia might be summed up as "paternalistic".

Peasants in …. the old Yugoslavia, were protected in structural terms: occasional agrarian reforms assured (as a reward for war services and consequently, as a basis for preserving authoritarian regimes) their small freeholds, enabling them to remain on the land (in sustained poverty), thus destroying one of the most important levers of modernization (rationalization and enlargement of estates, rural wage labour, generation of cheap industrial work force, etc.) (Lazic et al. (eds.) 1995:18)

The impact of World War II

As I noted in Chap. 3, there has been a general neglect of the social and economic history of the war-time period itself (as opposed to its military and political aspects). The years between 1941 and 1945 are treated as a blank historical hiatus from this point of view, their significance only measured in terms of the toll of damage and destruction which can be reckoned at its end, and as a liminal zone which separated the "First" from the "Second" (Capitalist from Socialist) Yugoslavia. The basic historical groundwork has not been done in order that any such appraisal could be attempted here. (See, however, Lampe and Jackson 1982:Chap. 13; Kaser and Radice eds. 1986:366.) It is important, nevertheless, to note some guide-posts which indicate that the experience of the war also left a legacy of significant continuity across these years.

First of all, a more or less systematic attempt was made to adjust Yugoslav agricultural production to German war needs (Brandt 1953). This had significant effects in two directions. Under the German Plenipotentiary for the Economy the requisitioning of food was in large measure organised through the pre-war administrative apparatus, such as the grain agency *PRIZAD*. "Yugoslav agriculture .... emerged from the Second World War with the apparatus of the central government's most powerful pre-war agency divided and discredited." (Lampe and Jackson 1982:547) The extreme unpopularity of this regime had a good deal to do with building the resentment and unco-operativeness of the peasant cultivator which was to prove a significant obstacle to the post-war state attempts to plan the agrarian economy, particularly the regime of compulsory deliveries and the collectivisation programme.

A good deal of the damage to the war time agrarian economy, measured by reduced production, was not simply a consequence of the impact of fighting. It also resulted from aspects of German economic intervention, such as resistance to the requisition of crops and the deportation of forced labour. "The hostility frequently to be found among food producers towards the authorities exacerbated the difficulty of farm procurement, quite apart from the purely economic tendency of food producers to withhold deliveries in times of scarcity." (Kaser and Radice eds. 1986:366-7) This was particularly the case in Macedonia, where food production was placed under the Bulgarian state agency *Hranoiznos* . (Lampe and Jackson 1982:544-45).

Against this should be set, however, the results of the efforts made by the occupiers to stimulate modern farming in some areas, especially the Banat, and the enhanced cultivation of some important crops such as sunflower seeds (Lampe and Jackson 1982:546). There is a tendency to explain changes in productivity and patterns of cultivation between 1939 and 1945 by reference to the introduction of socialist planning after the war. In many respects (at least where the modernisation of agriculture was concerned) the Communists only took over where the Germans left off.

The level of damage which war inflicted upon the Yugoslav countryside was enormous. Radice has estimated that agricultural production in 1946/7 in Yugoslavia was only 56% of its 1934-38 average (Kaser and Radice eds. 1986:371).

Vast quantities of farm machinery and other equipment, draft animals and livestock were destroyed, damaged or looted. The total reduction amounted to between 40 and 60 per cent of total pre-war holdings, e.g., 53 per cent of cattle, 67 per cent of horses, 52 per cent of hogs, 80 per cent of plows and harvesting machinery .... and 40 per cent of peasant carts. Nearly 40 per cent of the area under vineyards and fruit trees was seriously damaged. (Hoffman and Neal 1962:87; cf. Lampe and Jackson 1982:Chap. 13)

The effects of the war were extremely varied, ranging from almost complete destruction in parts of Bosnia, where the civil war had been experienced directly for long periods, to the relatively insignificant in large areas of the Vojvodina or Slavonia, which saw little fighting and the economy had been intimately tied into a regime of exports serving the needs of the German market.

Agriculture under "administrative socialism"

As I observed at the start of this chapter relatively little attention has been paid to the subject of Yugoslav agriculture either by indigenous or foreign social scientists. Indeed, indifference to rural affairs has become more pronounced over time. This neglect is especially curious in view of the salience of regional inequalities within the discussion of Yugoslav affairs. Yet Yugoslav agriculture has continued to play a major part in the transformation of Yugoslav society since 1945; and many of the themes which characterised that story in the inter-war years have retained their focal interest and importance across the Communist period. The most obvious and arguably the most deeply-seated of the factors making for regional diversity has been the cultural and economic gap between rural and urban Yugoslavia. The relative success or failure of attempts to bridge that gap have contributed as much as anything else to the growth of regional disparities in economic wellbeing.

Yugoslavia at the end of hostilities in 1945 was still overwhelmingly a peasant country. Although the proportion of the population which lived from agriculture had declined between 1921 and 1931 from 78.8% to 76.6%, the rate of population growth meant that in numerical terms the farm population had grown by around 1.25 million. Around 60% of the overall population increase had remained on the land: the percentage shift in the population dependent upon agriculture was only marginally downward over the wartime period, reaching 73.3% in 1945 (Stipetic 1982:168). These figures alone ought to indicate that any understanding of the transformation of Yugoslavia in the post-war years can not be attempted without addressing the experience of its rural population.

This situation began to change with the seizure of power by the Communists in 1945. Now the future of the rural economy was subsumed within a more general vision of the socialist transformation of society. "Socialist transformation" was equated fairly directly with rapid industrialisation, and in relation to this the countryside was regarded both as a resource to be exploited, and as the primary locus of the "class enemy". Two principal policies guided the realisation of this general aim in the immediate post-war period: further land reform and compulsory delivery of agricultural produce.

The basic framework of the second land reform was laid down in a decree of 23 August 1945 (Brashich 1954; Tomasevich 1958). Eight major categories of land were subject to expropriation into a land fund, which was then available for redistribution.[16]

1. Large holdings over 45 ha. involving the leasing of land or the use of hired labour.

2. Holdings of banks or other corporations.

3. Holdings of churches or other religious bodies in excess of 10 ha. of arable land.

4. Peasant holdings of arable land above a limit of 25-35 ha. depending upon the region and quality of the land.

5. Holdings of non-peasants, in excess or 3.5 ha.

6. Land which had been abandoned.

7. Holdings of German nationals confiscated under the decree of 21 November 1944.

8. Land confiscated by the courts from "collaborators" or other "enemies of the people". (Brashich 1954:47-8)

In all, 162,362 holdings were affected by this measure, yielding a fund of 1,566,030 ha. The largest contribution to the land fund was made by confiscation from German nationals, which accounted for around 60% of the affected holdings, and over 40% of the available land. This was followed by expropriations from large estates (15% of area) and ecclesiastical holdings (10.5%). Confiscation from peasants contributed less than 8% of the fund (mostly from Serbia, which had been untouched by the pre-war reform).

More than half of the fund was then disbursed to individual peasants (797,357 ha. or 51%), preference being given to those who had fought with the *partizan* forces. The great majority of allocations were of very small holdings (2.5-3.5 ha.) although bonuses were awarded to national heroes which might take their holdings up to around 10 ha.--43% of recipients were formerly without land. The remaining 49% of the land was distributed to various state agencies, including principally state afforestation programmes and a new socialist sector of state farms *(poljoprivredne dobre)* 288 of which were established on confiscated large estates, utilising 18.3% of the land fund.

A prominent stated aim of the land reform was to curtail the development of capitalism. Given the evidently weak development of rural capitalism in Yugoslavia at this time, this aspect of it would seem to be of rhetorical significance. In comparison with the first reform its achievements were relatively minor. Under the inter-war measures "more than 600,000 holdings with some three million persons over an area of almost 2,500,000 hectares were directly affected ....perhaps a fifth to a quarter of the area under holdings and between a fourth and a third of the population was directly concerned" (Brashich 1954:34-5). By comparison, the 1945-6 measures involved only about 1.5 million ha. And, except in Serbia, its impact upon the distribution of peasant holdings was marginal. Agriculture featured as just one component in a more general settling of accounts with fascism and its collaborators.

Possibly of far greater importance at this stage in shaping the relationship between the state and agriculture was the *otkup*, or system of compulsory deliveries of produce. The origin of this system lay in the wartime needs of the German occupation. Under severe drought conditions in 1945, and faced with the need to feed the cities while coping with the effects of war-time devastation, in 1946 a system of compulsory sales to the state at fixed prices was introduced, to replace the wartime requisitions (Wright 1986:5).[17] The *otkup* was extremely unpopular, and responsible more than any other action of the Communist government for the development of a sense of confrontation between the state and the peasantry. It was abandoned in 1952 as a part of the reconstruction of agricultural policy in the wake of the failure of compulsory collectivisation. As the *otkup* bore most directly (although by no means exclusively) upon sales of *grain* its impact was regionally very uneven.

The use of controlled prices created an adverse differential between agricultural and industrial goods. Wright has calculated that the ratio of the prices of agricultural to industrial products moved from an index value of 100 in 1947 to 48.6 in 1952, halving the relative purchasing power of agricultural income (Wright 1986:10). To this also should be added the impact of a steeply progressive system of taxation. The revenue from the taxation of agricultural income exceeded state investment in agriculture by a wide margin, thus exacting a net tribute for other sectors of the economy (Wright 1986:15).

The clearest contrast between the approach to agriculture taken by pre-war and post-war governments was the attempt to collectivise agriculture after 1948. This has often been represented as an impulsive response to the Soviet attack on the Yugoslav leadership, of May 1948. Ideological and practical failings on the agricultural front featured prominently in the Soviet allegations:

.... the leaders of the CPY are avoiding the question of class struggle and the checking of the capitalist elements in the village .... there is no mention of the question of class differentiation in the village; the peasantry are considered as an organic whole, and the Party does not mobilise its forces in an effort to

175

overcome the difficulties arising from the increase of the exploiting elements in the village. (Letter of the CPSU to the CPY, 4 May 1948; in Clissold ed. 1975)

At the Fifth Congress of the CPY in July 1948 a new programme was adopted, including a fourteen-point statement on "The Socialist Transformation and Advancement of Agriculture and the Cultural Uplifting of the Village" (Tomasevich 1958:169; Milosevic 1980:67).

The collectivisation programme built upon the institutional foundations laid down in the 1945 legislation, and provided for a number of state farms (*poljoprivredne dobre*) along the lines of the Russian *sovkhoz*, and for General Agricultural Co-operatives *(Opste zemljoradnicke zadruge--OZZ)* which had resembled the *kolkhoz* rather than the pre-war Yugoslav co-operatives after which they were named. Whereas in 1945 the former had been favoured as a "higher form" of socialist institution, within the new programme the "co-operative" (renamed Peasant Work Co-operatives (*Seljacke radne zadruge--SRZ*) became the bearer of change in the village.[18]

From a starting point of the 31 *SRZ* set up in 1945, these had expanded to 779, with over 200,000 members, in 1947. In this period collectivisation proceeded with some thought to the suitability of the type of land and crops involved, and with the consent of the participants. The precipitate commitment to collectivisation in 1948 drove these numbers up to nearly 7,000 *SRZ* with nearly 2.5 million members by 1950, by dint of propaganda, incentives, disincentives and downright bullying. Indications that all was not well emerged during 1951, with a succession of speeches by leading Communists addressing problems within the programme. It emerged that upon the expiry of the original three-year contracts with which many peasants had joined the *SRZ,* their members were withdrawing in large numbers. A further surge of propaganda, fiscal and other incentives, and credit subsidies failed to stem the retreating tide. Defeat was admitted in the "Decree on Property Relations and Reorganisation of Peasant Work Co-operatives" of 28 March 1953, in which year the number of *SRZ* had declined to 1,152 with a little over 300,000 members. "By 1954, the share of arable land held by collective farms had fallen to a mere 3 per cent" (Kaser and Radice eds. 1986: Vol. III, 11).

The reasons for the collapse of the collectivisation drive can be summarised as:

.... a combination of the effects of bad weather, inordinate haste, incompetent economic planning and political insensitivity. At the heart of that failure was the inability to see that collectivization involved far more than a mere transfer of property rights. The collectivization programme linked together the economies of scale to be achieved through the creation of large production units, and the elimination of chaos associated with petty private cultivation. What the planners omitted from their assessment of the situation was the fact that economies of scale could be realized only if the aggregation of production units went hand in hand with the heavy capitalization of agriculture (with investment in drainage, communications, and so forth as well as in machinery) and a total reorganization of management, the organization of work and budgeting procedures. As it turned out, the aggregation of "chaos" produced no more than larger-scale chaos. (Allcock 1980:204)

The first five years of socialist agriculture (1947-51), then, were broadly a disaster. In this period also the decline of agricultural population becomes more noticeable, from an estimated 11.1 million in 1945 to 10.3 million at the first post-war census of 1953 (total population rose in this interval by an estimated 1.89 million) (Stipetic 1982:168). At the same time, the gap was extended between the economic and social conditions of town and country. Equally significant inequalities emerged, however, between the situation of those employed in the socialist sector and the private peasant farmer. The former were unevenly distributed across the federation, concentrated in the richer agricultural areas in which land reform had facilitated the creation of extensive holdings which could be cultivated by relatively capital intensive methods. Of the 103,500 ha. allocated by the reform for the foundation of state farms, 41% was located in the Vojvodina. Of the 80,800 ha. allocated initially for the *SRZ*, 64% was also in the Vojvodina (Savezni Zavod za Statistiku 1989:205). This region was committed from the outset, therefore, to the technical and organisational transformation of its agriculture in the direction of mechanised and large-scale production for the market. In spite of their overt egalitarianism and the rhetoric of brotherhood and unity among the working people of Yugoslavia, agriculture served as one of the primary avenues through which regional differences were actively but unwittingly stimulated by the Communists.

Reappraisal--and stagnation

The *volte face* over collectivisation was followed by a period of political reappraisal. Compulsory sowing plans and the hated *otkup* were both abandoned in 1952, and discouraging taxes on the private peasant were replaced by a new system based upon the cadastral valuation of land--all of which offered incentives to increase production (Waterston 1962:23).

The socialist objectives of agricultural policy were by no means abandoned: merely implemented by more gradualist methods. As the revised Programme of the Communist Party of Yugoslavia stated in 1958:

> The policy of the Communist Party of Yugoslavia in the field of agriculture is composed of a gradual socialization process in agricultural production in terms of modern, socialist, agricultural organizations and other socialist forms which would arise in the evolution of that process itself and without arbitrary tampering in the private ownership of land. (Cited in Puljiz ed. 1972:22)

The new emphasis on gradual evolution was expressed in two concrete ways. A further land reform of 22 May 1953 imposed a ceiling (with some defined exceptions) on the private ownership of cultivable land of 10 ha. This yielded a relatively small fund of around 268,000 ha. the greater part of which came from disbanded collectives rather than directly from individual proprietors (Hoffman and Neal 1962:276).

By far the most important feature of the new orientation was the creation of the "General Agricultural Co-operatives" (*Opste zemljoradnicke zadruge--OZZ*). Although the small state farm sector also grew slowly in this period, from 1955 the *OZZ* took over as the principal instrument of the socialisation of agriculture.

> In order to induce peasants to join the general co-operatives, which are in any case attractive to them since they provide a variety of production, processing, marketing, purchasing, sales and other services farmers need, the authorities channel through the co-operatives most investment and other credits for

agriculture, subsidized fertilizers, fuel, machinery, improved seeds, breeding

stock and extension services. (Waterston 1962:24)

Participants in the scheme retained ownership of their own land, although the co-

operative was empowered to own land, and frequently took over the holdings of

former *SRZ*. These also attempted to rationalise production in some areas by leasing

land from individual proprietors.

By the end of the decade, however, in spite of these measures, the overall size of the

social sector in agriculture had actually decreased significantly. The total cultivated

area within the social sector had dropped from 2.3 million ha. to just over 1 million

ha.; the number of holdings had fallen from 26,130 to 5,121, although their average

size had grown from 9 ha. to 202 ha. (Defilipis, in Puljiz ed. 1972:71).

The really significant change which was taking place in this period, however, was

the rapid extension of market participation on the part of the peasantry. To some

extent this is suggested by the fact that the number of individual co-operators grew

steadily, reaching a peak of around 1.3 million in 1960 (Cukanovic 1971:143). "Many

co-operatives were merged with factory farms, which also took over their function of

co-operating with peasants ... large firms obviously have greater technical and

economic possibilities for co-operation than small co-operatives." (Defilipis, in Puljiz

ed. 1972:93). The relative success of agricultural policy in this period is indicated by

the fact that 1955-60 saw the most rapid overall growth of agricultural productivity of

the post-war years until the 1980s (Stipetic 1982:174; Savezni Zavod za Statistiku

1989:207, 224 and 225).

Although on the whole productivity was lower in the private sector, especially in relation to arable land, and above all in industrial crops, in other aspects of agriculture the individual peasant retained the greater share of the market, and sometimes achieved better relative results. Animal husbandry has remained throughout the post-war years primarily an affair of the individual proprietor, and the supply of milk, eggs, poultry products and much of the domestic supply of fruit and vegetables remained in their hands.

In spite of these suggestions of the vigour of Yugoslav farming, agricultural policy at this time amounted to little more than the fostering of decay. Agriculture remained among the poor relations from the point of view of investment. As the priorities of the government turned away from basic reconstruction, investment in agriculture rose from 2.5% of the total in 1955 to 4.2% in 1960. The real concerns of the state are made clear, however, in the rise of the share going to industry and mining, from 49.3% in 1955 to 53.8% in 1960 (Savezni Zavod za Statistiku 1989:130).

The census of 1961 told the tale in different terms. By that date the total population of Yugoslavia had reached 18.5 millions--an increase of 1.5 million since 1953. The agricultural population had fallen in this interval by more than a million, however, and now represented only a half of the total (Stipetic 1982:168; Savezni Zavod za Statistiku 1989:39). Whereas men had made up 59.7% of the active labour force in agriculture in 1953, by 1961 this proportion had fallen to 57%, as men were drawn increasingly into work off the farm.

Agriculture and economic reform

The general difficulties of the Yugoslav economy in the early 1960s, which resulted in a movement of policy away from Soviet-derived central planning mechanisms and towards the market, were reflected in agriculture.

The principal policy innovation in this area was the introduction of the *poljoprivredni kombinat* (agro-industrial combine). The new *kombinati* involved the vertical integration of the cultivation, processing and marketing of a range of types of agricultural produce. Sometimes they were created by the extension into manufacturing of the activities of the old state farms, or even agricultural co-operatives; sometimes a combination of both; and less frequently the creation of completely new enterprises.[19] Their rationale lay in a development of the justification for the *OZZ*, in offering to producers contractual assurance of the purchase of a stipulated crop, along with the provision of seeds, fertilisers and credit to the cultivator, and the purchase of machinery or other capital investment. Typically they offered the extension to the private peasant of the provisions of the state social security system. In this respect can be seen to have been directed as much at the incorporation of the peasantry into the socialist system, and to social control, as they were to the advancement of specifically economic objectives.

It is hard to give any general indication of the success of these projects either from the standpoint of their political or their economic goals, since Yugoslav statistics do not record their activities separately from other elements of the social sector. They certainly became a prominent and visible part of the rural scene, however, and one whose significance was repeatedly deferred to by politicians. In their impact upon the extension to the village of both market relations and to some extent industrial discipline, they can be regarded as illustrating the industrialisation of agriculture in this period.

Summarising the work of his collaborators in 1968, Bernard Rosier wrote:

The recent appearance of a technically developed and economically competitive peasantry is not illusory; but it is characteristic of a minority, and the majority of the peasantry remain enclosed in a system of production which is close to self-subsistence. The mental framework, attitudes and values remained for all those of the patriarchal family and the village. The contacts between town and country also do not make for a coherent transformation of this peasant mentality. Above all, among other reasons, it is necessary to note that these relationships find their place in a general culture in which the village is devalued .... (Rosier ed. 1968:286).

The decade between the constitutional and economic reforms of 1963-65 and of 1974-76 witnessed an acceleration in some aspects of the transformation of the Yugoslav village. The spread of patterns of consumption supported by enhanced prosperity, and the movement towards urban values in relation to some aspects of family life, went hand-in-hand with the persistence of deeply rooted traditional attitudes towards work. The peasants' relatively superficial integration into modern production subsisted along with their continuing exclusion from political modernity.

Whereas the gradual extension of social security provisions to the private peasant, through association with the socialist sector, may suggest a kind of political reconciliation between socialism and the private peasant, formerly seen as the last bastion of capitalism, in fact this was far from being the case. In large measure the defensive state of mind of the peasantry was reinforced by the entrenchment of official, ideologically defined, attitudes towards the peasant. "The peasantry and the village are .... denigrated and suspect. For years now the private cultivator has not been regarded as a proper producer, but as a proprietor, a petty capitalist, who has no place within a socialist system ." (Rosier ed. 1968:286) As agriculture remained dominated in many of its aspects by the small farmer, therefore, the sector almost inevitably remained relatively marginal to the concept of economic development which prevailed in policy-making circles.[20] This problem of the political difficulties surrounding private property in production was to persist until it was definitively addressed (too late) on the eve of the disintegration of Yugoslavia.

Perhaps the significance of the *kombinat* as an indication of the spread of genuine market relations was diminished in part by the tendency during the mid-sixties towards the regionalisation of the Yugoslav economy. Large quasi-monopolists appeared dominating the supply of processed food within each of the republics, such as *Gavrilovic* in Serbia or *Agrokomerc* in Bosnia-Hercegovina.

In the intercensal period 1961-71 the agricultural population of the country fell by more than 1.3 million, from 49.6% to 38.2% of the total (Savezni Zavod za Statistiku 1989:39). Possibly of greater significance is that fact that rural activity rates also declined steeply in this period, from 56.3% to 47.3%. It is during this period that political concern about the future of the countryside began to be reflected in academic activity, and particularly in the group surrounding the journal *Sociologija Sela* in Zagreb. A series of well-researched monographs subsequently documented the reduction in the rural population and the process of its "senilisation" (Suvar and Puljiz eds. 1972; Suvar 1973; Cvjeticanin ed. 1974).

It is in this period also that emigration emerges as an important factor affecting the Yugoslav labour market, as documented in the research of Ivo Baucic and others at the Centre for Migration Studies in Zagreb.[21] The agricultural population was significantly over-represented among migrants. By 1971 the agricultural population amounted to only 38% of the total: nevertheless, agriculture, forestry and fishing was the last reported occupation of 56.6% of migrant workers abroad in that year (Savezni Zavod za Statistiku 1989:202; Baucic 1973:68). Moreover, that over-representation was the more marked from the poorer regions: from Slovenia 35.6%, and the Vojvodina 42.8%, as opposed to 70.8% from Bosnia-Hercegovina, 70.1% from Kosovo and 64.5% from Macedonia. The significance of off-farm migration lies, among other things, in the fact that although debate about regional differentiation has been couched largely in terms of the positive impact of *policies*, in large measure regional backwardness can be accounted for in terms of neglect or indifference to important *sectoral* problems, significantly among them, the problems of agriculture.

This period also saw a slowing in the rate at which employment was created in the agricultural sector. In the decade 1955-65 social sector agricultural employment had run ahead of the Yugoslav average. The overall expansion of jobs in the decade had been 166%. Although agriculture lagged behind industry (184%), employment in the rural sector had grown by 179% (Savezni Zavod za Statistiku 1989:58-59). After 1965 the situation changed. The overall expansion of social sector employment fell to 130% over the decade, matched closely in the industrial sector (132%). New employment in agriculture grew by only 83%, however, overshadowed now by the growing new tertiary sector opportunities in finance (143%), the social services (144%), commerce (156%) and tourism and catering (159%).

It is a paradox of this process that the distribution of land-holding changed little, the number of holdings remaining roughly constant at around 2.6 million throughout the 1960s. Only 0.08% of holdings were in social ownership, representing around 19% of the agricultural area. The majority of the privately owned estates were very small, with more than 1 million comprising less than 2 ha, and 1.4 million between 2 and 10 hectares (Savezni Zavod za Statistiku 1989:201). The resolution with which private proprietors held on to their land is worth remarking upon, and several factors contribute to its explanation. The persisting difficulty of creating an adequate supply of urban housing to cope with the burgeoning urban population put great pressure upon those with urban jobs to retain their rural residence, as "peasant workers", regularly making quite long daily or weekly journeys to work.[22] The small size and basic conditions of many urban family apartments also led many otherwise urbanised families to keep their family residences in the country for recreational purposes--as *vikendice* (Poulsen, in Allcock, Horton and Milivojevic (eds.) 1992:61).

A significant feature of the rural situation is the fact that the cultivated area remained virtually unchanged throughout the 1960s: it is not the case that land was being abandoned to any appreciable extent.[23] The private cultivator remained a very important source of domestic fruit and vegetables and often other produce also (and serving either urban or even international markets) supplying the needs of family members in the towns.

The "Green Plan"

The emergence of concern about agriculture in the late 1960s and early 1970s came to be focussed upon the "Green Plan", launched in 1973. This envisaged a long term programme for the development of agriculture (1973-85) which would be funded by federal and republican investment, together with foreign loans. (The World Bank made a loan of $200 million for drainage and irrigation schemes in the Metohija basin.)[24] Across this period agricultural output was projected to rise by and annual rate of 2.8 percent.

The plan was certainly reflected in patterns of investment. In the period before the launch of the Green Plan agriculture was unquestionably the poor relation from the standpoint of investment, and this position was reversed after its introduction (see Table 5.1). The changed fortunes of this sector are especially remarkable, however, in view of the fact that after 1978, measured in *real terms*, the average annual change in general levels of investment actually went into relative decline, agriculture being the only sector to sustain real growth. In spite of the ostensible commitment of the policymakers to the agrarian economy, at least two factors should be born in mind which qualify this picture of a radical change of heart.

In the mid-1960s (in keeping with the wider process of economic reform) Yugoslav governments (both federal and republican) discovered the potential economic value of tourism. The Adriatic highway was completed in 1964, and the following ten years saw a massive increase in investment in tourism, particularly along the Adriatic coast

187

(Allcock 1983 and 1986). The boost to domestic agricultural production certainly did
not come from direct exports, which actually declined in relative importance during
this period (Savezni Zavod za Statistiku 1989:308). In large measure it came from the
expanding opportunities for indirect export "on the hoof" via the tourist. Hitherto
underdeveloped land (such as the Neretva delta around Opuzen) or abandoned land (as
in the Konavlje) became within a short period among the most productive in
Yugoslavia under the stimulus of the tourist market.

Table 5.1: Changes in the pattern of sectoral investment:
Yugoslavia, 1962-1985
(Annual average growth rates at 1972 prices)

	Overall	Industry & mining	Transport & comm'n	Agriculture & fishing
1962-1972	4.2	5.5	8.7	0.7
1972-1985	-2.0	1.3	1.0	4.0

Source: Savezni Zavod za Statistiku 1989:126-9.

A second, and related, factor in this period was the impact of emigrant remittances;
and during the 1980s the gradual reversal of the flow of migrant labour. Accordingly,
investment in the private sector was expanded enormously, as the gains from work
abroad were used to capitalise individual holdings (see Table 5.2).

Beginning with the reform programme in the mid-1960s there was a gradual shift in
official awareness of the need to stimulate market forms, and an easing of the

entrenched ideological opposition to the private sector. Although legislation was slow

to follow, the economic press was regularly taken up by discussion of the importance

of *mala privreda* (Bateman 1993).

**Table 5.2: Investment in machinery and chemical fertiliser on
Yugoslav farms: 1965-1985**

	Tractors on individual holdings as % of those in agricultural organisations		Use of chemical fertiliser on individual holdings as % of use by agricultural organisations
	N	Kw	
1965	27.5	16.6	11.1
1975	769.2	445.0	، 25.2
1985	1,871.0	879.8	29.5

Source: Savezni Zavod za Statistiku 1989:225.

Although there had always been informal evasion of the limits on land holding,

through the *de facto* consolidation of family holdings, changes in the law governing

the permitted size of individual holdings, and the numbers of employees other than

members of the household who might be engaged, had to wait until the eve of the

collapse of Yugoslavia, introduced in 1989 by the Markovic reforms. Nevertheless,

throughout the 1970s the individual farmer was encouraged by a succession of minor

shifts in both policy and practice. Efforts were made to stimulate further individual

producers to enter into co-operative agreements with socially owned enterprises, usually agro-industrial combines. Furthermore, credit provision to the individual proprietor by the banks became much more readily available. There remained, however, the obdurate obstacle of official resistance to the reform of laws relating to the private ownership of agricultural land and (of lesser significance in this sector) permitted levels of private employment.

Although it might seem appropriate in the context of a consideration of "market socialism" to include discussion of the market for land I will say little about it, largely because it has never been studied. As I have already suggested above, there was little change over the entire post-war period in the pattern of landholding.[25] Individuals building private houses typically either did so on land they already owned, or very often simply by expropriating unused common (socially owned) land--so-called "wild building", of which a fringe surrounded every Yugoslav town. Where socially owned enterprises acquired land this took place either through the *opstina*, in which case the price was largely an arbitrarily determined figure, or was subsumed under the communal role in investment, which was represented in the municipality's stake in the new enterprise. Agricultural co-operatives or *kombinati* acquiring land from private cultivators (usually for the rationalisation of holdings) did so with sufficient rarity for price formation to be almost entirely *ad hoc*. There simply are no statistics in the area.

Agriculture in the years of crisis

With the onset of economic crisis in the 1980s, and the adoption of the programme of *stabilizacija*, unemployment grew inexorably, stimulating a return to the farm. Under the programme of reforms introduced by the Markovic government in 1989, provision was made for the liberalisation of both the maximum landholding and the number of employees beyond the members of the immediate family, permitted to the individual land-holder.[26] There were signs (albeit extremely belated) of an acceptance of a positive role for individual enterprise in the economy, and more specifically of the inevitability of Yugoslavia's dependence upon the private sector in agriculture.

As the economic situation deteriorated, and the country spun into a vicious circle of rising inflation (the annual rate was estimated to have passed 2,000 per cent in 1989) individual plots became ever more important as a source of food for families, the value of whose nominal incomes collapsed. Systematic information is hard to come by concerning the significance of the village as a buffer between the family and economic hardship. Evidently land ownership remained an element of basic insurance for large numbers of Yugoslavs, during a period in which official earnings from urban and industrial employment sank in real terms to notional levels, and hard currency savings were gradually consumed (and then officially blocked).

On my own travels during this period, however, I was struck by the signs of the extensive reclamation for cultivation of abandoned land, including the laborious reconstruction of traditional terraces along the Dalmatian coast. Observation at any Yugoslav rail or bus station in a large city showed, on any arrival from rural areas, relatives or friends arriving laden with sacks and baskets of vegetables, wine, *ajvar*, hams, sausage or other domestic produce, depending upon the season.[27] During the period of *stabilizacija*, and even more so during the subsequent period of war, the survival of the urban population was assured largely through its continuing links with the village.

A study by Mrksic, based upon data for the "Third Yugoslavia" in November 1993, reported that a quarter of urban households still owned land, and that as many again engaged in "additional activities" related to agriculture (e.g. helping relatives) related to agriculture (Mrksic , in Lazic ed. 1995:48). For all strata agricultural production constituted the major type of "additional activity" of their members, although its proportional importance varied between social groups and regions, its relative significance being greatest among manual workers, the unemployed and pensioners (Mrksic, in Lazic ed. 1995:51-60).

There has to date been little comment on the impact of war upon the countryside, with the exception of the special edition of *Sociologija sela*, (30 (1/2) 1992) dealing with "war and reconstruction". This presents information solely relating to Croatia, but reports an estimate of the losses to agriculture and the food processing industry as US$ 1.3 million. War had affected 40 of the republic's 102 communes, and interestingly had borne most heavily upon rural areas--51.6% of the cultivated area. It was estimated that Croatia at that time had lost 35% of its agricultural productivity (Seda 1992: 20-22). Here too the village remained a vital "cushion" for the population as a whole, against the impact of war (Zupancic 1992:40-2). As Mladen Lazic put it succinctly in another context:

Thus the obstacle to modernization [he refers here to the peasantry] becomes, in times of crisis, a condition for survival, and even a positive basis for differentiation: the material position of the peasants relatively improved while the position of non-peasants with links to the village was at least able to be sustained (Lazic, in Lazic ed. 1995:18).

Interestingly, one response to this situation has been the demand that there should be a general re-evaluation of the countryside and its importance for the national interest (Budin 1992).

My own direct observations travelling in Croatia and Bosnia-Hercegovina in the immediate wake of the war suggest that the damage to agriculture may in some areas be catastrophic, with huge areas of depopulation consequent upon "ethnic cleansing", which will not be rectified readily by migration let alone the return of the displaced population. The physical damage has yet to be accurately estimated, and will take decades to repair. In parts of the Neretva Valley in the summer of 1996 there were no usable habitations, no animals were visible, and extensive areas had been subjected to a scorched earth policy. This picture needs to be compared with other areas, however, such as central Serbia or Macedonia, untouched directly by war, where the disintegration of the federation has actually resulted in a strengthening of their economic position *vis-a-vis* the towns.[28]

As in previous periods, war has remained for the rural population one of the most potent of the ways in which the wider world intrudes into the life and economy of the village. Impressionistic evidence suggests, however, that whereas this may constitute in some respects an acceleration of the process of globalisation, in other respects agriculture is forced back into pre-modern practices and patterns of exchange.

Conclusions

Far from being a kind of historical residuum of the modernisation process, a backwater of traditionalism left behind as industrial and urban Yugoslavia comes to be incorporated more closely into the global economy, agriculture has participated centrally in those processes. It may have been a declining sector in terms of its relative contribution to GDP or employment. Its labour force may have reduced and undergone "senilisation". Nevertheless, it has participated in all of the principal processes of transformation experienced by the Yugoslav economy and society more generally, playing a significant part in the corrosive and conflictual development of regional differentiation.

In this respect, the post-war period has seen an extension and intensification of the processes which were set afoot in the pre-war years. Agriculture and the rural population have become consistently, and at least until the "Wars of the Yugoslav Succession" almost completely, commercialised. There can be few remaining corners of the autarkic peasant economy (although perhaps these have been artificially strengthened by the recent war). The mixed household, in the sense of different household members working in rural and urban employment, or the phenomenon of the peasant worker, have eroded the economic separation of town and country.

What is more, the peasantry are now securely integrated into the network of international exchanges, although post-1945 government replaced the strategy of development based upon the export of primary products, by one based primarily upon industrialisation, in which the role of agriculture was to subsidise urban development. This process began with the reduction of the countryside to a situation of dependency with respect to urban and industrial centres; continued with the incorporation of migrants into the international labour market; was extended and intensified in many areas with the advent of tourism. The whole process has been undergirded by the steady expansion of the need for cash exchanges involving goods and services. Whereas in the First Yugoslavia mortgages and other forms of credit constituted the major point of articulation between the peasant and the modern economy, in the Second Yugoslavia this was replaced by the market, including the market for labour.

I have argued above that the phenomenon of rural capitalism was hardly developed at all in the pre-Communist period; and perhaps it is only with the decay of Communism that its construction on anything like a significant scale might begin. In the shadow of war, however, the prospects for the future are hard to assess. One thing is certain, however, and that is that the future of those states now emerging from the debris of war, and their place in a wider European economy, will be shaped in significant measure by the changing nature and role of agriculture.

Notes

1. Among writers dealing with the post-war period Hoffman and Neal, and Dirlam and Plummer, are exceptional in having each a respectable chapter on agriculture (Hoffman and Neal 1962; Dirlam and Plummer 1973). My own earlier brief review of the development of Yugoslav agricultural policy since 1945 remains the most systematic discussion in English (Allcock 1980). One of the drawbacks of the way in which Yugoslav society has been studied in the past is the over-concentration upon the system of self-management. This has tended to focus attention upon industrial organisation. The implicit model at the heart of self-management has always been "The Factory". This has made for the

invisibility of the rural economy, partly because agriculture has remained largely within the private sector (Warriner 1959).

2. I cover these issues more fully in Chapter 11.

3. The following discussion of the Ottoman rural economy is based, except where otherwise noted, on Tomasevich 1955; McGowan 1981; Lampe and Jackson 1982; Inalçik and Quataert eds. 1996.

4. Of the 1163 villages within the SR Macedonia, 314 (27%) were cultivated on a *ciftlik* basis, and a further 332 (28.5%) mixed *ciftlik* holdings with free peasant holdings (pp. 78-9).

5. The figures given by Tomasevich for 1897 record only 74 holdings in Serbia of more than 100 ha.

6. Slightly different figures from those of Tomasevich are given in Stojsavljevic 1965:35, although they are sufficiently close to suggest perhaps a common source.

7. The estate of Hugo Windisgrec contained 15,033 ju. of forest; that of Vincenc Turn contained 9,834 ju; and that of Karl Auersberg 3,032 ju (Stojsavljevic 1965:18). (One *jutar*, *jutro* or yoke, equals 0.5755 hectares.) For the Habsburg areas in general the studies by Stojsavljevic are an important resource. Stojsavljevic 1952; 1962 and 1965.

8. Tiltman (1936:46-7) reports an estimate that 90% of colonists in "the Croat regions" (presumably former Habsburg lands) were ethnic Serbs.

9. It appears than in relation to the northern territories Eric's figures are somewhat lower than the estimates of Franges. The additional charges which he cites might restore parity between the two estimates.

10. Land utilisation tended to become more intensive as a result of the Agrarian Reform. This generally took the form of a reduction in fallow land, on which cereals were grown for home consumption, in response to the pressure of peasant subsistence needs rather than growing marketisation.

11. Studies such as those undertaken by *Gospodarska sloga* in Croatia are a vivid witness to the almost desperate situation in which many peasants found themselves. Bicanic entitles one chapter of his celebrated *Kako zivi narod*, "Three fourths of the Croats have no beds" (Bicanic 1936 (1981); also Bicanic and Macan 1939; and Bicanic, Mihletic and Stefek 1939.

12. See Tomasevich 1955, Chap. 27. Slightly higher figures are given in Culinovic 1961:Vol.I, 231. Tiltman in his observation of Croatian peasants observes that of an average family indebtedness of 7-9,000 dinars per hectare (for all sizes of farm), roughly 2,500 were invested in buildings alone, "which is a higher figure than that found in any other part of Europe south of Hungary" (Tiltman 1936:47).

13. The ethnic bias of the Reform programme is open to different constructions. See Tiltman 1934:46.

14. See for example Kardelj 1959: Chap.7. One of the better treatments of the co-operative movement is provided by Stojsavljevic 1952.

15. Probably the foremost statement of the ideology of co-operation from the inter-war years is Avramovic 1924. See esp. p.73. See Jovanovic 1930:325 ff.

16. Several minor categories have been omitted here, which amounted to around 5% of the total area. See, however, Brashich 1954:49.

17. The system underwent a series of changes which it is not necessary to review in detail here, moving from an emphasis on compulsory sale of surpluses beyond a protected minimum necessary to sustain the producer's family, to (by 1950/1) a designated required sale of yield per cultivated hectare (Wright 1986:6-9).

18. There were four types of co-operative, although it is not necessary to review these differences here. See however Milosevic 1980:66-71; Brashich 1954:72-6. I have reviewed in detail the experience and problems of collectivisation in Allcock 1981.

19. Detailed studies of the establishment, including the capitalisation, of such enterprises are given in Rosier ed. 1968 and Milosevic 1980.

20. A rare study of private enterprise in the Yugoslavia is Grbic 1984. (See also Gams 1987.) The relative lateness of this material indicates the political sensitivity of the topic. See my essay on the private sector in Allcock, Horton and Milivojevic eds. 1992.

21. A substantial bibliography of studies on economic migration was published by the Centar za Istrazivanje Migracija, Zagreb. Haberl ed. 1979.

22. In 1981 only 23.5% of Croatian households lived exclusively from agricultural incomes: *but only 26% lived exclusively from non-agricultural incomes* (Stipetic, Vajic and Novak, 1992:13). It seems to have become the norm to combine agricultural and non-agricultural earnings to the point at which it is misleading to speak of "peasant workers" as an interesting if rather marginal social category. See also Mrksic, in Lazic ed. 1995.

23. The total agricultural area declined from 15 million ha. in 1960 to 14.7 million in 1970, and the total cultivated area from 10.28 million ha. to 10.15 million ha. in the same period (Savezni Zavod za Statistiku 1989:206-7).

24. I have been unable to trace information as to what proportion of foreign investment (as opposed to aid) was directed into agriculture. My impression is that the sums are relatively small. Lampe, Prickett and Adamovic (1990:206) allude only to the general neglect of the sector—"premature and over-concentrated industrial development". Rosier and his collaborators imply that investment in the large "Belje" *kombinat* which they studied in Baranja during the reform period was funded entirely by Yugoslav banks (Rosier ed. 1968:161-2).

25. It is important to note the extreme political sensitivity of information relating to land transfer, going beyond the obvious official caution which attached to this question under the socialist regime. The subject of the transfer of land from Slav to Albanian ownership both in Kosovo and western Macedonia was a hot potato which nobody wanted to grasp.

26. The legal framework was laid down in the *Zakon o preduzecima* of January 1989. Chapter IV dealt with self-employment and agriculture. The details of changes in the law in many relevant respects were deferred for determination in each of the republics, and consequently there was room for a considerable degree of variation. See Kosovac, Grahovac and Radosavljevic eds. 1989.

27. Nearly half of all households were engaged in "additional activities" of one kind or another in the "grey economy". There were 0.66 "registered engagements" per household, and 1.40 such "engagements" per household reporting additional activities (Mrksic in Lazic ed. 1995:47-8).

28. It may be noted that Milosevic has been able to sustain his electoral hold on "Serbia proper" throughout the 'nineties largely on the basis of the solid support of a rural and small town constituency, relatively untroubled by the ravages of war, and secure in the market for basic foodstuffs.

5

THE MOVEMENT OF POPULATION:

TERRITORY AND POWER

The importance of population

No complete sociological or social-historical account can be constructed of any

society, let alone of Yugoslavia, without taking into account the essential ingredient of

population. It is people, physically embodied and distributed spatially in specific

numbers, who experience economic development or democratisation, who develop a

sense of ethnic identity or enter into conflict. There can be no process of

modernisation without the bearers of modernity. Yet the topic of demography has

suffered from a relative neglect within sociology.

In relation to the Balkans, however, it is of practical as well as theoretical importance

to counter this neglect. There is a tendency in contemporary nationalistic accounts of

the region, which filters into journalism and popular histories, to treat relationships

between people and land as at least in principle static. The notion of "historic lands",

to which particular ethnic groups are presumed to be primordially attached, has played

a large part in political discourse since the mid-nineteenth century. Consequently,

people often talk as if the population movements set in motion by the Yugoslav war of

the 1990s are an aberration which can be contrasted with a normal stability.

Populations have always been in movement; their numbers, spatial distribution and demographic structures are typically and normally in process, sometimes in ways which bear directly upon modernisation. The range and significance of emigration from the region has been one of the factors which illustrate its constant involvement in wider patterns of social change, including those which can be described as "globalisation". In our bid to achieve a sociological understanding of the South Slav region we neglect these particular processes at our peril.

A complete history of population movement has yet to be attempted for any region of the Balkans, although there has been significant work in this area.[1] Any enterprise of this kind would be an enormous task which would require linguistic and statistical skills which are beyond my own capability. The purpose of this chapter is to stake a claim for this kind of study as an important component of the sociological and historical understanding of the Yugoslav region.

Four types of population movement

The word-spinners of romantic ideologies of nationalism have made much of the importance of the antiquity of settlement in their attempts to legitimate the power of ethnic groups over territory. Objectively there is no identifiable group in the Balkans today who could claim to the satisfaction of archaeologists or anthropologists to represent the autochthonous settlers of the region.[2] The earliest peoples of whom we have much historical knowledge are the Dacians, Greeks, Illyrians and Thracians. Although each of these groups has been claimed as the ancestors of a contemporary nation in the Balkans (Romanians, Greeks, Albanians and Bulgarians respectively) there is no case in which the continuity of that connection is not clouded by the admixture of other peoples. The story of the Balkans has been from the earliest time that of the migration and mutual assimilation of peoples. The fact that there are not states extant in the region inhabited by nations who call themselves Dardanians, Moesians, Morlachians or Rascians is explained by the accidents of political history, and not because the one-time occupants of these formerly specific regions, or claimants to these identities, have left no genetic descendants who might have carried their names into our own day.[3] The traces of the lives, languages and identities of autochthonous historical peoples have been typically obscured by more recent and powerful arrivals

Under this general rubric of the normal processes of migration and assimilation it is possible to separate analytically five broad types of movement, illustrated in the following discussion. These have been of particular importance in the social development of the Yugoslav region.[4] (i) Conquest and the establishment of new state structures has brought in new ruling strata and other settlers associated with them. (ii) As a consequence, war has also been a significant factor in the displacement of older indigenous groups, driving them to seek living space elsewhere. (iii) These processes can typically be looked at as relatively clearly bounded events. By way of contrast, however, there have been slower and less distinctive processes of drift ("metanastasis"), usually in search of better economic conditions. (iv) Although conceptually related to the third type, it is worth treating the far more dramatic population changes associated with modernisation, especially in the rise of industrial cities, as *sui generis*. (v) Finally, I look at differential rates of population growth and suggest something of their potential significance. Through this survey it becomes evident that the patterns and causes of mobility change with the process of modernisation, but mobility and the mixture of peoples are themselves nothing novel.

Conquest and the changing character of new elites

One of the historical clichés which frame understanding of the Balkan Peninsula is that it stands at the frontier of contrasting cultural traditions associated with the two great Empires which governed the region for so long--the Ottoman and the Habsburg. They expanded into the region at roughly the same time, subordinating in their different ways the scatter of local states.

Ottoman penetration can be dated from the Battle of Maritsa (near Edirne) in 1371, although the image of the wave of Islam sweeping across the Balkans must be qualified by a realisation of the length of time taken to complete the process. An independent Serbian state was not finally subordinated until 1459, when Smederevo was taken: the greater part of Albania had fallen by 1478: Bosnia and Hercegovina held out rather longer, with the *banat* of Jajce submitting only in 1528. In the following year the Turkish advance was repulsed from the walls of Vienna. Turkish expansion was reversed during the seventeenth century, and the Treaty of Carlowitz, in 1699, established the frontier between the Ottoman and Habsburg domains roughly along the modern northern border of Bosnia. After further wars against the Habsburg Empire, the Treaties of Passarowitz (1718) and Sistova (1791) fixed the western border of Bosnia and Hercegovina along lines which have remained unchanged except in minor detail until the present day.

The demographic impact of Turkish rule was highly variable, partly because of the character of the Turkish system of land-holding, and partly because of the great differences in the political and social context within which the Ottoman elite found itself at different points in this extended process of expansion and contraction. Initially the Ottoman order imposed a thin stratum of military aristocrats (*sipahi*, or spahis) onto the mass of the indigenous peasantry (*reaya*). The non-Turkish, largely Christian, population came to be administered subsequently by their own ecclesiastical authorities, through the system known as *millet*.[5]

On the whole the Turks did not set out to impose Islam through wholesale forced conversion: they were more interested in booty and compliance. The nationalistic interpretation of history which has come to predominate since the late nineteenth century throughout the region has tended to play down the factor of conversion, emphasising the importance of resistance to "the Turkish yoke" in the formation of national identity. There were substantial local exceptions to this, however, especially in Bosnia and Hercegovina, the Sandzak of Novi Pazar and Macedonia where large numbers of the Slav peasantry did embrace the religion of their conquerors.[6] The fact that there are today well-established communities of Serbo-Croat speaking Muslims in Serbia, Macedonia and Montenegro as well as Bosnia-Hercegovina, attests to a dual process. There was a widespread, continuous and spontaneous drift towards the Islamisation of the Slav population in these regions, which went hand in hand with a similarly significant but unspectacular Slavicisation of the Turkish diaspora. A significant exception to the spontaneous character of this process was the intermittent imposition of the *devsirme*, or "tax in children", by which the Ottoman administration recruited children from Christian families for training in the civil and military administration of the Empire, some of whom rose to the highest positions.

The demographic and social balance between Muslims and Christians began to change significantly during the seventeenth century, as the frontiers of Islam were pushed southwards. Members of the Ottoman aristocracy formerly settled in Hungary, Transylvania and Oltenia moved southwards in search of land. The steady contraction of opportunities for enrichment and mobility through military service gradually turned the Muslim military elite towards a redefinition of the relationship between themselves and the peasantry which resembled more closely that of landlord and tenant. Many moved to towns, making a living as artisans or merchants. This process, which affected both Muslim and Christian peasants, increased the social distance and political conflict between the ruling stratum and their subordinates.

The demographic impact of Ottoman rule was not only felt in terms of the superimposition upon Slav rural society of a Turkish and Muslim ruling elite. Its indirect effects were also felt in the creation of functionally specialised ethnic minorities. Particularly during the first two centuries of Ottoman rule, the Turks confined their activities largely to military leadership, administration and the clergy, whereas other activities came to be identified often with specific linguistic or confessional groups.

Trade was especially important in this respect, as the enormous demands of the administrative centre of Istanbul required the creation of a vast network of supply, to that trade came to be shared between Ragusans, Greeks, hellenised Vlahs and, after the expulsion of the Jews from Spain in 1492, Sephardic Jews. Salonika remained one of Europe's most important centres of Jewish settlement up to the Balkan Wars (57%

of the population ca. 1900) (Magosci 1993:107-110). Skopje, Sarajevo and Travnik all had large Jewish colonies linked to trade. Consequently almost every town of any significance would have its quarters (*mehale*) occupied by these trading groups.[7]

Similar processes of subordination to new elites can be seen at work in the Habsburg lands. While the Nemanjic dynasty was building a Serbian state the Slovenes were incorporated into the short-lived Bohemian Empire of Ottokar. This fell to the Holy Roman Empire following the defeat of Ottokar at the Battle of Marchfeld in 1278. The March of Styria was then bestowed upon the Habsburg family, who in 1335 also acquired Carinthia and Carniola. A small Croat kingdom, established under Tomislav (923-8) and centred upon the Adriatic cities of Nin and Biograd, flourished until 1089, when a dispute over the succession was resolved by appeal to king Ladislas I of Hungary. Related to the Croatian royal family, he himself took the throne of Croatia in 1091, inaugurating the historic tie between Croatia and the Hungarian crown. Following the collapse of Christian (especially Hungarian) resistance to the Ottoman forces as the Battle of Mohacz (1526), the Diets of both Croatia and Slavonia elected Ferdinand of Austria as king. For almost four hundred years Croatia-Slavonia was to be integrated into the Habsburg state.

In Dalmatia and Istria the story was more complex. Comparatively wealthy and well-fortified maritime and mercantile cities (such as Cattaro, Zara, Sebenico, Spalato and Ragusa) were able to resist absorption by the tide of Slav migrants, retaining for the most part an allegiance to Byzantium, and a cosmopolitan culture of their own. Although the Hungarian king Koloman claimed the crown of "Croatia and Dalmatia", Venetian interest in the control of the Adriatic coast was always able to qualify and challenge that claim. Until the extinction of Venetian power by Napoleon in 1797 the political history of Dalmatia can be summarised as a contest for control between Venice and Budapest. It has become a cliche of historical writing about the region that Dalmatia became "a Slavonic land with an Italian fringe".[8] While this observation needs to be heavily qualified, recognising that the urban civilisation of the Adriatic cities was in many respects an amalgam of Slav and Latin culture which was *sui generis*, it is undoubtedly the case that this coastal fringe was also a world apart from its peasant hinterland.

As a consequence of these developments the upper strata throughout the Habsburg lands were typically separated by a cultural gulf from their peasant subjects at least as wide as that between Ottoman Turks and their Christian *reaya*. Although the Croatian nobility were often successful in retaining their titles to land and power under Habsburg rule, they underwent a rapid process of assimilation.

> Since the destruction of the Zrinjski and Frankopan families, Croatia was left with practically no national aristocracy. The existing higher nobility was either of foreign origin or cosmopolitan in outlook and did not embrace the cause of Croatian nationalism in the same spirit that the Hungarian aristocracy had embraced the Magyar cause. (Gazi 1973:132)

The alien character of aristocratic culture was probably most severely marked in Slovenia.

A key demographic difference separating Ottoman and Habsburg lands, however, was the position of trade and the professions. Although to some extent non-Slav groups were over-represented in trade and the professions throughout the Habsburg lands, they never became as closely identified with specific ethnic enclaves as in the Ottoman cities. There were substantial Jewish settlements, for example, in Zagreb,

Osijek and other large towns throughout Croatia (principally Ashkenazim) although nowhere did their numbers reach 5% of the total.[9] The lack of a religious barrier between elite and non-elite meant that a small Slav middle class was able to emerge in the cities, composed not only of merchants but also including a small number of professionals, especially teachers, lawyers and priests. Their numbers remained very small indeed until the middle of the nineteenth century, although they exercised a disproportionate influence on cultural and political development.

In the case of both of these imperial elites, and the groups associated with their arrival, their numbers were typically small in relation to the surrounding mass of Slav peasants, and the rates of mutual assimilation often slow. A combination of the social distance between aristocrat and peasant, differences of religious faith, language, and the segmented character of rural society, generally inhibited this process. Nevertheless, their impact was profound, shaping legal and political systems, languages, economies, and wider patterns of culture well beyond the point of collapse of the Empires and the expulsion or flight of many of their representatives. Even though these former ruling groups may be reduced in the modern world to the position of decaying and insignificant minorities, their importance continues at the level of *identities*. As we shall see below in Chapter 10, in the process of forming contemporary nations these former elites and their clients have often continued to provide a symbolic (although sometimes negative) focus for the definition of the identity of the South Slav nations.

War and the displacement of the defeated

The natural concomitant of the arrival of new elites and the imposition of new political structures has been the displacement of the defeated. These are but two sides of the same coin. Movements of this kind have been extremely widespread, especially when one takes into consideration the effects of the suppression of numerous peasants' revolts which have punctuated Balkan history, and of war. I shall concentrate upon the major "tidal" movements of population which since the middle ages have been set in motion by wars and conquest.[10]

The arrival of the Turks in the late fourteenth and throughout the fifteenth and sixteenth centuries sent a series of shock waves across the Balkans, displacing the indigenous populations northwards and westwards. Some of the resulting migrations were of a long-range character; and Albanian colonies in southern Italy date from this time, as do settlements of Croats in central Italy and the Austrian Burgenland (Gradisce). Macedonia suffered from serious depopulation at this time, which is one reason why in the modern period substantial populations of Turkish speakers are still to be found settled in the region (Inalçik, in Inalçik and Quataert eds.1994: 14; Bourchier 1911:217).[11]

As the frontiers of Ottoman control began to contract during the seventeenth century, both Turks and Islamicised locals withdrew southwards. The density of Muslim population in Bosnia, the Sandzak and Macedonia was augmented appreciably during this period, although the increasing harshness of the Ottoman regime and the associated peasant unrest, combined with the effects of war and disease, resulted in an appreciable overall decline of population. Lampe and Jackson estimate that from a peak of around 8 millions in the sixteenth century, the population of the Balkan

Peninsula fell by the mid-eighteenth century to 3 million.[12] Changes in the structure of the Ottoman system of military land-holding appear in part at least to be linked to these population movements.

During this process of contraction of the Ottoman Empire further waves of Slav refugees were set into motion. A primary stimulus in this respect was the advance of Austrian forces into the heart of the Balkan Peninsula during the 1680s. Most of Hungary was freed from Turkish control between 1686-7, and Habsburg armies pressed southwards, taking Skopje. There were widespread uprisings by the local Slav populations against the Turks. The invaders were pushed back after 1691, however, and fearing Turkish reprisals many local Slavs chose to follow the retreating Austrian armies northwards.

The most celebrated of these movements took place in 1691, when a series of migrations from the areas around Pec, Prizren and northern Macedonia, estimated at between 30-40,000 families, crossed the Danube into southern Hungary. Here the emperor Leopold I granted them religious liberty, a measure of self-government under their own *vojvode* (leaders), and permission to settle the land in return for their readiness to undertake military service. What appears to have been an initial expectation that this arrangement would be a temporary one, however, was undermined by the reversal of the gains made by the Habsburg forces south of the Danube and Sava. These settlers were integrated (together with earlier refugee populations) into a "Military Frontier" (*Militärgrenze* or *Vojna krajina*), owing direct allegiance to the Emperor and separated from the normal Hungarian civil authority.[13]

Following the expulsion of the Turks from Austria-Hungary in the seventeenth century, the Habsburgs began a systematic attempt to recolonise Croatia and Slavonia.

This was achieved in the main by implanting rural settlements from elsewhere in the Empire.[14] Consequently throughout Croatia and Slavonia, and the Banat and Baranja, were to be found colonies not only of Hungarians, but also Czechs, Slovaks, Ruthenes, and above all Germans. Austrian and Hungarian interests came directly into conflict in this region, as the latter had expected a reestablishment of Hungarian authority and the return of territory to Hungarian settlers. Especially after the war of 1715-18, however, when the Habsburgs gained control of the "Banat of Temesvar", the distinctive status of the "Military Frontier" was enhanced, strengthening Austrian control. An elaborate programme of colonisation was set in motion, supported by land reclamation and the construction of communications, in a region which had remained largely a marshy wilderness under the Turks. Magyars were actually forbidden to settle in some areas: but in addition to Serbs, colonists from throughout the Austrian lands (including Italians, Cossacks, Catalans and even some from Alsace-Lorraine) were brought in. As a consequence of these developments the ethnic composition of the population both this "Vojvodina" and large areas of Slavonia has remained complex to this day.

The Military Frontier also acquired in this period a special significance in the development of Serb culture. Historically the centre of Serb ecclesiastic life had been the Patriarchate at Pec. The events described above coincided wit the rise to influence in Istanbul of the "Phanariotes"--Greek speaking functionaries in the service of the Sultan. They used their position in order to press for the hellenisation of the Orthodox Church more generally. Taking advantage of Serb support for Austrian campaigns against the Ottoman Empire succeeded in 1766 in securing the abolition of the Serbian Patriarchate and the reversion of its authority to the Greek Patriarch. During the eighteenth century, therefore, the centre of Serbian ecclesiastical life (and cultural life more generally) moved northwards, across the Sava, to the new Serb settlements in the vicinity of Novi Sad.

Migrations induced in this way have operated throughout the history of the region to rework the pattern of settlement more or less subtly in almost every part of the region. Dalmatians backed the Habsburgs against the French during the Napoleonic wars, and many migrated into Bosnia-Hercegovina in order to avoid French rule after 1809 (Eterovich and Spalatin 1970:36). The Austrian occupation of Bosnia-Hercegovina following the Congress of Berlin in 1878 also prompted a substantial exodus of Muslims (Bougarel 1995:87; McCarthy 1995). Emigration from Macedonia in the wake of the suppression of the Ilinden uprising of August 1903 laid the foundation for today's colonies in Australia and Canada (Draganof 1906:39-40).

The demographic impact of war has continued to be felt across the region in the twentieth century, notably in that fact that the three decades between 1912 and 1945 saw the Balkan Wars, and the First and Second World Wars. The toll exacted by each of these conflicts was enormous, in terms of disease and displacement as well as the more direct casualties of war. In the Balkan Wars Serbian military losses were in the region of 15,000 men, while more than 16,000 were carried off by disease (largely epidemics of typhus and cholera) (Kennan 1993 [1913]:395).

These figures pale into insignificance beside the losses endured between 1914 and 1918. It has been estimated that "Serbian military losses were 275,000 or close to 40 percent of all mobilised men, and Montenegrin losses approximately 25,000". Including civilian deaths (especially the estimated 150,000 victims of the typhus epidemic of 1915) "the loss of life caused directly and indirectly by World War I in

Serbia and Montenegro was between 750,000 and 800,000" (Tomasevich 1955:222-3; see also Lampe and Jackson 1982:521). Because of the decomposition of the Habsburg Empire in 1918 it is harder to estimate the impact of war upon these parts of the South Slav lands. A figure of 150,000 military losses for the South Slav areas of the Dual Monarchy has been suggested (Tomasevich 1955:223).

The wider disruption caused by war in terms of forced migration, displacement and the wider impact upon demographic patterns has been controversial, but was clearly very considerable (Tomasevich 1955:220-6; Lampe and Jackson 1982:330-5). The acquisition of Macedonia, Kosovo and Bosnia-Hercegovina by the new Kingdom of Serbs, Croats and Slovenes, however, set in motion further attempts to stimulate the "repatriation" of "Turks" in which uncalculated numbers of Muslims (regardless of their mother tongue) were expelled in campaigns which have come to be known more recently as "ethnic cleansing" (McCarthy 1995: Malcolm 1998).

More appalling still was the devastation wrought by the Second World War. There has been considerable controversy over the scale of losses between 1941 and 1945. The official estimates by Vladimir Zerjavic, and for a long time accepted as authoritative, placed the total demographic loss to Yugoslavia as 1,696,000, which was composed of 1,027,000 casualties, which included both losses through military action and the victims of concentration camps and other atrocities. Roughly a half of this figure was made up of civilian victims (cited in Denitch 1996:32-33).[15] These figures have been challenged subsequently as being too high, and Franjo Tudjman has placed the figure for total demographic loss from all causes as between 700,000—800,000. These discussions of the impact of war take into account the displacement of population as well as casualties. Zerjavic estimated that some 669,000 persons emigrated as a result of the war, and Tudjman offers 500,000. I believe that Zerjavic's figures on this count are probably closer to the truth. It is necessary not only to count the more direct and immediate transfers of population, such as the estimated 298,000 *Volksdeutsche*, 130,000 Italian "optants", or 17,000 Poles who left in 1945. To these should be added those who fled the country ahead of the Axis invasion of 1941 (estimated at 250,000), and those who accompanied the retreating German armies northwards in 1945.

Extending the relevant time-interval a little, we find that in the period up to 1957 the displacement of Muslims was renewed with some vigour, resulting in the expulsion of perhaps as many as 195,000 Turks, Albanians and Serbo-Croat-speaking Muslims. At the end of the Greek civil war Yugoslavia also received a large number of Slav speakers from Greek Macedonia, who had sided with the defeated Communist forces.[16]

Although the longer term effects both of war itself and its associated "ethnic cleansing" of the recent wars can not yet be calculated, there is little doubt that we are contemplating here a demographic catastrophe of a similar order. It has been estimated that anywhere between 100,000-300,000 people have been killed in the fighting, although there is a very substantial amount of uncertainty about these figures. Estimates of the numbers displaced by the war are also partly hypothetical.[17] In June 1996 (after refugees had already begun to return to their homes) the UNHCR reported that within former Yugoslavia they were planning on the basis of 522,800 refugees, 1,240,000 "internally displaced persons", and a total level of demand on their services (including "war affected vulnerable cases" of 3,162,800 (UNHCR Information Notes, No.6-7/96: 4). They also estimated that for Bosnia-Hercegovina alone 686,533 persons were refugees in other European countries, and that 642,800 refugees from Bosnia-Hercegovina were located within the other republics of former Yugoslavia (UNHCR *Information Notes*, 10-11). In other words, roughly a third of the pre-war population of that republic were refugees.

Large tracts of the Croatian *krajina* and Bosnia have been depopulated, with an estimated 150,000 displaced from the former *Krajina* by "Operation Storm" of August 1995 as well as the more widely publicised "ethnic cleansing" of the earlier phase of the war. There is every reason to believe that the demographic effects of the war of 1992-95 will be at least as long lasting as those of former centuries.

Spontaneous drift or "metanastasis"

These developments contrast strongly in both their causation and their consequences with the spontaneous drift of population, although the two may be connected. Taking a very long view, there was a general drift of population northwards from the fifteenth century onwards (Naval Intelligence Division 1944-5: Vol. II, 201; Hersak 1993). These movements have taken place, not in the form of the readily documented migration of thousands of families, but as almost imperceptible and rather individualistic relocations.

The scale and importance of these movements was noted by the Serbian geographer and ethnographer Jovan Cvijic, in connection with which he coined the phrase "metanastasic movement".[18] The primary form of such migrations has been movement from areas in which grazing is more plentiful or reliable, or into more fertile from less fertile arable areas.[19] Typically there is a tentative quality about them. Based upon the traditional Slav *zadruga* (extended family), representatives locate better land in scouting movements, and a portion of the herd, or a branch of the family, moves into the new-found home, often on a temporary basis over a few seasons, before the *zadruga* is reformed in a new base, or a permanent division is agreed upon.

Instead of repeating Cvijic's findings here, as these have been cited widely in the anthropological literature of the region, it will be useful to draw attention by way of illustration to more recent work by Jovan Trifunoski in Macedonia (Trifunoski 1988). Three things are interesting about his findings.

First of all, they are supported independently by the incidental observations of travellers in the region from an earlier period. In spite of Albanian nationalist claims to the effect that "Albania" traditionally extends to the east of a line drawn between Bitola and Skopje, Albanian settlement east of the Ohrid and Prespa lakes and the river Crni Drim seems to have been relatively thin in the early years of the nineteenth century.[20]

Secondly, an oral tradition regarding the origins of families, not infrequently extending back well over a century, is relatively common, making it possible to speak with precision and assurance about the origins of Albanian settlers in western Macedonia today.

Thirdly, whereas contemporary Macedonian Slav stereotypes accounting for the growth of the Albanian population invariably focus upon the higher fertility of Albanians, a high proportion of the expansion of population does appear to be due to in-migration, and of a type described by Cvijic. In many cases these have involved quite long-range movements, with a large number of the Albanian settlers interviewed by Trifunoski from western Macedonia tracing their origins to the Albanian regions of

Llumi, Peshkopi and Mat (Trifunoski 1988:51-2). Although the *zadruga* is usually discussed as a specifically Slav institution, Trifunoski notes that it is the strength of this tradition of familial solidarity among Albanians which supports this type of incremental movement.

Recalling that even at the end of the Second World War three quarters of the population of Yugoslavia were engaged in peasant agriculture, "metanastasis" may be assumed to have accounted for an appreciable proportion of the distribution of population, especially of the central highland regions of the country, until very recently. Its slow and incremental character, involving the penetration of ethnic minorities, has often resulted in their assimilation and the transformation of ethnic identity.

This kind of movement is of particular potential interest in relation to the large-scale displacement of population between 1991 and 1996, which has once again left large areas almost denuded of population. Undertaken with the intention that this kind of "ethnic cleansing" will "rectify" the ethnic balance of an area, past experience suggests that a land-hungry peasantry will move spontaneously into vacated regions, producing patterns of settlement which are possibly widely at variance with those originally sought.

Modernisation and the flight to the towns

Substantial as other forms of population change have been, the twentieth century introduces new varieties which are qualitatively different, associated with the gradual incorporation of the region into more global patterns of economic exchange, and the

218

creation of the modern state. A key difference between the population movements

which I have considered above and those which are associated with the process of

modernisation is the role which explicitly formulated policies play in the latter. There

are two dimensions to this question; the political and the economic. Under the rubric

of political change we confront the impact of the development of the modern state:

under the rubric of economic change we encounter industrialisation and urbanisation.

An important attribute of the modern state is the range of tasks to which it addresses

itself in its work of "surveillance". A primary task of government in such states is

typically recognised as being the "management of the economy"--a project which

could not have been encompassed by the imagination of pre-modern politicians. The

concept of a "welfare state" is significantly different from the paternalistic notions of

the responsibilities of The Prince, which characterise earlier stages of political

development. For the first time it becomes possible, not only technically but also

conceptually, to speak of "population policy".[21]

A vital characteristic of the creation of the Yugoslav state (the first attempt at the

construction of a modern state in this region), as I argue in later chapters of this book,

is that it has suffered from a key deficiency in its failure to institutionalise citizenship.

The close identification between the state and particular "charter" ethnicities has

resulted in an endemic problem of the position and rights of ethnic minorities. As a

consequence of this failure, attempts to manipulate the ethnic composition of

population , in the interests of the stability of state control, have been a recurring and

explicit concern of policy.

The first of such attempts occurs immediately after the Balkan Wars, and continues

with the foundation of a united South Slav state, with the expulsion of Germans from the Vojvodina and Slavonia, and the "repatriation" of "Turks". The management of ethnic balance was one of the most important features of the land reform programme of the inter-war years. This involved the attempt to move Slav populations into those regions which were then dominated by non-Slavs (primarily Kosovo and the Vojvodina), and the attempt to detach Macedonia from Bulgaria, by implanting a Serb population, especially in the eastern parts. The fact that these attempts were often unsuccessful, in that the implanted settlers were regarded as intruders by the locals if they stayed, and in any case often preferred urbanisation to the "internal exile" of colonisation, does not detract from our understanding of its original intention (Ivsic 1926:359-68: Brashich 1954).

The collapse of the "First Yugoslavia" saw if anything an intensification of this idea, in monstrous proportions, with a series of attempts to impose ideal ethnic identities upon the fragmentary states which were established on the ruins of Yugoslavia. This was particularly the case in Croatia and Bosnia-Hercegovina, where the *Nezavisna Drzava Hrvatska* (*NDH*, or Independent State of Croatia) engaged systematically in what today would be recognised as "ethnic cleansing" of the non-Croatian population, through the most brutal means possible.[22]

In the post-war reconstitution of Yugoslavia, the manipulation of population for political ends was undertaken once again in the guise of land reform after 1945. On this occasion the ethnic dimension was subordinated to socialist ends. It was by no means absent, particularly in the cases of the repatriation of Italians from Istria, and "Turks" from the south. Land reform was also linked, however, to the policy of the collectivisation of agriculture. In this case the colonists were often seen in terms of the implantation of politically reliable, former partisans, who would carry into the countryside the correct proletarian consciousness. The ethnic dimension was present even here, however, in a negative form. The counter-intuitive movement of population was regarded as desirable precisely because it weakened the tie between ethnicity and territory; hence there was a transfer of people from the "economically passive" areas of Hercegovina, Macedonia and Dalmatia into the Vojvodina.

The "ethnic cleansing" which has accompanied the break-up of the "Second Yugoslavia", therefore, should be understood neither as some alien novelty within the Balkan context, nor as a reversion to some atavistic consciousness. Whereas in some respects it continues practices which have become widespread and indeed routine throughout Balkan history, this type of displacement of population by war in many ways should be understood as *a specifically modern phenomenon*. It exemplifies the problems of which can emerge when the development of the capacities for "surveillance" of the modern state is not matched by the concomitant development of citizenship.

The linked processes of urbanisation and industrialisation are also to be regarded as specifically modern, in the sense discussed here. Cities and manufacture have both been vital features of the social and economic landscape of the Balkans since ancient times. In post-war Yugoslavia, however, the creation of an industrial and urban society became explicitly linked to the building of socialism. These developments were not confined to "industrialisation" in its narrower sense, but extended to include such developments as the creation of the tourism industry. The pattern of spatial distribution of population along the Dalmatian coast, in particular, was dramatically altered, especially after 1965, by the deliberate fostering of tourism by republican and federal governments, in the attempt to gain income in convertible currencies (Poulsen

221

1977; Allcock 1983a). Urbanisation was no longer a spontaneous, slow drift to the towns but a deliberately stimulated transfer of population away from the perceived backwardness of a peasant society (Hoffman and Hatchett 1977).

The "socialist transformation of the village" was not limited to changes in property relations (the diminution of private land-holding) but was to be extended to encompass the industrialisation of agrarian economic relations.

Table 3.1 The growth of Yugoslavia's major cities: 1931-1981

	Cities of > 50,000 N of cities	% of total pop.	Cities of > 100,000 N. of cities	% of total pop.
1931	8	5.0	3	3.8
1981	37	23.8	14	17.4

Source: Savezni Zavod za Statistiku, 1989:52

The steady incorporation of the region into global systems of exchange also intensifies another type of population movement--international migration. Whereas long-distance migrations have been a permanent feature of Balkan society, the nineteenth century heralds the emergence of an international labour market. Surplus agricultural labour begins to move not only into adjacent towns in search of the means of survival, but to cross continents. The ravages wrought in the 1890s by phylloxera upon the wine trade in Dalmatia precipitated the first of these massive movements of emigration, although more general pressure of population upon the resources of the land also boosted the export of surplus labour both before and after the First World War (Balch 1910; Willcox 1931; Warriner 1964).

These developments were continued and indeed intensified in socialist Yugoslavia. Large numbers of Yugoslav workers left the country in search of work as *Gastarbeiter* across Europe and elsewhere, providing relief to the country's growing problem of unemployment, supporting the standard of personal incomes at a level unusual in eastern Europe, and helping to service Yugoslavia's regularly adverse balance of trade through the remittance of their earnings abroad. The census of 1971 reported that 790,500 Yugoslav workers were "temporarily" employed abroad (Baucic 1973:36). The decline of the countryside became a national political concern especially in Croatia. With 21.5% of Yugoslavia's population in 1971, Croatia contributed 34% of the country's workers abroad (Baucic 1973:38-9). In this way the Yugoslav labour force came to be included directly into the international labour force in a manner which subverted the public distinction between socialist states and capitalism.

Differential population growth

The problem of over-population in the Balkans became noticeable in the period before the First World War. The number of inhabitants in the region had been growing steadily since the middle of the nineteenth century in a pattern familiar to demographers and sociologists. A typical balance between high birth rates and high mortality (especially infant mortality) began to be upset by the relatively rapid decline of the latter, as a consequence of better diet, improved communications, housing, sanitation and medical provision.

The population of Serbia rose from 1.7 million in 1878 to 3.02 million by the outbreak of war in 1914. From the census of 1921, when an agricultural population of just over 9.2 millions was recorded, to that of 1931, when the Yugoslav population was reported to be around 10.7 millions, the numbers settled on the land expanded by 15% (Stavrianos 1958:420 and 594-7; Vuco 1968:47). The annual average rate of population growth in Yugoslavia between the wars was 1.43%, or more than three times that of Britain or France in the same period.

By western European standards the Balkan countries did not have particularly high densities of settlement: but the large proportion of the country which was not agriculturally productive, and the extensive and technically primitive methods of cultivation in most areas, meant that the pressure of population was *relatively* high. Consequently, although the overall density of population in Yugoslavia per square kilometre was only 56, according to the 1931 census, the density of the *population dependent upon agriculture*, per square kilometre of *farm land*, was estimated to be around 140. In addition to this, as Tomasevich has pointed out, particular regions of the country had much higher densities than the average. The most favourably situated of the *banovine* (prefectures) was Dunavska, where the agricultural population per 100 ha. of cultivated land hovered around the 80 mark throughout the inter-war period. By way of contrast, in the Primorje region, the level rose from 235 in 1921 to 251 in 1938 (Tomasevich 1955:322). Rapid population growth caused increasing demands to be made upon agriculture, while at the same time ensuring that the surplus remaining above the subsistence needs of the population was too small to be used to fund the improvements needed in agricultural stock or technique.

Throughout the inter-war period a number of agrarian economists and other commentators debated hotly the implications of this situation.[23] Their diagnoses were used in order to justify not only the land-reform in general but in particular the colonisation programme. It was generally agreed that the countryside was "overpopulated", but there was no unanimity regarding the level of population which could be regarded as "surplus to the needs of agriculture", and little concurrence as to the appropriate methods for arriving at such estimates. A widely quoted investigation by Wilbert Moore, during the first half of the decade, reported levels of "surplus" agricultural population for five eastern European countries: Yugoslavia 61.5%; Bulgaria 53.0%; Romania 51.4%; Poland 51.3% and Hungary 22.4% (Moore 1945:63-4). Doreen Warriner agreed that all of southern and eastern Europe, with some regional exceptions, could be said to suffer from a measure of overpopulation in the period, and the upland areas of Yugoslavia were probably among the worst-affected in this respect.[24]

Examining the distribution of farms by size in relation to measures of population density it is clear that there does appear to be a definite association between the number of very small farms and the degree of population pressure. (See Table 3.2) The "passive" areas of the karstic coastal region showed the highest rates under both of these headings (Primorska, Zetska), while the broad and relatively sparsely populated Vojvodina (Dunavska) rated relatively lowly. These patterns are closely linked to the development in the post-war period of flows of migrant labour entering the international labour market, and the process of urbanisation, discussed above.

Since the war, partly as a result of the alleviation of direct pressure on the land as a result of urbanisation, the political attention devoted to population matters has altered its focus. Widespread concern was expressed in the 1970s about the "senilisation" of the rural population, and the danger that Yugoslavia would no longer be able to sustain the level of agricultural activity necessary to feed itself. These concerns have been voiced with particular vigour in Croatia, where there has been a long tradition, linked to the Croatian Peasant Party in the period before 1941, which identifies Croatian culture especially with the rural milieu. (Nejasmic 1991; Stambuk 1991. See also the special edition of *Sociologija sela*, Nos. 79-81, 1983.)

More significantly, debate switched from the rural/urban differences to ethnic differences, and in particular to the conspicuous discrepancies between the very low birth rates among (for example) Slovenes and the unusually high rates among rural Albanians.

Table 3.2: Agricultural population per 100 ha. of cultivated land, and the percentage of farms having less than 1 ha. of land, by banovina, in 1931

Banovina *	Agricultural population per 100 ha. of cultivated land	Percentage of farms having < 1ha. of land
Zetska	243	18.0
Primorska	235	33.4
Dravska	191	20.3
Moravska	156	9.7
Drinska	154	14.6
Savska	151	17.4
Vrbaska	150	11.4
Vardarska	144	17.6
Dunavska	81	15.9

Spearman's rho=0.6167 (significant at 5%).

Source: Adapted from Tomasevich 1955:322 and 387.

* Since it was predominantly an urban area the figures for the prefecture of

Belgrade have been omitted.

The nature and significance of these developments were firstly underestimated, and secondly misrecognised. Differentials in population growth undermined systematically policies directed at the correction of regional economic imbalances (Vojnic, in Akhavan and Howse eds. 1995:77-99; above pp. 000-000). Furthermore, a rather oversimplified version of these trends became used as a means of generating anti-Islamic (especially anti-Albanian) prejudice in many areas of Yugoslavia, and the fertility of Muslim women used as a symbol of the "threat" to Yugoslavia. Population matters have returned to the political agenda in almost every republic of the former Yugoslav federation, however, and in each case ethnic differentials in rates of reproduction have been close to the heart of controversy.[25]

Conclusion

There is a tendency to look at issues relating to population as rather peripheral to sociology. Along with the physical geography of a region sociologists are often prepared to take demography as no more than a matter of general background relevance. Incorporating this chapter into this book I suggest that the subject is far more important than this.

In subsequent chapters of this book I turn to questions relating to the development of states and nations in the region, and to the relationship between state and nation. A good part of the discourse about nationality, national identity and the claims which nations might have on territory, hinge upon assumptions about the spatial distribution of population. A glance at the enthographic map of Yugoslavia before its disintegration indicates that there is no simple link between peoples and land.

Several problems become clear when one considers the historical processes by which populations have come to be distributed as they are. It becomes possible to challenge the authoritative character of nationalistic mythologies, exposing their claims for what they are. Nevertheless, it becomes apparent why the attachment to these essentially pre-modern concepts of the state is so dangerous in the Balkans. It becomes easier to understand the processes of the displacement of population which have characterised the recent Yugoslav wars, in pursuit of the realisation of these mythologies. Finally, it places at the centre of attention in considering the future of the region the urgency which attaches to the creation of civic rather than ethnic bases for state-building in the region.

Notes

1. Of great interest is the attempt by a Croatian sociologist to sketch a general history of population movement for Croatia (Hersak: 1993). His bibliography in English, French, German, Italian, Russian and Serbo-Croatian, provides a valuable basis for further and fuller research. Several aspects of this question are covered, and essential background bibliographical material assembled, in Tasic and Stosic eds. 1989. For a very useful summary of material relating to the formerly Ottoman areas of the region (and a valuable discussion of the methodological problems of working with historiographical resources in this area) see Palairet 1997:Chap. 1.

2. Some aspects of the very early history and pre-history of the region relevant to this discussion are considered in Cunliffe 1994; Stoianovich 1994; Wilkes 1992; Tasic and Stosic eds. 1989.

3. See Koledarov 1977, esp. the maps on pp. 295, 305, 308 and 310. Also the map on p. 169, illustrating Carter's essay in the same volume. See also Pribichevich 1982:69; Durham 1928:13-4. In addition to his historical summary of the movement of peoples into Bosnia, Noel Malcolm raises several important general methodological points on this issue (Malcolm 1994: Chap. 1). It is not surprising that students of the "primordial" character of ethnic identities are able to trace back into the ancient world the symbolic ancestry of its contemporary inhabitants. They typically neglect the related issue, however, of the historical *erasure* of identities. Noel Malcolm has much good sense to say on these issues in his recent book on Kosovo (Malcolm 1998), which reached me too late to be used systematically in the preparation of this chapter.

4. Of course, in practice these types have been closely intertwined with each other, and I separate them here only in order to aid exposition.

5. Several useful discussions of Ottoman landholding, and especially the millet system, are available: see Inalçik and Quataert eds. 1994; Castellan 1992; Lampe and Jackson 1982; Sugar 1977. This element of Ottoman social organisation has had profound significance for the subsequent development of the relationship between ethnicity and political culture in the Balkans. The *millet* system in its full form was, in fact, a relatively late development. It is important to realise that in the early stages of Ottoman conquest the primary line of differentiation was not between "Christian" and "Muslim", but between Ottomans and the rest.

6. The balance between immigration and conversion in accounting for the existence of a Muslim population in the region has been a matter of some historical controversy. Although the number of Turks in relation to the total population may well have been small it is nevertheless now acknowledged to have involved substantial numbers of migrants. For a survey of the discussion, see Todorova 1996: esp. pp. 61-4. Also Todorov 1983: Chap 3. Inalçik, in Inalçik and Quataert eds.1994:35 cites the view of Vryonis that Ottoman penetration of the Balkans was not "a typical military conquest ... but an ethnic migration of nomadic peoples of substantial numerical proportions".

7. Other occupations which tended to be associated with specific groups were cattle-droving (Vlahs), masonry and wood-carving (Macedonians), silversmithing (Albanians), and ironwork (Albanians and Gypsies).

8. The phrase originates with Freeman (ed.) 1903:115. It is important to acknowledge that, whereas pockets of "Balkan Latinity" persisted in Dalmatia until recent times, these peoples were not necessarily speakers of Italian, but perhaps more often of ancient dialects more closely related to Vlah. See, Naval Intelligence Division 1944: Vol. II, Fig. 13, 45; Winnifrith 1987: esp. 28-9.

9. Lampe and Jackson 1982: Chapter 2; Naval Intelligence Division 1944 Vol. II, History, Peoples and Administration, 252-3; Malcolm 1994: Chap. 9; also Magosci 1993: Chap. 1.

10. A useful summary of these is provided by Hersak 1993:290-1. Hersak's work, incidentally, contains a glaring illustration of the ways in which work of this kind can be corrupted (knowingly or otherwise) by its subordination to nationalistic projects. Whereas it can be generally accepted that there has been a long-term and widespread process of the assimilation of Orthodox Vlahs to Serb identity Hersak appears to write the Serbs out of the picture almost completely, replacing them across the central Balkans by "Vlahs". The discussion of demography has become highly politicised in Croatia in relation to the republic's bid for independence. See also, for example, Klanac 1992; Nejasmic 1991.

11. As in the Habsburg areas, the establishment of a "Military Frontier" went along with the settlement of troops also within the Ottoman lands. This process took place in two stages, however, in the latter case. The settlements in Macedonia date from the late fourteenth century, when this region did, in fact, represent a frontier of Ottoman expansion (Inalçik, in Inalçik and Quataert eds. 1994:13-14). The later establishment of "kapetanates" in Bosnia does not appear to have had an equivalent demographic significance, but was more a matter of military organisation (Malcolm 1994:90 and 122). These were abolished in 1835.

12. Macedonia was affected with particular seriousness by disorder in the early seventeenth century (Inalçik, in Inalçik and Quataert eds. 1994:25). These depredations typically affected the lowlands more severely than they did the upland regions. Consequently periods of depopulation were typically followed by periods of the resettlement of the lowlands by waves of immigration from mountainous areas. I believe that this is the basis for the somewhat perverse theories of "social character" originally popularised in Tomasic 1948, and recently revived in Mestrovic 1993.

13. Rothenberg 1960 and 1966. See also relevant plates in Magosci 1993. Serb settlement north of the Sava-Danube dates from the arrival of the Turks in some places. Srsan reports that the Ottoman armies which occupied Baranja in the early sixteenth century were composed in large measure of "Rasani" (Serbs) in the service of the Sultan, many of whom settled there. See Srsan 1993:74-75; also McGowan, in Inalçik and Quataert eds. 1994:648-9.

14. Some of these settler populations were far older, however, such as the German colony in and around Kocevje (Gotschee) which dated from the mid-fourteenth century.

15. A concise survey of the literature is contained in Djilas 1991:125-127. The field is an extremely contentious one for two principal reasons. In the first place it is not always clear to what claims about numbers of victims refer. Do they claim to record Serb victims, or all victims; do they account for those killed in camps such as Jasenovac, all victims of *Ustasa* terror, or all civilian victims; do they cover events in Croatia, in the *NDH*, or all of Yugoslavia; do they claim to operate on the basis of documentary sources, or (as in the case of the work of Tudjman) a method based upon demographic differentials? The problems ramify well beyond this list. Difficulties at least as great as these attach to the fact that the casualties of the Second World War have come to be matters of great current political sensitivity, as nationalistic parties have sought to use such figures as ammunition to discredit their contemporary opponents. All that one can do in using these sources is to caution the reader about their contentious status. On the question of population transfers in the Balkans during the Nazi occupation, see Magosci 1993:plate 48 and pp. 164-68.

16. See my essay in Luciuk and Kenzer eds. (forthcoming) for a fuller account of population movements in the wake of the Second World War. On the expulsion of Albanians in this period, see the survey of the problem provided in Malcolm 1998.

17. The UNHCR estimated in February 1993 that within the territory of former Yugoslavia, in addition to the more than 2 million of whom they had records, perhaps a further 93,000 persons were unregistered. Recognising that their criteria exclude several types of involuntary displacement, at this time also they reported that they were "assisting" approximately 1 million other individuals not classed as "refugees". By July 1996, at the height of the problem, approx. 687,000 refugees were being accommodated in countries outside former Yugoslavia.

18. Cvijic, *Balkansko poluostrvo*, excerpted in the single-volume selection of his work, 1965:202-5. On the antiquity of these processes, see Hammond 1976. Whereas he derives this term from the Greek phrase which simply means "the movement of place", it is clear that his interest is in these long-term and incremental drifts of population.

19. I do not consider here the related issue of transhumant migrations, which are seasonal in character. The process under consideration here refers to permanent resettlement. See, however, Stoianovich 1994:61-6; McGowan, in Inalçik and Quataert (eds.) 1994:647.

20. For early nineteenth century observations on the limits of Albanian settlement, see for example, Hobhouse 1813: Vol. I, map facing 1, and 169. "It (i.e. Albania) extends in no part more than 100 miles in land, and in the southern districts not more than 30" (Leake 1814:255-6). The ethnographic cartography of the region has produced some widely discrepant results, but I believe that my contention here is supported in general terms. See Kennan ed. 1993: maps in the Appendices. Also Wilkinson 1951 and Strupp 1929—although in each case the author's primary concern is with the distribution of the Macedonian Slav population.

21. "Natalistic" policies, of encouraging women to have large numbers of children, and opposition to birth control, are to be distinguished from "population policies" and are typically rooted in *pre-modern* attitudes.

22. For an incomplete, but detailed, consideration of the displacement of population during the Second World War, see Kulischer (ed.) 1943.

23. Tomasevich 1955: Chapter 16; Vuco 1968: esp. Chap. II "Sazrevanje krize, 1924-1930". On the wider debate, particularly the literature in German, see Warriner 1964: Chap. III, "Overpopulation"; Kirk 1946; Mitrany 1945, Chap. III; Tiltman 1936.

24. Warriner studiously avoids committing herself to figures in her discussion of the topic: her chapter is a well-considered critique of the whole exercise of estimating over-population.

25. I return to these issues in relation to the subject of "traditionalism" in Chap. 10.

6

NEW CLASSES FOR OLD

New perspectives for old

The question of stratification in Balkan societies raises in intensive form the problem which I have mentioned already in connection with the process of economic modernisation, namely, the need to disengage sociological analysis from the primarily ideological concepts in which it has become encased. The work done by Yugoslav sociologists is often of a high technical standard and clearly in touch with intellectual developments in the discipline. Nevertheless, the dominant position of the League of Communists in Yugoslav cultural life between 1945 and 1990 had an impact upon this area of sociology more than any other. The question of class is so close to the heart of Marxist orthodoxy that the agenda of social science has often been constrained to accommodate to a political definition of the nature of social reality and the course of its transformation.

The requirement that social differences should be conceptualised within a Marxist framework imposed a certain schematic framework upon history. The history of the region had to be forced onto the procrustean bed of a general movement from feudalism, through capitalism, to socialism, in ways which robbed all three terms of sociological and historical precision. Whereas at first sight it may appear that the description of pre-modern Balkan society in terms of "feudalism" is unexceptionable, for a variety of reasons it is sociologically problematic.[1] Difficulties arise in relation to the application of this term both to the Ottoman and Habsburg systems, as they operated in the Balkans.

No attempt was made on the part of Yugoslav sociologists to really address the problems of theorising pre-capitalist social formations in the Balkans.[2] "Feudalism" was generally used in order to frame (basically) nineteenth century history, and for the less advanced areas of the region even the period immediately preceding unification. This tended to foreshorten the long period during which a predominantly agrarian society was nevertheless being steadily drawn into a monetised economy and inserted into international patterns of exchange and the attendant changes in stratification.

Four features are common to processes of social differentiation across the entire Balkan Peninsula, however, in this transitional and pre-modern period.

1. It is necessary to place in the foreground of analysis *strata other than the military and landholding aristocracy*. The growth of the central state and the power of its servants, the role of the merchant, and of local urban intelligentsias within these larger social formations, do not find an adequate place in sociological models of "feudalism".

2. Both the rising urban strata and the older landholding aristocracies, *especially* in the Habsburg lands, failed to develop a coherent, shared ethnic consciousness. The

potential for class formation was everywhere frustrated by the *political and cultural fragmentation* of the upper strata.

3. *Stratification hierarchies tended to peak outside of the region itself*, so that in important respects an account of Balkan society in the early modern period which limits itself to the Balkans must remain sociologically incomplete--one might say "decapitated".

4. I have already made reference to John Lampe's characterisation of the structural consequences of the mutual confrontation of the two great empires in the region as "imperial borderlands" (Lampe and Jackson 1982: esp. Chap. 9). Certain characteristics of class formation in the region reflect this *confrontational* relationship.

Consequently, I offer a reinterpretation of the history of stratification in the South Slav lands which attempts to revise this rather politicised version of sociological analysis, and challenges the conceptualisation of the development of stratification in terms of three discontinuous stages. I also draw attention to some hitherto unrecognised patterns of continuity or even recurrence. Finally, I suggest some ways in which developing patterns of inequality have been implicated in the break-up of the Yugoslav state.

Social hierarchy under the Habsburgs

The Slovene lands during the nineteenth century can be said to exemplify very well Anderson's general account of Austrian absolutism (Anderson 1979: Part II, Chap. 5).

Beneath the ruling landed aristocracy there emerged during the later nineteenth century urban strata, particularly of professionals such as the clergy, lawyers and teachers, as well as petty traders. The task of the state was to reconcile their growing aspirations and real economic weight with the interests of the rural-based aristocracy. The stratum of landed magnates was primarily Austrian in identity, however, having ousted or absorbed the indigenous Slav aristocracy in the Middle Ages. There was a disjunction between this germanised, but rather cosmopolitan, aristocracy oriented culturally towards Vienna (and indeed the rest of Europe) and the essentially *local* purview of the urban middle class, marked after the Napoleonic period by the consolidation of the Slovene language. The problem for Austrian absolutism was to maintain the authority of the state in the face of processes of differentiation. They were aided in this task by the internal divisions within the urban middle classes, as the more advanced capitalistic sections of these strata were themselves typically not Slovenes but nationals whose homeland was elsewhere in the Dual Monarchy.[3]

In the Croatian lands the pattern was complicated by the division between not only Austrian and Hungarian jurisdictions, but also between civil and military Croatia. The commercialised agriculture practised by many Magyar landlords contrasts with the economic conservatism of the aristocracy in the Slovene lands, whose estates preserved huge tracts of forest for the sporting pursuit of game, or where commercialism did gain a toe-hold, the extraction of lumber. In some areas extensive cultivation on good soils lent itself to the more rapid development of modern agriculture, and it is here that the early stirrings of capitalistic cultivation can be detected, discussed in previous chapters.

Social hierarchy in civil Croatia-Slavonia and the Vojvodina resembled in one respect that found in Slovenia, in that the focus of aristocratic life lay in Budapest or Vienna rather than in Zagreb. Ethnic divisions between Magyar and Slav, however, sometimes cut across and sometimes reinforced incipient class divisions. Whereas the emerging capitalist class in the countryside were largely Magyar, the cultural and economic life of the urban middle classes was marked by linguistic divisions between Magyar, German and Croatian communities.

These features were largely absent from the *vojna krajina* (the most obvious reflection of the status of the region as an "imperial borderland"). As a consequence of the protracted struggle between Magyar and Turk by the end of the seventeenth century large parts of the Croatian lands were almost depopulated, so that a primary problem during the eighteenth century was the retention of labour. Attempts to resolve the problem by importing settlers from other parts of the Empire (and from the Ottoman lands), described in the previous chapter, made for a unique ethnic diversity. Here one finds an almost complete absence of towns of any size, a peculiar uniformity of land-holding patterns, based upon the *zadruga*, and the prominence within the few urban settlements of the military (who were often of the Orthodox and not the Roman Catholic faith). It is partly because of the high level of militarisation of this region that some other Balkan parts of the Austro-Hungarian lands manage to develop in rather unmilitaristic ways.

Culture and society in Dalmatia also bore several distinctive features. Both the rural aristocracy and the urban mercantile class were (except in Dubrovnik) heavily Italianised--"a Slavonic land with an Italian fringe". The urban, mercantile elite was here, unusually, the summit of the stratification hierarchy, not a stratum of rural

landlords whose identities and loyalties were focussed largely elsewhere.

Social hierarchy under Ottoman absolutism

Ottoman absolutism exhibited one feature which differentiated the "Asiatic" version

from the Habsburg variety. The aristocracy traditionally and juridically did not have

the kind of permanent attachment to estates which characterised their western

European counterparts, lacking heritable fiefs. During the centuries of Ottoman

decline the *timar* holders moved in one of two directions from their original military

constitution: either they became tax-farmers, or began to convert their holdings into

hereditable estates, which divided (and therefore weakened) the ruling stratum. There

emerged regional political magnates (the so-called *ayans*) whose power might be

based either on tax farming or *ciftlik* holdings (and the tendency to the *de facto*

heritability of estates). Either way there was an element of usurpation about their

situation which frequently placed them in conflict with both the Sultan and the

peasantry.

In Bosnia and Hercegovina, although the local landlord stratum of agas and begs had

originated in the Ottoman feudal cavalry, they were recruited in very large measure

from indigenous Serbo-Croat speaking stock. After 1630, when jannissaries gained

the entitlement to marry, they increasingly moved into the cities, losing in the process

their specifically military vocation and coming to be absorbed into the artisanate or

the mercantile groups. Consequently, Bosnian society lacked the linguistic underscoring of the differences between social strata found in the Habsburg lands, replacing it to some extent by a confessional divide, although this mapped imperfectly onto the pattern of social hierarchy.

The shared culture of Islam was not an entirely unifying force. Sarajevo (and other towns such as Travnik) grew up as important mercantile and administrative centres, which possessed a distinctive civic culture, partly based upon Islam, but mixing Islamic and Christian communities. Rural and urban leadership groups were internally divided along ethno-religious lines, institutionalised within the. Ottoman social order in the *millet* system, and often segregated into different *mehale* (neighbourhoods). Even more than in the Habsburg lands, therefore, Ottoman society was characterised by a pattern of vertical segmentation which cut across hierarchy, which gave to it an "estate basis" (Stoianovich 1963:294).

Recent scholarship has sought to emphasise the distinctive characteristics of Bosnian society, as the primordial basis for a contemporary Bosnian identity (Donia and Fine eds. 1994; Malcolm 1994; Pinson ed. 1994). My own reading of history results in a more ambiguous picture. Networks of trade extended outside of Bosnia (and in any case, a good proportion of the mercantile stratum were rather cosmopolitan types such as Ragusans). The specifically Ottoman orientation of administration, and the use of the Turkish and Arabic languages in administration and culture, to some extent resulted in a situation similar to that which I have noted in the Habsburg lands, in that the pyramid culminated elsewhere. After 1878, however, the Austrian administration gave a considerable stimulus to the consolidation of *local* leadership, cutting the link with Turkey, but in this period the stratum of Austrian and Croatian functionaries expanded enormously, adding further to structural complexity and the potential for conflict.

The land-owning stratum in Bosnia and Hercegovina certainly do appear to have developed a greater sense of local social identity than in the Sandzak, Kosovo and Macedonia, where they were far more heavily turcicised, and where other urban professional and commercial groups were more weakly developed. In these regions far more than in Bosnia-Hercegovina the process of *ciftlik* building fragmented the rural aristocracy and blurred its outlines.

Montenegro is a curious exception to all of this, in view both of the entire absence of anything which could be called a feudal aristocracy, and the insignificance of other elite groups based in cities. Elite formation took place around a very small circle of tribal chieftains, whose power and prestige did not depend entirely upon their control over land, but heavily upon other forms of "symbolic capital" (Bourdieu 1977:177-183 and 1990: Chap. 7). Clan loyalty was still the primary medium of politics, and the few merchants seem to have been generally ethnic outsiders. These characteristics are shared by the regions of mainly Albanian settlement.

Serbia is also entirely distinctive in its social structure. The gradual extension of independence from the Porte went hand in hand with the forcible expulsion of the former Turkish landholding aristocracy. The redistribution of their estates, however, did not result in the creation of local landed magnates, but a highly egalitarian spread of peasant landholders. Around the court, however, there emerged a class whose fortunes depended in part upon this process, in two ways. Some gained considerably

241

from commercial transactions over the disposal of land. Others made money from the growing peasant indebtedness, as moneylenders.

Serbian agriculture became quite rapidly commercialised. Trade was not monopolised by foreign ethnic enclaves (although many were Austrians) but retained in the hands of a local commercial elite known as the *carsija*, whose mixed Serb-Cincar membership developed close links with the crown and its functionaries. The clergy, although they retained an ambivalent relationship with other elite groups, did not develop the community of interest with a stratum of large landowners, as in the Slovene and Croat lands, where the Church counted among the largest proprietors. During the nineteenth century there also emerged a very small but cohesive secular urban intelligentsia (Guzina 1959 and 1960). Serbia and Montenegro were consequently the only parts of the South Slav lands which were not characterised by the ethnic alienation of the upper reaches of society.

A further feature of Serbia, as of Montenegro, was the pervasive militarisation of society. Military experience was not differentiated to particular either socially or geographically distinct social groups. Military skills, and even until the last quarter of the nineteenth century the ownership and control of the means of violence, were distributed throughout the state, the defence of which depended primarily upon a *levée en masse*. In this respect both Serbia and Montenegro, as well as parts of the Croat lands, can be said to encapsulate in their social structures essential attributes of "imperial borderlands".

The chimera of Balkan capitalism

In its attempt to find an ideological basis for the notion of socialist revolution, Yugoslav social science has lent itself to the task of providing a narrative of the "development of capitalism". The basis of this project in Marxist theory was overlaid by nationalistic agendas, which sought to demonstrate the historical basis for the greater "advancement" of Croatia and Slovenia in comparison with the "backwardness" of the former Ottoman lands. In this endeavour (as I have already outlined) it exaggerated the significance of the early industrialisation process in these regions. It generally neglected to point out that the most important dimension of the insertion of the region into the capitalist system was neither the import of foreign capital, nor the creation of indigenous classes of "capitalists" and "proletarians", but the incorporation of the region's producers of primary products into international pattern of exchange. The most characteristic local representatives of capitalism in the South Slav lands before their unification were the merchant and the moneylender, followed by the miller and the brewer. The manufacturer, and even the capitalistic agrarian producer, competed for a rather distant third place.

In as far as it is appropriate at all to speak of "capitalism" in the Balkans before the unification of the South Slavs, capitalistic activity was everywhere intimately intertwined with government. "Far from being an autonomous force, capitalism was dependent upon the largesse of government bureaus (*sic*) and ministries, and government officials were rarely 'large' unless business was kind in turn." (Stoianovich 1963:336)

One other important factor might inhibit the sociologist from embarking too freely on an analysis in terms of class, even having recognised these qualifications. To speak of "class" in sociology is to speak not only of economics but also of *culture*. The possibilities for the creation of anything resembling class consciousness, culture, organisation and action in the Balkans were severely limited, not only on the part of a potential bourgeoisie but any other class, by three features.

Hierarchies tended to culminate outside of the region, not only because different areas were incorporated into different state structures (Ottoman, Austrian, Hungarian or Venetian) but also into the spheres of influence of different economically advanced European states (particularly Germany, Britain, France and Italy). The relatively small number of local representatives of capitalism were typically no more than the "foot soldiers" of "armies" based elsewhere.

Indigenous elites (in this case largely the middle strata) were chronically divided not only by their dispersion across different states, but also by the diversity of their cultural heritage. Their identification with projects of formalising and institutionalising local languages, or their adherence to competing faiths, ensured that it would be difficult for them to cohere around any common project. Bosnia is a microcosm of the problem, where during the latter part of the nineteenth century banks were created along confessional lines. In Croatia the tourism trade was characterised by competition between Magyar and indigenous Slav capitals. The point is also made by a consideration of the biographies of South Slav intellectuals, especially those who acquired a higher education. Those who were educated in St.

Petersburg or Paris brought to their home-land a mental set quite different from those who were educated in Vienna or Budapest.

It is important to realise the relatively small scale of urban settlements in the Balkans until very recently. One of the most important features of the social relationships and identification of the great majority of those who might have aspired to "bourgeois" status was their primary attachment to *locality*. There were few settlements which were large enough to count as "cities". In Croatia in 1910 only seven exceeded 15,000 inhabitants (Klemencic ed. 1993:108). Only Zagreb and Belgrade at this time had populations larger than 100,000, and only the Vojvodina had a significant proportion of its population living in settlements greater than 5,000. (Tomasevich 1955:174; Also Todorov 1983: Chap. 19, and pp. 338-9.) In the light of this information perhaps Kostic's study of the provincial town Bajina Basta conveys well the general shape of "bourgeois" society in the nineteenth century across the entire region—a mixture of lndowners, shopkeepers and artisans (Kostic 1955-57:137). Parochialism is important as an enduring characteristic of Balkan society. The development of *class* society necessarily involves a process of "disembedding" from locality, and the experience of class as an "imagined community" which extends well beyond the circle of face-to-face relations (Anderson 1991). The cultural gap separating the cosmopolitan Greek-speaking *Cincar* or Jew, or Austrian merchant, from the local Slav *zelenas* or inn-keeper was much deeper than that represented by language alone.

Unification in 1918 brought with it important new developments. The process begun in Serbia after independence was extended, whereby elites considered to be aliens were expropriated and ejected. In the lands acquired by Serbia after the Balkan Wars

(Kosovo, the Sandzak and Macedonia) the expulsion of "Turks" expanded to take in many who did not consider themselves to be ethnic Turks, but who were marked by their adherence to Islam--Muslim Slavs and Albanians (McCarthy 1995). The land reform programme expropriated the estates of Magyar, Austrian and Italian proprietors in the Croatian lands and Slovenia.

The definitive overthrow of the "absolutisms" of Austria-Hungary and the Ottoman Sultanate eliminated, in large measure, not only foreign landowners, but also a substantial stratum of servants of the state, both civil and military (together with a sizeable component of the economic elite). In this way it is possible to speak of the "decapitation" of stratification structures in the region. This is a recurring and important feature of the development of stratification in Yugoslav history, whereby incipient class formation is repeatedly frustrated or diverted.

One very significant variant of absolutism survived into "capitalistic" Yugoslavia, however, and that was the Serbian ruling stratum. It is not unreasonable to characterise pre-unification Serbia as a somewhat idiosyncratic variant of absolutism. Because of the circumstances of unification the Serbian state was able to bring this stratum virtually undamaged into the new, unified South Slav kingdom. A major problem was presented by the demands of adjusting the relationship between fragments of the former urban middle classes in the Austro-Hungarian Empire and the newly established hegemony of Serbian absolutism. The nationality problem in inter-war Yugoslavia yields convincingly to analysis in terms of a bitter conflict between these two class fragments.

It is partly this process of decapitation which enables Yugoslav social scientists to speak so unambiguously about the post-unification period as the age *par excelence* of the development of capitalism in the region. A significant proportion of those who were expelled have been defined within Marxist rhetoric as representing the last stages of "feudalism", definitively abrogated under the land reform programme. This embodies a crucial confusion, however, from a sociological point of view, in that a substantial part of the decapitation process also removed from Yugoslavia key representatives of *capitalistic* production in agriculture and manufacturing. To a significant extent their role in the integration of the region into capitalism was then taken not by indigenous entrepreneurs, but by the state and its functionaries. The insertion of the First Yugoslavia into international capitalism as often as not took the forms of the government loan and the provision of expertise. The characteristic manifestation of this process in the context of Yugoslav stratification, therefore, is not the indigenous *capitalist* but the foreign *technical specialist*--say, the mining engineer.[5]

The creation of the unified state not only resulted in the massive inflation of the number of state functionaries but also enhanced the position of other strata. There was a burgeoning of the local intelligentsia--lawyers, doctors, teachers, journalists. The expansion of the Universities contributed significantly to elite formation in this period. Universities in Ljubljana and Zagreb trace their origins to institutions founded in the sixteenth and seventeenth centuries, although they were later suppressed. The University of Zagreb was reconstituted in 1905, and Ljubljana in 1919. Belgrade was established as a *Visoka skola* in 1863, subsequently acquiring University status, and spawning dependent faculties in Subotica and Skopje in 1920 (Dedijer et al. 1974:553; Naval Intelligence Division 1944: Vol. II, 231). By 1938 there were around 20,000 students in higher education in Yugoslavia. Representatives of this "humanistic intelligentsia", typically heavily influenced by western European ideas, were frequently active in politics, including the Communist Party. Movements of peasants and workers were invariably led by dissident intellectuals, who distanced themselves culturally from the commercial or official elites.

The most powerful section of the indigenous bourgeoisie was still mercantile, however, rather than industrial or cultural throughout the inter-war period. The growth of a bourgeoisie was also partly fuelled by the investment of compensation paid to landlords expropriated by the land reform. A domestic manufacturing class begins to emerge in this period, and with this a small manual working class, especially in the northern cities, although with important outposts in centres such as the Macedonian tobacco industry.

For the inter-war period we have available census data covering the occupational structure of the population of the new unified South Slav state. Mirkovic has produced corrected figures for the censuses of 1921 and 1931, and his results are summarised in Table 6.1. These figures do not map directly onto stratification, of course. What is remarkable about them is, firstly, the extremely small proportion of the population who are in non-agricultural occupations, and secondly the fact that the numbers of those employed in infrastructure, administration (not to mention "rentiers and pensioners") at least keep pace with the expansion of "industry and handicrafts". During the years of the depression also the numbers of insured workers actually declined (from 605,065 in 1930 to 520,980 in 1933, before recovering again to 616,209 in 1936 (Mirkovic 1952:51 and 53).

Table 6.1: Changing occupational structure in Yugoslavia, 1921-31

Occupational category	1921 %	1931 %	% change in number
Agriculture, stock-raising and fishery	75.9	72.5	-12.7
Industry and handicraft	9.8	11.7	+40.3
Trade and credit	3.2	2.9	- 7.5
Transport and communication	2.0	2.5	+53.6
Public service and the free professions	3.5	4.1	+37.6
Military	0.5	0.3	-15.0
Workers without indication of profession	1.4	1.4	+17.2
Rentiers and pensioners	2.3	3.1	+57.2
Other (including unemployed)	1.4	1.5	+22.1

Source: Mirkovic 1952:7 and 17.

Although during the Communist period in Yugoslavia an elaborate quasi-academic establishment grew up around the "history of the workers' movement", and it is undeniably the case that before their suppression under the *diktatura* free trade unions formed and conducted a number of hard-fought strikes, notions of class formation have to be applied with considerable caution. The "working class" was small, regionally fragmented, and incompletely differentiated from its peasant origins.

In dealing with peasantries in relation to stratification it is always important to bear in mind the significance of characteristic life-processes of the farming family. Peasants acquire and loose land over the course of their lives for a variety of reasons. Juridical processes (especially where there is division upon the death of the proprietor) impose upon estates a cycle of accumulation followed by decay. Family

fortunes are affected by birth and death, and above all by the available supply of

useful labour within the family. Crops and cattle have good years and bad years

(Galeski 1972). The fluidity of family fortunes, and the difference between the

mechanisms which generate or threaten economic security for the peasant and the

worker, means that the social and cultural boundary between the city and the country

remains far more vivid and significant than any differences within and between

peasant communities.

The peasantry never acted politically independently of groups of intellectuals and

small business more generally, although presenting themselves as "peasant parties".

What we have emerging in the inter-war period is a form of populism, which

emphasises the idea that what unites both "the people" and competing elites is the

sense of the unity of "the nation": ethnic differentiation subverts class consciousness

across the board.

Inequality and Communist revolution

The experience of the *partizan* struggle has frequently been the object of comment as

transforming the class basis of Yugoslav society. It is a common observation that the

period between 1941 and 1945 in Yugoslavia compounded three conflicts which,

while linked to each other, should be identified by quite different characteristics.

There was a "war of national liberation" (*narodna oslobodilicka borba--NOB*) fought

by Yugoslavs against the occupying forces of the Axis powers; an inter-ethnic civil war, which had to do not only with the conflict between Serbs and Croats, but in which the relationship between state and nation was at issue across the entire Balkan peninsula; and a process of socialist revolution, in which the Communist Party and its allies attempted to seize power in order to transform the social and economic structure of the country. The historiography of each of these dimensions of the conflict remains controversial.

The interpretation of events in terms of socialist revolution became a standard component of Yugoslav historical and social-scientific writing, framing the character of post-war Yugoslav society. Accounts of the social transformation associated with the rise to power of the Communist Party tended to give pride of place to the "working class", although the industrial working class in Yugoslavia was relatively small before 1941. So much is perhaps recognised in the tendency of post-war ideological discourse to refer to the "working people of Yugoslavia"--which term also nicely accommodates in populist fashion peasants, functionaries and intellectuals.

Although representatives of the radicalised industrial working class may have played a prominent part in its leadership, the *partizan* war was won by a peasant army. "It has been estimated .... that peasants constituted about ninety percent of the Partisan forces and over half of the 1946 Party membership" (Zukin 1975:117; also Trouton 1952:196-8). There can be no pretence, however, that the Communist revolution in Yugoslavia was a "peasant revolution", in that it was unquestionably led and directed by an elite group who were rarely drawn from the peasantry. The Antifascist Council for the National Liberation of Yugoslavia (*AVNOJ*), elected by the National Assembly at Bihac in November 1942, contained six barristers, six professors, four doctors, one engineer, five priests, four writers, five journalists, three regular officers, sixteen peasants and four industrial workers (Trouton 1952:197).[6]

Between the wars the peasantry were subject to processes which *cut across class formation*, enhancing the sense of *national* consciousness and differentiation. If anything that experience is more consistent with the concept of *massification*, by which the boundaries and identities of groups are blurred in relation to each other.[7] In that respect, the wartime experience should be regarded as a continuation of that of the inter-war period, rather than as a revolutionary departure from it.

The other side of the coin represented by massification is the concept of an elite.[8] War produced yet another cycle of the process of class "decapitation". Former landowners, proprietors and state functionaries were driven out. They were replaced by a rapidly constituted new elite formed out of the massified residue of society. The early *partizan* military formations (the "proletarian shock brigades" formed in December 1941) were formed around a core of active Communists, including many from the industrial working class (Milivojevic 1988:3-7; Gow 1992:33-5). The military apparatus and the organisation of the Party itself, served as important means of mobility for many former manual workers and peasants, but they were joined in these settings by other, middle class, groups (Cohen 1989: Chap. 2).

This new elite was therefore an aggregate of professionals, the technical intelligentsia, white collar workers, manual workers and peasants, which was homogenised into an all-Yugoslav character as well as being given the stamp of party functionaries. It was solidified around a common *experience* rather than a shared class background, cultural heritage or specifically economic base. A condition of advancement within the new order was the minimisation of ethnic, religious and regional particularisms, exemplified by Tito himself, who was born of mixed Slovene-Croat parentage.

The war took some people from rural backgrounds, and moved them into urban environments and even elite status: but that does not mean that those left behind in the countryside were radically altered in their class orientation by war. They were returned after the war to the villages, there to become once again the objects of policy, identified after the first flush of land reform with the backward residue of private property, and facing no other expected destiny than their disappearance as a group.

What the war did was to deliver a new "political formula" by which the new elite were able to legitimate rule.[9] The victory of the Communist Party of Yugoslavia in the armed struggle was taken as legitimating the moral and legal basis for their ruling Yugoslavia, as the leaders of a movement which, through its opposition to fascism, and unified under the slogan of "brotherhood and unity", claimed to have brought together all the peoples of the country into a "national liberation struggle".

As significant in this process of legitimation was the immediate post-war period, and especially the break with the Cominform. The break with the Soviet Union and its allies created an enormous problem within the Communist movement (Banac 1988). After an initial attempt to demonstrate good Left credentials, in the collectivisation programme, there was a wholesale retreat from the "war against the peasant". The peasantry were effectively bracketed from politics, and politically insulated from society--neutralised, and confirmed in their semi-autonomous status as a peasantry.

An end was brought to early attempts to promote levelling, and a rhetorical switch made to an emphasis upon national unity through common participation in self-management. In this respect, although dressed as socialist theory, "workers' self-management" can be construed equally as a *populist* concept, which has to do with the diminution of class differences, and the blurring of levels of hierarchy. Its ideological focus is upon *participation* rather than *equality*.

The experience between 1941 and 1951 did four things with respect to stratification. It confirmed the symbolic isolation of the peasantry (although in practice they were undergoing a gradual and inexorable incorporation into the wider process of economic modernisation). It created a stratum of party-state functionaries and endowed them with an effective political formula. Between the two, it promoted the general massification of society, and obfuscated processes of the creation of class identities, through an ideological preoccupation with the common involvement of the "working people of Yugoslavia" in the building of a "self-managing society". Finally, because of the real sensitivities left in the wake of war, the question of ethnic stratification was effectively bracketed, making it difficult for Yugoslav social science to tackle openly and honestly this issue until the impending break-up of Yugoslavia made it unavoidable.

The development of social differences in the "Second Yugoslavia"

In this section I will explore the development of stratification in Yugoslavia from the 1950s to the disintegration of the federation, largely through the eyes of Yugoslav sociologists. There are two reasons for taking this approach. Yugoslav sociologists

have done a lot of work in documenting social differences in their country. There has

in any case been little relevant work done by outsiders, and that which there is heavily

dependent upon data supplied by Yugoslav colleagues, and discusses the problems

largely in the same terms.[10]

I explore four aspects of the question in turn. (i) I review the *dominant models of*

socio-economic inequality which have been used by Yugoslav social scientists. (ii)

Starting out from these, I will explore the development of *patterns of inequality under*

socialism in Yugoslavia. (iii) I then attempt to formulate some conclusions about the

overall *shape of stratification in Yugoslavia*. (iv) Finally, I examine the bearing which

the discussion of inequality might have upon the collapse of the Yugoslav state.

i) Models of inequality in Yugoslav sociology

Before 1965, independent sociological theorising of inequality in Yugoslavia was

impossible. The attempt by Milovan Djilas to broach the problem in his celebrated

collection of essays *The New Class* brought down the ire of the Party upon his head,

and resulted in his expulsion and disgrace (Djilas 1957: also 1959). His work was

controversial because he confronted openly the question of the manner in which

access to power through the Party could be seen to be acquiring a measure of

permanence and transferability. It could also be used in order to affect the economic

situation (and life chances more generally) of an emerging elite. In these respects, and

in that they also had access to institutionalised control over the means of production,

Party functionaries as a group might be seen as acquiring the characteristics of a "new class".

The fate of Djilas ensured that discussion of inequality in Yugoslavia remained within a stultifying framework of Marxist orthodoxy for nearly a decade. In works purporting to be sociological, only one "class" was discussed (the working class-- *radnicka klasa*), although there is also mention of "strata" (*slojevi*). The relationship between these concepts was not considered systematically. There were descriptive accounts of occupations and occupational structures, but largely detached from sociological theory.[11]

The period of economic and constitutional reform in the 1960s brought with it a wider liberalisation in politics. The position of Yugoslav sociology began to change; and since 1965 issues relating to stratification, class and inequality have featured strongly within Yugoslav sociology (Allcock 1975). The conference of the Yugoslav Sociological Association in Split in 1966 took this area as its theme.[12] The first major empirical investigation of inequality took place also at this time (Popovic ed. 1977).[12] Several Yugoslav sociologists have secured international recognition for their work in this field (e.g, Ivan Bernik, Bogdan Denitch, Mladen Lazic, Vojin Milic and Josip Zupanov).

One work which was influential in stimulating debate was Stipe Suvar's *Socioloski presjek jugoslovenskog drustva*, in which he introduced the conceptual distinction between the "working class" and a "counter-class" (*radnicka klasa* and *kontraklasa*) (Suvar 1970). Suvar presents us with a tripartite model of stratification: the working class, a "counter-class" and the small producers with their own means. The working class (*radnicka klasa*) are all those employed persons engaged in direct production, distribution and trade--at the time some 31% of the economically active population. The small producers, with about 56%, were composed mainly of the peasantry, with a small number of urban self-employed, mainly craftsmen and petty traders (who only made up just over 1%). The remaining 12% were described as the *kontraklasa* ("counter-class").[13] They included administrative functionaries, financial workers, managerial personnel in industry, members of the defence forces and the "humanistic and technical intelligentsia" (Suvar 1970:18).

Suvar's model is basically a simple oppositional one--*kontraklasa/radnicka klasa*. As an historical anachronism the small producers are gradually being absorbed into the ranks of the working class (the big expropriators having been expropriated) and therefore present no major political or sociological problem. As direct producers who control (with little exception) only the labour power of themselves, and sell on the market the product of that labour, they do not exploit the labour of others and share basically the same interests as the working class.

The *kontraklasa* is composed of: "all those who still live off alienated surplus labour, particularly if in a monopolistic fashion they establish the volume of surplus labour at their disposal in society" (Suvar 1970:16). Although the distinction between productive and non-productive labour has been criticised for its conceptual confusion, it does figure as an important component for the consideration of stratification in state socialist societies.[14]

Probably more common within Yugoslav sociology has been a model of stratification which depicts society as a ladder of hierarchically arranged groups, based upon the division of labour. To these are applied the term "social strata"

(*drustveni slojevi*) rather than classes. They are typically referred to by a mixture of

terms covering economic function, qualification level and property ownership. A

landmark in that respect was the study by Mihailo Popovic and his colleagues at the

Institut drustvenih nauka in Belgrade (Popovic ed. 1977). This investigation (limited

in its scope to Serbia) produced an image of Yugoslav society which is in many ways

very Weberian (although Weber is never credited by the authors). We are shown a

complex array of what are basically status groups, based upon the division of labour,

but one which does not fall into a simple hierarchy. They are differentiated not only

by their economically-determined life-chances (or "class situation") but also by life-

style, interest, social power, class consciousness and ideological orientation.

Five reasonably consistent divisions emerge from their study. These are: peasant and

small business proprietors; peasant-workers and unskilled manual workers; skilled

workers and routine white-collar workers; professionals; and the leadership stratum.

(The social and economic position of both the peasant-workers and the routine white-

collar workers, however, is particularly subject to shifts and ambiguity.)[15] This

approach has provided a model for other important pieces of empirical work on

Yugoslav stratification (for example, Lazic 1983; Elakovic and Brangjolica 1985;

Popovic ed. 1988).

Suvar's approach operates within an orthodox Marxist framework. The key to

increasing inequality lies in the capacity of the non-productive workers to alienate the

surplus product of the others. The alternative approach, while recognising the

continuing importance of private ownership as a factor in the determination of life-chances, treats this as only one factor among many which interact in the shaping of a hierarchy of strata, which is not broken by any single outstanding line of differentiation. Inequality is therefore to be explained in terms of an accumulation of impetus coming from a number of analytically separate sources.

These two approaches hold out to us alternative hypotheses about the route which post-1945 Yugoslavia has taken out of the condition of massification to which I referred earlier. Suvar's *klasa/kontraklasa* model poses the central questions as to whether (*pace* Djilas) Yugoslav society did begin to crystallise as a class-divided society under Communism, and if so, what was the basis of that division. The Popovic study (and others like it) depict a society which has replaced the condition of massification by one of openness and mobility, and increasingly unified around a system of values, based upon equality of opportunity, which can contain an increasing actual disparity of economic and other life-chances.

ii) Patterns of inequality under socialism

The notion of equality has always featured prominently in the ideals of socialist movements, and governments committed to socialism. Although there has always been acceptance of either the pragmatic necessity or desirability of some economic differentials, socialists have compared the relative equality of socialist societies favourably with the relative inequality of capitalist or feudal states (Lane 1971; Matejko 1974; Bauman 1976; Kende and Strmiska eds. 1987). Socialism has never been defined exclusively in these terms. The Programme of the League of Communists of Yugoslavia stated that, "Socialism cannot be equated with the realisation of the principle of equality and freedom, although striving for equality and freedom is a vital element in its ideology" (League of Communists 1959:95). Nevertheless, progress towards equality has been cited as evidence of the genuineness of the country's claim to be advancing towards socialism (Denitch 1976:10). Claims to have advanced equality were important elements in the legitimation of its socialist regime (Pesic 1988).

In the years after the 1941-45 war, documentation of the progress which Yugoslavia appeared to have made towards greater equality was therefore hailed with interest by both Yugoslav and non-Yugoslav social scientists. A comparative study of income distribution by the UN in 1965 showed that in 1951 in Yugoslavia the incomes of qualified white-collar workers were only 25% more than those of unskilled industrial workers, whereas the incomes of skilled manual workers were only 5% lower than those of qualified white-collar workers (cited in Parkin 1971:173).

The theory of "associationist socialism" with which the system of "workers' self-management" was trumpeted following its introduction in 1953, argued that it represented a fuller realisation of socialist ideals than that encountered elsewhere in eastern Europe. The theme of equality played an important part in that argument, in this case with an emphasis on equality of power through participation (Horvat 1969; Drulovic 1978; Pesic 1988). The development of self-management was seen as relevant to questions of *social equity* in that the increasing engagement of citizens in the control of public utilities and services, as well as the original vision of control over the means of production, was construed (in Durkheim's phrase) as an equalisation of the "external conditions of competition".

These original egalitarian tendencies were soon eroded. The 1965 UN study pointed out that by 1961 the average income of highly-skilled manual workers had risen to about two and a half times that of the unskilled worker. The incomes of the highest-qualified white-collar workers was then about three and a third times that of this base: the average incomes of all white-collar workers was higher than that of the majority of manual workers. (Unqualified white-collar workers were 135% of the base: although *skilled* manual workers were 160% of the base.) Later studies, taking other measures of income differential, show a continuation of this movement (Drulovic 1978:94-99). A Slovene study of 1971 showed a ratio of between 1:6 and 1:7 between the lowest and the highest incomes (Popovic ed. 1977:16; also Jambrek 1975:57-58).

Of particular note is the growing differentiation between the incomes of groups of manual workers. By 1984, according to official statistics, the most highly-paid group of workers were taking home 156% of the national average wage, whereas the most poorly paid were taking home only 72% of that standard.[16] Pipeline workers (to take a specific example) were taking home about half as much again as the average wage: workers in personal and domestic service were taking home three quarters of that standard.

These figures generally leave out of account the private sector which, particularly after the economic reform of the mid-1960s came to display a much greater range of inequality than did the social sector. Many elderly peasants in subsistence agriculture, for example, were receiving very low incomes indeed, whereas some private entrepreneurs (especially in sectors such as tourism) were found, by the mid-1980s, to be among the highest paid in the country with incomes well above those of the public sector. In a Serbian survey 45% of the private sector respondents described their incomes as "high" or "very high", and 64% of them accepted that this was "adequate" (as opposed to only 17% of manual workers) (Bogdanovic 1988:76-7).

If we take into account the significance of unemployment, the degree of real poverty in parts of Yugoslav society across the post-war period must emerge. Beginning with the economic reform, unemployment emerged as a persisting and significant differentiating factor in Yugoslav society. Those registered as seeking employment rose from fewer than 250,000 before 1966, and doubled over the next decade (Savezni Zavod za Statistiku 1989:70). In 1985, after Yugoslavia had experienced the effects of the second "oil shock", the figure passed one million. As Yugoslavia entered its last decade of economic crisis, unemployment became a serious social and economic issue, reaching 8.2% in 1991 even in prosperous Slovenia, and in Serbia in 1990, 16,4% (although in Kosovo 38.4%) (Dawisha and Parrott1997:150 and 208). Rates of unemployment support have been meagre, and during the late 1970s and 1980s were relatively unresponsive to the rapid deterioration of the value of money.[17]

Individuals' life-chances, and their social consciousness and identity, are shaped by more than their pay-packets. Of particular significance in Yugoslavia, because of the emphasis which has been placed there upon participation, is the distribution of *social power*. Here too it is possible to document growing differentials between strata. The problem was pointed out as long ago as 1973 by Vuskovic who showed that unskilled and semi-skilled workers were heavily *under*-represented in workers' councils, and that those with the highest professional qualifications were heavily *over*-represented

(Vuskovic 1976). With the exception of very highly-skilled manual workers the participation of skilled manual workers was also falling.

The same points were made by Neca Jovanov in his extensive investigation of the causes of strikes in Yugoslavia (Jovanov 1979:78-9). According to Jovanov's data, the manual worker was gradually being squeezed out of the formal mechanisms of the exercise of social power. As his study demonstrates, the strike became more and more accepted as the political weapon of the manual worker, taking their efforts out of the formal system of political participation.

Differences of social power were considered systematically by Popovic and his colleagues. They reported on the participation of members of their sample in the League of Communists, in self-managing bodies, and in other representative institutions such as local communities (*mjesna zajednica*) or chambers of commerce. Their results show very clear differences between occupational groups (Popovic ed. 1977:59-62). Participation is at token levels for peasants and the self-employed, and rises to very high rates among the "leadership group" (*rukovodioci*). Clear breaks are to be seen between skilled and unskilled manual workers, and between manual and most non-manual workers, and between these groups and the leadership stratum. Aggregating their data into a scale of social power, they found that 87-93% of peasants and the self-employed, peasant-workers and the unskilled (but not *skilled*) manual workers, were ranked as "low" in social power (Popovic ed. 1977:61). Subsequently, in a large number of studies, "Yugoslav sociologists unequivocally concluded that distribution of influence (power) in the Yugoslav 'self-managed' work organizations is oligarchical in character" (Sekelj 1993:40). These findings unsurprisingly correspond to widespread feelings of powerlessness and dissatisfaction (Sekelj 1993:41-51).

A useful illustration of the manner in which the distribution of social power relates to the distribution of other services, enhancing the life-chances of some groups, is revealed by differences in access to housing. Accommodation has always been chronically in short supply in urban localities, and a matter of persisting primary concern, although it has been the subject of little comment in the English language literature. Reporting a study completed in 1971, of two locations in Zagreb, Caldarovic notes the systematic differences to be observed between the housing of different strata in terms of the average surface area of the apartments, the average number of residents per flat, the average number of households per flat, the average number of persons per flat, the average number of persons per room, and the average surface area per resident (Caldarovic 1987:162).

A study by Sekulic in the late 1980s reported that more than 80% of those in leadership positions enjoyed the benefit of housing obtained through their occupational position, whereas only 20% of unskilled or semi-skilled, and 22% of skilled workers, were housed in this way.[18] The relatively clear spatial segregation of strata also reported by Caldarovic, differences in the quality of accommodation available, and its accessibility, are broadly characteristic of all areas of Yugoslavia, and have remained so after its disintegration.

These data point to an important general but rather understudied aspect of the structure of inequality in Yugoslavia, namely, the failure of the system to develop progressive redistributive mechanisms. This notion is commonplace in the discussion of inequality elsewhere; yet there has been little serious consideration of it in Yugoslavia. (See, however, Drulovic 1973:Chap.7.)

In general Yugoslavia has been slow to develop an awareness of the need to tackle questions of redistribution in dealing with internal inequalities. Although health care was free in socialist Yugoslavia, medicines were not. Although educational access was in principle open, there was nothing like the level of grant aid available in Britain. No adequate system of unemployment insurance was created. Vuskovic pointed out that the proportion of workers receiving financial assistance while unemployed actually fell between 1966 and 1971, from 12.7% of those registered as unemployed, to 3.4% (Vuskovic 1976:38). Although this proportion then rose steadily after 1974, by the late 1980s it still stood at less than a third of the total. What is possibly more remarkable is the fact that the proportion of those so assisted fell with the duration of their unemployment (Savezni Zavod za Statistiku 1985:140). The average value of assistance given in this manner in 1984 was only 28% of the average personal income for the federation as a whole.

For a long time the self-employed peasant was excluded from the social security network, unless linked to it through a co-operative agreement with some social sector enterprise. Otherwise it was necessary to make provision through private insurance for these needs. This situation was only changed on the eve of the fall of the "Second Yugoslavia".

Another aspect of this question which could be developed at length is the function of taxation in redistribution in Yugoslavia. Fiscal means played very little part in redistribution throughout the life of socialist Yugoslavia: indeed, they were largely regressive in character (Prout 1985). Unearned incomes were not taxed at all; and the arbitrary and erratic structure of the system provoked a great deal of controversy and dissatisfaction, especially in connection with the taxation of the self-employed. (Allcock 1992:407-12).

One important study casts light on these issues (Vukotic-Cotic 1991). Examining data for 1988, she shows that the effect of transfers on final income is quite uneven, varying not only between agricultural and non-agricultural households, but between the rich and poor. Agricultural households received 15.4% of their final revenue in transfers, 54.2% of which was received in kind. Non-agricultural households received 23.3% of their final revenue in transfers, only 5.4% of which was in kind (p.4). "Social transfers are oriented toward the urban population, and the more one moves from urban to rural areas the less important they become" (p.9).

Her data document the general point made above about the relative disadvantage of rural families, and demonstrate the unevenness of transfers between strata. The picture varies depending upon the type of benefit in question; but the general conclusion of her complex quantitative argument is that "the distribution of social transfers among social groups is more unequal than the distribution of original revenue" (p.7). In other words, such redistributive mechanisms as there were in Yugoslavia actually served to enhance rather than reduce social differences.

It is clear that economic differences, differences of social power, and differences in the distribution of a variety of goods and services affecting life-chances, have been a persisting feature of Yugoslav life. The experience of Communism has not reduced these appreciably, and the indications are that since the break-up of the federation if anything these discrepancies have been generally increasing.

iii) The shape of stratification in Yugoslavia

It is one thing to establish the existence of inequalities under Yugoslav socialism: but the question remains as to their sociological character. Although Yugoslav social scientists have tended to operate with two models of the stratification process, as I have indicated, neither of them can give an adequate account of these.

At the most general level, it is important to take into consideration the processes of *vertical segmentation* which have cut across this *horizontal layering*, with the effect that neither models of "classes" or of "strata" properly represent the pattern of differentiation which has emerged. One of the crucial areas of deficiency lies in the manner in which the rural-urban divide is handled, particularly with respect to the significance of "mixed" households. The second lies in the reluctance of Yugoslav sociology to confront fully and openly the question of ethnic stratification.

The phenomenon of "mixture" goes well beyond the problem of the "peasant worker", who has been of interest for a long time within Yugoslav sociology, identified often as a harbinger of the eventual incorporation of the peasantry into the working class (Kostic 1955). This group has also been of great interest to anthropologists with an interest in their role in cultural transmission, both as the potential bearers of modernity into the village, and as the agents of the "peasantisation of the towns"--the persistence of traditionalism within a supposedly modernising milieu (Halpern and Halpern 1972; Simic 1972). "Mixture" has also been discussed in

267

relation to stratification, and all sociological discussions of stratification in Yugoslavia assume that "mixture" is to be understood in terms of the "peasant-worker", who is to be located on a single vertical continuum, somewhere between the peasant and the industrial worker.

This is understandable, in view of the generally low status accorded to agriculture, but inadequate. A study by Danilo Mrksic shows that part-time involvement in agricultural production includes a very wide range of social groups, with a variety of different attachments to farming. This constituted the largest area of activity for all those who declared "additional activities", regardless of their occupational category (Mrksic 1995:75). This observation is noteworthy because it questions the assumption that it is possible to segregate the "private" from the "social" sector of the economy, and the "rural" from the "urban", in such a way as to yield distinct "strata". Cultivation of the land maps only incompletely onto social hierarchy, contributing to life-chances and economic security of families and individuals at all levels of society.

Extensive consideration has been given, especially around the period of the break-up of Yugoslavia, to the question of regional inequalities. The argument over the funding of regional under-development, however, has tended to ignore *its implications for stratification*. In 1947 Slovenes received about 175% of the federal average *per capita* income, whereas workers from Kosovo received about 53%. By 1978, however, this discrepancy had grown to about 195% of the national average for Slovenia and as little as 29% for Kosovo (Singleton and Carter 1982:221). My own calculations for more recent years suggest that on the whole the picture did not change. The rate of divergence might have slowed, and the specific regions varied a little in their relative disadvantage. If we look at the incomes of specific groups of workers within the republics and provinces, we find much greater discrepancies. The most highly remunerated group in Slovenia were receiving more than twice the average wage for the whole federation, whereas the most poorly paid group (actually in Macedonia, not Kosovo) were receiving less than half of the federal average (202% as opposed to 49%) (Savezni Zavod za Statistiku 1985:142-5 and 466-8).

The general differences in levels of economic development across Yugoslavia tended to endow groups with the same economic function with markedly different life-chances. Outwardly similar economic situation of groups could also conceal considerable differences in their real sociological character. Economic conditions affecting, say, the private sector are very different depending upon whether one is talking about the prosperous Adriatic tourist zone or a small inland market town. A market gardening area close to a big city does not offer the same conditions for the private agrarian producer as those experienced in a close to subsistence peasant farming region in the backwoods. Terms such as "artisan" and "peasant" should therefore be used by sociologists with some caution, and with imaginative construction of their regional and indeed their *local* content and significance.

Taken together with the presumed tendencies towards the regionalisation of the Yugoslav economy , these factors militated against the formation of any sense of common class identity across a wide range of the social strata identified in sociological studies.

My second point concerns ethnic stratification as we are more familiar with it. Work on this topic has been underdeveloped in Yugoslavia for reasons which are not hard to imagine. There has been discussion concerning the composition of elites, and in particular the alleged over-representation of Serbs and Montenegrins within federal structures, or in Croatia at the time of the "Croatian Spring" (Cohen:1989). There has been very little attention paid, however, to the *systematic* interaction of ethnicity and privilege or under-privilege.

All of the republics of Yugoslavia experienced processes by which membership of one ethnic group or another has either degraded individuals or consigned them to privilege, although this has been a largely unacknowledged part of the process of inequality. In part these patterns have been derived from historical ethnic antagonism, such as the extension of Albanian settlement into Macedonia. Often they have been linked to the extension of patterns of migrant labour into the more prosperous areas, for example the influx of Bosnian workers to Slovenia.

Studies done on "ethnic distance", although not relating *directly* to stratification, are relevant indirectly here.[19] Such studies indicate: (1) that ethnic distance has increased over time, from the low level reported by Fiamengo and Supek in the early 1960s to the study by Kuzmanovic three decades later; (2) that ethnic distance varies together with the ethnic diversity of the population—highest in Slovenia and lowest in Croatia; and (3) that acceptability varies with region, history and the nature of the relationship (it might be possible to accept Roma as neighbours or even friends, but not as superiors at work or as figures of political authority) (reported in Kuzmanovic, in Lazic ed. 1995). These claims are partially reinforced by information about patterns of intermarriage in Yugoslavia (Mrdjen 1996).

It is hard to infer actual behaviour from studies of ethnic distance. If there is a relationship, however, it is reasonable to hypothesise that ethnicity bestows proportionately greater advantage or disadvantage in ethnically more homogeneous areas than in mixed areas. If this is the case, we should expect to find that Serbs would have experienced little disadvantage in multi-ethnic Osijek, or Croats in Banja Luka, but that they would both be at a disadvantage in the relative homogeneity of Maribor. Ethnic distance, and consequently the privilege or disprivilege which attaches to ethnicity, should be lower in the relatively cosmopolitan cities, and greater in the countryside (lower in Zagreb than Varazdin, or in Belgrade than Vranje, or in Ljubljana than Celje).

The limitations of understanding inequality in terms of the two dominant models of stratification are not confined, however, to the issues raised by the overlaying of patterns of vertical segmentation (rural-urban differences, regional differences, and patterns of ethnicity) onto models of horizontal strata. The evidence also points to a succession of problems relating to the ways in which particular "classes" or "strata" are conceptualised. I consider three such areas here: the manner in which the private sector is handled; the problem of giving an adequate account of the *kontraklasa* or leadership stratum; and the contradictory evidence relating to the processes of class formation among manual workers and routine white-collar workers.

First of all, the *klasa/kontraklasa* model is wrong in banking on the steady absorption of the *privatnik* into the working class. Writing in the late 1960s perhaps Suvar could be forgiven for this assumption. Numbers employed by the private sector did indeed decline across the interval described by Suvar. There was a fall from 3.04%

of all employed persons in 1945 (3.58% of the economically active population), to 1.91% of employed persons (2.29% of those economically active) in 1975. Taking employers and their employees together, a similar picture is obtained. The numbers of proprietors and their employees fell from 2.9% of the economically active population in 1951 to 2.1% two decades later. Had Suvar examined more carefully trends in employment, however, he would have discovered that the lowest year for private sector employment was actually 1963, and that following the economic reforms the individual entrepreneur began a steady recovery.

Similarly, there was a decline in the percentage of total investment made by the private sector from about 19% in 1960 to around 16% by 1980, but rising in following years to more than 20%. My own work on the tourism sector illustrates the steady growth in the importance of the private sector both in providing employment and as a source of investment in the decades following the economic reform of the 1960s (Allcock 1992: esp. Table 13.2). Whatever the situation of the private entrepreneur, even before the collapse of Communism, there was little reason to believe that we were witnessing the declining remains of a stratum which was on the way to absorption into the working class.

Although it may have been true for some time that the overall economic significance of the private sector declined in agriculture, the individual entrepreneur remained massively important. Indeed as the Yugoslav economic crisis advanced during the 1980s (and above all after the collapse of socialist Yugoslavia) this trend towards decline was reversed decisively. Because of the action of factors which are not revealed directly in the statistics (the way in which private property configures with other sources of economic advantage) it is reasonable to assume that throughout the post-1945 period self-employment continued to contribute significantly to the real inequality between families.

Sociological studies which reflect upon the role of the private entrepreneur seem to miss the point, in two other respects. There has been a tendency to equate private property with traditionalism. This comes about in part because of an unacknowledged tendency to assume that self-employment = the peasantry. This is to overlook those other areas of the economy, such as construction, transport, tourism and a wide range of personal services, where the investment is often being made by the most outward looking and "modernising" sections of the population. In many cases the establishment of private sector businesses is premised upon capital, technical skill and social experience gained through migrant labour in western Europe or elsewhere. Furthermore, a good deal of what was in effect "private enterprise" within socialist Yugoslavia concealed the use (or abuse) of social property. Borrowing the firm's equipment for moonlighting jobs, especially in areas such as construction, transport and mechanical or electrical services, was (and probably still is) endemic.[20]

The view required by socialist ideology that the self-employed are a distinct stratum typically located at the bottom of the stratification ladder therefore bears scant relationship to reality. Ownership or non-ownership of private property must be seen as part of a rather wider picture. Taking into considerations patterns of family association, life-time economic trajectories of individuals, and the fluidity of the boundaries between different areas of the economy, any assumption that it is possible to identify clearly and stably differentiated, horizontally layered, social formations tends to fall apart.[21]

A further question of this kind is posed when we turn to discussion of the so-called "new class" or *kontraklasa*. The designation of the changes wrought in 1945 as "revolution" is more than mere socialist rhetoric. Nevertheless, it is important to recognise the difference between this revolution and that imagined in the Marxist classics (Lazic ed. 1995:8-9).

The collapse of the old order and the triumph of the new, between 1941 and 1945, in "decapitating" the former system, left a vacuum which was filled by an *ad hoc* congeries of individuals created by the experience of war rather than by any organic process of socio-economic differentiation. I have suggested that it is more appropriate to conceptualise the upper stratum of post-war Yugoslav society as an *elite* rather than a class ("new" or otherwise). The concept is useful for two reasons. It recognises that whatever it is that constituted the basis of their position and cohesion as the upper strata of Yugoslav society, it was not "property". The nature of "social property" has provided a barrier, rather than a window, to clear discussion, which on occasions has come close to seeming impenetrable (Horvat 1969: Chap. IV; Grbic 1984:13-69; Gams 1987).

The concept of "elite" is also perhaps more congruent with the approaches taken by non-Yugoslav sociologists considering the nature of inequality in "real socialist" states. Bauman, for example, prefers to identify the uppermost stratum in terms of "officialdom". (Bauman 1974; see also Lane 1971; Matejko 1974; Kende and Strmiska eds. 1987.) Here the root dimension of inequality has been identified not in terms of the expropriation of surplus value but in terms of inequalities of *power*, or as Bauman puts it, "the differentiation of opportunities of action". The League of Communists, it should not be forgotten, ruled as a *party* and not primarily as a *class*.

Giddens' notion of the centrality of the systems of "surveillance" provides a potentially useful approach here.

> "Surveillance" I take to mean two closely related phenomena. One is the collection and organisation of information that can be stored by agencies or collectivities and used to "monitor" the activities of the administered population. The second is the direct supervision or control of the activities of subordinates by superiors in a particular organization or range of social settings. (Giddens 1987:174)

Although Giddens notes with respect to "actually existing socialist societies" that as yet "surveillance .... has to be theorised", his conceptualisation of the primary dimension of inequality in these terms is suggestive (Giddens 1987:181-2).

A third alternative is provided by the work of Pierre Bourdieu, which draws our attention to the importance of control over "symbolic capital" and the means of "symbolic violence" (Bourdieu 1977:171-83; 1990: Chap. 7). The centrality of processes of ideological control in states such as Yugoslavia would appear to be amenable to analysis in these terms. It might be assumed that the principal resource at the disposal of the League of Communists was control of the terms of discourse over a wide range of aspects of life.

Perhaps the incomplete overlap between these ways of focussing the issues should be welcomed rather than regretted. It draws our attention to the possibility that, instead of trying to find a single structuring principle which will permit us to frame unambiguously processes of elite formation in Yugoslavia, we are confronting the results of a configuration of related but analytically and empirically separable developments, best described in the words of Peculjic as a "conglomerate of different privileged strata" (Peculjic 1979:155). This is not a "new class" which is in the process of formation. It is precisely the *fluidity* of the system, and the *incompleteness* of its formation, which is deserving of sociological comment. This is supported by the results of empirical studies , which have consistently revealed significant differences between components of the elite in terms of both life-chances and value-orientations. Commonly groups of "leaders" (*rukovodioci*) are to be distinguished from managers and professionals, or from a "humanistic" and a "technical" intelligentsia.

An additional factor which casts doubt upon the utility of conceptualising social differences in Yugoslavia in terms of class is the information available about social mobility. Class formation depends upon the ability of groups to pass on advantage to following generations. These more static depictions of inequality in Yugoslavia have been complemented by investigations of social mobility. (See, for example, Hammel 1969; Saksida, Caserman and Petrovic 1974; Denitch 1976; Bogdanovic 1988) These studies (especially those conducted in the earlier years of the development of the "Second Yugoslavia") tend to show quite high rates of mobility. This is understandable in view of the coincidence of processes of rapid urbanisation and industrialisation, together with the creation of a new socio-political system. Nevertheless, although there may have been a secular tendency to closure of the elite in later years, this does not seem to have advanced to the point at which one might speak with confidence about the formation of a *class*.

One of the few areas in which it might be appropriate to speak of class formation in Yugoslavia, however, is among the manual working class. The evidence suggests that ideological and attitudinal patterns here underwent a complex development. Particularly during the 1970s there were signs that Yugoslavia was coming to be increasingly radically divided at the level of political culture, and that the apparatus of self-management was falling more and more into the hands of groups which did not represent the ordinary worker.

Jovanov concluded his series of studies of strike action in Yugoslavia in the mid-1970s. His conclusions are interesting, in that they show that roughly 80% of strike action involved only workers engaged in direct production in manufacturing industry (with the greater part of the difference being made up by routine white collar or technician support staff) (Jovanov 1979:153). His own surveys show that the vast majority of strikes were directly about wages, or issues relating very closely to the determination of wage levels. The strike rate varied enormously from industry to industry. Those with the heaviest strike rates (especially textiles and woodworking) were those with the lowest wage levels, and also those with the most disadvantageous position in international markets. (Hence official explanations of strikes in terms of the local unwillingness of management to actually operate the mechanisms of self-management can at best be very partial.) An additional very significant factor emerging from these studies (under-rated by Jovanov himself, but clear from his data) is the importance of a tradition of industrial militancy dating back to the pre-war period. This helps to explain the relatively high strike rates in mining and engineering.

A distinct political culture can be seen to be emerging which was characteristic of manual workers in industry, who participated less and less in the formal mechanisms of self-management, experiencing steadily growing alienation from the system. This hypothesis of gradually crystallising class culture is consistent with Bogdanovic's observation that in more recent years the manual working class had the highest rates of self-reproduction of all strata, entering generally speaking only the lower-non-manual strata (Bogdanovic, in Popovic ed. 1988). Two factors must be considered, however, which strongly qualify this picture.

There have been recurring disagreements between Yugoslav sociologists about the interpretation of the relationship between manual workers and routine white-collar workers. The problem occurs not primarily at the level of the distribution of economic rewards, but at the levels of political attitudes and life-styles. The differing approaches Bogdanovic calls the "Belgrade variant" and the "Zagreb variant" (Bogdanovic, in Popovic ed. 1988: esp. 31-32). The first of these postulates a relatively clear division between white-collar and blue-collar workers, along lines familiar to sociology in western Europe and North America. The second tends to group the two categories together, emphasising the distance between both groups and the upper strata, thus approximating to the Suvar model. Whether the issue is to be resolved in terms of methodological differences between the studies in question, empirical differences in the character of the social structures of each region, or differences of theoretical orientation on the part of the researchers, evidently a degree of ambiguity remains about the relationship between these groups.

These issues are brought into focus when we look at the overall *direction of change* which might be presumed to have characterised stratification in Yugoslavia after 1945. In his contribution to Popovic 1977, Dragomir Pantic looks at the values and ideological orientations of their sample. At the end of a complex factor analysis he produces the graphical representation of his findings reproduced in Figure 6.

[Figure 6 about here.]

Two independent dimensions are identified which he labels "liberalism/etatism" and "traditionalism/self-management". There is a clear hiatus between the values of the two self-employed groups in his sample, and the various strata engaged in the socialist sector of the economy, which appear to be ranged in an even continuum, differentiated relatively little with respect to their liberalism. The leadership stratum, who might be expected to express ideologically idealised responses in this direction, stand out as separated by a long gap from the other groups with respect to their values on the other dimension. Although Pantic emphasises the continuous nature of this series by connecting the groups with a line which projects a "direction of social and ideological transformation" (there is a commitment, in other words, to a notion of a developmental sequence) his data might equally be read as confirming the ideological diversity of incipient classes.

Siber's ("Zagreb") study, on the other hand, concludes that there is great diversity in the distribution of social attitudes (Siber 1974). He identifies three attitudinal dimensions by means of factor analysis, which he labels "pro-system/anti-system", "egalitarianism" and "centralism/decentralism". The first two of these yield interesting contrasts between strata in their political outlook. The first dimension differentiates higher functionaries as (unsurprisingly) strongly "pro-system", and the private sector proprietors as equally clearly "anti-system". Other groups occupy a rather undifferentiated middle ground. On the second dimension it is the intelligentsia which tends to be most inegalitarian, the functionaries who occupy the middle ground, and manual workers and peasant cultivators find themselves sharing the egalitarian position. In short, in contrast to the Belgrade study, here there is no clear and uniform tendency towards a crystallisation of attitudes on a class basis, as similarity and difference vary depending upon which dimension which one selects.

Taking all of these considerations together, it is hard to see a clear and unambiguous process of the structuration of inequality emerging from the conditions of massification which characterised Yugoslav society between 1945 and 1990. There is rather the *potential* for development in several contrasting directions. Whatever might be the future for society in the region which was Yugoslavia, however, these processes were probably interrupted and diverted decisively by the disintegration of the Yugoslav state after 1991.

Inequalities as a factor in the break-up of Yugoslavia

Although only a short historical period has elapsed since the collapse of Yugoslavia, it is possible to suggest several ways in which patterns of inequality were relevant to that event. Sharon Zukin has identified the problems arising from the attempt to balance "equity" and "efficency" as the major problem which faced socialist Yugoslavia (Zukin:1980). This assessment appears to be supported, although approached in rather different terms, by Josip Zupanov. His principal contention is that the Yugoslav crisis (which subsequently came to wreck the country) sprang from the tension between "that which ought to be" and "that which is"--between the normative prescriptions about institutional order on the one hand, and the way things actually worked (Zupanov 1983). This gap encompasses Zukin's problem as one part of a wider problem. Zupanov identifies four "dimensions to the crisis".

> At the normative level: (1) the concept of associated labour within the framework of social ownership of the means of production; (2) the co-ordination of decisions within the economic system on the basis of self-managing agreement, to which also is subordinated commercial co-ordination from one political centre; (3) the absence of vertical social differentiation, and in that regard not only classes but also functional elites and social strata ....; (4) class-based solidarity of the various nationalities and national groups, by means of which national exclusiveness and antagonism are completely overcome.
>
> (Zupanov 1983:34-5)

In contrast to these normative ideals, however, the *actuality* of Yugoslav society consisted of:

(1) ....actual behaviour in the economy is conducted according to an entrepreneurial conception, and the logic of means, profit and hierarchy. .... (2) .... in actuality co-ordination is either neglected, or by means of the division of the market, or on the basis of state intervention. Both the market and state intervention signify definite natural social processes which automatically reproduce themselves once they are planted in the system. (3) Society is evidently stratified: and even if perhaps it is not possible to speak of the existence of classes in the marxian sense, there exist other forms of stratification .... by which functional elites have some class characteristics. (4) .... national exclusivism and antagonism almost wrecked the ship in the sixties and early seventies. .... in more or less concealed forms they continue today, drawing their strength from the unconscious and irrational layers of conduct. (Zupanov 1983:35-6)

The existence of these contradictions between the normative and the actual, according to Zupanov, resulted in a crisis of both legitimacy and continuity for Yugoslav society. Social change takes place without reference to normative ideals, and society is reduced to the status of a series of temporary social arrangements which at any moment may be called into question. Certainly his generalised description of the problem bears a very close fit with the results of Magid's study, conducted at about the same time, in which he contrasts the widespread acceptance of the legitimacy of the *system* with growing scepticism about the probity of those who occupied positions within it (Magid 1991).

Although Zupanov's analysis is not confined to processes relating to inequality, the significance which he attributes to "functional elites" and their failure does focus attention on the centrality of such processes to the Yugoslav crisis. The extensive discussion which has raged about the causes of the downfall of Yugoslavia has focussed repeatedly upon the failure of the elite (see esp. Cohen 1989; Sekelj 1993). There were two broad areas in which it can be said that the old elite failed of legitimacy. The first is implied by Zukin's remark, above. The sudden failure of the economy challenged the expectations about equity which were built into the system. The proposed Markovic plan, and the broad movement towards private enterprise and the open market, deeply threatened the economic security of most Yugoslavs. From being one of the most secure countries in Eastern Europe Yugoslavia suddenly became very insecure indeed. The images of unjustified inter-republican differentials resulting from the supposed inequities of "Belgrade" may not always stand up to analysis, but they were important as expressions of the growing belief that the expectations of ordinary Yugoslavs were failing to be matched by experience.

The second area of elite failure is found in the region of ethnicity, and is most clearly underlined by the deteriorating situation in Kosovo. Kosovo symbolises as does nothing else the failure of the Yugoslav state to embody its own normative ideals. In part these were perhaps unrealisable in view of the contradictory nature of the distinction between "nations" and "nationalities", and the inevitability of conflict over the anomaly of a situation in which the Albanians were a local majority, but had no recognised "home" within the system. The federation found itself forced to uphold the demands of Serb populists in order to defend the autonomy of other republican elites within their own bailiwicks. The state became identified with blatant repression, and the prisoner of one of the most anti-modern segments of Yugoslav society--Kosovo Serbs.[22]

Could the country have been saved by a "circulation of elites" in a more orderly fashion? The suggestion of Vesna Pusic is interesting here, that an alternative business elite was waiting in the wings (Pusic 1992). I doubt it, as even if she is correct in her belief that a technically able elite stood in waiting, they could only have come to power through mechanisms provided for within the system the legitimacy of which was already in question. Furthermore, a business elite could only have secured its position (presumably through the ballot box) on the basis of appeals to the analysis of Yugoslavia's problems which was already proving so unpalatable under Markovic.

The evidence of post-disintegration Yugoslavia suggests that, in spite of her suggestion, business managers were in any case insufficiently differentiated from the old political elite to strike out on an independent line either of ideology or action. Post-disintegration experience tends to indicate, on the contrary, a moving-together of the political and economic leadership groups rather than their disaggregation. In fact, freed from the constraints of socialist ideology, it is perhaps only now that the "new class" is coming to be just that.

The brief experience of "post-communism" suggests that at least in some areas the former officials may have been in a position to benefit disproportionately from the redefinition of property relations. The popularity of the "management buyout" as a route to privatisation has resulted in the confirmation of privilege and unequal rewards, so that former "red executives" now find themselves sharing a social space together with the rapidly emerging group of private entrepreneurs. Under these circumstances perhaps quite novel changes have been set in motion. Nevertheless, with respect to the experience of socialist Yugoslavia there are clear reasons why one might also be reluctant to speak of the formation of *the* elite.

In the editorial introduction to the volume of essays on *Yugoslavia in Transition*, my colleagues and I committed ourselves to the view that:

> The "collapse" of Yugoslavia is heralded in several places. .... the complete collapse of a social system is a relatively rare phenomenon, and one for which there are well-documented historical preconditions. Such a catastrophe requires either or both the active hostility of at least one very powerful external enemy, and the complete loss of resolution and cohesion on the part of its ruling stratum. (Allcock, Horton and Milivojevic 1992:3)

Writing in the spring of 1990, the fall of the Berlin Wall suggested that the first of these preconditions was lacking. Plainly we overestimated at that time the extent to which the Yugoslav elite did possess adequate resources of "resolution and cohesion". Our error on that occasion might be taken as powerful evidence for the fragmentation of the Yugoslav elite, and certainly of the fact that it had failed to develop anything like a coherent class consciousness. An important effect of growing regionalism was to create a pattern of vertical segmentation which cut across strata, inhibiting solidarity and the co-ordination of action. The "Second Yugoslavia" was torn apart not by the welling-up of supposed antagonisms from below, which its leaders were unable to contain, but in large measure by the rivalries which split into irreconcilable factions its ruling stratum.

Notes

1. There has been considerable debate among historians and sociologists about the legitimate extension of the term "feudalism". It is inappropriate to engage with this discussion here, but note the contrast between the approach in terms of ties of political dependence emphasised in the seminal work of Bloch (1962), and the analysis of a "feudal mode of production" in the Marxist tradition, exemplified by Hindess and Hirst (1975).

2 See three widely-used Yugoslav textbooks: Fiamengo 1971; Goricar 1970; Lukic 1970.

3. The shape of social stratification was dictated in large measure by the pattern of land-holding, upon which I have commented already in Chapter 4.

4. Kostic warns us that it is difficult to be confident about the occupational position of people in this period, because they would quote different descriptions of themselves for different purposes, and many of those with urban occupations would also own land.

5. Such as those described by Rebecca West following her visits to the Stari Trg mine—part of the Trepca complex (West 1967 [1942]: Vol. II, 312-24).

6. *AVNOJ* had a deliberately "national front" character which gave it a composition untypical of the Communist Party leadership itself. More systematic consideration of these issues is given in Cohen 1989: Chap. 2, and esp. 116-25. Cohen notes (Table 2.7) that whereas 61.1 % of participants in the *partizan* movement were from peasant backgrounds, their representation on the Central Committee of the KPJ varied between 2.6% in Oct. 1940 and 4.8% in 1948.

7. On the concept of "massification", see Kornhauser 1954; Giner 1976.

8. The term has not been popular among Yugoslav social analysts, possibly because of its association with anti-Marxist thinkers. Cohen has effectively defended the continuing utility of this concept for the analysis of post-war Yugoslav stratification, and analysed the way in which the structures which that term describes were laid down during the war (Cohen 1989). See also Barton, Denitch and Kadushin 1973, Denitch 1976; Magid 1991.

9. Reference is often made to the "partizan myth". It is important to note the difference between Mosca's concept of a political formula and that of "myth" (Mosca 1939). "Myth" in this political context is too close to Sorel, for whom myths were "not descriptions of things but expressions of the will". "When we act, it is because we have created an entirely artificial world, in advance of the present, consisting of movements which depend on us." (Sorel 1908, cited in Stanley 1976:204 and 205.) Whereas Mosca's "formula" is retrospective, and grounded in history, Sorel's "myth" reaches into the future, and requires that we live out in the present that which exists only in the projection of our imagination. What we have in the ideological utilisation of the *partizan* experience in Yugoslavia is the former.

10. It is worth singling out for reference as particularly useful, however, Parkin 1971; Benson, 1972; Cohen 1989.

11. Probably the most characteristic study of this period is Ilic 1963. Examples of treatment of the issues in this period see the widely used textbooks of Fiamengo (1971:245-60 and 381-88); Goricar (1970:341-88); and Lukic (1970:413-20).

12. See the series of publications which appeared under the general title *Covjek i sistem*, which devoted a substantial amount of space to these issues (Supek and Pusic (eds.) 1975-77). See the thematic issue of *Sociologija*, XXIV(2-3), 1982; also the useful review of the literature in this field

provided by Sekulic 1983, by Popovic ed. 1988, and by Lazic 1995. A prestigious, politically-sponsored conference on the issue was also held in 1984, which resulted in a substantial collection of essays: Pojatina ed. 1986

13. The distinction can be traced in its essentials to Saint Simon. Is the *kontraklasa* a class (one which is *opposed to* the working class) or is it *a non-class*--like the logician's "p" and "not-p"? This is left fundamentally ambiguous. While serving as a professional sociologist at the University of Zagreb, the author remained a loyal and active member of the League of Communists and rose to occupy several of its highest posts. His sociology faced both ways!

14. See, for example, Lane 1971; Bauman 1974. Branko Horvat dismisses the distinction between productive and non-productive labour as having "no theoretical meaning or justification whatsoever" (Horvat 1969:123). He bases his own analysis upon the position of "the bureaucracy", the power of which rests in part upon its character as a "closed corporation" (Horvat 1969:19-21).

15. At one point they describe the routine officials as part of a "socialist middle class", along with other white-collar workers. In this way they are separated from the "direct producers" who "in greatest measure possess the characteristics of a class" (Popovic ed. 1977:40-1). Also on this occasion they group the peasant-workers along with other *privatnici*. These groupings are not uniformly consistent with their subsequent empirical analysis. See below pp. 000-000 for further discussion.

16. Based upon income statistics published in the *Statisticki Godisnjak SFRJ*, 1985. I am aware of the methodological limitations of sociological research based upon such material.

17. Lydall points out that Yugoslav workers had to be unemployed for a year before receiving benefit (Lydall 1989:44).

18. There are interesting differences, however, in that only 38% of those in positions of *economic* leadership enjoyed this kind of benefit (as opposed to *political* functionaries) whereas 45% of highly-skilled manual workers in industry were housed in this way (Bogdanovic, in Popovic ed. 1988:52).

19. "Ethnic distance" is a modification of the broader concept of "social distance", developed by Bogardus, which addresses the question of the mutual acceptability of groups. It is measured by constructing a scale from responses to questions about the degree to which members of one group might be acceptable to members of another, ranging from permitting them to enter the country to close kinship.

20. The problem is mentioned by Vuskovic (1976) although I know of no reliable, systematic data, and there probably can be none.

21. There is a vital need in assessing both the extent and mechanisms of inequality to consider family processes. As I have already noted in relation to Caldarovic's work on housing, a very high proportion of accommodation units in Yugoslavia contained more than one household, although these are typically kin-related. What is more, for all strata of society economic activity rates for women have been relatively high, and indeed tend to rise with social status. It would have been good to be able to comment more fully upon the significance of family processes. Unfortunately Yugoslav studies typically sample on the assumption that the "head of the household" is a male, and questions about the *household* economy are not regularly and systematically analysed. See for some incidental comment, however: Zukin 1975:36-45 and Appendix.

22. The role of Kosovo in the break-up of Yugoslavia is argued most fully and adequately in Magas 1993. I think that she overstates the importance of this factor, although it has undeniably been on central relevance. These issues are discussed more fully in Chapter 10.

7

STATE FORMATION AND THE INTERNATIONAL ORDER

States and the system of states

"*Jugoslavija je okruzena brigama*"--Yugoslavia is surrounded by woes. With this pun Yugoslav diplomats once delighted to introduce audiences to the basic facts of life about their country and its position in the system of states. The pun lay in the fact that the Serbo-Croat word for "by woes" (*brigama*) is an anagram of the initial letters of the country's seven bordering states. The idea is more than a humorous conceit, as it contains in germinal form a fundamental truth about the development of the system of states in the Balkan region. On the one hand, the South Slav peoples have been surrounded by others who have seen themselves as having an interest in the area, and consequently the right to intervene in the shaping of its political progress. On the other hand, the interests of the South Slavs themselves could only be realised in relation to spaces and peoples surrounding them.

One of the ironies of modernity is embodied in this *aperçu*. The modernising process is constituted in part by the formation of states; but the interests which find expression within any one state can only be realised within a wider process of the constituting of other states. States do not emerge in isolation, but intrinsically and necessarily as components of a *system* of states.

The view of state-formation which has come to predominate in the past has tended to portray states as embodying the political will, or sense of identity, of peoples. For this reason, in the modern world, we often speak of the "nation-state". This basically romantic notion is founded upon the idea that states emerge as if in accordance with some kind of historical inner necessity. In this approach, state-formation is at least in part a teleological process which finds its motivating purpose in national identities.[1] This continues to be a problem, although to a lesser extent, even in more recent "constructivist" approaches to state and nation.[2]

The romantic view of a teleological link between nation and state does not lie well with the understanding of state formation as it is theorised within the sociology of modernity. Charles Tilly insists that: "since states always grow out of competition for control of territory and population, they invariably appear in clusters, and usually form systems" (Tilly 1990:4). Much the same point is made, although approached from a different angle, by Anthony Giddens.

> The sovereign power of modern states was not formed prior to their involvement
> in the nation-state system, even in the European state system, but developed in
> conjunction with it. Indeed, the sovereignty of the modern state was from the
> first dependent upon the relations between states, in terms of which each state
> .... recognised the autonomy of others within their own borders.
> (Giddens1990:67)

Within this latter approach, states are seen as no more than nodes within a global process: they are invariably parts of *a system of states* which (at least potentially and in principle) is global in its extent. Paradoxically, the particularisms which we normally think of as characteristic of states depend upon a process of globalisation.

States do not emerge simply because there are nations which, like the boll weevil, are "lookin' for a home". Nations acquire their national consciousness at least in part because human communities find themselves caught up in the crystallisation of states and the relationships between them. The relationship between state-formation and nation-building is thus a dialectical one. I will have a great deal more to say in Chapter 10 about the development of the diverse forms of national consciousness in the Balkans. In this and the next two chapters, however, I concentrate upon the state, and begin by considering the globalising characteristics of state-construction.

In considering the process of state formation in the Balkans I exclude from discussion the mediaeval period. The modern nations of the region are in the habit of founding their pedigrees upon primordialist arguments, tracing the historical association between peoples and territories to states which flourished before the division of the region between the two great empires.[3] Nevertheless, feudal states of this type were of a very different character from the modern state, and from a sociological point of view bear little resemblance to states as we know them.[4] Any continuity with the process of state-formation in the modern era was definitively broken by the incorporation of the entire region into the two multi-ethnic "world-empires" which dominated the region until 1918.

The attention given to these mediaeval polities by nationalistic historiography typically blinds us to their generally ephemeral character. The average longevity of the dozen Balkan dynasties of the mediaeval period for which details are listed by Fine, was in the region of 126 years. Five lasted for less than a century; and the overall picture is skewed by the exceptional durability of the Serbian Nemanjas, who ruled for nearly three centuries (Fine 1983 and 1987: Appendices).[5] In several cases these formations feature later in my account as providing resources for the symbolic construction of the nation in the nineteenth and twentieth centuries. They have no place within the discussion of my present problem.

"Imperial borderlands" and the "Eastern Question"

I have already made reference to the utility of John Lampe's description of south-eastern Europe in terms of "imperial borderlands", describing a key characteristic of their development during the hey-day of the two great empires (Lampe and Jackson 1982: esp. 278-322). These empires can be considered to some extent to have acted as retarding factors on state-formation throughout their territories, and not only along their mutual borders. Their interest on this occasion, however, lies more in the fact that the configuration of imperial confrontation itself provided the essential features of the context within which a system of states developed in the region.

During the eighteenth century the character of these "borderlands" altered fundamentally as a result of the aggressive expansion of Russia into Central Asia. Following a succession of wars between the Ottomans and Austria, the border between these two Empires became more or less stabilised on the Danube-Sava by the Treaty of Belgrade (1739). Although Vienna continued to cherish ambitions for further expansion into the Balkans, these were expected to be as much at the expense of Venice as Istanbul. After periods of war, lasting from 1768-74 and from 1787-92, however, the Russian Empire advanced its borders against the Porte as far as the Danube delta.

> The Treaty of Jassy (1792) is a turning point in Near Eastern history. It marks the advent of Russia as a great Near Eastern power. When Catherine the Great came to the throne the Black Sea was a Turkish lake. Before she died it had become a Russian-dominated lake. (Stavrianos 1958:197)

Russia was then in a position as never before to influence developments in the Balkans (Jelavich 1991).

The "Eastern Question", which occupied the minds of European foreign offices so obsessively during the nineteenth century, is often represented as reflecting the internal decline of the Ottoman state, to which the formation of new nation-states within the Balkan region was a response. The conditions under which new states could come into being were determined fundamentally, however, by the competition between the major European powers, including Russia, for control over territory and trade. It is possible to point briefly to the diversity of ways in which these contextual factors can be found at the root of this process, for all of the Balkan states which achieved independence before the Congress of Berlin.

Serbia was the first Balkan country to embark on the process of state-formation. I have suggested in a previous chapter that during the late eighteenth century the trade of the northern part of the Ottoman state underwent a substantial northward reorientation. Particularly in response to the Napoleonic period in western Europe, this trade in goods was expanded to encompass the "trade" in ideas. The construction of a new state became possible, however, not because somehow a more advanced stage of development of national consciousness had been achieved in this region, but precisely because ideas about national identity took root at the conjunction of expanding economic opportunities, and at a location where the three spheres of imperial influence (the Russian, Austro-Hungarian and Ottoman) met in conflict. The Serbian uprisings of 1804-1813 and 1815-1817 took place against the background of the Napoleonic convulsion of Europe, and in the open expectation that it would be possible to take advantage of Austrian and Russian ambitions to expand their own influence at the expense of the Porte.

The shape and timing of Romanian independence owed a good deal to its location as an "imperial borderland" between Russia and Turkey. The Crimean War (1853-56) can be understood as continuing Russian expansionist ambitions towards the Straits, and western European attempts to contain these.

> Ostensibly the Crimean War was fought to maintain the integrity and independence of the Ottoman Empire. Yet the immediate effect of the war was the unification of the Moldavian and Wallachian Principalities into the autonomous kingdom of Rumania. (Stavrianos 1958:339):

Curiously Romanian independence was favoured both by Russia and a variety of western European interests. The Tsar sought to secure recognition from the Porte of his right to style himself the defender of the Orthodox throughout the Ottoman

Empire, and defender of the Holy Places in Jerusalem. His sponsorship of an independent, Orthodox, Romania can be seen as the outworking of that ambition. On the other hand, an autonomous Romania held out the expectation of an independent buffer state between Russia and the Balkans. Romania dates its emergence as an independent state from the election of Alexander Cuza as head of both the principalities of Moldavia and Wallachia in 1859, thus bringing about their *de facto* unification. The groundwork for this event had been laid already, however, by the compromise with which the conflict of the great powers had already been resolved.

The advance of Greek nationalism illustrates yet another aspect of this wider process. The motor of the development of Greek national consciousness was the large Greek-speaking mercantile diaspora, spread throughout Asia Minor, the Black Sea ports and well into Central Europe. This social base has sometimes been interpreted as giving to Greeks a cosmopolitanism which made them particularly effective as a conduit for the transfer into the Balkans of currents of western European political thought. There is a sense, however, in which the peculiar ambitions of the Greek national movement placed it out of line with the general movement of European nationalisms. Frequently the fact has been overlooked that the *"Megali Idea"* which emerged within this cultural milieu can not be reduced to a conventional demand for the creation of a national homeland in the Balkans for Greeks. It aspired rather to the recreation of the Byzantine Empire. In this can be seen mirrored not only Greek geographical dispersion but also the ambivalence of their position, between the narrower nationalisms of other Balkan communities and a wider vision of political possibilities derived from their awareness of the need for structural reform within the Ottoman

Empire. The Greece which was recognised as a monarchic state by the London Protocol of Feb 1830 fell far short of these larger ambitions. The birth of the Greek state, therefore, can not be regarded solely as the flowering of some national ideal, but as its failure within the context of the emerging system of states in the contested Balkan space.

The Porte itself was not indifferent to such wider currents of change in Europe. The *Tanzimat* (reform) process which was begun in 1839 under Sultan Abdul Mejid, and directed by his Vizier (from 1845) Rejid Mustafa Pasha, was in large measure precipitated by a growing realisation of the relative advancement of the western European powers at the levels of economic development, political organisation, and military technology. The *Hatti-Sharif* of Gulhane, promulgated in 1839, set out to address the administrative backwardness of the Empire. Its significance lay, however, in the extent to which it raised expectations of change among the subject peoples rather than in the changes which it actually wrought.

The state-formation process in Bulgaria is to be understood in part in relation to this context. Russian ambitions for expansion were expressed in a succession of attempts to make territorial gains in Central Asia and the Black Sea region. In the Balkans, however, exploitation of the tensions between the religious communities provided the principal point of leverage. The *Hatti-Humayun* of February 1856 extended religious toleration in the Ottoman lands, very much in response to Russian pressure. In significant measure, therefore, the crystallisation of Bulgarian national consciousness took place under Russian sponsorship, initially through the pursuit of ecclesiastical autonomy. This bore fruit in the declaration in 1870 of an independent Bulgarian

Exarchate, which laid the foundations for the subsequent consolidation of a Bulgarian national state during the 1880s.

By the time of the Bosnian-Hercegovinian uprising in 1874, the failure of the internal Ottoman reform process was evident, and the expansion of the ambitions of the Balkan national states was under way. The conditions under which these infant states had come into being, however, were set very much by the balance between the conflicting economic and territorial ambitions of the Great Powers. Similarly, the speed and direction of the dismantling of the territory of the Ottoman Empire, now seen as definitively in decline, were also regulated as much by factors external to the region as by the strength and scope of the drive of Balkan peoples themselves towards national self-determination.

Left to themselves, even so, the internal processes of state-formation in the Balkans may well have reached their natural resolution more quickly.[6] The Treaty of San Stefano of 1878, concluding the war which resulted from the Bosnian uprising, anticipated the exclusion of Turkey from the Balkans. Fearful of the creation of a large Bulgaria, which was perceived as a Russian client state, the intervention of the western Powers secured at the Congress of Berlin of the same year the restoration of *de jure* Ottoman authority, as a means of containing Russian influence in the region. This deferred the final delineation of the system of states in the Balkans until the end of the Balkan Wars in 1913 (or even the post-war settlement after 1918). What the Congress of Berlin actually achieved was little more than the protracted misery of the populations of Macedonia and Thrace, exposing them over a period of thirty five years to the terroristic competition between neighbouring indigenous states without the effective presence of Ottoman power to enforce order.

The Great War and the formation of a unified South Slav state

It is frequently said that the historian is better able to understand the developments of the past because of the advantageous optics afforded by the passage of time. Hindsight is always 20/20 vision. Yet this retrospective view distorts rather than extends and deepens our view of the past. We are readily tricked into thinking of historical events as if they were the results of historical necessity. We have become used to thinking that the demise of the Austro-Hungarian Empire was inevitable, and that the emergence of independent states in southern and eastern Europe was somehow the result of a natural process. Looking at the Habsburg Empire from the standpoint of 1914 rather than that of 1919, however, we have no reason to believe that this was so. Neither are we able to assume that when its dismemberment was agreed upon by the Great Powers, a unified South Slav state would necessarily be among its successors. The creation of the "Kingdom of Serbs, Croats and Slovenes" in 1918 can be seen as the outcome of a complex interaction between the global context of the First World War, and a process of negotiation between the several local elites, seeking to optimise their own positions within the space framed by these general developments.

In the pre-war period it seemed that the Austro-Hungarian Empire was still quite vigorously expansionist. Who, observing the annexation of Bosnia-Hercegovina in 1908, would have suspected political decrepitude?[7] The annexation could be seen as a part of a policy practised consistently and energetically over a period preceding the Great War by which Vienna sought to head off, limit and even reverse the expansion of a strong, independent South Slav state in the Balkans. The government of the Dual Monarchy shared with other European powers the aim of limiting Russian access to and influence in the Mediterranean through potential client states such as Bulgaria and Serbia. The annexation of 1908 can be seen as the practical outworking of this policy.[8] Its culmination was the Austrian ultimatum to Serbia following the assassination of the Archduke Ferdinand in Sarajevo in 1914, which was so readily seized upon as a *casus belli*. There is little doubt that the Dual Monarchy hoped to secure the ruin of Serbia as a leading force in the Balkans, and the establishment there of its own hegemony.

The pattern of rivalries between the European powers underwent a complex development in the years before 1914. By August 1914, however, a configuration of two competing alliances was in place: the "Entente" (France, Britain and Russia) against the "Central Powers" (Germany and Austria-Hungary).[9] The declaration of war by Austria on Serbia triggered a series of declarations and counter-declarations, in which the reasons for engagement were progressively distant from Sarajevo, and spread like ripples on the surface of a pond across the whole of Europe and beyond.

i) Serbia at the outbreak of war

Serbia was the only part of the South Slav lands, with the exception of the tiny Montengrin kingdom, to enter the 1914-18 war as an independent state. This fact was of crucial significance in shaping both the creation of the state and the course of the inter-war political struggles in Yugoslavia. Successive expansions had taken the form of the incorporation of new peoples and territory into a Serb state, little concession having been made to non-Serb elements who had found themselves included in its compass. Indeed, each territorial enlargement was accompanied by the more or less forcible ejection of alien (primarily Muslim) elements. Expansion in 1913 brought into the state significant Muslim groups in the Sandzak of Novi Pazar, "Old Serbia" and Macedonia (although the majority of the population of the region was of the Orthodox faith).[10] Under the brief period of Serb rule after 1913, whatever they may have thought of the matter themselves, the population of these regions were to become Serbs. "Macedonia" did not exist, except as a vague geographical concept; and the area incorporated after the Balkan Wars was designated simply as "South Serbia".

An important point to note is that this process of expansion still left a very substantial proportion of the Serb diaspora outside of the borders of the state. In Bosnia-Hercegovina the Orthodox "who are unanimous in calling themselves Serbs" made up 43% of the population in 1893 (Olivier 1911: Chap. V esp. 103). While falling short of an absolute majority of the population (35% of which were Muslims and 21% Catholics) the Orthodox were the largest confessional group in the provinces. Serbs were also settled in large numbers in the Austro-Hungarian lands--in Dalmatia, the Vojvodina and the former Military Frontier regions. The census of 1910 recorded more than a million of them: 462,516 in Croatia-Slavonia and 644,955 in Hungary itself (Seton-Watson 1962:417).[11] As Serbia had a population estimated at around four and a half million in 1913, roughly a third of all Serbs were located outside the 1913 borders of the country (Petrovitch 1915:17).

The royal assassinations in Sarajevo on 28 June 1914 were committed by a group of juvenile extremists in pursuit of the unification of Bosnia with Serbia. They had been armed and incited by a faction within the Serb military who were discontented with the conduct of Serb policy in "South Serbia", and intent upon using the occasion to embarrass their own government (Seton-Watson 1926; Dedijer 1967). The event thus dramatised the importance of this dispersion of Serb settlement, and brought together in its precipitation of a general European conflagration the interpenetration of the local and global dimensions of state-formation.

The Austrian armies invaded Serbia on 13 August, but were defeated at the Cer Mountain, permitting the Serbs themselves to cross the Drina into eastern Bosnia. An Austrian counter-offensive in September drove them back to the point at which Belgrade was taken briefly in December. This victory was short-lived, however, and by the end of the year the invaders had once more been cleared from Serbian territory.

Faced with a third assault by the Central Powers now including Bulgaria, and weakened by the effects of an epidemic of typhus, in October 1915, Serb resistance collapsed. The Serbs were compelled to retreat through Albania; and after a hideous experience crossing the mountains in the depths of winter the remnants of the army were evacuated to Corfu. There can be little doubt that when the government of Serbia was forced into exile in 1915, they took with them the hope that the eventual outcome of war would be the restoration of the Serbian kingdom, if possible with borders expanded to incorporate more of the large Serb diaspora. In these circumstances it is understandable that Serbian politicians should have seen the creation of a new state in 1918 largely in terms of the unification of a dispersed population of Serbs into a common state, and as the culmination of a century-long project initiated by Karadjordje. In his "Nis Declaration" of September 1914, Prime Minister Pasic clearly acknowledged the aim to "create out of Serbia a powerful southwestern Slavic state" (Banac 1984:116). In doing so he recapitulated the long-standing Obrenovic vision of Serbia as a "Balkan Piedmont" *vis-a-vis* the Habsburg South Slavs, assisting in their liberation and incorporation into an enlarged Serb state (Pavlowitch 1971:42).

ii) South Slavs in the Dual Monarchy at the outbreak of War

For Croats, Slovenes and Bosnians the problem which framed their view of the future was the position of the South Slavs within the Austro-Hungarian state. Slovene experience was quite unlike that of the Serbs. They had no great mediaeval state to which they could look as a precursor of coming independence. Slovene aspirations with respect to the political future of the Austro-Hungarian Monarchy were by no means uniform, but on the whole they looked for the defence of Slovene cultural autonomy within the Empire (Rogel 1977).

The idea that the various South Slav peoples shared a common cultural heritage is a very old one which is certainly traceable to the end of the eighteenth century.[12] Its development during the nineteenth century, particularly in the wake of Napoleon's "Illyrian Provinces" took place principally at the hands of literary figures, especially those such as Jernej Kopitar and Ljudevit Gaj, who were preoccupied with the systematisation of the various South Slav languages.[13] It was not until much later that South Slav unity began to take on a practical political form. In 1904 a number of Croat deputies led by Ante Trumbic and Franjo Supilo decided to ally themselves with Hungary against Austria in return for specific political concessions, particularly the incorporation of Dalmatia into Croatia. A resolution to this effect was adopted at a conference in Fiume (Rijeka) in October 1905; and subsequently a number of Serb deputies were persuaded to support this move, thus bringing about the first effective Serbo-Croat alliance. Although the idealism expressed in this event descended in part from the earlier "Illyrian" idea, the deputies who joined on that occasion were more interested on the whole in hard-headed political horse-trading. It reflected an effective political compromise, and was, of course, confined to the Austro-Hungarian regions.

The profile of Croat politics was changed radically by the founding in 1904 of the Croatian People's Peasant Party (*Hrvatska pucka seljacka stranka--HPSS*) led by the brothers Ante and Stjepan Radic (educated men but from a peasant family) (Gazi 1962-3:Livingstone 1959). In addition to proposing in its platform a wide-ranging series of social and economic reforms aimed at improving the lot of the peasantry, the *HPSS* introduced into Croatian politics a new concept of "the nation", and a new type of politics. The Radic brothers (particularly Ante) were largely responsible for this reorientation with their importation of Russian populist concepts, identifying the nation with the peasant and seeing in the peasant the repository of moral virtues which had been eroded by urban and western ways. The first success of the new party was felt in the 1908 elections.

The Magyar-Croat compact broke down after two years, but the Serbo-Croat alliance stayed intact through the elections of 1908, effectively undermining the earlier Magyar policy of playing off Serb against Croat. In the election the alliance took 57 seats, the conservative "State's Rights" party of Frank took 24, and the fledgling *HPSS*

7. Unable to obtain an electoral majority the Hungarians obtained the dissolution of the *Sabor*, and Croatia was ruled by decree, the constitution being suspended in 1912. This result encapsulated the pattern of Croatian politics in the few years remaining before the outbreak of war. The opposition were still divided between those who were inclined to accept co-operation with Hungary in return for concessions to Croat independence, and those who believed that the lesser danger lay in closer relations with Austria--the Frankists and the *HPSS*.

These latter groups were in turn radically divided in their concept of the nation. The Frankist view was in one sense not "nationalist" at all, since the focus of their political creed was the defence of certain constitutional traditions. This stood clearly apart from the mystical populist concept of a free nation of peasants advanced by the Radic brothers, which lacked specific constitutional reference beyond a diffuse republicanism. In its emphasis on social and economic reform and the importance of the peasantry determining their own affairs clearly the party operated on a different plane from the rest of Croatian politics in this period. The diversity of Croatian politics was therefore shaped much more by differences of attitude towards Austria and Hungary than by concerns about the relationship between Croats and other South Slav peoples. These differences were clearly indicated by party reactions to the war. While the Serbo-Croat alliance was reduced to embarrassed silence, both the Frankists and the *HPSS*, although for quite different reasons, supported the war.

The course of Austrian occupation had left the population of Bosnia-Hercegovina increasingly divided on ethno-religious lines, so that no clear voice could be heard pleading the cause of the provinces in relation to war and its possible outcome.

Bearing in mind the diversity of objectives and views of an ideal future state which characterised different sections of the political class in the South Slav lands at the outbreak of war in 1914, their union in 1918 might seem rather like a wedding in which the groom ends up married to one of the bridesmaids instead of to the bride. The precise circumstances in which unity came about, therefore, require some comment.

iii) Unification as a response to the course of the War

At the outbreak of war a number of politically active people fled from the Habsburg areas, principally to Italy. In Rome they were organised, together with several expatriates and foreign well-wishers, into a "Yugoslav Committee", chiefly as a result of the enthusiasm of Dr. Ante Trumbic, a former Mayor of Split and a member of the Dalmatian Diet and the *Reichsrat* in Vienna.[14] They set out on a programme of education in the capitals of Europe, hoping to persuade statesmen to take into account the aspirations of the subject nationalities of the Habsburg Empire when it came to a peace settlement. Frano Supilo was particularly energetic, and it was through his efforts that in London the scholar Robert Seton-Watson, and the political editor of *The Times*, Henry Wickham Steed, were recruited to the cause.

The war did not begin well for the South Slavs. The rapid reaching of a stalemate in France, and the evaporation of hopes for a speedy end to the war, impressed both sides with the need to widen the conflict. Italy was persuaded, with the promise of large territorial gains in the eastern Adriatic, to join the Allied cause by the secret Treaty of London, in 1915.[15] (Earlier attempts to secure Bulgarian support were headed off by the Central Powers, with whom Bulgaria threw in her lot in 1915, encouraged by the possibility of territorial gains in Macedonia.) During a visit to St. Petersburg, Supilo stumbled across news of the secret negotiations which were to lead to the Treaty of London. The year 1915 therefore saw a picture of deepening gloom developing for the South Slavs.

The German breakthrough at Gorlice (and the consequent Russian withdrawal from Poland) and the disaster at Gallipoli, both boded ill for the Balkans. In the autumn of 1915 von Mackensen was able to launch his successful attack on Serbia, in concert with the Bulgarians. The failure of the Russian offensive of June 1915 had already depressed Serb confidence. The final blow was delivered in the spring of 1917 by the overthrow of the Russian imperial regime. Russia had hitherto been the principal champion of Serbia among the Great Powers, and without the support of St. Petersburg the Serbs were in urgent need of friends.

Although military developments held, on the whole, no better news for the Yugoslav Committee than for the Serbs, the entry into the war of the Americans in April 1917 was taken as a favourable omen by those working for a settlement based upon self-determination for the subject peoples of the Habsburg Empire. America had been a signatory neither to the Treaty of London, nor that of Bucharest. The US government therefore did not regard itself as committed in the negotiations for peace to the honouring of either agreement.

It was from this position of extreme weakness that the Serbian Prime Minister Pasic and the Radical Cabinet invited the Yugoslav Committee to Corfu, seeking for a common programme, and on 20 July 1917 the "Corfu Declaration" was issued, calling for the union of all South Slavs in a common democratic state. This was to be a constitutional monarchy under the Karadjordjevic dynasty, including in its constitution guarantees of the cultural autonomy of the various peoples. Such was the gap which at this stage separated the two sides that the declaration remained at the level of a very general statement of intent (Laffan 1918:266-7).

Momentum towards the disaggregation of the Dual Monarchy began to accelerate in April 1918, when a "Congress of Oppressed Nationalities" was organised in Rome, in which the Yugoslavs were actively represented. The rights of subject peoples to self-determination were affirmed in its concluding pact; and aspirations for the creation of a Yugoslav state were given subsequent public support by the Italian government, which hoped to weaken the resolve of Croatian regiments still fighting on behalf of the Habsburgs (Stavrianos 1958: 575). In May the South Slav members of the Vienna *Reichsrat* constituted themselves as a "Yugoslav Club", and issued a dramatic manifesto calling for the unification of all Serbs, Croats and Slovenes living within the Monarchy into a single state. Although they did not openly challenge the legitimacy of the crown, in the circumstances of war this can be considered an act of some courage.

The war in the Balkans underwent a major change in September 1918, with the opening of a new offensive on the Salonika front. After a fierce struggle, Bulgaria surrendered on 30 September. Although Austria held out doggedly against the Italians until French reinforcements turned the tide in November, the Dual Monarchy had already begun to collapse (an event as momentous as that of the fall of the Berlin Wall seventy years later).[16]

The political elite groups representing South Slav interests declared themselves to be free and independent. The Slovene *Narodni svet* (National Council) met in Ljubljana in August. Under the leadership of the Yugoslav Club in the *Reichsrat* a provisional government was established in Zagreb, known as the *Narodno Vijece* (National Council) in October. In October too the *Sabor* acted to stop rioting by declaring an independent union of the Croat lands (Banac 1984:128).

The situation in Croatia and Bosnia-Hercegovina rapidly disintegrated into disorder, with bands of armed deserters disturbing the countryside more in the manner of bandits than freedom fighters. The *Vijece* had few resources at its disposal to restore order, and what was more disturbing was the fact that the advancing Italian forces began to occupy areas even in excess of the expectations of the Treaty of London. Under these circumstances the support of the Serbian army held a definite attraction, although the prospect of the presence of Serbian troops was not universally welcomed.

A Great National Assembly in Cetinje on 26 November declared the deposition of King Nikola and unification of Montenegro with Serbia under the Karadjordjevic dynasty (Banac 1984:285).

When in the winter of 1918 the leadership of the *Vijece* approached the Serbian government, in accordance with the principles of the Corfu Declaration, offering the establishment of a joint state, the Pasic cabinet vigorously rejected any suggestion that the word "Yugoslav" should be used in its title. They were on no account willing to submerge their identity as Serbs in the new order. The title adopted by the new state, for this reason, was the cumbersome "Kingdom of Serbs, Croats and Slovenes". Having surmounted this hurdle, there were still enormous difficulties in finding agreement about the basis of the new state. Consequently, the loyal address read to Aleksandar on 1 December 1918 was limited to the broadest of generalities, with all the detail to be resolved by decision of a Constituent Assembly (Banac 1984:138).

It is worth commenting further on the problems of Croatian representation. The *Sabor*, an institution which was inextricably identified with the constitutional order of the defunct Dual Monarchy, was marginalised in the early stages of developments by the Yugoslav Committee, which had assiduously and effectively cultivated its contacts with the Foreign Offices of the Entente powers. The Committee was not a formally constituted and accountable body but an impromptu collection of individuals brought together by shared common concern. They were emphatically not a government in exile. What is more, they were a highly skewed selection of Croatian political opinion with, for example, a heavy over-representation of Dalmatians.[17] The figures who remained within the country (members of the *Sabor* such as Svetozar Pribicevic, but above all Radic) had perhaps a rather better appreciation of popular feeling, but were relatively marginal to the process, and often opposed it.

When Allied victory was finally secured in 1918 it seemed certain that Serbia would gain in population and territory at the expense of the defeated Habsburgs. The Serbs had a recognised government in exile, and had won a respected place among the victors, not only through their heroic early resistance to Austro-Hungarian attack, but more particularly through their participation on the Salonika front. A large portion of the South Slav lands, however, were still considered part of the Dual Monarchy, and South Slav regiments had fought (not always unwillingly) on the side of the Central Powers. Croats and Slovenes could therefore, in the eyes of the powers at the Paris peace conference, be considered as "the enemy", and their lands as "enemy territory".

Understanding of the situation of the South Slavs within the former Habsburg

territories was diminished by the plurality of voices (the *Narodni svet*, the *Narodno*

vijece and the Yugoslav committee), and their unclear constitutional legitimacy.

iv) *The South Slavs and the Peace negotiations*

President Wilson's ideas about the self-determination of peoples have often been

construed as setting the tone for the peace conferences. His famous "fourteen points",

however, left unstated the identity of the units which had the right to self-

determination. In spite of the fact that the vocabulary of diplomacy at the time was

that of nation-building, what actually emerged was a compromise with pragmatic

interests of the Powers, which tended to consider the implications of the existence of

states rather than *nations*.

Whereas victory in 1918 assured the position of the Serbs, Britain and France still

remained committed to the Treaties of London and Bucharest, and did not approach

negotiation in the spirit of President Wilson's principles of self-determination. As a

result of their lightning defeat by the Central Powers between September and

December 1916, the Romanians were hardly in a position to argue for the full

implementation of Bucharest. It was a matter of considerable importance to the

Italians, however, to press for the enforcement of the terms of the Treaty of London,

which would have guaranteed naval control over the entire Adriatic. Trieste and

Fiume would have secured control over a considerable portion of the trade of central

and eastern Europe.[18] Preventing the emergence of a strong and unified South Slav state, which could have challenged both of these objectives, therefore became the primary objective of Italian foreign policy.

The birth of a unified South Slav state may be conveniently dated from the address of the *Narodno Vijece* of Zagreb to the Regent, Prince Aleksandar, in 1 December 1918. Yet in January of the following year the Allied invitation to send delegates to the Paris conference was addressed to "the kingdom of Serbia". Recognition of the new state was only secured with difficulty. Not only were the Great Powers reluctant to prejudge the decisions of the conference, but they also placed very high value upon allied solidarity. Hence Italian obduracy in refusing to recognise the new state was effectively used to prevent general recognition for a long period (Baerlein 1922; Lederer 1963).

The Italo-Yugoslav aspects of the post-war settlement were indeed the most protracted and difficult of all the negotiations. The basic framework of the agreement with Italy was laid down in the Treaty of Rapallo, which was only signed in December 1920. D'Annunzio's occupation of Fiume (which blocked one of the kingdom's primary export outlets) was not finally conceded until January 1924. Several factors stimulated the final resolution of the Italo-Yugoslav border, including the establishment of the Hungarian Soviet in May 1919, and the progressive diversion of President Wilson's interests to other ends. The electoral defeat of Wilson in November 1920 contributed in no small way to the collapse of Yugoslav resistance. For both Italian and Yugoslav governments, however, the growing pressure of domestic events compelled them to reduce the amount of attention paid to diplomatic problems.

Although Italian opposition constituted the most serious of the obstacles to the shaping of the new South Slav state, there were issues of varying degrees of difficulty to be overcome with respect to most of its borders. The contentious issue of the Klagenfurt basin, and the future of its Slovene-speaking population, was only determined by plebiscite in October 1920. Peace with Romania was concluded relatively unproblematically in Paris in June 1919; but the settlement with Hungary regulated by the Treaty of Trianon of June 1920, whilst it provided for large concessions of population and territory by the Hungarians, fell well short of Serb claims. The Treaty of Neuilly (November 1919) which concluded hostilities with Bulgaria resulted in substantial revision of the 1913 borders of the two states. The Albanian border was the most contentious of all: and a minor war continued in effect in northern Albania until Yugoslav troops were compelled to withdraw in July 1926. The definition of the space to be occupied by the future Yugoslavia, therefore, can be seen to have been the resultant of a complex of territorial problems involving the interests of all of its neighbours as well as those of the major powers.[19]

I have given a good deal of space to the events of the war, and its impact upon the unification process, for three reasons. In the first place, we are not dealing here with the results of some spontaneous upsurge of national feeling. Union was negotiated by elite groups with little if any democratic reference to a popular base. (Only the Serbian government was a formally constituted government with any kind of electoral mandate.) The new creation was the result of pragmatic negotiation between cliques. Consequently the relationship between state and nation remained problematic throughout the entire inter-war period. The state's mandate was in the first instance

313

legalistic rather than popular. The main actors were recruited from quite different state systems, however, each with different legal traditions respecting the nature of the state.

Secondly, when union did come about, it was realised at the hands of groups which came from established political traditions in which the nature of politics was defined essentially in terms of the nation. The problem was, however, that each represented very different concepts of what it meant to be a nation.

Thirdly, these developments underline clearly the manner in which Yugoslav politics can not be separated from the context of European politics. The notion that a unified state was simply imposed upon unwilling people by the Paris conference is a fantasy on the part of extreme nationalists. Unification is unintelligible without its context, however, and took place as a result of a complex interaction between "internal" and "external" political processes, so that the creation of the new kingdom might best be described as a local adaptation to the exigencies of a wider European settlement. In that respect, the formation of Yugoslavia bears comparison with the delineation of all of the other states in the region.

The "First Yugoslavia" in the Balkan political space

i) Redefining the Balkan space

In examining the position of the "First Yugoslavia" in the Balkan political space after 1918 two general patterns become clear. The process of constructing a system of states in south-eastern Europe is defined by three primary new features: the redefinition of the political space vacated by the Habsburg state; compensation for the virtual elimination of Turkey as a significant player within that space; and a fundamental realignment of forces occasioned by the consequences of the Russian revolution.[20]

Following upon the disintegration of the Habsburg Empire, it was necessary to bridge the difficult gap between the aspirations of the wide range of nationalist movements which had figured in the pre-1914 political configuration of the Dual Monarchy, and the actual delineation of new states.[21] Germany emerged in the period, however, as a new continental power, moving into this vacated space. The demise of the Ottoman state as a major Balkan player encouraged Italy to move into the vacuum in North Africa, in the Middle East, and in the Balkans. Post-revolutionary Russia was not in a position to resume the contest for territory which characterised the Tsarist period, having been forced to accept relatively disadvantageous terms in the peace settlements. The new Communist Russia pursued its ambitions by other means, however, and through the *Comintern* conducted an ideological offensive which sought to exploit class divisions across the entire continent.

The reasons for the failure of the "First Yugoslavia" are frequently ascribed to *internal* factors, and in particular to the inter-ethnic struggle, and the incompatibility between the different concepts of the state which were brought into it. It is important not to divorce the internal political processes which characterised the region from *external* developments, however, and to treat the latter as mere "context". Whereas there is some substance in this view, it is vital that we grasp two other points.

Firstly, the fragility of democracy was a *general* feature of European politics at this time. This condition was to some extent made worse by the preoccupation of the major democracies with their own internal or imperial problems, leaving them relatively indifferent to the interests of the Balkan states. Richard Crampton has made the general point that: "War, when it came, was not caused by east European instability; as in 1914 it was caused by great powers taking advantage of east European political fragility for their own purposes" (Crampton 1994:32).

Secondly, we tend to look at democracy in our own age through the rather dogmatic prism of Fukuyama's "end of history", however much we may challenge that notion at a theoretical level. Between 1918 and 1938 there seemed to be nothing inevitable about the advance of democracy. Indeed, in part democracy lived under the shadow of the Great War. The post-war settlement, widely experienced as unjust in those states which had suffered the loss of territory, population and prestige, tended to blame their condition on the action of the democratic powers.

The elements of *ressentiment* fused with the sense of anxiety resulting from the general instability of the system of states in southern and eastern Europe to give rise to authoritarian nationalist movements across the continent.[22] In this light the failure of the "First Yugoslavia" can not be reduced to the effects of Serb "hegemonism", which was as much a symptom as a cause of the problem. The focal issue of domestic politics in Yugoslavia was not one of democracy *versus* authoritarianism, but a clash of rival styles of authoritarian populism, all of which to some extent found their roots and models elsewhere.

ii) Yugoslavia and its neighbours

The provision of several international treaties notwithstanding, there was no firm conviction among their neighbours in the immediate post-war period that Austria and Hungary really had relinquished hope of Habsburg restoration: indeed, the Emperor Charles made and attempt to regain the throne in 1921. This, together with the continuing awareness of Hungarian irredentism, motivated the formation of the "little Entente" between Czechoslovakia, Romania and the South Slav kingdom between August 1920 and June 1921. These concerns were further activated by Italian sponsorship of a scheme for the reunion of Austria and Hungary, briefly floated in 1933-34, until the subsequent rise of fascism saw these fears eclipsed by others.

Even Austria and Hungary themselves had to struggle to reach a new self-definition, and an accommodation within the new order. For both of them this was immensely difficult. By the Treaty of Trianon Hungary was striped of 75% of its territory and 60% of its population (although the greater part of these were not ethnic Magyars).[23] There was incessant agitation for revision of the treaty. Hungarian domestic politics fluctuated between the extremes of the Communist-led republic of Bela Kun (March-August 1919) and a succession of militaristic, authoritarian governments beginning with the Horthy "Regency" and ending with the fascism of Donány (1936-38). The Austrian republic also rapidly collapsed into fascism, partly facilitated by the close links between the Dolfüss government and Mussolini.

The constant involvement of Italy in Albanian affairs, and Italian occupation of the Dodecanese, contributed to the sense of instability in the Balkans, and the Pact of understanding signed by Greece, Romania, Turkey and Yugoslavia in February 1934 was a reflection of a shared sense of threat from that quarter.

In good measure the reasons for insecurity can be found not only in the attitudes of states outside the region towards the Balkan countries, but equally in the problematic status of their own borders. The new Kingdom of Serbs, Croats and Slovenes was by no means the only state for which the apparent rationality of its borders was in doubt, and the compatibility of its diverse populations was in question. I many respects the problems experienced by the South Slavs only encapsulated perhaps in a more intense form those of the region as a whole.[24]

The consequences of the Balkan Wars had not had the time to register internationally before 1914. The Macedonian situation, however, remained unacceptable to the Bulgarians throughout the inter-war years (the new borders were if anything generous to the Greeks from an ethnographic point of view). *VMRO* remained an active agent in Bulgarian politics, creating a virtual state-within-a state in the Pirin region, from which armed incursions were regularly mounted into Yugoslavia and Greece. The organisation created a major preoccupation for Belgrade, reflected in the high level of militarisation of Macedonia, and even destabilised the Bulgarian state itself. The struggle for Macedonia created a chronic state of insecurity and mutual suspicion.

> The Balkan entente of 1934 could never become effective as an international
> instrument because Bulgaria, its eyes still set on Macedonia and the Dobrudja,
> would not recognise existing frontiers as permanent whilst other states would
> not accept Bulgaria into the pact until it did. (Crampton 1994:37)

It is a measure of the extremity of the situation that, following the formation of the Rome-Berlin Axis in October 1936, the quest for security among the Balkan states led to the Yugoslav-Bulgarian treaty of friendship of January 1937. Instability in relation to Macedonia was not solely attributable to the Bulgarian position: it was also partly fuelled by the barely concealed aspiration of Serbia for an outlet to the sea at Salonika, which the Axis powers exploited in 1940-41 as a lever to persuade the Yugoslavs to join the Pact.

Even though a pattern of independent states had to some extent been created in the Balkan region before 1914, the configuration of circumstances which prevailed after 1918 made for a largely new and unstable situation. Attempts to create regional alliances foundered on the juncture of conflicts of interest of different external states and the irreconcilability of different local goals. The upshot of this is that the inter-war period affirms the existence of a number of states in the Balkans, but without permitting the crystallisation of a *system* of states.

iii) The wider picture

When the final disintegration of the Austro-Hungarian and Ottoman states exposed the Balkan region to a new fluidity in the pattern of state-construction and inter-state relations, the position of the major powers also emerged as an important factor which impinged upon this process.

The problems posed by the need to create a new and stable system of inter-state relations in the Balkans was exacerbated by the situation of Germany after 1918. The defeat of Imperial Germany was followed by a punitive peace, which rested upon the assumption of German guilt for the war. Consequently huge reparations were imposed upon the country, and it was deprived not only of its imperial possessions in Africa, but also suffered territorial losses in Europe. It proved to be impossible to enforce the payment of reparations, in spite of the French occupation of the Ruhr in 1923, and their rescheduling under the Dawes Plan of 1924. Although they were abandoned in 1929 under the impact of world economic depression, these humiliations had already taken effect, watering the seeds of Nazism.

From 1934, under Nazi leadership, Germany found a range of opportunities to extend its diplomatic and economic influence in the Balkan region, taking advantage of the indeterminacy of the situation there, and the unwillingness or inability of the other major European states to counter that influence. After the trade agreements of 1933 and 1934, therefore, Yugoslavia found itself in a position of growing embarrassment, with a widening discrepancy between its pattern of trade and investment, which tied it ever more closely to the Axis powers, and its foreign policy commitments to the other Balkan states.[25] The real possibilities of sustaining effective independence from the Rome-Berlin Axis faded rapidly when the *Anschluss* of Austria in March 1938 gave Yugoslavia a common border with the Third Reich. As the Italian invasion of Greece in October 1940 collapsed ignominiously, pressure on the Yugoslavs to ally themselves with the Axis mounted. One by one all of the country's neighbours were pressed into the alliance, until in March 1941 the Yugoslav government finally acceded, precipitating the *coup d'état* of 27 March, which pulled the country into war.

In a different way the role played by Russia in the new European order was almost as disturbing. The Romanov policy of territorial expansion was replaced by one of evangelical Communism. Under the conditions of political disorder in the wake of war, the possibility of Communist revolution spreading beyond Russia itself seemed very real. There were brief left-wing uprisings not only in Hungary, but also in Berlin and the "People's Republic of Bavaria" in 1919. A wave of strikes swept Europe between 1919 and 1923. Although the real prospects for the export of revolution were, in retrospect, far more limited, the foundation of the *Comintern* (The Third International) in 1919, and in 1923 a Soviet-led Peasant International (the *Krestintern*), were seen as harbingers of an extending Communist influence (Mitrany 1961). Within Yugoslavia the Communist Party secured 58 seats in the Constituent Assembly of 1921 (the third largest representation), before it was banned. The visit of Stjepan Radic to Moscow, where he established links with the *Krestintern* in June 1924, continued to fuel the fires of anxiety about Communist subversion.

More disturbing than the perceived threat of internal destabilisation by the Communists, however, was the behaviour of the Soviet Union on the international scene, in what was seen as its extreme unpredictability. Running counter to the pre-1914 pattern of alliances, the German-Soviet friendship pact of April 1926 startled Europe. Fears of Bolshevik indifference to international order in Europe were confirmed by Soviet co-operation in the division of Poland in September 1939, following the further non-aggression pact with the Reich in August. The days of Russian sponsorship of Serb autonomy were over, and no support could be expected from that quarter for Balkan stabilisation.

The relevance of the USA to the situation is of a rather different order. American intervention had been a determining factor in the outcome of the First World War. The economic ruin of the European states as a result of that war left the USA in a new position, as the leading capitalist state in the world, notwithstanding the low levels of US investment/credit in the Balkan countries. The general tone of American politics was one of introversion, however, which perhaps is not unnatural in view of the fact that the USA itself was racked by economic crisis throughout much of the inter-war period. For this reason it is too early at this stage to speak of "superpower" status. In spite of its potential for influence America was relatively indifferent to the region; and no effort was made to influence Balkan developments.

British and French attention was concentrated on the oil resources of the Middle East, as well as on their own internal political problems, such as the British preoccupation with Ireland. After their involvement in the occupation of the Ruhr, French thinking on defence matters fell into the "Maginot mentality". The Balkans were left to stew in their own juices, too internally divided and too economically weak to create their own momentum of economic development, and exposed to German intervention. There is some evidence of British activity behind the 27 March coup in Yugoslavia, but its ineptness and lack of real insight into Balkan realities is indicated that its success immediately had an effect opposite to that which was intended.

The collapse of the "First Yugoslavia" is often seen as a foregone conclusion in view of the severity of its internal problems, and in particular the Serb-Croat conflict. There is considerable room for doubt as to whether the Cvetkovic-Macek agreement, and the Serbo-Croat compromise, could have heralded the achievement of an acceptable constitutional balance. It is relevant to point out, however, the "First Yugoslavia" was ended by external invasion and not by its own divisions. It is only under these conditions that internal fascism was able to become a significant force within Yugoslavia, with all the consequences which followed from that for the subsequent internal development of the country.

The rise of Socialist Yugoslavia and the Cold War

The historiography of post-1945 Yugoslavia has been periodically wracked by debate about the course of the war and its outcome. For most of the time there has been a kind of orthodoxy which explains the recreation of the Yugoslav state in 1945 in terms of two primary factors: the superiority of *partizan* forces in the "National Liberation Struggle", and the determining role of Allied (mainly British) intervention in their support. The two strands are brought together in the celebrated anecdote from Fitzroy McLean, in which he relates a conversation Winston Churchill:

> "Do you intend," he asked, "to make Jugoslavia your home after the war?"
>
> "No, Sir," I replied.
>
> "Neither do I," he said, "and that being so, the less you and I worry about the form of government they set up the better. That is for them to decide. What interests us is, which of them is doing most harm to the Germans." (Maclean 1949:202-3)

Debate has centred upon the soundness of Churchill's judgement, and the possibility that this was influenced by politically interested distortion of the military picture, the extent to which *partizan* forces did offer an effective challenge to German occupation, the role of the Red Army in supporting Communist victory in Yugoslavia, and the justice of the outcome, based upon a succession of allegations that one party or another was involved in collaboration with the occupier. There remain large significant *lacunae* in historical writing about this period, especially in the lack of any objective and systematic study of either the *NDH* or the Nedic regime in Serbia. [26] In spite of these difficulties I believe that the main outlines of the orthodox account remain unchallenged.

Regardless of the means by which this was achieved (and their "fairness" is irrelevant to historical explanation) Tito's Communist forces did ultimately demonstrate their military superiority. That they did so was in significant measure due to the external backing which they received, although from a military point of view the tide may be considered to have turned in their favour with the capitulation of Italy in 1943. Both of these factors ultimately acquire the weight of their significance from the broadest contours of the war in Europe rather than the local balance of forces. The entry of the Soviet Union into the war on the Allied side after the collapse of the Hitler-Stalin Pact in 1941 brought into play an army of some 360 divisions--the full military might of the Red Army.[27] Entry of the USA into the war after Pearl Harbour ensured that the course of the war was determined by a truly global balance of forces. The decisions of the leaders of the Allied powers on the conduct of the war were made within a global context, in which Yugoslavia featured as a very marginal element. The famous back-of-the-envelope agreement between Churchill and Stalin, to the effect that Yugoslavia fell "50/50" across their respective spheres of influence, is a vivid illustration of this. Once the decision to open a second European front against Germany had been made, which committed the main Allied offensive to Normandy (and not, in Churchill's phrase, the "soft underbelly of Europe") then Yugoslavia was assured its place as a diversionary irritant rather than as a primary determining arena of action. There is no comparison between the significance of events in the Balkans after the opening of the Salonika Front in 1917, which was a truly decisive event, and the impact of *partizan* warfare between 1941 and 1945.

Internal factors were not totally irrelevant to the course of developments. It is evident that the Royal government in exile was both divided and inept: and if the Communists were adopted as preferential partners by Churchill it must be acknowledged that this was in part because of the political failure of the former, as well as the military inferiority of Mihailovic (Jukic 1974).[28] As in the period after the First World War, Croatia (in the form of the *NDH* regime) found itself defined among the ranks of "the enemy", and denied any independent voice in negotiations. The fact that other parts of Yugoslavia had been (at least nominally) under other occupying powers (Bulgaria, Germany, Italy and Hungary) resulted in their having no formally constituted voice either. At both the *de jure* and *de facto* levels, therefore, the Tito-Subasic coalition represented the only practicable way in which voices other than those of the victorious *partizani* could be engaged in the negotiation of the future shape of the state.

Although there were matters to be sorted out in the peace negotiations, these were of marginal relevance in a process which had been shaped principally by the overall course of a global war. The words of Draza Mihailovic in his final statement to the court in July 1946 have often been quoted. "Destiny was merciless towards me when it threw me into the most difficult whirlwinds. I wanted much, I began much, but the whirlwind, the world whirlwind, carried me and my work away." (Cited in Tomasevich 1975:471) Mihailovic is far from being the only Yugoslav to whom these words might be said to apply. The "whirlwind", it is important to note, was not his adversary Tito, but the "world whirlwind" of global war.

In spite of the "50/50" agreement there is little indication of Allied influence on the course of Yugoslav affairs in the immediate post-war years. Yugoslav abandonment of Trieste was enforced. Nevertheless, the fact that Tito was in unquestioned control within Yugoslavia meant that the transition from nominal coalition to a socialist state was effectively unopposed. There appears to have been no appreciable international impact on the Yugoslav dispute with Albania, and Yugoslav forces shot down US aircraft with impunity. These untoward events certainly did nothing to impede the massive transfer of aid to Yugoslavia through UNRRA.

The strength of the Communist position is revealed in the brushing-aside of the formal trappings of royal participation in government, following the hollow formality of the elections of 11 November 1945, in which voters were presented with a single government list. A republic was proclaimed on 29 November, and the constitution of the "Federative Peoples' Republic of Yugoslavia" on 31 January 1946.

The break with Stalin is interesting, and not only because it reveals the relatively strong position of Tito in comparison with the other Socialist states.[29] The episode has most typically been commented on from the point of view of its marking the emergence of Tito as the "Balkan strongman". It also reveals, however, Yugoslavia's marginality in the newly established continental balance of power, each side of the

"Iron Curtain". Yugoslavia was indeed able to survive economic and political exclusion from the Socialist bloc, and sustain its independence--but at the cost of the collapse of its main foreign policy planks--support for the Greek civil war, and the project of Balkan federation. Both of these were hastily abandoned. After a period of insecurity and uncertainty featuring the short-lived Balkan Pact with Greece and Turkey in 1954, the Yugoslavs "discovered" non-alignment in 1955.

In the inevitable period of re-evaluation following Tito's death there has been a tendency to dismiss the NAM as a quirky individual obsession of the Marshall, and as no more than evidence of his concern for self-aggrandisement. This is to a large extent misplaced as a judgement on Yugoslavia's relationship to the NAM, and its significance for domestic politics.

The Communist Party of Yugoslavia had been compelled to come to terms with the delicacy of the problems posed by the ethnic diversity of the region early in the war. It moved rapidly from the mainstream CP line of denigrating nationality as a bourgeois distraction from the essential unity of the working class, and particularly under the influence of the Slovene ideologist Edvard Kardelj, came to build recognition of national diversity, and the legitimacy of national identity, into the main frame of the ideological and political structure of the country. As early as the first meeting of the Anti-Fascist Council for the Liberation of Yugoslavia (*AVNOJ*), in November 1942, the need for a federal solution to the problems of political order in any post-war settlement was accepted. Indeed, the Yugoslav state came to be defined as an association of nations in which the Communist predeliction for collectivist concepts was extended rather than challenged. The putative unity of the "working people of

Yugoslavia" was legitimately qualified by their division into *nations*, without being undermined by any recognition of their diversity as individual *citizens*.

This capacity to incorporate recognition of the central importance of nationality into the ideological orthodoxy of Yugoslav Communism thus simultaneously added to the effectiveness of its legitimacy while sowing the seeds of future national conflicts. It is to the first of these consequences that membership of the NAM centrally relates. The policy of using a world platform to insist upon the right of self-determination of peoples, and the significance of the anti-colonial struggle, not only underlined publicly the determination of the Yugoslav Party to maintain its independence from Moscow; it also entrenched at the domestic level the primary political importance of the nation. Non-Alignment provided an ideological parable on the international plane of the correctness of the regime's stance with respect to national identity within Yugoslavia.

These developments illustrate vividly the need to consider the evolution of Yugoslav politics in relation to its global context. There is a constant dialectical movement between internal events and their international environment. Important features of the domestic political course of the country (the adoption of federation and the nationalities policy, the collectivisation of agriculture and its abandonment, and the introduction of self-management) along with the creation of the Non-Aligned Movement, all stem in part from Yugoslavia's position within the newly emerging system of states under super-power domination. Federation, self-management and non-alignment in particular come to be bound together into a coherent ideological formula which (as "Titoism") legitimated the rule of the LCY both domestically and internationally.

It seems undeniable that an important component of the impetus towards the creation of self-management was the fact that domestic political legitimation (particularly within the Party) interpenetrated the need for wider legitimation within the international Communist movement. Given the need to turn towards the West for support, self-management offered the possibility for a totally ambiguous presentation, depending upon the audience. Within Marxist discourse it could be advanced in terms of the greater approximation of Yugoslavia to the Marxist utopian aspiration of the "withering away of the state". To Western audiences, however, it could be delineated in terms of participatory democracy which broke significantly with Soviet traditions.

The whole configuration was given a kind of stability (even immobility) by virtue of its insertion into the overall configuration of the Cold War, which brought to a temporary halt local processes of the formation of a system of states. That "freezing" experience has had enduring consequences, in that it may now be hard to address the international consequences of any renewal of the unfinished processes of ethnogenesis among Kosovar Albanians, Macedonians and Slav Muslims.

The break-up of Yugoslavia in its global context

In other chapters of this book I have touched upon a variety of aspects of the significance of the insertion of Yugoslavia into wider economic, political and cultural contexts across the post-war period. In particular I remind the reader of the importance of the international dimension of Yugoslavia's economic crisis during the 1980s. In conclusion, however, I want to address the issue of the significance of Yugoslavia's position within the process of formation and change of the system of inter-state relations for its disintegration after 1989.

Communism has been a powerful factor making for the integration of Yugoslavia: but this has been treated in a very one-sided fashion during the period of the disintegration of the country. A powerful, but false, mythology attributes the "death of Yugoslavia" more or less directly to the death of President Tito who (depending upon which version of the myth one takes) either ensured the cohesion of the country by means of his charismatic personality, or "kept the lid on" by the application or threat of force.[30]

There is a strange mystique about the causal factors which might be involved here. Ten years elapsed between the Marshal's death in 1980 and the break-up of the country, which suggests at the very least that other factors of cohesion must have been active. The second explanation overlooks the fact that the greatest challenges to the state during his lifetime (the crisis years of 1968, and of 1971-2.) were largely handled without the obvious involvement of force, except in that the state always has at its disposal ultimately the application of force. These matters were settled by political means. Force was resorted to increasingly during the 1980s, especially in dealing with the deteriorating situation in Kosovo.[31]

I would prefer to argue that the relative stability of Yugoslavia between the mid-1950s (the reconciliation with the Soviet Union) and the early 1980s had more to do with the fact that an extremely supportive international context made for a stability which enabled domestic problems to be handled generally speaking by negotiation, without opposition being construed as a direct challenge to the state. What is remarkable about the period between 1968 and 1971-2 is the relative ease with which, faced with an extremely serious political challenge, the authority of the centre was reasserted without any obvious threat to the stability of the state.

This situation changed relatively quickly following the introduction of Gorbachev's *glasnost* and *perestroika*, and the "Solidarity" struggle in Poland, in the late 1980s, and dramatically in 1989, with the sudden collapse of Soviet hegemony in eastern Europe. It then emerged that one of the most powerful of the cohesive factors governing Yugoslav politics had been the external threat of possible Soviet intervention, along the lines of East Germany in 1953, Hungary in 1956, the Prague Spring of 1968, and Poland before the Jaruzelski take-over in 1981. The significance of the change lay not only in the clarity with which it emerged that there was no immediate and continuing threat of Soviet discipline, but relatedly in the raising of the price which western governments were prepared to demand for continuing subventions to the Yugoslav state.

The bloody collapse of the federation in 1991 has been blamed in part upon the ambiguity of the signals which were given by other significant states to the Yugoslavs, about their perception of events in the country, and in part upon their failure to intervene effectively to stifle war when it did flare up. International unanimity about the importance of preserving the integrity of international borders on the eve of the secession of Slovenia and Croatia was interpreted as supporting the action of the federal government in deploying the Yugoslav People's Army (the *JNA*) to prevent the break-up of the state. Nevertheless, it is important to note that the regional system of states was reflected in the entire post-1945 evolution of the configuration of relationships which was manifested in Yugoslavia after 1989.

There is a puzzling incongruity between Yugoslavia's progressive integration into the wider European networks of economic and political relations (the move towards European Associate status, and participation in the Alpe-Adria group, for example) and the irrelevance of these things when the internal integrity of the state was finally put to the test. The fact of the matter is that Yugoslavia and its place within the European order were simply taken for granted by its more powerful European neighbours. The implications of the coincidence of a rapid deterioration of the economic security of the population, and the disappearance of key elements of the country's external political framework, were not appreciated.

As I have suggested elsewhere, a key factor making for the collapse of Yugoslavia was the dreadful rigidity of its internal political structure, and its consequent chronic inability to adapt to both internal and external change. The changing pattern of *inter-state* relationships interacted with such *internal* factors, to produce an uncontrollable spiral of disintegration, so that when the external environment permitted and even compelled change, the internal structure was not able to cope with it.

I have already cited the view taken by my editorial colleagues and me in our 1992 volume *Yugoslavia in Transition*, to the effect that the complete collapse of a social system requires either or both the active hostility of at least one very powerful enemy, and the complete loss of resolution and cohesion on the part of its ruling stratum (Allcock, Horton and Milivojevic 1992:3).[32] There are two relevant respects in which, with hindsight, we can be said to have misjudged the situation. First of all, we overestimated the resolution of the elite, and in common with the majority of commentators at the time anticipated that the most likely consequence of a further development of intra-elite conflict would be the reestablishment of authority through military intervention—"another Jaruzelski" (Milivojevic 1988). Possibly of greater significance is the fact that we failed to appreciate the difference between the *active presence* of a powerful external enemy and the *complete absence* of an externally supportive framework of the system of states. The threat of Soviet intervention was removed after 1989: but this was replaced by he "triumph of the lack of will" which characterised the response of the international community to the Yugoslav crisis (Gow 1997). The disintegration of the Yugoslav federation was acutely revealing of the weaknesses in particular of European institutions, and the gap between their aspirations and what they were in fact capable of delivering.

The sociological interest and relevance of developments does not lie only in whether or not European and American political leaders were imaginative, responsible, resolute, or characterised by clear vision or a developed sense of moral values.[33] It is in this respect misleading to characterise this situation in terms of a failure of political will. The problem lay in the characteristics of the regional and global system of states, caught in a state of transition between the stability of the Cold War confrontation of power blocs, and some (as yet undefined) new pattern.[34]

Notes

1. This kind of account is commonplace in relation to the states of the Balkan region. A good example is Singleton 1985. It is important to note that my remarks here relate to the *modern* state, which is significantly different from the dynastic states, which in the mediaeval period emerged around a combination of the military power (or marital opportunism) of great families (Elias 1994 [1939]: Vol. II, "State Formation and Civilization").

2. The best concise explanation of "constructivism" I have encountered is Cornell and Hartmann 1998, esp. Chap. 4.

3. For the concept of "primordiality" and its significance, and the relevant background in the literature, see my discussion in Chap. 10. See also Cornell and Hartmann Chap. 3.

4. Elias 1994 [1939]:311 draws our attention to the falsity of projecting anachronistic ideas about law and justice onto the past. His observations are well taken with respect to the Balkans.

5. These figures must be taken as no more than approximations in view of the uncertainty which surrounds the dates of several of these rulers. In several instances the continuity of the "dynasty" is also in question.

6. It is interesting to compare the dates of the foundation of the Serbian and Greek independent states (around 1830) with the relatively late consolidation of the modern state in some other parts of Europe. Italian and German unification only take place in the 1870s. On the dimension of state formation the "backward" Serbs and Greeks were ahead of the supposedly "advanced" Czechs, and even parts of Germany. It is worth reflecting upon these issues in the light of Anderson's treatment of "creole" nationalities. Anderson 1991: Chap. 4.

7. Note in particular Austria's success in forcing the evacuation of Scutari at the end of the Second Balkan War.

8. Up to the beginning of the war the historian R.W. Seton-Watson was convinced that the perpetuation of the Monarchy was not only likely but *necessary*. See Hanak 1962: esp. 24 ff; Macartney 1968:784. I have relied heavily in this chapter upon the following, unless otherwise cited: Crampton 1994; Crampton and Crampton 1996; Davis 1996; Hobsbawm 1994.

9. By the end of 1914 Turkey had also aligned itself with the latter.

10. For further information on the religious dimension of developments, see Malcolm 1998 (with specific reference to Kosovo); McCarthy 1995; Jelavich 1954; Anarkis 1963; Dragnic, in Kerner (ed.) 1949: Chap. 12.

11. There are serious problems of accurate reckoning here, but the figures will do as a "ball park" estimate. Seton-Watson also indicates that there were substantial numbers of Serbs left in other countries of the region not incorporated into the new kingdom. An ethnographic map was presented to the peace conference detailing Serbian estimates of the extent of these, reprinted as an appendix to Vosnjak 1917.

12. I have in mind here the work of Paisii Hilendarski, in his *Slavianob'lgarska istorija* of 1762, and that of Jovan Rajic, *Istorija raznih slavenskih narodov, napace Bolgar, Horvatov i Serbov* of 1794-5. See Lord 1963:259.

13. For accounts of the development of the different South Slav languages, see Comrie and Corbett eds.:1993.

14. Although historians typically refer to "The Yugoslav Committee" I have found it hard to pin down exactly who they were. Their social and political composition is interesting, in which connection see the list of those who signed the Manifesto in London in May 1915, provided in Petrovitch 1915:11-12. Jankovic and Krizman list 11 named individuals, but add *i drugi* (and others) (Jankovic and Krizman 1964:11) See also Sepic 1970:563-74; and the article in the *Jugoslavenska Enciklopedija*.

15. Romania was embroiled on a similar basis by the Treaty of Bucharest in 1916.

16. Preoccupied as we tend to be in Britain with events on the Western Front, we overlook the fact that "half a million men died at Caporetto .... The Austrian army was broken in Italy" (Davis 1996:90708).

17. In many histories the Committee is identified more with its British sympathisers than with its core of active members. Eterovich and Spalatin make a great deal of the significance of the number of participants with American connections (Eterovich and Spalatin 1970:77).

18. The Treaty of London did not specify that Fiume should become Italian. The campaign to secure Fiume was the subsequent creation of an irregular force of Italian nationalists led by the poet Gabriele D'Annunzio. Even so, they pressed their claim as vigorously as if it had been agreed by the Treaty.

19. The position of Turkey in the region (with which Yugoslavia did not actually have a common border) was stabilised by the Treaties of Sevres, in 1920, and Lausanne in 1923.

20. I have relied on two useful surveys on the international situation in the inter-war period: Crampton 1994: Part I; Davies 1196: Chap. XI.

21. One of the best sources for the study of this period remains Seton-Watson 1962.

22. Of the 30 states of inter-war Europe (excluding Turkey and the micro-states) 18 experienced some form of dictatorship between 1917 and 1939. Davis 1996:1320.

23. Crampton and Crampton 1996:77 give a somewhat different estimate, but the nature of the problem is not altered thereby.

24. An excellent review of these issues is provided in Magosci 1993: maps 38-43.

25. The most authoritative review of these developments is still Hoptner 1962.

26. Tomasevich once informed me that his study of the Chetniks (1974) was projected as the first volume of a trilogy, which was to have covered all the contending local forces. With the exception of Cohen's rather polemical contribution (1996) it remains the only significant study in this area. The virgin territory of Soviet archives has still to be exploited. The range of scholarship in this area (in English) is usefully surveyed in Horton 1990.

27. By November 1941 the Germans had suffered around 730,000 casualties on the Eastern Front.

28. Both Churchill and Stalin seem to have underestimated the strength on the ground of Tito's forces, both politically and militarily. They both urged caution upon him, and coalition with the Royalist forces.

29. There has been some historical comment on the precursors of Yugoslav autonomism before the dispute with the Cominform (Maurer 1991).

30. Sekelj (1993) refers with consistent irony throughout his work to "the charismatic individual"—without naming him!

31. It is relevant to the history of the Kosovo struggle that the Kosovar Albanians have had no powerful external patrons.

32. It should be noted that the passage in question was actually written in April 1990.

33. For examples of this kind of moral critique of the response of political leaders outside of Yugoslavia, see Almond 1994; Mestrovic 1994.

34. The problem was revealed clearly in the confusion manifested by analysts presenting evidence to the Select Committee of the House of Commons, about just what was the form in which we should understand that system. (See House of Commons 1992 and 1992a.)

8

DIMENSIONS OF POLITICAL MODERNITY:

THE FAILURE OF DEMOCRACY

"Democracy" and political modernity

The collapse of Communism in eastern Europe has prompted and fuelled widespread discussion of a "transition to democracy" in the region. Whereas the release from Soviet hegemony in some other former "real socialist" countries appears to have gone along with the creation of a democratic political culture, this process has not been replicated in Yugoslavia (with the possible exception of Slovenia). In order to explain this we need to specify what we understand by "democracy". An approach to the study of democratisation within a sociological framework must be distinguished from that of political philosophy, which is primarily concerned with normative ideals. I am addressing here, however, descriptive and theoretical issues which arise in relation to the process of political modernisation.

 Sociological interest in democracy and democratisation appears as a primary topic in the work of all of the "founding fathers" of the discipline. Following in the tradition established by these writers, the mainstream of sociological writing about democracy embodies the assumption that *representative forms* are an important indicative and constitutive element of the modernisation process in general, but on their own, however, they do not exhaust the modernisation process in politics. It is necessary to add two other developments, namely the emergence of a relatively independent *civil society*, and the institutionalisation of general criteria of *citizenship*.

What is possibly the most famous definition of democracy (although one which in its aphoristic simplicity has never been accepted into the canon of social science) is Abraham Lincoln's phrase, that it has to do with "government of the people, by the people and for the people". Its simplicity conceals an essential difficulty: for whereas one can take it for granted that government is "of the people", government "by the people" and "for the people" presuppose quite different models of politics. The first we might call "participatory democracy", and the second "representative democracy".

On the whole *participatory* democracy has been treated with suspicion in sociology. Direct participation in government has been thought to be possible only in relatively small, face-to-face communities. In more complex societies, which are necessarily both differentiated and hierarchical, a vision of general participation has been regarded as a populist or socialist utopia. This is held to be the imagery of mass society or totalitarianism, in which the rhetoric of solidarity masks the reality of manipulation. It is the concern with democracy as *representation* which has dominated political sociology. Here the central theme around which interest has revolved has been *individualism*.

In the work of Karl Marx, democracy was conceptualised as one aspect of the wider process of the creation of bourgeois society, reflecting in the realm of politics the determining individualism of the market place. To a large extent this approach was subsumed in the sociology of Max Weber, who located democracy largely in relation to his discussion of the problem of legitimation in modern societies. Democracy was deemed to be characteristic of "legal-rational" order, and its development intimately bound up with the over-arching process of rationalisation, of which it could be seen as one facet of its specifically political dimension (along with bureaucratisation).

Emile Durkheim's approach was in many ways very different. Representative democracy actually fails Durkheim's test of modernity, because it throws up only representatives of sectional and local interest. By virtue of their representative status they cannot embody a *general* vision of social interest, and express those general and transcendent states of the *conscience collective* which are ideally manifested in the state. To reduce the state to the mere expression of the popular will was to diminish its proper functioning. His vision of advanced societies as structured around corporate groups presupposes that these are better fitted to the defence of true individualism than is the homogenising process of democratic politics. Nevertheless, Durkheim does interpret the emergence of representative democracy as a stage in the development of individualism. Democratic forms play a key part in breaking the monopoly power of established feudal and absolutist authority, in which power is vested particularistically in the link between lineage, locality and (often in Europe also) religious confession.

All of these approaches to democracy find powerful echoes today in Anthony Giddens' account of modernity as intimately linked to the emergence of expertise, and its disembedding from particularistic social contexts. One might say that political representatives can be regarded as "political experts", who by virtue of their elected and representative status are set free to operate outside the limitations of the political institutions of feudalism or absolutism, within a much wider spatio-temporal context. In this way democratic institutions do function (as Marx diagnosed) alongside the market and in an analogous manner as the most characteristic features of modern societies. As Jean Baudrillard expresses it dramatically: "the drugstore and the polling booth, the geometric spaces of individual freedom, are also the system's two mammary glands" (Baudrillard 1988:39). In their role as sustaining "the system", the market and electoral choice are both important in endowing modern societies with their superior flexibility and adaptability. These characteristics are only partially attributable, however, to the market-like attributes of representative democracy. They depend at least in equal measure upon the development of civil society and citizenship.

The importance of "civil society"....

When we start to examine the structural changes which are implied in the democratisation process, from a sociological point of view, we find ourselves attending to a configuration of relationships and processes which have been called "civil society". The multi-stranded nature of this concept has been summarised very well by Edward Shils.

> This idea of civil society has three main components. The first is a part of
> society comprising a complex of autonomous institutions--economic, religious,
> intellectual and political--distinguishable from the family, the clan, the locality
> and the state. The second is a part of society possessing a particular complex of

relationships between itself and the state and a distinctive set of institutions
which safeguard the separation of state and civil society and maintain effective
ties between them. The third is a widespread pattern of refined or civil manners.
(Shils 1991:3-4).

There has been a good deal of discussion on the importance of civil society, in
response to the changes in eastern Europe, particularly concerning its possible
importance as a cause of change. Where this discussion has focussed upon
Yugoslavia, however, as often as not it has been couched in terms of a relatively crude
understanding of the theory, giving greatly exaggerated importance to the role of
fashionable but ephemeral and marginal dissenting groups, and avoiding almost
entirely discussion of the significance of larger patterns of institutional differentiation
of the kind suggested by Shils.[1]

What is meant by "civil society" is illustrated well by the judiciary. In modern
societies law is no longer the prerogative of religious functionaries (based upon
traditional and charismatic factors), and neither is it administered by a landed
aristocracy through manorial courts, reflecting simply the power of an agrarian ruling
class. Law becomes rationalised as the special field of expertise of trained
functionaries, who whatever their origins might be in other elite strata depend for their
authority upon their expertise and their independence from other organs of the state.[2]
There is an intimate connection between democracy and the rule of law. The law
stands apart from both rulers and people, proving an impersonal framework for, and
normative regulator of, their action and inter-relationships.

Other institutional areas have attracted similar attention for their significance as effective components of civil society, not only the "economic, religious, intellectual and political" institutions mentioned by Shils, but regularly and notably the media of mass communication.

As Keith Tester has pointed out, there is a sharp contradiction at the heart of the phenomenon of civil society. On the one hand it is dependent upon the state for its existence and the defence of its functioning. On the other hand, it offers a permanent and effective challenge to the state (Tester 1991:96). This "paradox of modernity", nevertheless, is part of its strength as well as its political weakness. The importance of this edifice of civil society lies in the diversity of ways in which institutions can combine or adapt independently of each other and the state, or act as checks and balances against each other, contributing greatly to the distinctive adaptability of the modern state.

It should not be forgotten that Shils also draws attention to the element of *civility*, echoing the work of Norbert Elias on the "civilising process" (Elias 1994 [1939]). The general institutionalisation of norms of civil behaviour is essential as a medium through which potentially conflictual relationships can be managed across a wide range of social contexts. Like money, civil manners are important as a universal medium of social exchange, where individuals are called upon to interact with each other across a diversity of situations which are no longer embedded within their own local habitus.

In approaching a definition of what I understand by "citizenship", particularly as that understanding has a direct bearing upon the empirical argument which follows, I am content in this context to rest with the definition set out elegantly by T.H. Marshall. "Citizenship is a status bestowed on those who are full members of a community. All who possess the status are equal with respect to the rights and duties with which the status is endowed."(Marshall 1992 [1950]:18).

Civil society is an essential complement to citizenship, in that human identities and interests cannot be exhausted by citizenship itself. It is an essentially contentless category. Robert MacIver, in his discussion of citizenship, deploys the image of the highway, which allows all people to go about their business but without prescribing exactly what that business might be (MacIver 1926:482). Unless there is an institutionally protected space (civil society) which lies between the state and the more direct face-to-face relationships of kinship and neighbourhood, however, reduction of human beings to nothing but the category of citizen can end in totalitarian vacuity. This situation has been characterised as "mass society", in which, deprived of contact with substantial intermediate groups, individuals are reduced to anomic atoms, available to manipulation either by the state or by totalitarian mass movements (Kornhauser 1959; Giner 1976). Civil society endows citizenship with content, which is otherwise no more than a dangerous void. On the other hand, civil society without citizenship is a recipe for fragmentation and unregulated conflict between groups, with no institutionalised point of reference regarding the limits of the claims which each may make upon the other, or upon their constituent members.

The central thesis of this chapter and the next is that there has been a failure of political modernisation in Yugoslavia. I understand that concept to refer not only to the relatively weak development of representative institutions, but extend it to include also the underdevelopment of civil society (including "civility"), and the failure to institutionalise a sense of citizenship. The first of these areas is the subject of this chapter, and the second will be dealt with in Chapter 9. The reason for this division is not arbitrary, but emerges from the claim that the process of political modernisation in the region has followed an uneven course, with change taking place at different speeds along its different dimensions. This unevenness of development has had a direct bearing on the eventual break-up of the Yugoslav federation, so that it is important to give it adequate recognition.

Representative institutions before the unification of the South Slavs

During the break-up of Yugoslavia after 1990 both Slovenes and Croats were loud in their insistence upon the differences of political heritage which supposedly separate them, as former citizens of the Austro-Hungarian Empire, from the Ottoman legacy of their less favoured neighbours to the South and East. Among the significant contrasts which were affirmed were the relatively advanced development of democratic parliamentary government in the western European tradition under the Habsburgs, in comparison with the backwardness of the Ottoman regions. It was argued that these deep-seated disparities, artificially cloaked during the failed experiment of the two

Yugoslavias, both survived the period of unification, and constituted a major political

fault-line which made for the ultimate disintegration of the Yugoslav state.

My argument is that these claims are, for the most part, an ideological distortion of

history. Slovenia and Croatia also displayed relatively rudimentary development of a

culture of democratic representation before unification. Some of the distinctive

characteristics of the Yugoslav state which should be regarded as directly conducive

to its failure can be traced to the Habsburg as much as to the Ottoman inheritance, and

some are distinctively local, making the contrast between Croatia and Slovenia as

interesting sociologically as that between the Austro-Hungarian and Turkish

traditions. What is more, the damage to the foundations of civil society and

citizenship can be laid as much at the door of Royal (and supposedly "democratic")

Yugoslavia as that of the country's older cultural heritage.

i) The Slovene lands

One of the most characteristic sins of nationalists is a tendency to anachronism--to

reading back into distant history the features of their contemporary situation. Two

important features of the Austro-Hungarian political system should be noted in

assessing claims of Slovene political "advancement" in the nineteenth century. Along

with many other peoples of Europe the Slovenes began their slow journey towards

representative democracy during the revolutions of 1848. Participation was limited

throughout this period, however, to an extremely narrow electoral base. In Carniola in

1861 an estimated 8% of the population were enfranchised, although "in practice the

percentage was even smaller" (Dedijer *et al.* 1974:376). Although the reforms of 1871 were greeted as providing for a "genuinely parliamentary government", under the Franchise Act of 1873 only an estimated 5.9% of the population enjoyed the vote (Macartney 1969:605). Until the granting of universal manhood suffrage in 1907 the franchise was limited by a series of qualifications based upon residence, literacy and property-ownership or the payment of taxes. These tended to favour disproportionately the German-speaking and urban population.

Furthermore, the representative structure did not provide for direct election to the *Reichsrat* in Vienna. The enfranchised population chose representatives to local and regional assemblies, most significantly the *Landtage*. These in turn sent delegates to the capital. The Slovenes were distributed unevenly across several *Lände*: Carinthia, Carniola, Istria, Gorizia-Gradisca and Styria. Only in Carniola did Slovenes constitute an undisputed majority, where in 1883 they acquired the majority in the Landtag, mixing elsewhere principally with Germans, Italians, Magyars, Croats and even Serbs. Even under the democratic constitution of 1907 the division of electoral districts was carefully crafted in order to weight the distribution of seats in favour of certain ethnic groups--primarily Germans. Hence only 40,000 voters were required as the basis for one German representative, whereas 50,000 were thought necessary in order to justify one Slovene representative (Kann 1964: Vol. II, 223).

The *Landtage* had a multi-cameral structure, dividing into four Curia (Chambers); these were composed in turn of great landlords (defined by the tax value of their estates), of holders of wealth other than in land, and of representatives of urban and of rural communities. The system was balanced in such a way as to favour the landed magnates. The resulting combination of these factors made for the marginalisation of the majority of the Slovene population from the electoral process. As political groupings formed almost exclusively upon ethnic lines, and the dominant land-owning stratum contained few Slovenes, the *Reichsrat* never saw more than one Slovene representative between 1867 and 1907.

It was at the level of *local government* that Slovene political activity was manifest, and effectively so. By 1890 the Slovenes controlled all the rural districts in Carniola, except the German ethnic islet of Gottschee and one other, and even most of the towns, including Laibach itself, where they gained the majority on the Municipal Council in 1882 (Macartney 1969:645).

Austro-Hungarian politics was dominated by the question of ethnic balance throughout the nineteenth century: every issue or measure which confronted the legislature was scrutinised minutely from the point of view of its prospective impact upon the balance of power between the constituent nationalities of the Empire. Under these circumstances it is hardly surprising that the political configurations which emerged within the representative bodies at all levels from the communal to the imperial had an ethnic character.

The Slovene voice in politics was principally that of the Slovene People's Party. For a variety of reasons Slovene representatives tended to be somewhat illiberal and clerically-oriented Catholics, with a pronounced loyalty to Vienna which frequently brought them into conflict even with other Slav parties (Macartney 1969:645; Kann 1964: Vol. I, esp. 301-2). The party was created in 1895 from a union of Slovene Catholics and a fraction of the Christian Social Party (Naval Intelligence Division 1944, Vol. II, 339). Shortly, the electoral monopoly of the People's Party began to be challenged by the Slovene Liberals, and in the elections of 1907 the latter were strong

enough to secure 5 seats--still very much the junior partner to the People's Party's 18

(Macartney 1969:794).[4]

The history of democratic political representation on the part of the Slovenes,

therefore, is not a long one. The political class within the Austro-Hungarian system

comprised a small elite from which, in the nature of the case, Slovenes tended to be

excluded. Consequently, there are no long-standing traditions of Slovene political

democracy, with the significant exception of participation in *local* government, which

could set them off significantly from their fellow South Slavs in the period before

unification.

ii) The Croat lands

Turning to the early character of politics in Croatia it is possible to identify several

similarities with the Slovene situation, by virtue of their common subordination to

Habsburg rule, but also some significant differences. The habit of linking Slovene and

Croat experience as part of a common "Habsburg" legacy, which can be set off

against a contrasting "Ottoman" inheritance in politics, can be as misleading as it is

instructive. The political experience of Croatia was affected by three important factors

which were not present in the Slovene lands: the distinctive constitutional situation of

the Croat lands; the different structure of the Croat political class; and the different

configuration of ethnic politics.

Whereas (with very minor exceptions) the development of Slovene political life had

to do with the position of the areas of Slovene settlement as Austrian crown lands, the history of Croat politics is complicated by the link between Croatia and the Hungarian kingdom. A personal union of the crowns of Croatia and Hungary had been arranged in 1089, following the death of the last Croatian king. Although Croats had tended to include Dalmatia within their understanding of the historical "Croat lands", these had long been Venetian possessions (with the exception of the Ragusan Republic). By the Treaty of Campo Formio (1797), however, these Venetian territories were ceded to Austria, and following the interruption of the Napoleonic period Austrian control was reasserted in 1815. With the dismantling of Napoleon's "Illyrian Provinces", the Military Frontier was also re-established, separating "civil" from "military" Croatia, the latter also constitutionally under the direct authority of the Austrian crown. The course of politics in Croatia throughout the nineteenth century, therefore, was marked by shifts in the relationship between German and Magyar elements within the Empire, between which emergent Croatian nationalism found itself caught and divided.

As in Slovenia, the political class in Croatia was extremely small. Nevertheless, Croats played a far more significant role within it. The noble Estates had survived the vicissitudes of the wars against the Turk, and against Napoleon, retaining their sense of identity, although crucially this identity was defined in *juridical* rather than in ethnic terms. What is more, Croats had not been marginalised within the urban middle strata to the same extent as had the Slovenes, and participated in appreciable numbers in the ranks of the upper clergy, the commissioned ranks of the armed forces, the urban professions and the mercantile bourgeoisie. It is possible to speak (with some qualification) of a Croatian middle class.

The salient ethnic division for the Slovenes lay (with minor exceptions) between "Teuton and Slav" so that the ideological self-image of the Slovene national movement represented their people in terms of "a bulwark against Germany" (Vosnjak 1917). Although to some extent this is reflected in the Croat self-image as an *antemuralis Christianitatis* against the Ottomans, the development of Croat national identity was complicated by the need not only to place this identity in relation to both Germans and Magyars, but also in relation to Serbs. What is more, the historical diversity of Croat experience rendered problematic the task of defining a single, specifically *Croat* identity in the face of strong *regional* identities.

Croatian political opinion in the period between 1848 and 1868 was divided between "autonomists, southern Slav unionists, pro-Magyars and imperialists" (Kann 1964: Vol. I, 253). Consequently party organisation was fragmented between the National Party, the unionists, Rightists and an Independent National Party. These divisions became particularly acute in the events surrounding the constitutional revisions of 1860-61.[5]

In June 1867 the major national struggle within the Empire, between Austrians and Magyars, reached a temporary compromise in the *Ausgleich* (balance, or reconciliation), by which Magyar authority in Croatia was conceded by the Crown. Moderate Hungarians realised the importance of a negotiated settlement of the constitutional issue with the Croatians, and under the leadership of Francis Deák, concluded the following year a historic *Nagodba* (compromise) with the *Sabor* (Assembly). Within the constitutional framework laid down by the *Nagodba* Croatian autonomy was enhanced, and many ambiguities concerning the status of Slavonia resolved. Although the *Nagodba* signalled a more adequate representation of Croatia's interests within the Empire it would be mistaken to identify this event with any process of democratisation. "If anything, in the decades just before 1878, the direction of internal policy had been toward a kind of bureaucratic totalitarianism," (Pinson ed. 1994:86).

The intensity of party conflict and the amount of noise created over these constitutional questions in Croatia should be placed into their context, by reference to the fact that the electorate amounted (in the estimate of Seton-Watson) to fewer than 2% of the population--50-60% of whom were state officials. "Croatia presents an example, probably unique in Europe, of perpetual juggling with the franchise. .... Public voting and tax qualification which was extremely high for so poor a country, made 'freedom of election' in Croatia a mere farce." (Seton-Watson 1911:104-5) Throughout the nineteenth century the political contest was largely confined to the upper strata of society, centred upon constitutional issues rather than the electoral process, and was divided chronically by the lack of any common constitutional life encompassing civil Croatia-Slavonia, the Military Frontier and Dalmatia.[6]

At the turn of the century, however, the brothers Ante and Stjepan Radic embarked upon an entirely new political project, which bore fruit in 1904 with the foundation of a "Croat Peasant Party". This not only broadened the base of participation but also significantly redirected political effort towards economic and social issues--primarily the condition of the agrarian population. Broadly sympathetic to the notion of an Austrian-led federal state in which a Great Croatia would find its place, the brothers Radic derived their ideas not from the *arcanae* of constitutional and legal history but from a sense of the community of interest of the most numerous stratum of the population, spread across the Balkan peninsula. The electoral reforms of 1908 lowered the property qualification for voting, expanding at a stroke the electorate from 45,000 to 222,000 (Macartney 1969:769). In the elections of October 1908 the Peasant Party secured 9 seats.

It should be evident from the foregoing sketch that there is little basis for describing the history of representative politics among the Croats before unification in a South Slav state as "democratic".

iii) Pre-unification politics in Bosnia-Hercegovina

In turning to the "Ottoman" regions of the Balkans it is important to note the differences of political culture and experience between them. Bosnia-Hercegovina had four decades of Austrian administration after 1878, unlike the Sandzak, Kosovo and Macedonia, from which the Turks were only expelled in 1912. Serbia began its autonomous road of political development in 1815; and Montenegro had evolved independent political institutions over an even longer period. If the simple contrast between a "Habsburg" and an "Ottoman" political legacy is problematic in relation to differences between Croatian and Slovene experience, the internal differences between the "Ottoman" lands present this view with an even stronger challenge.

The Vienna government expected that occupation of Bosnia-Hercegovina would be a relatively simple operation, effectively and directly fulfilling the aim of preventing further Serbian expansion in the Balkans. Count Andrassy, the Austro-Hungarian Foreign Ministry at the time, is reported to have said that he expected that occupation could be achieved with "a platoon headed by a military band" (Macartney 1969:592). In the event, the modest force originally despatched for the purpose was soon increased to 150,000, suffering over 5,000 casualties.

Because Austrian occupation of Bosnia-Hercegovina did not constitute a formal incorporation of these provinces into the Dual Monarchy until 1908, representative institutions were late to emerge there. The two provinces were made a crown land, which meant that it was governed by a Commission set up under the joint (Austro-Hungarian) Ministry of Finance. For the most part the former Ottoman structures of administration remained in place. Austrian concern to provide regular administration led to the setting up of a *vakuf* commission in 1883, with the aim of providing a proper accounting framework for these Islamic charitable institutions.[7] Resentful of this external intrusion into their affairs, Muslim leaders under the leadership of Mula Mustafa Dzabic organised in order to resist the imposition of state control here, and to counter legislative proposals with their own. The nature of this movement indicates that they were able to build upon a base of already existing, informal local associations.[8] The country-wide organisation which emerged ("in effect, an embryonic political party") held an assembly in Budapest in 1900 (Pinson, in Pinson ed. 1994:107-8; Malcolm 1994:147). A further stimulus to the development of Muslim political consciousness and organisation was given by the thorny issue of conversion, particularly as this had a bearing upon the competence of traditional Islamic courts (Pinson, in Pinson ed. 1994:100-3). Here, however, state interference under the somewhat crude disguise of supporting "Bosnian" institutions, in which Muslims had a privileged place, was more effective in stimulating Orthodox and Catholic resistance than in building a solid sense of Bosnian identity.

The annexation of 1908 permitted Bosnia-Hercegovina to participate more fully in the process of constitutional reform which was taking place elsewhere in the Dual Monarchy. In 1909 the Muslims won their battle for a representative *vakuf* administration. Political parties were formed at this time also: the Muslims leading with their Muslim National Organisation in 1906, and Serbian and Croat organisations following in 1907 and 1908. The following year the first Bosnian parliament was elected (albeit on a somewhat restricted franchise) forming in 1911 a government based upon Muslim-Croat coalition.

Although forming under rather different historical circumstances, representative institutions in Bosnia-Hercegovina carried into unification the same primary characteristics as those which marked those in Slovenia and Croatia. The organisation of representation took place almost exclusively in relation to ethnic groups, although frequently in the form of traditionalist resistance to the state.

iv) The Sandzak, Kosovo and Macedonia

Rudimentary as the experience of representative government may have been in the annexed provinces, it went well beyond that which was available in those regions which were only separated from the Porte in 1913--the Sandzak, Kosovo and Macedonia. Two important points are nevertheless worth making about these areas.

In the first place, there had been a kind of political activity within the region, associated with the internal decay of the imperial establishment, notably, several popular movements which grew up in the *Tanzimat* period (1878-81), stimulated by the abortive reform process within the Ottoman empire. The Young Turk challenge was mounted in significant measure from within Macedonia.[9] Such political organisation as had developed among modernising Turks, however, had been directed towards the reform of Turkish institutions. Even the autonomism of the Macedonian Slavs expressed through IMRO, and that of the "League of Prizren" organised by Kosovar Albanians, in the period following the Congress of Berlin, were principally directed towards constitutional reform under the Sultan rather than fully-fledged secession. The emergent voices in support of greater Albanian authority, what is more, tended to be raised on behalf of the entrenchment of traditionalism (the *saria* courts and the customary law of the *Kanun*) rather than the advance of modern representative institutions (Malcolm 1998: 221-7).

When these regions found themselves cut off from Turkey in 1913 it was necessary for those who remained (and an appreciable proportion of the political class left after the Balkan Wars) to reorient themselves completely in relation to new political tasks and discourses in a newly unified South Slav Kingdom. In the absence of any form of representative politics within the Ottoman state, the various Slav and Greek movements for autonomy or national independence in Macedonia took the form of secret societies, typically employing terrorist methods. Far from being simply virgin lands in which the ground had not yet been prepared for modern representative institutions, in Macedonia these processes had been thoroughly subverted.

v) Representative institutions in pre-unification Montenegro and Serbia

If the attainment of manhood suffrage is taken as the mark of representative

democracy, then Montenegro achieved this status no later than some of its Balkan

neighbours. Its constitution of 1905 paved the way for the election of the first

Montenegrin parliament (*Skupstina*) the following year. The question is, of course,

more complex than this.

Until the territorial expansion of the country confirmed at the Congress of Berlin,

Montenegro was small enough for its inhabitants to bring their grievances in person to

be heard by their Prince, seated under an ancient elm in Cetinje. The first Montenegrin

constitution of 1868 had marked the first significant moves in the diminution of the

power of tribal elders, and ushered in a kind of belated, miniature absolutism, in

which the Prince conducted a very personal rule, aided by a relatively small circle of

officials.

The territorial gains of 1878 posed for Montenegro new and serious structural

problems, in that for the first time tribes and territories were brought into the state

who had slender historic links with the country, and even looked primarily toward

Serbia. Simultaneously, Montenegro's widening contacts with the outside world

produced a small number of young men with an education acquired in European

Universities, whose attitude toward the monarchy was impatient, to say the least. An

unlikely alliance emerged between the traditionalism of the north-eastern pastoralists

and the urban radicalism of the educated and expatriate Montenegrins, which

transformed the country's politics within a decade. As one contemporary put it, the

country became "the stage of .... explicit collision between Serbdom and

358

Montenegritude, between love of freedom and reaction" (quoted in Banac 1984:277).[10]

The *Skupstina* of 1906 was soon divided on party lines, between the Club of National Deputies (*klubasi*), who although Serbophile in orientation were invited as the majority group to form the first government, and the royalist *pravasi*, of the True People's Party (Banac 1984:278-9). These groups in later years were to become more popularly known as the "Whites" and the "Greens" (*bjelasi* and *zelenasi*). The embryonic party politics of Montenegro, therefore, can be seen not only to be divided along the axis of traditional/rural vs. progressive/ urban. This conflict also had to do with the basic legitimacy of the state, rather than simply the orientation of policy within a structure the legitimacy of which was generally above question, and in this respect stands in clear contrast to Serbia.

The idealisation among educated Montenegrin youth of Serbia as the land of freedom strikes oddly upon the ear of those habituated to the stereotypical opposition between the political advancement of the Habsburgs and the backwardness of the Ottoman Balkans. Yet their perception in 1910 would not have been entirely without substance. Although so often relegated to the ranks of the backward Ottoman regions of the Balkans, with respect to the development of representative institutions, Serbia presents an odd combination of the development of party politics within a parliamentary system which resembles more than any other region of the Balkans western European models, and extreme archaism.

The Serbian uprisings exemplify patterns which are in many respect typical of the Ottoman political process. The court and administration of Milos Obrenovic replicated features which would have been familiar to any Pasha. The personalisation

of rule illustrated very well the phenomenon which Max Weber termed "*Kadi-*

justice", noting its marked contrast of principles with those of rational systems

(Weber 1978: 976-78).

> The Kniaz resided at Kragujevac .... was surrounded by his family and heads of
>
> government treating them like servants, even on occasions having them flogged.
>
> Any thought of constitutional government was alien to him .... Until 1833
>
> Milos' Serbia had every characteristic of being the Kniaz' very own extended
>
> domain, patriarchally administered using traditional peasant hierarchies and
>
> without any codified laws. (Castellan 1992:292)

The traditional village and local assemblies (which had previously been of great

importance in providing a measure of self-government) were nominally extended to

embrace a *Skupstina* for the principality, but even after Milos was forced to accept a

constitution in 1835 (revised in 1838) Serbian government continued to resemble in

its essentials Ottoman autocracy rather than European constitutional monarchy

(Petrovich 1976:157). The Prince governed through a Council of State, which was

appointed by him: the *Skupstina* could be called at his will, and had few real powers.

The operative divisions in political life were between the small circle of those who

participated in government and those who were excluded from it. Loyalties were

formed on the lines of shifting patterns of personal patronage.

In 1867 Turkish garrisons were finally withdrawn from Serbia, and the constitutional

development of the country gathered pace. The accession of Milan in 1868 was

followed by the granting of a new constitution which placed at its centre the

360

Skupstina, and provided for certain civil rights.[11] The elections of 1869 were actually

contested by "parties", including a "Liberal" group, which via Vladimir Jovanovic and

other western-educated intellectuals brought a new ideological infusion into Serbian

politics (Stokes 1975:158-9). It was only in the 1880s, however, when representative

institutions were sufficiently institutionalised, and political factions sufficiently

advanced beyond the level of personal followings based upon patronage, that "the

parliamentary period of Serbian politics began" (Stokes 1990:21). From about 1875

onwards it is possible to trace the development of Nikola Pasic's Radicals and

Liberals as organised groupings, and subsequently a Social Democratic Party (1892).

By this period the principal Serbian parties had developed a specifically *ideological*

focus which differentiated them from the nationalistic parties of both Croatia and

Slovenia. It is not just that the Radicals were characterised by a rooted opposition to

the Obrenovic dynasty: debate about the nature and extent of civil liberties was an

important theme of party controversy. This bore fruit in the new constitution of 1888-

9, which expanded the power of the *Skupstina*, abolished the appointed members,

provided for secret ballots, and widened the scope of civic freedoms (Petrovich

1976:441-3). The fact of a fairly wide franchise (although short of universal suffrage)

facilitated real popular contest here.

On the surface, by 1910 Serbia looked very much like a relatively modern

constitutional monarchy, judged by the forms of its political life. Indeed, measured by

the standard of the existence of representative institutions alone Serbia should be

considered the most "advanced" of all the South Slav lands. The real oddity of the

Serbian situation is that beneath a surface of modernity ran another, powerful current which contradicts this picture entirely. This is exemplified by the extent to which state authority was effectively undermined by the famous "Black Hand" (*Crna ruka*, or alternatively *Ujedinjenje ili smrt*—"Unification or Death"). This secretive organisation, composed largely of military officers, thoroughly penetrated government to the extent that its chief (Col. Dragutin Dimitrijevic-Apis) was appointed head of intelligence of the Serbian General Staff in 1913. Despising the civilian government, *Crna ruka* was involved actively in the support of nationalistic work both in Bosnia-Hercegovina (including the Sarajevo assassinations of 1914) and Macedonia, as well as within Serbia itself. Its power was only broken by the Salonika Trials of 1917.

Nowhere is the fragility of the Serbian state more dramatically underlined than in the murders by members of *Crna ruka* of Alexander Obrenovic and his Queen Draga, in 1903, finally excluding the dynasty from Serbia and restoring the Karadjordjevic line. It is probably the impact of this event more than any other that fixed the image of the primitivism of Serbian political culture, for both public opinion and scholarship in western Europe (Allcock, in Allcock and Young eds. 1991:186-7). What this material indicates is that "democratisation" in any purely formal sense is not adequate as an index of political modernisation. Although Serbia went into the new unified South Slav state confident in the superiority of its experience as a democratic state over many of its new partners, it brought with it another legacy. This was the legacy of a deeply entrenched substructure of corruption, manipulation and violence, which constituted a threat to democracy at two levels. It subverted democratic processes while it remained undetected, and delegitimated them when its presence and importance was revealed.

The populist pattern of inter-war politics

The historical legacy which the different South Slav peoples brought into the unified kingdom in 1919 provided very weak foundations upon which modern representative political institutions could be based. Generally speaking the experience of representative government which involved more than a tiny fraction of the population dated only from the turn of the century. Where, as in the Serbian kingdom, manhood suffrage had been in operation for at least a generation, the shell of democracy was eaten from within by alternative political structures based upon secrecy, corruption and violence. Setting out from this noticeably insecure starting point, the bruising experience of constitution-making between 1919 and 1921 (described briefly in Chapter 7) fixed Yugoslav inter-war politics on its course in two respects. It cast political conflict in the mould of opposition between the representatives of *nations* (or at least, ethno-confessional groups). Furthermore, it set Yugoslav politics upon a course of assuming that opposition to the *government* meant opposition to the *state*. In this respect it is useful to introduce the notion of "populist" politics, as providing some kind of pointer to a distinctive and continuing characteristic of political life in the region.

The concept of "populism" has had a long, chequered and above all controversial history in the social sciences (Ionescu and Gellner 1969; Allcock 1971; Canovan 1981). The term is useful not as a label which identifies a clearly defined ideology or programme, but because it alerts us to certain characteristic problems or processes.

Populism arises where the terms of reference of politics are under challenge. Hence its historical association with the threat to rural society posed by modernisation, urbanisation and the rise of capitalism.

Populist movements typically centre their attention upon "the people" as a totality, and the *exclusion from the political community* of those who are deemed to be not of "the people"--whether these are big business, foreigners, city folk or non-peasants in general. There is a process of *delegitimation* of political opposition within the community which comes about as a result of the elevation of "the people" to the status of an ideal political community, and the minimisation of its internal diversity.[12] The consequences of setting politics into this populist mode are inevitably inimical to the advancement of both citizenship and civil society. The rooted opposition between "the people" and their antonym (however that "Other" might be conceived) necessarily results in a denial of any possibility of recognising their equal claims to citizenship. Civil society is also threatened because there can be no legitimate interposition of interests between the state and "the people". Groups and institutions must be identified either with the "bloc" which exercises state power (and which must be ousted from their position of domination) or with "the people" themselves.

The inter-war period in Yugoslavia thus stands in an ambiguous relation to the process of political modernisation. On the one hand this is the period *par excellence* of the building of "imagined communities", and hence the incorporation of people into groups with temporally and spatially extended identities wider than those of kinship and locality, as individuals become "disembedded" as responsible political agents from local collective identities. On the other hand, it actually retards (and perhaps in some cases even reverses) the development of effectively institutionalised representative democracy.

With the sudden accession of general representative democracy in the region after 1919, the inter-war period in Yugoslavia saw a succession of attempts to define the political community in exclusive and homogenising terms. Politics came to be not about differences of aims and methods within a taken-for-granted institutional framework, but *about the legitimacy of the institutional framework itself.* The history of politics in Yugoslavia between 1919 and 1941 can be understood in terms of a succession of exclusions, withdrawals, and attempts to redefine the terms of reference of political life, rather than constructive engagement with issues which were common to a community whose boundaries and interests and rules of political conduct were agreed.

In addition to the proposal which was eventually adopted as the "Vidovdan" Constitution, nine other constitutional models were laid before the Constitutive Assembly which met to determine the shape of the newly unified state in 1920-21 (Boban 1992:23-28). Confronted with the difficulty of securing support within the Assembly for a confederal constitutional model, however, Stjepan Radic and the Croatian Peasant Party withdrew from the proceedings.[13] Although they did contest the elections of 1923 (gaining 70 seats) the party did not return to parliamentary participation until 1924 (Banac 1984: 399-403). During this period of non-co-operation Radic tried unsuccessfully to find support abroad for his political position, and for a time affiliated his party to the Comintern-sponsored "Green International" of peasant parties. At the time Moscow favoured the break-up of Yugoslavia and the creation of a federation of Balkan peasant states. This attracted Radic, but he quickly

withdrew on the realisation that it would tie Croatia into the Balkan rather than the

Central European sphere (Singleton 1985:148). For the suspicion of treason which this

visit raised he spent a brief period in prison.

The Communist Party of Yugoslavia too performed respectably in the elections to

the Constitutive Assembly: with 58 seats they formed the third largest representation.

In March 1921, however, the results in ten of the 45 seats which the party had gained

in local elections in the Belgrade region were declared invalid; and as a consequence

in July a group of Communist Youth assassinated Milorad Draskovic, the Minister of

the Interior (Lampe 1996:139). The party was immediately subjected to general

proscription (although it continued after 1923 to operate through a "front

organisation", the Independent Workers' Party).[14]

The last elections under the "Vidovdan" constitution were held in September 1927.

Although the previously dominant Radicals lost seats (partly as a result of a

corruption scandal surrounding the son of Nikola Pasic, and the death in December

1926 of this charismatic leader of Serb nationalism) it was no easier to put together an

effective working coalition. Party co-operation became steadily more difficult to

establish.

> The Skupstina degenerated into a bear garden. Insults and personal abuse were
>
> used in place of reasoned argument. When insults were thought to be
>
> insufficient, blows were exchanged. Finally recourse was had to the gun. On 20
>
> June 1928, during a debate on government corruption, a Montenegrin Radical

deputy, Punisa Racic, produced a revolver and shot Pavel and Stjepan Radic and three other opposition deputies. (Singleton 1985:150)

The opposition deputies withdrew from the Assembly, and an alternative parliament was set up in Zagreb under Radic's successor to the leadership of the Croatian Peasant Party, Vladko Macek. Although government staggered on under the Slovene Anton Korosec, it was evident that no working consensus could be arranged without constitutional restructuring. The King invited Macek for discussions concerning the kind of arrangement the Croats would find acceptable: but the Crown could not stomach the degree of federalism which Macek demanded, and the latter was unwilling to compromise to meet the degree of unity in the state expected by the King. On 6 January 1929 he announced that the Constitution was abolished (together with the assembly and all political parties), and a temporary Royal dictatorship was promulgated.

There began a period in which all popular institutions were suspect. Aleksandar believed that it would be possible to create a viable state if only the "impediments" could be removed which stood between the people and the monarchy. Consequently not only was the activity of political parties suspended, but trade unions, cooperatives and even the gymnastic societies were controlled. "Yugoslavia's experiment in parliamentary democracy had ended in a fashion similar to that of Bulgaria, Romania, Poland and Greece" (Singleton 1985:150). Opposition figures were arrested and imprisoned, although several (including Ante Pavelic, the leader of the Croatian fascist organisation *Ustasa*) fled abroad.

A nominal return was made to constitutional government in 1931, in which an attempt was made to eradicate historical regional differences and identities through the creation of ten *banovine* (prefectures). These cut across ancient boundaries in a deliberately arbitrary fashion, and replacing familiar names of provinces or states by the names of their principal rivers. The elections of November permitted only parties which fielded candidates in all constituencies. The combination of the practicalities of this demand and the boycott of the process by several parties resulted in there being only one list—that of the government's "Yugoslav National Party". While making gestures in the direction of a return to parliamentary life, therefore, the period is marked by the attempt of the state to control and regulate it, by both legal and extra-legal means.

The abrogation of democracy by the crown produced a response in kind: and in October 1934 Aleksandar was assassinated (along with the French Foreign Minister Louis Barthou) upon his arrival in Marseilles for a state visit. Subsequent investigation revealed collaboration between the *Ustasa* and the Bulgarian IMRO (pursuing their grievance over Macedonia), aided and abetted semi-officially by both Italy and Hungary.

Elections held in 1931 and again in May 1935, however, were democratic in name only, based upon less than universal adult suffrage, without secrecy of the ballot, and under strict conditions placed upon the operation of political parties. Croat representatives once again boycotted the Assembly. Indeed, the new government led by Milan Stojadinovic can be seen in some respects as taking the country even further from democracy. He reorganised the ruling party as the *Jugoslavenska Radikalna*

Zajednica (JRZ--Yugoslav Radical Union), bringing together a wing of the Serb

Radical Party with Korosec' Slovenes and the Yugoslav Muslim Organisation in a

marriage of convenience. Initially it seemed that Stojadinovic might be able to reach

an accommodation with the Croats, endeavouring to establish a *Concordat* with the

Vatican, although this conciliatory move was headed off by the intervention of the

Orthodox hierarchy. Many political prisoners were also given amnesties.

Nevertheless, the JRZ soon began to acquire the trappings of a fascistic movement,

creating a green-shirted, paramilitary organisation which adopted the "Roman" salute,

with Stojadinovic styling himself *Vodja* (Leader). The combination of his fascist

leanings, his pro-German foreign policy and his advocacy of the *Concordat* alienated

large sections of Serb support, however, and by January 1939 the Regent, Prince Paul,

felt compelled to replace him, calling upon Dragisa Cvetkovic to form a new

government.

Cvetkovic was chosen precisely because Paul felt that he had the capacity to

negotiate an effective compromise with the Croats. In August 1939, in a rapidly

deteriorating international situation, what was to all intents and purposes a new

constitution was endorsed by the *Skupstina*. The *Sporazum* (agreement) negotiated by

Cvetkovic and Macek provided for the reorganisation of the system of *banovine*

introduced under the dictatorship, uniting the regions with substantial Croat majorities

into a single entity, *banovina Hrvatska*. This had substantial autonomy, with its own

restored *Sabor* in Zagreb, accountable to its own governor (*ban*). It has been a matter

of some speculation amongst historians as to whether this new federal structure might

have provided the basis upon which the "First Yugoslavia" might have begun to erect a stable and functioning democratic order. The two years during which it was able to serve before the country was dragged to its destruction in the Second World War were insufficient to give any definitive answer to that question.

The anti-Communist rhetoric of the period following the collapse of the Socialist Federation has tended to present that process in terms of a return to the task of building democracy which was interrupted by war and Communism. This view scarcely bears examination. The inter-war years should rather be characterised in terms of the atrophy of democracy than its inception, with representative politics, if anything, weaker at the end of this period than at its beginning.

The political legacy of war: 1941-45

It was not simply the case that "democracy" in Yugoslavia was overthrown by "Communism" between 1941 and 1945: the description of pre-war Yugoslavia as "democratic" stretches the term considerably. (In that respect Yugoslavia differs from, say, Czechoslovakia.) The Yugoslav state was overthrown by external invasion, precipitated in large measure by the character of the country's international context.

"Democratic" politics had in any case been considerably discredited by the pre-war experience. Everywhere under the occupation by the Axis powers collaboration was also justified in the name of popular democracy, yet nowhere did these regimes live up to the credentials which they claimed. Consequently, neither the pre-war not the war-time exposure to "democracy" left any appreciable residue of loyalty, and paved the way for the acceptance of Tito's regime in 1945.

Under conditions of war one might expect that no development of political institutions was possible. Indeed, the complex interaction of the collapse of the state, foreign invasion and revolutionary struggle might be expected to have resulted in the total dissolution of political order. Nevertheless, the experience of war did provide experiences which were relevant to the subsequent creation of a political culture.

The experience of war provided, first of all, the substance for the founding "political formula" of the Yugoslav state after 1945. In many respects this set off Yugoslavia from other states in eastern and central Europe. When Yugoslavia emerged from war in 1945, the victorious *partizan* movement, led by Tito, had earned a valuable capital of legitimacy. This reserve was to last it for four decades. War also provided the consolidation and *esprit de corps* of a new political elite, reinforcing its sense of a right to rule.

Although Communism has been associated with the centralising power of the state, the war itself made in part for the restoration of the *local* basis of politics. The chaos of the shifting struggle threw people back upon their own resources. Beyond that, the commune (*opstina*) grows out of the *partizan* system of temporary government--the "Committees of National Liberation".

The struggle between indigenous forces has also left its own legacy. It has been said that more Yugoslavs were killed by other Yugoslavs than by the occupying forces. This has endowed present day conflicts with a peculiar bitterness, as political opponents come to be cast in the mould of wartime opponents--*Ustasa* and *cetnici* have re-emerged as political epithets. Represented in the categories of the wartime struggles, contemporary opponents become *prima facie*, fundamentally, illegitimate.

The raw materials for demonisation are all too readily to hand. In this respect the period entrenches the populist dichotomisation of politics rooted in the pre-war years, in which "the people" were depicted as standing opposed to the "Other".

Since 1945 the armed forces have enjoyed a particularly privileged position within the Yugoslav system. It is no exaggeration to say that their importance as a political force has been comparable to that of individual republics. Within the Praesidium of the League of Communists the armed forces were represented on exactly the same level as were the republican delegations; and although excluded from the federal Presidency, the Yugoslav National Army continued to have an effective voice in the conduct of affairs. The wartime experience has left its mark in the form of the general militarisation of society, reflected in the doctrine of total people's defence (Milivojevic 1988 and 1988a; Milivojevic, Allcock and Maurer eds. 1988). The diffusion of military awareness, and even more significantly of military skills, was a highly significant resource when it came to the break-up of the federation--especially, ironically, in supposedly anti-militaristic Slovenia. For these reasons the period 1941-45 has to be considered as more than a "chaotic gap" (Pavlowitch 1971). It was a period of transition the characteristics of which are partly understandable in the light of the pre-war decades. It also lays an important foundation for the course of development of political structures and culture in the post-war years.

Communist hegemony and the one-party system

The settlement of 1945 made nominal provision for the establishment of a multi-party democracy in Yugoslavia. Under the Tito-Subasic agreement, although the king was prevented from returning until and unless invited, the country was ruled nominally by a coalition of parties (a "Popular Front") charged with the reestablishment of constitutional order (Irvine 1993:241-50). The trappings of compromise were quickly swept away, however, the legitimating screen of cross-party co-operation set aside, and the Communist Party of Yugoslavia established as the single ruling party. The constitution of 1946 laid the foundations for a basically Stalinist state. In many ways the regime was regarded both in the east and the west as a model of Communist orthodoxy, and the Tito regime as particularly obdurate.

Although electoral processes continued to be a regular part of the Yugoslav political scene, they ceased to have a democratic character for the next forty years. It is worth commenting here, however, upon two related aspects of Yugoslav politics—the nature and significance of dissent and the sociological character of the institutions of "delegation" which were created.

It is fundamentally mistaken to equate Communism in Yugoslavia with a monolithic political orthodoxy, which is to be contrasted with the debate and diversity supposedly characteristic of democracy. It is possible to find both massive uniformity of opinion within a system of democratic representation, and vigorous diversity on some issues within single party systems. The issue is not whether or not there is "dissent", but how change is managed institutionally and legitimated. The Communist movement had a long and fraught history of dissent in Yugoslavia. Party discipline has been a precarious achievement throughout the greater part of its history. When Josip Broz was nominated to the post of Secretary General of the Yugoslav Communist Party in 1937 it was quite explicitly with the remit of "tidying up" the Cold Comfort Farm of political factionalism for which the party had become a by-word. National divisions were particularly problematic, but internal conflict was by no means confined to these. This story of internal dissent continued into the post-war years.

The expulsion of the CPY from the Cominform in 1948, as a consequence of the refusal of the Yugoslav leadership to accept discipline from Moscow, came as a shock to all observers. It has been treated chiefly as of interest for its significance in international relations: but as Banac has pointed out the dispute also placed enormous strains on internal discipline (Banac 1988). In the years which followed there was a protracted struggle to root out the *ibeovci* (supporters of the *Informbiro*).[15]

Party discipline was further strained by the campaign of forced collectivisation of agriculture upon which Yugoslavia embarked the following year, partly as a means of demonstrating the socialist credentials of the regime. In 1950 the first steps were taken in the creation of the famous Yugoslav system of "workers' self-management" (*radnicko samoupravljenje*). The accommodation of this ideological novelty was one of the reasons behind the constitutional reform of 1953. These events brought with them the most intense intra-party discussion over the characteristics of socialism, the nature of the political possibilities open to Yugoslavia, and above all the nature of the Party itself.

The severity of these divisions became briefly apparent in 1953-4, when the Vice-President of the Party and one of its leading ideologists, Milovan Djilas, broke ranks

374

with the publication of a series of highly critical articles in the party paper *Borba*.

These pieces, together with his subsequently published book *The New Class*, mounted

a thoroughgoing moral and political critique of the emergent leadership stratum, and

ensured his political disgrace and imprisonment. Djilas became a *cause célèbre* as a

"dissident"; but the attention paid in the West to his personal dissent diverted attention

from the deeper and more widespread party disunity which his gesture both expressed

and precipitated.

The mounting economic problems faced by Yugoslavia during the early 1960s added

to the pressures for diversity within the country's politics. The steps taken to extend

regional decentralisation and to introduce "market socialism", in the form of the new

constitutional law of 1963, and the economic reform package of 1965, brought with

them new conflicts. The severity of these is suggested by the sudden dismissal of

Aleksandar Rankovic from his position as head of the security services in 1966,

accused of the abuse of his powers.

In many respects the reform programme was a resounding success. The late 1960s

were a period of unrivalled prosperity for most Yugoslavs; and this new economic

freedom was accompanied by a measure of political liberalisation. This was expressed

in publications as diverse as the Catholic paper *Glas Concila* and the philosophical

journal *Praxis*, as well as in much more open debate within the League of

Communists itself. Some indication of the range of toleration which was achieved can

be gleaned from the contents of the journals *Gledista* (founded 1959) and *Nase Teme*

(founded 1956).

These halcyon days were relatively short-lived. By the turn of the decade the return

of severe economic difficulties found the regime exposed and threatened once again

by outspoken dissent, and the participation of students in the international movement

of unrest during 1968 was met with a very heavy-handed response (surveyed in Popov

1989). When reaction to the country's economic problems began to take the form not

only of the demand for radical economic liberalisation, but linked to the demand for a

massive extension of national independence, the result was a vigorously enforced

return to centralised political control by a variety of means.

The most widely reported and dramatic of these movements of dissent was the

MASPOK (masovni pokret--mass movement) in Croatia during 1971-72. The LCY

replied with the suppression of the cultural organisation *Matica Hrvatska*, which had

been revived in 1967 particularly with the aim of sustaining the sense of identity of

Croatian migrant workers abroad, which had become increasingly significant as the

medium for expression of Croat nationalism. It also led a thorough purge of the

Croatian LC, most notably expelling from the party the republican Secretary Savka

Dabcevic-Kucar, and the Prime Minister Mika Tripalo.

Whereas press and academic attention were caught be events in Zagreb, the same

process was repeated at a more discreet level throughout the federation. For example,

in Slovenia the pro-reform Kavcic was removed, in Serbia the liberal leadership of

Marko Nikezic and Latinka Perovic was replaced, and in Macedonia the

Milosavljevski faction was ousted on similar grounds (Rusinow 1977).

In fact, the regime appears to have differentiated between *individual liberty* on the

one hand (at which level considerable freedom of expression was permitted) and the

376

representation of collective and *organised opposition* (which was met with repression). This distinction is illustrated well by the experience of the celebrated *Praxis* group of philosophers. Academics were permitted to develop and disseminate quite radical critical views regarding the regime, and to meet openly with foreign colleagues at such institutions as the Korcula Summer School and the Dubrovnik Inter-University Centre. As soon as they were suspected of mobilising into organised opposition as an incipient political party, however, the group was disciplined.

Students could indulge in the familiar western youth cultural experiences of "sex 'n drugs 'n rock 'n roll"; but the student demonstrations, led and organised with the intention of producing political change, were clamped down upon. Even industrial strikes could be tolerated for as long as these remained entirely spontaneous and uncoordinated.

The relevance of the contrast between dissent and freedom of organisation is underlined by the characteristics of the "delegate" system. The system which developed over the post-1945 years eventually evolved an elaborate structure of elections within a pyramid of delegation, beginning with the neighbourhood (*mjesna zajednica*) and the organisation of associated labour (*organizacija udruzenog rada*). The anti-democratic nature of this structure does not lie in the fact that although in theory it was possible for delegates to be selected who were not members of the League of Communists, in practice it was possible for the process to be largely co-ordinated by party activists. (After all, so much could be said about the role of parties in almost any representative system.) The point is that the normative basis of the system is that of *participatory* rather than *representative* democracy. Not all representatives are delegates. The latter are expected to carry into the arena of political decision-making the direct reflection of the "will of the people". It presumes a solidaristic community the interests of which can be expressed through delegation. Its basis is not (in Max Weber's terms) "legal rational" as in the case of representative democracy, but charismatic. It is not the legality of the formal process which provides legitimation, but the notion that the delegate is somehow imbued with the spirit of those by whom he or she is delegated.

It is important to note two features of the delegate system in Yugoslavia. From the introduction of the 1963 constitution onwards it became relatively commonplace for the election of delegates to be contested by alternative candidates, although it was necessary for their "suitability" to be vetted in a process managed by the Socialist Alliance. As April Carter has pointed out, however, these alternative candidates in practice (especially in the liberal climate of the reform years, were likely to represent a hard-line approach to Communism, rather than pressure for greater "liberalism" in the system (Carter 134-5).

The liberal model of democracy recognises not only the real existence of social diversity and the plurality of interest, but sees democracy as important because of its relative efficiency in delivering both legitimated agents and courses of action in a political market place. The model of participatory democracy espoused by the Yugoslav system rests, however, on an ideal of "a uniform social interest" (Carter 1982:6). "Dissent" is acceptable in such a system because it can be represented as the voice of the individual. There can be no legitimate *organised* opposition, however, as

378

this denies the concept of such a "uniform social interest"—the only voice of which was the League of Communists.

As Yugoslav politics came to be framed more and more in terms of opposition between *republics* within the federal system, however, that "uniform social interest" was steadily reduced to the interest of "the nation". In this respect, therefore, the ending of the Communist one-party system in 1990, and its replacement by multi-party competition, can be seen not as a move towards the recovery of a democratic tradition interrupted by an interlude of totalitarianism, but as the continuation in another form of the long-established pattern of populist politics which had flourished in the First Yugoslavia. As Zarko Puhovski has pointed out, there is a profound continuity in this respect in Yugoslav·political life in the dominance of the spirit and ideology of *collectivism*, as opposed to the individualism of the western tradition of democracy (Puhovski 1995:122).[16]

It is undoubtedly the case that the delegate system remained firmly managed up until the end of the Second Yugoslavia, and that political change when it did come had to be initiated largely as a challenge to the system rather than as its natural evolution in a more democratic direction. In the first series of contested, multi-party elections which took place between April and December 1990, 202 parties were registered throughout the whole federation. Of these, 94 included the word "democratic" (or its derivatives, including phrases such as "social-democratic") in their titles (Allcock 1991a). Nevertheless, instead of heading the transition to a representative democracy which could provide solutions to the rigidities of the Communist period, the "democratisation" of Yugoslavia coincided with its violent break-up in war. The reasons for this apparently contradictory development are best understood by placing these events within the context of a discussion of civil society and citizenship.

Notes

1. I have in mind here specifically the widely-cited work of Tomc and Mastnak. See my critique of their work in Allcock 1995.

2. It is a curious fact that although the study of law featured centrally in the works of the founders of sociology it has become relatively marginalised more recently.

3. Several of the ideas developed in this chapter were first aired before the Conference on "Citizenship and Cultural Frontiers", held at Staffordshire University, September 1994. I am grateful to colleagues who participated in that occasion for their critical comment.

4. Barker insists that the history of these groups is rather longer than this, tracing the Liberals back to an earlier Progressive Party, and arguing that the People's Party can be traced back to 1868 (Barker 1960:81). For additional discussion of early party formation in Slovenia, see Dedijer *et al*. 1974:390-91.

5. The so-called "October Diploma" and the "February Patent". See also Gazi 1973 as a valuable summary of the events covered in this section.

6. It is important to emphasise that the greater part of the energies of political debate in Croatia throughout the nineteenth century were not directed towards the enlargement of the franchise, but the

position of the Croatian state in relation to the Hungarian Crown. This story is far from being a Balkan version of the British struggle for the "Great Reform Bill", as the old political class were largely indifferent to *popular* representation in their concern to defend their historic privileges.

7. As Pinson puts it: "the vakifs were allowed to continue to function, though the Austrian administration tried to introduce somewhat more precise bookkeeping methods than had previously been the case" (Pinson, in Pinson ed. 1994:95). Pinson suggests (p.105) that one source of Mulsim organisation was the *Kiraethane*, or benevolent society and reading room. The Austrian approach seems to bear many strong resemblances to the typical British approach to the colonies, of "indirect rule".

8. Robert Donia has provided a detailed examination of the emergence of Islamic "factions", pressure groups and eventually parties in Donia 1981. See also Pinson, in Pinson ed. 1994:96.

9. Khalidi notes, in relation to the Porte's apparently exceptional sensitivity to political change in Macedonia, that: "Rumelia and Macedonia were not only Turkish provinces but the homeland of most of the leaders of the CUP." Khalidi 1977:221; see also Palmer 1992:203-5.

10. Although perhaps there is a measure of hyperbole in the assessment of a contemporary figure, Marko Dakovic: "Montenegro became the stage of bloody conflicts, rebellions, protests, bombs, executions, chains, persecutions ... " (Quoted in Banac 1984:277).

11. Although the value of these in practice was limited. See Petrovich 1976:367-9. The attitude of government to opposition is illustrated with brutal frankness by a letter of Ilija Garasanin: "Tell them simply to consider minding their own business instead of concerning themselves with what the Government is charged with doing" (Petrovich 1976:271) See also Dedijer *et al.* 1974:382-84.

12. Mouzelis goes beyond the terms of this discussion to add to discussion of the typical circumstances which generate populism, and typical characteristics of the populist movement (Mouzelis 1986). Greskovits (1995) introduces yet another dimension in terms of the intrinsically populist character of the content of economic policy. For a recent comparative account of populist movements in eastern Europe which brings out these features, see Held 1996.

13. The intransigence of his approach had been signalled already by the change in the name of his party in December 1920, from the "Croatian People's Peasant Party" to the "Croatian *Republican* Peasant Party".

14. In a statement reminiscent of FranjoTudjman's response to opposition victories in 1997 in Zagreb, Draskovic insisted that "Communists cannot have the capital city's government in their hands" (Lampe 1996:139-40).

15. The scars were still visible upon sections of the LC throughout the post-war years, especially in Montenegro.

16. I return to this point at the end of the next chapter.

9

DIMENSIONS OF POLITICAL MODERNITY:

THE FAILURE OF CIVIL SOCIETY AND CITIZENSHIP

The key to the failure the process of political modernisation among the South Slavs

lies not only in the retarded character of representative institutions, and their failure to

look beyond populist collectivism and a managed form of participatory democracy. It

lies equally in the lack of a viable civil society, and the related failure to develop a

sense of citizenship. I take "civil society" in this context to refer to all three of the

components identified by Shils (above, p. 000).

As in the case of representative institutions there were significant differences

between the political histories of the various regions which came to be included in the

Yugoslav state with respect to the development of civil society. Once again, however,

these do not map neatly onto the Habsburg/Ottoman divide, and neither do they

correspond simply to differences in the development of representative democracy.

In general terms the pervading weakness of civil society and citizenship throughout

the South Slav lands can be explained by the fact that all institutions below the level

of the state came to be strongly linked to patterns of ethnic difference. Consequently

there was a tendency to reinforce social cleavage along these traditionalistic lines,

rather than contributing to flexibility and stability by creating the possibility for cross-

cutting structures of identity and co-operation. This broad generalisation, that the

rudimentary bases of civil society tended to become conflated in the *ethnie*, holds true of both of the great historical traditions which contributed to the political formation of the peoples of the region.

The underdevelopment of civil society before 1945

If Slovene political life is considered from the point of view of the rudimentary formation of civil society, two particular institutions are noteworthy—the Church and rural co-operatives.

The Church became particularly effective in eroding Austrian cultural domination in the second half of the nineteenth century. Bishop Slomsek was appointed to the reorganised see of Lavant in 1857. A strong Slovene nationalist, he lost no opportunity to ensure that vacancies within his diocese were filled, as far as possible, by Slovene nationals. He was so successful that eventually Slovene priests predominated even in the German-speaking towns. The importance of the Roman Catholic Church in the subsequent development of Slovene politics is suggested by the prominent part which clerics played in party leadership and organisation, especially Fra Janez Krek and Monsignor Anton Korosec.

Equally significant was the development, especially during the 1880s, of the co-operative movement. Created partly at the initiative of the Slovene People's Party, and inspired in large measure by its Christian roots, these ostensibly economic organisations came to serve a much wider social and communal function, and outdistanced the party itself in their significance (Zidaric 1939:44-5).

The advancement of Slovene national consciousness under the Habsburgs owes more to these developments than to conventional political parties and representative politics. Slovene party life was relatively weakly developed; as was the Slovene press, which circulated to a small urban readership. The focus of the Slovene national movement was the *parish*, which along with the co-operative society gave it both a strongly local focus and a defensive character. In fact, Slovenes tended to be rather supportive of imperial institutions, and there was little impetus behind the kind of nationalism which aspires first and foremost to the creation of an independent state.

Educational and cultural institutions were not particularly well-developed as elements of civil society. Although it is true that levels of literacy were notably higher among Slovenes than the other South Slav peoples, education in the Slovene language was only available to the level of the *gimnazium*. Austrian centralist policies ensured that higher education was only available elsewhere, and in the medium of German, until the refounding of Ljubljana University in 1919 (Naval Intelligence Division 1944: Vol. II, 231; Magosci 1993:100-103).[1] Unlike the Croats and Serbs the Slovenes had no Academy. A *Matica* (cultural centre) was founded in Ljubljana in 1863, and a national theatre in 1892. Following the "Slovene national renaissance" of Kopitar (d. 1844) and Preseren (d. 1849) there was actually a slackening of the vigour of Slovene urban cultural life in the second half of the century (Kann 1964:529-30).

Such intermediate, autonomous institutions as there were displayed two important characteristics which would subsequently limit their effectiveness. The major economic and judicial institutions, which were largely identified either with nascent industrial capitalism or with Habsburg absolutism, were relatively marginal to the interests and identities of the mainly peasant Slovene population. (In any case, these would undergo considerable disruption and disorientation following the unification of the South Slavs in 1918.) Institutions within which Slovenes were integrated tended to be centrally concerned with the defence of national identity *vis-a-vis* the perceived encroachment of German or Italian cultures. As a consequence of these features,

Slovene political life acquired a rather one-dimensional and closed character within which context economic, religious and local political identities tended to be conflated.

The development of Slovene cultural institutions faced an additional problem following the unification of the South Slav kingdom. Unlike the Serbs and the Croats, many Slovenes were left outside the boundaries of the new kingdom. National cultural institutions had been concentrated in the towns, and by the creation of new state boundaries the majority of Slovenes were cut off from important centres of national cultural life—especially Trieste (Trst), Klagenfurt (Celovec) and even Vienna, to which Slovene intellectuals had gravitated. It was not until after 1945 that Slovene cultural life began to recover from the effects of this drastic fragmentation.

The distinctive features of social structure in the Croat lands gave to the rudiments of civil society there a character quite different from that in Slovenia. The specific constitutional position of Croatia meant that Croatian cultural life was less threatened by magyarisation than the Slovenes were by germanisation. The greater development of urban middle strata also made Zagreb the centre of a lively cultural life. It acquired its own Museum in 1841, and the following year the *Matica Hrvatska* was founded. An Academy of Sciences and Arts was founded in 1868. In proportion to the Croat population also the provision of *gimnazije* was better than in the Slovene lands, and a University was created in 1874.[2]

A highly significant factor in the development of civil society in Croatia was the Roman Catholic Church, in that (unlike the Slovenes) the Croats had their own provinces, based in Zagreb and Zadar. Archbishop Josip Strossmayer (1815-1905) became one of the great ideologists of Slav autonomism within the Habsburg state, and because of this has been generally revered as one of the spiritual ancestors of the Yugoslav idea.

The long history of the coastal trading cities meant that along the Adriatic coast, and especially in Dalmatia, there was a strong sense of *civic identity*. (This feature was also present in the settlements of the former Military Frontier, such as Karlovac.) An important element in this respect was the development during the last quarter of the nineteenth century to found civic Chambers of Commerce. In towns which emerged as centres of tourism there were often associations for the beautification of the place and the improvement of civic amenity (Allcock 1989).

Although noted for its bureaucratic formalism, the judiciary did enjoy a degree of independence within Austria-Hungary, and a certain sense of professionalism had developed. The real limitations of this, however, and the proneness of judicial institutions to political interference, might be said to be illustrated well by the infamous "Agram" and "Friedjung" Treason Trials, in which it was demonstrated that the courts had been subverted for political ends (Jelavich and Jelavich 1977:257-8).

The peasantry, lacking the levels of literacy found in Slovenia, only lately became involved in the co-operative movement, however, and its association with the Croatian Peasant Party gave it the populist tone of a mass movement quite different from the communalism of the Slovenes (Zidaric 1939:49-50). While noting the radical discrepancy between town and countryside, the large towns in Croatia saw the greater development of the institutions of civil society before the First World War than any other part of the subsequently unified South Slav kingdom. Despite its greater complexity of structure and diversity of composition, however, civil society in Croatia, as in Slovenia, tended to boil down to a configuration of overlapping and reinforcing demarcations of the Croat/non-Croat divide. The modest scale of these developments, and their discouragement by the state in the Habsburg lands, is suggested by Jozo Tomasevich, who concludes that, "from the point of view of the

South Slavs the Habsburg Empire was worse than a bad stepmother" (Tomasevich 19955:145-6).

For very different reasons, but in effect even more radically, the basis of civil society also tended to collapse into ethnicity within the Ottoman sphere of influence. Here particular importance attaches historically to the Ottoman institution of *millet* (Sugar 1977:44-5; 74-7; 271-82). Ecclesiastical organisations were fostered by the state, giving to them a range of functions of an educational, administrative, judicial and even fiscal character, anticipating in some respects the policy of "indirect rule" characteristic of the British Empire. Reflecting this structure, Ottoman towns were often also divided into distinct *mehale* (quarters) adding through their spatial segregation to the visibility of ethno-confessional difference. Thus in Bosnia and Hercegovina, for example, Sarajevo was the seat of archdioceses for both the Orthodox and Roman faiths, and it was through the Churches that *gimnazije* were promoted—for the Orthodox in Sarajevo and for Catholics in Sarajevo, Travnik and Livno.[3]

Particularly as a result of the confrontation with Austrian administration (as noted in the previous chapter) the Islamic community began to acquire a vigorous defensive organisation, initially around the juridical status of the Islamic institution of *vakuf*. A marked consequence of Austrian occupation (especially after annexation of the provinces in 1908) was the greater crystallisation of ethnic divisions, with the foundation of explicitly confessional co-operative societies and even banks. The *millet* system thus continued to be vitally important in imposing a pattern of confessional segregation on all kinds of political, economic and cultural activities, long after the displacement of Ottoman authority (Bougarel 1996:27-8).

The imprint of the *millet* system was especially important in Macedonia, but with the difference that here the Orthodox community was torn apart after 1878 by the contest between the Greek and Serb Churches and the Bulgarian Exarchate for the loyalty of the flock. Rather than offering the rudiments of civil society, ecclesiastical and educational institutions here became proxies through which neighbouring national states carried on the fight for territory until the division of the remaining Ottoman lands on the Peninsula was determined in 1913.[4]

Gale Stokes has remarked upon a fundamental contradiction of Serbian political life: "How is it possible to seek modernity through nationalism when that nationalism placed its faith in a decidedly unmodern peasantry?" (Stokes 1990:181). In this he suggests that the constitutive elements of civil society in Serbia such as they were took the form of the dogged persistence of traditionalist institutions, such as the village community and its assembly.[5] The evolution of an independent state here, however, resulted, in a kind of absolutism by which both the former Ottoman institutions of *millet* and *mahala*, as well as these traditional rural institutions, were in fact eroded only to be replaced by the paternalistic direction of the crown. While elevating the peasantry to the status of a central ideological symbol (as Stokes indicates) the state undermined the real independence of local institutions. It was traditional*ism* that came to provide the principal obstacle to the modernisation of the Serbian countryside rather than tradition.[6]

In marked contrast to the part played by the Roman Catholic Church in Slovenia and Croatia, where it served as the active focus for the formation of Slav national identities against the dominant German and Magyar cultures, the Orthodox Church in Serbia developed a close association with the state. It too lent its weight to cultural traditionalism, opposing for more than a quarter of a century the introduction of Vuk

Karadzic's linguistic reforms. Rather than providing the stimulus to a modernising development of popular education in the vernacular, therefore, ecclesiastical institutions within Serbia itself constituted a dead weight inhibiting cultural and political change (Wilson 1970: Chap. XIX). It is significant that the most vigorous development of Serb cultural institutions throughout the greater part of the nineteenth century (with the exception of the University of Belgrade) was found among the Serb diaspora in the Habsburg lands, especially Srem and Backa, and not in the kingdom itself. For a long time Sremski Karlovci in the Vojvodina was a more important centre of Serb culture than was Belgrade.

The co-operative movement began in Serbia earlier than in any other part the South Slav lands, and in many respects experienced its strongest growth there. The existence of an independent Serbian state, however, and the strength of the indigenous mercantile *carsija* as the centre of economic power against which it came to pit its energies, meant that unlike in Slovenia and Croatia co-operation did not acquire the nationalistic edge which it did elsewhere. Its ideological thrust targeted the opposition between town and country, and the exploitation of the *opanke* (peasant moccasins) by the *kaputas* (wearer of a city coat). The line of political cleavage lay between rural and urban interests, portraying the significance of co-operation principally in terms of the deployment of traditional village solidarities to resist the corrosive effects of economic modernisation. In as much as co-operation can be regarded as an embryonic component of civil society in Serbia, therefore, its function was to hold modernity at arm's length. Political and social life in Serbia in the cities remained suffused with the spirit of clientilism, which while offering a cultural resource for utilising or resisting the state, did so on the basis of the extension of the traditionalistic solidarities of patronage rather than the creation of modern public institutions.

In Montenegro, as in the remaining areas of the Ottoman domains (the Sandzak, Kosovo and Macedonia) there was little that could be characterised as civil society in any form. The administration of justice in Montenegro and in the predominantly Albanian areas remained embedded within the clan system. It is evident that the response among Albanians in Kosovo to the threat of the partition of Albanian-speaking areas, following the Congress of Berlin, was largely organised and led through an alliance of chieftains, upon which the small coterie of western-educated and urbanised nationalists had difficulty in making an impact (Malcolm 1998).

If the legacy of civil society was relatively weak before the creation of the Kingdom of the Serbs Croats and Slovenes in 1918, little was done in the inter-war period to remedy this deficiency. Indeed, as with the undermining of representative democracy, in some respects the experience of the First Yugoslavia can be said to have set back this aspect of the process of political modernisation.

The historical traditions of the two indigenous monarchies (Serbia and Montenegro) had favoured a rather centralised state in which intermediate institutions had played little part. The other regions brought into the kingdom suffered in some measure from the "decapitation" of their elites, and consequently the weakening of the capacity of such elements of civil society as they may have contained in the face of the paternalistic habits of Serbian institutions. This was particularly the case after the proclamation of the royal dictatorship. The federations of co-operative societies, as also the trades unions, were subject to government interference (Naval Intelligence Dvivision 1944: Vol. 2, 278.) Even the *Sokol* gymnastic societies were reorganised as a state-wide federation, supervised by the government (Naval Intelligence Division 1944 Vol. 2. 234). These traits of "Great Serb hegemonism" have often been presumed to characterise the principle obstacle to the creation of civil society in the

First Yugoslavia, and so some extent this view is justified. It would be a mistake to regard it as the whole picture, however, and other factors should be taken into consideration. Equally if not more important was the failure to create any integrative institutions which extended effectively across the whole state.

Reorganised and unified in 1919, the Orthodox Church was given a new statute in 1931, by which senior ecclesiastical appointments were ratified by the crown. The formal proximity between Church and State before this date was rendered closer by the personal friendship between Patriarch Varnava and the king, before the death of the former in 1930 (Naval Intelligence Division 1944: Vol.2, 221). In 1930 also the position of the Muslim community was regulated by the creation of the office of *Reis-ul-Ulema*, who was nominated by the crown. All ecclesiastical affairs came under the supervision of a Department of Religions, although the controversial failure of negotiations to reach a Concordat between the Yugoslav state and the Vatican (finally defeated by Orthodox resistance in 1938) indicated clearly that there were significant degrees of difference between the political positions of different faiths. Ecclesiastical politics was directed far more to the goal of limiting the perceived influence of other faiths than it was to defending in general the freedom of belief and worship.

The press (often associated with particular parties) was censored by a law of 1929, and its implementation seems to have run unchecked ahead of provision in the law (Beard and Radin 1929:250-3). Its application was also thoroughly uneven. "A communist advocating a revolution that is not likely to happen is quickly imprisoned; a government editor advocating murder goes scot free" (Beard and Radin 1929:253). Nevertheless, censorship does not seem to have constituted the only limitation on the Yugoslav press in this period. Beard and Radin remark that: "Ably edited, independent in politics, avoiding sensationalism, lively with witty cartoons, and sober with serious articles on economic and literary themes, it (i.e. Belgrade's *Politika*) may fairly be said to rank with the best in Europe." (Beard and Radin 1929:254). *Politika*, however, was one of the few papers which circulated in all parts of the kingdom. "Since the parties tend to localism and the papers are party organs, provincialism is inevitable" (p. 255). It was the extreme fragmentation and localisation of the press, as much as censorship, which prevented its emergence as an effective force in politics.

Although the co-operative movement was potentially very powerful as the organised representative of rural society, it too was seriously weakened by fragmentation.

In some places Croat and Serb Co-operatives faced one another across the street of a small town. .... Further, in some areas there were two or more associations operating simultaneously, as for instance in Slovenia, where one association, originally founded by priests, was still very closely connected with the Catholic Church, whilst the other, almost as long established, had some, though not an extreme, inclination towards socialism and secularism. (Trouton 1952:161).

The same problem afflicted the trades unions. In spite of the suppression of the Communist Party, unions were permitted by law. To a significant extent the cause of their ineffectiveness lay not in the hostility of the government, which for the time might be said to have been quite favourably disposed towards organised labour.[7] There were, however, no fewer than five separate associations of unions, only one of which (the *Ujedinjenje Radnickih Sindikata*, based in Belgrade) operated across the entire country. Two others were centred in Zagreb (one affiliated to the Croatian Peasant Party), and two in Slovenia (Naval Intelligence Division 1944: Vol. 2, 278).

The same fragmentation afflicted the law. A ministry for the unification of law was created in 1919, charged with the task of producing proposals for the reconciliation of the country's diverse legal systems. Although it had managed to deliver recommendations for the unification of a code of criminal procedure by 1926, its

work was overtaken by events, and its operation suspended by the royal dictatorship.

> With respect to private law, therefore, the Kingdom is still, in fact, a federation
>
> in which the laws of the several sections--Serbia, Croatia and Slavonia,
>
> Slovenia, Dalmatia, Bosnia and Herzegovina, and Voivodina--remain in effect
>
> within their respective jurisdictions. (Beard and Radin 273)

In many ways the situation remained unchanged by 1941. Without a unified system of

law and code of practice it was hard to develop an integrated legal profession.

Estimates of the degree of independence of the judiciary vary over time. Writing in

1928, shortly before the proclamation of the *diktatura*, Beard and Radin reported that:

> Judicial processes .... are openly conducted and extensively reported in the
>
> newspapers. Able counsel can apparently be secured for the defense of the
>
> accused. At all events, at the great trial of communists held in the early winter
>
> of 1928, the defendants had distinguished lawyers to represent them and the
>
> proceedings, including the testimony and exhibits, were amply covered in the
>
> press reports. (Beard and Radin 251-2).

Reflecting the experience of the second inter-war decade, however, Cohen suggests

that during the period of the First Yugoslavia the independence of the courts was

systematically subverted (Cohen 261-262).

The Universities enjoyed a rapid expansion during the inter-war years. Yugoslav

academic institutions not only earned respectable intellectual credentials, but enjoyed

an important measure of organisational freedom. They were certainly places in which

critical social ideas circulated and were debated freely and openly.

> The universities were the only bodies within the educational system which
>
> retained some autonomy. Although financed by the Ministry, the universities

elected their rectors and deans and appointed their professors through their senates, subject only to confirmation by the Minister. The assured position of the university teaching-staff was reflected in that of the students, whose claim to independent action through their corporate bodies was tolerated to some extent even during the most strict years of the Dictatorship. This made possible the expression of student interest in politics at a time when censorship virtually suppressed such interest in other sections of the community, which enhanced the already great prestige of the universities amongst the people at large. (Trouton 1952:173).

Even so, they remained relatively insulated from each other, with Belgrade, Zagreb and Ljubljana forming relatively self-contained centres of intellectual and cultural life, reflected in the continuing existence of rival Academies.

The centralising predisposition of government, and especially the royal suspicion of all institutions which stood between king and people, certainly did nothing to promote the health of civil society before the collapse of the kingdom in 1941. Equally dangerous, however, was the non-existence of any integrative capacity on the part of those institutions which did flourish. Divisions of loyalty and identity were everywhere reinforced along the same regional and ethno-confessional lines precisely by the structure of civil society. It is important to note a third problem, however, which is of general relevance in evaluating the significance of civil society with respect to the modernisation process. It is possible that institutions might develop between the state and the family and locality which are in fact thoroughly traditionalistic in outlook, and which represent the vestiges of resistance to modernisation in a number of ways. (The most effective voices of political opposition in inter-war Yugoslavia were, after all, the Croatian Peasant Party and the Yugoslav

Muslim Organisation.) This was certainly the case with a number of aspects of social development in Yugoslavia between 1918 and 1941. Civil society should perhaps be regarded as a necessary but not a sufficient precondition for political modernisation, which on its own might well be at odds with other aspects of structural and cultural change.

The failure of civil society in the Second Yugoslavia

The range of components which could possibly be considered as relevant to the creation of an effective civil society is considerable. There is insufficient space in this book to cover them all comprehensively. I confine my discussion in looking at the Communist period of Yugoslavia's history to what might be regarded as the most important or interesting from a sociological point of view, looking at the judiciary, the media of mass communication, religious institutions and self-management. My argument in each case points to significant continuities of structure and process across the two Yugoslavias.

i) The judiciary

In spite of the insistence of the "founding fathers" of the discipline upon its importance, and its centrality to the modernisation process, the study of law has occupied a relatively minor place in the subsequent development of the discipline. An extremely important aspect of structural differentiation, and the development of an effective civil society, has been the establishment in modern societies of a strong and independent judiciary. As a component of civil society, the law is one of the features which in modern society is most important in the realisation of the conditions for liberty sought by Mill. There is an intimate connection between democracy and the rule of law. The emergence of an independent judiciary is a particularly important part of the modernisation process. It is one component of the general development of systems of expertise, replacing elements of traditionalism and charisma. It offers norms of rationality as the basis for the regulation of relations between groups and individuals, and between them and the state. Impersonal criteria, impartially applied across the range of social contexts and members of society, can be regarded as the heart of the rule of law. Nobody is "above the law". It is also the precondition for the effective implementation of claims of citizenship, and in that sense especially relevant to political modernisation. In that respect an independent and effective judiciary has to be regarded not just as one element of civil society but as a general precondition for its functioning.

In spite of its undoubted theoretical significance, however, it is a remarkable fact that the law has received hardly any attention by students of Yugoslav affairs. "The judicial sector of the state bureaucracy, and the elite bureaucrats who function in that sector, are among the most neglected topics of political research on Yugoslavia and Eastern Europe" (Cohen 1989:257).[8] Amid the flood of works discussing the break-up of Yugoslavia there is hardly any mention of its legal system, with the significant exception of Vojin Dimitrijevic's assessment of constitutional factors (Akhavan and Howse eds.1995).

The establishment of the Communist regime in 1945 did bring with it the creation of a formally unified judiciary, unlike that which had characterised Royal Yugoslavia, but the foundation in theory for this arrangement was very different. Marxist theory postulated that law had its basis in class rule, as did the state. Just as progress towards socialism could be measured by the "withering away of the state", so too a "withering away of law" could be expected within a society in which the bourgeoisie had been ousted from rule (Lapenna 1964).

Instead of a class function, the general social function emerged as the most important one. In other words, the basic characteristic of Yugoslav State and Yugoslav law is the fact that this State and that law are withering away.
(Blagojevic 1977:2)

The judiciary "holds up a mirror to society" (Trajkovic 1984:7); and accordingly must reflect the specific character of Yugoslavia. The "basic characteristic … which makes it specific in relation to all other systems of law, is its self-management character" (Blagojevic 1977:3). These general principles were reflected in two features of the system.

There was a clear move away from the notion of a fully professional judiciary. At each tier of the judiciary full-time personnel were elected by the appropriate level of legislative assembly, and stipendiary judges generally worked as members of a panel along with lay assessors (*sudije-porotnici*—"judge-jurors").

Although reform of the legal system conducted between 1951 and 1954 did result in the raising of educational levels of judges, and a degree of professionalisation, the institution of the "judge-juror" still functioned to provide a strong element of direct democracy, a check on the autonomy of the judiciary, and a means of ensuring effective Party influence over the judicial process.

The new constitution of 1963 emphasised legality, and in particular introduced a Constitutional Court, but this body had only a quasi-judicial character. Even after the removal of Rankovic in 1966, when the intelligence services were brought under the scrutiny of legislative bodies, the possibilities for political influence over the judicial process were little reduced. The appointment of judges was for a period of eight years.

Both initial appointment and reappointment were by election in the appropriate level

of legislature, following a process of candidature managed by the Socialist Alliance.

Although by then judges were required to possess appropriate University

qualifications and legal experience, it remained a criterion of successful candidature

that they should demonstrate their "moral and political suitability for office", which

typically in practice meant membership of the League of Communists. Despite the

existence of constitutional affirmations of the independence of the judiciary,

therefore, the reality of this is called into question by the fact that:

> data reported for 1979-80 with respect to over 8,000 judges and other judicial
>
> officers indicate that 87.2 percent were members of the League of Communists:
>
> 84.7 percent in the law courts; 93.2 percent in courts of associated labour; and
>
> 93.7 percent in public prosecutors' offices (Cohen 1989: 280-81).

The professionalisation of the judiciary itself, although undeniably significant from

the 1960s onward, remained qualified in effect by the continuing importance of the

lay "judge-juror", of which there were 54,149 in post in regular courts, and 3,594 in

the economic courts, in 1987 (Savezni Zavod za Statistiku 1989:434).

The continuing effective politicisation of the judiciary in Yugoslavia is clearly

signalled by the results of a rare study conducted by Uglesa Zekovic, which asked

judges to list the major factors making for the advancement of a career in the

judiciary. Their responses are summarised in Table 8.1. The politicisation of the

system was guaranteed by the extremely powerful institution of the Public Prosecutor

(*javno tuzilastvo*) which was "closely connected with, and often recruited from the

Intelligence Services, the Military, and the Secret Police"(Cohen 1989: 267). Both of

these features ensured the subordination of the judiciary to "the people" and of

autonomous legal reasoning and norms to "proletarian" culture.

399

Table 8.1: Opinions of Yugoslav judges concerning the five major factors for advancement in a judicial career.

Ranking of factors	Judges in the		Presidents of Courts (N=78)
	Communal Courts (N=642)	District Courts (N=224)	
1	Socio-political activity	Socio-political activity	Personal and principles
2	Personal and professional principles	Support from the local power structure	Socio-political activity
3	Professional competence	Personal and professional principles	Diligence in work
4	Support from the local power structure	Membership of the LCY	Professional competence
5	Diligence in work	Professional competence	Support of the local power structure

Source: U. Zvekic, cited in Cohen 1989: 286.

The ability of the judiciary to act as a constituent of civil society as opposed to a simple transmission belt for the will of the state is, of course, also conditioned in significant measure by the legislative framework which it is required to administer. Here also it is clear that in Yugoslavia the law provided in practice considerable means to control the freedom of speech, assembly and the action of the citizen. In this respect the limitations of the judiciary to meet the conditions necessary for it to function effectively as an element of civil society abut directly upon the failure of the communications media.

ii) The media of mass communication

Superficially, Yugoslavia appeared to have experienced after 1945 the revolution in communication which is characteristic of modernity. In 1987 Yugoslavia boasted 2,825 newspapers with a total circulation of some 2.7 million copies. There were approximately 5 million radio receivers and 4 million TV sets, served by 202 radio stations, with TV centres in each of the republics and autonomous provinces. There were papers for the various religious confessions and in the languages of the national minorities (Ramet 1992a: Chap. 4; Thompson 1994: Chaps. 1 and 2; see also Zavod za Statistiku 1989:388-95). Although described as "economic propaganda" in order to give it a recognised niche in the system of Marxist ideology, advertising was a prominent feature of all media of communication (Topham 1981). Several distinctive features of the structure and operation of the media in Yugoslavia merit closer attention.[9]

A feature of the Yugoslav media was the lack of any federal network of communication. In 1990 only 5 papers had circulations exceeding 100,000. Television broadcasting was organised on a republican basis, and even quite small towns had their own radio stations. Fragmentation matched the process of political decentralisation, with the diversity of titles reflecting not only the structure of republics and provinces but also accommodating the pattern of local ethnic minorities. Only the League of Communists' daily *Borba* (Struggle) appeared in both Latin and Cyrillic scripts, continuing a tradition established under King Aleksandar. The prestigious *Politika* (founded 1904) was printed in Cyrillic, and remained a Belgrade-centred paper. Although to some extent diversification reflected the "highbrow/popular" distinction characteristic of the broadsheet/tabloid division in the British press and elsewhere, the dominant characteristic of the Yugoslav communications media remained (as in the pre-war years) their parochialism, and a tendency to reinforce local and especially ethnic identities. A Press Law enacted in 1985 never managed to counter these wider decentralising tendencies, which have re-emerged if anything in a more intense form within the independent successor states.

The long tradition of censorship in Yugoslavia antedates the Communist period. The legal framework for the press was, in this respect, ambiguous.[10] The 1974 constitution insisted that "the freedom and the rights of man and citizens are limited only by the equal freedom and rights of others, and by the constitutionally affirmed interests of the social community" (Basic principles, II, Article 153). Given the position of the League of Communists as the "organized leader of the ideal and political powers of the working class in the building of socialism" (Basic principles VII), and hence presumably as the guardian of these "constitutionally affirmed interests", the point of balance between individual rights and collective discipline remained unclear.

Within the criminal code of the federation the delineation of offences such as "counterrevolutionary activity" (Article 114), the commission of "hostile propaganda" (Article 118), and especially "association for the purposes of hostile activity" (Article 136), gave ample scope for interpretation in such a way as to suppress any attempt at the expression or organisation of fundamental opposition. Article 133 made provision for prosecution for "verbal delicts", and regularly earned for Yugoslavia the opprobrium of civil rights groups. (Internal party discipline, of course, could be used to sanction those who were regarded as subversive of party order.) The 1974 Law on the Cinema stated (Article 38) that films may not be shown "the content of which offends against public morality, or has a negative influence on the upbringing of the young". Although that restriction may be regarded as relatively commonplace in the majority of European democratic states, the law also banned films "the content and ideological-aesthetic tendency of which runs contrary to the human, cultural and educational aims and needs of a socialist society". The generality and looseness with which these limits are specified is noteworthy. In practice also local authorities became adept at the deployment of apparently innocuous legislation (such as that designed to protect public health) in order to limit the activities of those of whom it disapproved (such as alternative youth cultures). Despite the existence of these means of control, however, visitors to the country were often struck by the relative freedom of expression in Yugoslavia, which extended to religious controversy and soft pornography as well as a certain diversity of political views.

By law publishers were required to lodge copies of galley proofs with the censor before publication, but the small size and inefficiency of the censor's office meant that this kind of intervention was infrequent. The major newspapers were published under the auspices of the Socialist Alliance, and the republican Associations of Journalists were also in a position to exercise control over their members. Ninety percent of accredited journalists in 1987 were members of the LC (Ramet 1992a:61). Consequently the burden of control was exercised largely through self-censorship. The vigilance of members of the LC in publishing houses occasionally resulted in "spontaneous" refusal to print material at the point of production. There were controversial cases of post-publication repression, the most frequent targets of which were the student papers—during the 1970s the Belgrade *Student*, and subsequently *Mladina* in Ljubljana. Unusually, as during the "Croatian Spring", titles were closed as a direct result of political intervention.

During the 1980s the conflicts emerging in Yugoslavia found expression in the media, which both precipitated political conflict by airing controversial views on sensitive subjects, and in doing so exposed the repressive habits of the League of

Communists.[11] The Feb. 1987 edition of *Nova Revija* attracted enormous attention because it carried items on the nature and future of the Slovene republic. The editor was fired--although the new editor and his executive council subsequently endorsed its policy. *Katedra* published an interview with Milovan Djilas in March 1987; and in April 1987 *Mladina* published allegations that the Army was preparing a plan for the arrest of political undesirables in Slovenia, in an attempt to suppress the growing movement towards democratisation.

A key development in the struggle for communication took place in relation to the autonomy of Kosovo in 1987, when TV Belgrade installed its own team instead of accepting networked reports from TV Pristina. The inter-republican rota arrangements broke down altogether in 1988, initiated by the withdrawal of TV Zagreb. This retreat from freedom was accelerated as disintegration approached. The situation of the press in Serbia became more difficult after the rise to power of Slobodan Milosevic. The editors of *Duga*, *NIN*, *Intervju* and *Svet* were all replaced within a year of his taking office. In the summer of 1988 the editor of *Politika* was replaced by a Milosevic nominee. *Borba* bucked the trend towards political clientship. A new editor took over in 1987, who took the paper from being a pliable mouthpiece of the LC, to critical and independent journalism. By 1989, however, the federation-wide media had been reduced to *Borba*, the news agency *Tanjug* and the short-lived *YUTEL*. The Zagreb government set up its own news agency in November 1990, *HINA*, to serve the interests of the Tudjman regime, undermining Tanjug's operations in Croatia. A pro-Milosevic editor in chief was appointed to *Tanjug* in December 1991.

A new press law introduced in November 1990, as part of the reform programme of Ante Markovic, abolished the constitutional provisions making for censorship, and permitted private ownership of the press, including foreign participation. Soon new independent titles began to appear (eg. *Vreme* in Belgrade, *Globus* in Zagreb). For a variety of reasons, however, they have found it hard to create a counterbalance to the general pattern of state domination of communication.

The post-Yugoslav republics have all adopted constitutions which affirm rights to the freedom of expression. In some cases these broad constitutional provisions are amplified in specific legislation. Croatia, for example, adopted a "Law on Public Communication" in April 1992, which includes provision for a Council for the Protection of the Freedom of the Press. In spite of the existence of liberal constitutional frameworks for the operation of the communications media, all of these states have encountered problems in the creation of a free press.

The creation of new states has left intact the old media, staffed in the main by the same journalists, so that old habits of patronage and self-censorship fade slowly. This situation is not improved by the fact that the officials of ruling parties often tend to act much as did those of the old LC. Croatia has pleaded the exigencies of the war as a reason for the failure to implement the provisions of its own press law, relating to the creation of a Council for the Protection of the Freedom of the Press. In Croatia also the process of the privatisation of former "social property" has been used in order to interfere with the composition of management boards. Attempts were made by the ruling Croatian Democratic Union (HDZ) to control the regional daily *Slobodna Dalmacija* and the current affairs weekly *Danas* in this way. The satirical weekly *Feral Tribune* has been the target of repeated legal harassment, as has the radio station 101.

In Serbia, Belgrade challenged effectively editorial independence in 1989 of TV stations in Titograd, Pristina, and Novi Sad. The distribution of broadcasting frequencies and the technical specifications of transmitters has been used as a device to control radio and TV stations critical of government, such as B92, and the setting of exorbitant license fees has operated to deter new and independent entrants to the market. During the war transmitters became important military objectives, especially in Bosnia, in the effort to ensure the control of information and opinion as well as territory and the movement of people. The offices of *Oslobodjenje* were a prime target of the Serb besiegers of Sarajevo.

Control of TV and radio became particularly important during the war, as the depressed economic situation of ordinary people throughout the former federation placed the print media beyond their reach. Efforts to control the flow of news through these means were to some extent limited by the relatively indiscriminate nature of broadcasting. Citizens of Zagreb could watch and listen without difficulty to Serb transmissions from Banja Luka. The attempts of the Serbian government to co-opt *Borba* came unstuck when its former journalists launched a rival paper, *Nasa Borba* (*Our Borba*), and only drew attention to the heavy-handed oppressiveness of state interference. The result was similar everywhere--the spread of a general popular cynicism and distrust of all media.

The ending of the war brought no sign of immediate improvement. Such was the disquiet of the Office of the UN High Representative in Bosnia, during the run-up to elections in Republika Srpska, in 1997, that troops of the UN "Stabilisation Force" (S-FOR) took over control of transmitters in order to ensure a more balanced flow of communication. In Serbia journalists have regularly been the target of intimidation by both "heavies" employed by political parties, and by economic racketeers. The harassment of *Feral Tribune* and other alternative voices in Croatia has continued. An attempt was made in Serbia to introduce a new and restrictive press law in 1997, which was defeated in the courts.

The obstacles to the creation of a free press have not only been of a political character, however, and economic difficulties have perhaps been equally significant. The prevailing depression of living standards has meant that few citizens can afford the cost of a newspaper. The press remains either dependent upon subsidy (which opens opportunity for political interference), or (as in Slovenia, with its very small potential readership) permanently on the verge of economic unviability. The press has failed everywhere to emerge as an element of civil society, but not only because of direct attempts to control its content by the Communist and post-Communist authorities. Yugoslavia inherited a relatively weak and divided tradition of journalism; and more to the point, the development of communications has reflected the more general process of social and political fission which has characterised many other aspects of Yugoslav society.

iii) Religion

The war in Yugoslavia has been depicted not infrequently as an "ethno-religious" struggle--in other words as a conflict between peoples who are primarily constituted as confessional groups. This case has been made with particular vigour by Paul Mojzes and by David Sells (Mojzes 1994; Sells 1996). It is also implied by the interpretative framework advanced by Samuel P. Huntington, in terms of a "clash of civilizations", as his "civilizations" (which supposedly come into collision in the Balkans) are defined by reference to the religious cores of their historical cultures (Huntington 1997).

Sabrina Ramet has listed four senses in which religion can be seen as a constitutive part of the identities of peoples in the region (Ramet ed. 1989:299). Religion provides the historical core of the culture of most groups. It acts as a badge of identity, distinguishing "us" from "them". Religious figures have been in the forefront of the development of the national languages and literatures of the region. Historically the clergy have often played leadership roles, as among the most educated and articulate members of the group, in explicitly nationalist and other political movements.

In the post-1945 period in Yugoslavia the League of Communists adopted a generally hostile attitude towards religion. Religious education was discouraged, even at an informal level, and the religious press was radically curtailed. The training of the clergy was strictly regulated, and an attempt was made to manipulate them in relation to their respective ecclesiastical hierarchies through the creation of Associations of Priests. Religion was denied any place in public life: and although the constitution proclaimed freedom of religious belief the expression of this was confined to the private sphere. Nevertheless, the Communists recognised the historical and cultural importance of religion, and were prepared to countenance and even encourage certain of its aspects.[12] Three of these have been of particular importance.

The first was the creation of a Macedonian church. The task of winning the "national liberation struggle" imposed upon the Communists an early commitment to a federal structure. There are competing theories as to the intentions which lay behind the particular pattern which emerged: one view sees the task in terms of the need to ensure adequate representation for Serbs: another emphasises the supposed need to contain them, and redress the balance of their pre-war domination. Whichever interpretation one chooses, there was a need to consolidate the balance between different republics within the federation. The official institutionalisation of the "Macedonian literary language" as a way of clearly differentiating Macedonians from Serbs was supplemented by the sponsorship of an autonomous Macedonian Orthodox

Church, which separated from the Serbian hierarchy in 1967. (Similar, although so far unconsummated developments have made their appearance in Montenegro since the break-up of Yugoslavia.)

In a similar manner, the LC can be seen actually to have sponsored Muslim ethnogenesis, as a means of regulating the competition between Serbs and Croats in Bosnia-Hercegovina. There seems to have been little if any serious consideration given to the possible alternative, of attempting to build a purely *regional* and civic identity; and in the absence of any realistic possibility of designating Bosnians as a special linguistic community, religion once again was identified as providing the appropriate symbolic core of a group identity.

A relatively neglected, but nevertheless influential factor which has served to foreground the religious element of ethnic identities in the post-1945 period has been tourism. In the search for visible evidence of local heritage which could be developed as tourist sights, religious monuments have been given great prominence. The definition of Yugoslav identities to outsiders has largely taken place through the medium of the great monastery or church, or ecclesiastical art or other treasures. Huge sums of money have been expended by the state, therefore, in the preservation of the religious heritage of the Yugoslav peoples, ironically by an avowedly atheist regime, in pursuit of the entirely secular goal of earning foreign exchange.

Consequently, while the link between national identity and religion was feared and actively discouraged in relation to Serb and Croat identity, there were ways in which the action of the regime operated in such a way as to entrench this link, in other respects. It has often been remarked upon that Communism acted in Yugoslavia to *contain* the seething pottage of ethnicity. In this respect, as in many others, however, the actual effect of state policy with respect to religion has been to emphasise the specifically religious lineaments of national identity, ensuring that with the eruption of conflict in an ethnic framework it would also have a religious colouring. Consequently, as an element of civil society religious institutions in Yugoslavia have been limited in three directions.

At certain times, and in some respects, the free development of religion has been subject to repression and restriction. These experiences have either alternated or coincided uneasily with efforts to co-opt the churches as allies of the state in the creation of the federal system. By entrenching the link between confessional and ethnic identity, the regime has acted to reinforce the vertical cleavages in Yugoslav society which in other respects have consistently made for its fragmentation.

As a result, in the period during and following the break-up of the Yugoslav federation, religious institutions have found themselves (not always unwilling) collaborators in the creation of new ethnically homogeneous states, defined in large measure by confession. Although the leaders of all three major confessional groups issued pleas for moderation toleration and peace, during the course of the Yugoslav wars, none of the ecclesiastical authorities have publicly challenged the central political objectives in pursuit of which war was being waged. Almost without exception the disintegration of the Yugoslav state has brought religion closer to the state than at any time in the past, so that its credentials as an effective component of civil society have been reduced rather than augmented.

iv) Workers' self-management

The paradox of the 1960s and 1970s is that the steady movement towards the constitutional elaboration of self-management saw a rapid growth in the expression of economic dissent through industrial disputes (Jovanov 1979). Industrial "dissent" was tolerated (albeit at first reluctantly, and never given legislative and institutional approval). Self-management was able to tolerate these expressions of dissent while acting to subvert class organisation in opposition. Strikes expressed a cumulative dissatisfaction which was localised in particular sections of the work-force. The system prevented horizontal organisation which might have united these expressions of dissatisfaction into an effective movement. The "unions" (*sindikati*) developed quite a different view of their role, as primarily concerned with issues of welfare, and were in any case effectively co-opted by the party as *de facto* "managers of self-management".

Here we see the real political interest of the self-management system. It actually institutionalised a structure of vertical segmentation. Horizontal organisation (the aggregation of class-based interest into political action) was subverted by the encapsulation of segments of the work-force into their own-place of employment. This was carried to an extreme under the regime of *oourizacija*--the fragmentation of former "enterprises" into "basic organisations of associated labour" (*osnovna organizacija udruzenog rada--OOUR)* after 1976. Within this context they were grouped together with other groups of employees and management having a variety of quite different interests in the nature and outcome of the production process.

This might be called the "paradox of participation". A great deal of attention has been directed towards the significance of workers' self-management as a form of industrial organisation which maximised participation.[13] The greater the degree of their commitment to the system, and to participation within the official structures of self-management, the more workers were separated from each other, and the chances of the collective self-defence of their interests at a level wider than the plant was diminished. Although superficially a prime candidate for consideration as an

411

important factor in the development of civil society in Yugoslavia, in effect workers' self-management was one of its most powerful limiting factors. Its centrality to the ideological foundations of the Yugoslav system, whatever else it was possible to say or publish in Yugoslavia, ensured that it was never acceptable to question the validity of self-management.

It is quite a different story when one turns to the Chambers of Trade (*Privredne komore*). These are a severely neglected aspect of the structure of Yugoslav economic life. At the level of management it was possible to organise into effective groupings; and these came to represent a distinctively "business" view, very often with an effective voice These operated, however, with a local focus, largely communal but also republican. Trade unions were able to operate only as formal agencies, and ironically in a socialist state were largely emasculated through their fragmentation. The Chambers, however, represented a powerful articulation of interest which were important partly because of their effectiveness in by-passing the structures of self-management. Ironically, they can be regarded as a significant though rudimentary component of a genuine civil society. Both of these developments confirmed the *localisation* of politics, which was given institutional sanction through the much more frequently commented-upon republicanisation of political structures.[14]

Citizenship

Introducing the concept of "citizenship" I have already cited Marshall's definition: "Citizenship is a status bestowed on those who are full members of a community. All who possess the status are equal with respect to the rights and duties with which the status is endowed". At the heart of the failure to modernise of the Yugoslav state has been its inability to institutionalise citizenship. This has several historical sources, both pre-Communist and Communist.

In my discussion of the pre-unification history of the South Slavs I have already pointed out that the extension of citizenship to all adult members of society was weakly developed in all regions. In all regions political culture came to identify people with specific collectivities, membership of which over-rode in some way any claim to the status of citizen. Everywhere the basis of political division was drawn along ethno-religious lines, although the sources of exclusiveness were different.

In Austria-Hungary, the exclusion of the South Slav peasantry from political participation came about as a pragmatic consequence of the combination of economic disprivilege and lack of competence in one of the major languages of the Empire, and not as a *direct* consequence of ethnicity. A Slovene landowner, for example, enjoyed privileges equal to those of his Austrian neighbour; and a Serb merchant in Dalmatia was, from the standpoint of citizenship, on an equal footing with his Croat business partner, perhaps the proprietor of a hotel. The system was thus in theory relatively open. In those areas which brought with them the legacy of the *millet* system, however, habits of political thought tended to operate on the principal of the mutual insulation of relatively exclusive political communities, whose interests it was the function of the state to reconcile. The extension of the Serbian state had taken place along with the more or less forcible expulsion of Turks (and often other ethnic minorities also), which produced a territory the exceptional ethnic homogeneity of which is visible today.

The contrast between the two traditions is made starkly by noting the comparison between the experience of Bosnia-Hercegovina under Austrian administration, and of the areas successively incorporated into the Serbian kingdom. For all its faults, the rule of the Common Ministry of Finance in Sarajevo attempted to institutionalise the formal equality of citizenship of adherents of the three faiths.[15] In the growing Serbian state, however, the designation of the new territories as "Old Serbia" and "South Serbia" symbolically disbarred from full citizenship all those who, on the basis of language or confession could not be assimilated to the category of "Serb". While introducing a formal equality of citizenship throughout its territory, the Kingdom of Serbs, Croats and Slovenes did nothing to efface these traditions.

Although it may appear that the rhetoric of Communist order, which sought to base its legitimacy on the "working people of Yugoslavia", might have served to promote a sense of citizenship, this was not in fact the case. Political rights and duties were by no means evenly distributed. Above all, the status of membership of the League of Communists marked out some for privilege. The institution of *nomenklatura* and its related more informal consequences may have been less developed in Yugoslavia than in some other "real socialist" states, especially the Soviet Union. Nevertheless, membership of the LC and its associated "socio-political organisations", and especially occupancy of position as a functionary, was undoubtedly the key to enhanced "life chances" in a number of ways, as well as to enhanced effectiveness in the political sphere. The absence of codes of civil manners worked together with these practices to reinforce the importance of patterns of clientship (*veze*) which ensured that one was able to claim "civil" treatment on the basis of particularistic and traditional criteria where one could not do so as of right, simply as a citizen.

What is more, the apparent egalitarianism of the phrase "the working people of Yugoslavia" also concealed devices of both exclusion and status enhancement. The structure of participation in Yugoslavia allowed in effect for plural voting. Those who were employed permanently in the social sector of the economy were entitled to additional opportunities to register opinion which were not available to the unemployed, the self-employed or those who were not seeking employment (perhaps engaged in full-time child-care or house work, or in retirement). The degree of disenfranchisement was most pronounced, of course, in the case of self-employed rural households, especially those which were not heavily engaged in co-operative association with the social sector. This sense of exclusion was used intermittently throughout the Communist period to create the atmosphere of a political crusade against reaction and the enemies of socialism. The concept of "class enmity" marked the early campaigns of nationalisation, but also surfaced in opportunistic drives against "managerialism", "technocracy" or "enrichment" at different times.

The most important solvent of citizenship in post-1945 Yugoslavia, however, was probably nationality. The understanding of the state as comprised primarily of nations and nationalities rather than of individual citizens was rooted directly in the heritage of pre-unification politics. It was an accommodation made by Communist collectivism to older collectivisms. The division between "nations" and "nationalities" inevitably consigned some to the status of second class citizenship--as guests within a state whose primary hosts were its eponymous nation. (This distinction is examined further in the next chapter.)

The Communist Party had been compelled to come to terms with the delicacy of the problems posed by the ethnic diversity of the region early in the war. It moved rapidly from the mainstream CP line of denigrating nationality as a bourgeois distraction from the essential unity of the working class, and particularly under the influence of the Slovene ideologist Edvard Kardelj, came to build recognition of national diversity into the main frame of the ideological and political structure of the country. As early as the first meeting of the Anti-Fascist Council for the National Liberation of

415

Yugoslavia (*AVNOJ*), in November 1942, the need for a federal solution to the problems of political order in any post-war settlement was accepted. Indeed, the Yugoslav state came to be defined as an association of nations in which the Communist predeliction for collectivist concepts in politics was extended and not challenged. The putative unity of the "working people of Yugoslavia" was legitimately qualified by their division into nations, without being undermined by any recognition of their diversity as individual citizens. So thoroughgoing was the movement of effective power from the federation to ethnically defined republics, that from its initial position of founding its power on a dominant *class* Yugoslav communism retreated into a system based upon the power of dominant *nations* (Puhovski 1995:124).

This capacity to incorporate a recognition of the central importance of nationality into the ideological orthodoxy of Yugoslav Communism thus simultaneously added in the short term to the effectiveness of its legitimacy, while sowing the seeds of future national conflicts, by entrenching at the domestic level the primary political importance of the nation. It has also permanently and decisively subverted the possibility of developing an understanding of the importance of the full equality of citizenship.

Civility and "civil manners"

There is a danger in introducing the dimension of "civility" or "civil manners" as a criterion of comparison, in that it may well be misunderstood as indicating a prejudiced disparagement of some groups. As with Norbert Elias' use of the term "civilisation", however, it is intended as a dispassionate description of the phenomenon in question. "Civility" is not necessarily a morally superior mode of comportment. What is at issue here is simply the potential of civil manners to provide a medium for the management of discourse which by virtue of its impersonality permits interaction across a wide range of settings and between individuals drawn from a diversity of contexts. We are dealing at the level of manners with the same kind of development which at the level of organisation is represented by the shift from personal dependency to bureaucratic responsibility, and at the level of economics by the shift from barter to monetary exchange.

As the term itself suggests, civil manners have been associated in this region as elsewhere with urban development. It is not by accident that the terms "civility" and "urbanity" are linked both etymologically and historically. "Civil manners", generally speaking, may be seen to have been more widespread and thoroughly institutionalised in the Austro-Hungarian lands, although this is a contrast which in some respects maps onto rural-urban differences, and reflects the greater development of cities in the north and west (especially the Adriatic coast). Consequently the question can not be reduced entirely to the contrast between former "Habsburg" and former "Ottoman" regions.

In Bosnia-Hercegovina it seems to be the case that an important feature of the alliance between the Austrian administration and the former Muslim ruling stratum was that the indigenous Islamic traditions of civility, commented upon so frequently by foreign travellers in the region, were preserved (Samic 1960).[16] This feature provides an important contrast with other formerly Ottoman areas in the South Slav region. In this respect, the legacy of "incivility" in Serbian politics is not something which can be attributed to the direct legacy of Ottoman rule. Serbia had no great Ottoman cities, such as Sarajevo: Belgrade was a frontier garrison town and trading post. The genesis and ultimate success of the early Serb uprisings against the Turk is to be found in the weakness of Ottoman administration in this peripheral region, and the breakdown of the hold of the ruling elite. Consequently the poverty of civil life which lurked behind the apparent advancement of representative institutions there must be understood as an *indigenous* feature, and not as a legacy of "The Turk".

In my treatment of stratification I remarked upon an important feature of the history of the region in general, and this is the recurrent "decapitation" of elite structures. In modern times the rise of nation-states, the unification of the South Slavs, and recently the creation of a Communist federation have all been accompanied to some degree by the ejection of members of the former ruling strata. These "decapitations", which have included the expulsion of Turkish administrators, litterati and merchants as well as Austro-Hungarian bureaucrats, professionals and capitalists, have entailed in large measure the elimination of those groups which have been the repositories of greater civility in conduct and communication. The most dramatic of these episodes was the accession to power of the Communists, which placed in the highest ranks of society those drawn from a variety of social backgrounds.

In his study of the new elite in post-1945 Yugoslavia, Lenard Cohen notes that whereas in the First Yugoslavia the majority of elite members had been recruited from the families of professionals and functionaries, this pattern changed after the Communist take-over. Seventy-two percent of the officer corps in 1945 had occupational backgrounds as peasants or workers, and 43.8% of members of the Central Committee of the Communist Party in 1948 were from similar backgrounds (Cohen 1989:117 and 119). Although it is certainly the case that intellectuals were heavily over-represented in leadership positions, so too were industrial workers, and the *partizan* movement and the Party came to be important avenues of mobility for those from manual working backgrounds both urban and rural. This does not mean that they simply brought into political life the codes of conduct appropriate to the families of peasants or workers. The military and the party were themselves powerful agencies for socialisation which overlaid "background" factors with their own *esprit de corps*.

There are important characteristics of the loyal Communist party worker which stand in clear contrast to "civil manners", especially where these are reinforced by codes of military discipline. Civil manners are universalistic, whereas the Party (and army) inculcate *esprit de corps*. Civility is valuable because it smoothes the way to the negotiated management of differences, whereas the Party thrives on a culture of confrontation; and the unquestioning obedience to authority, which is not to be negotiated but simply accepted.

Civility is able to separate the specific situation from the total condition of the individuals concerned. In this respect the dealing between professionals and their clients is exemplary of civility. (The doctor's "bedside manner" is only one specific application of the general norms of civil conduct.) The contrast between party membership and non-membership is, however, one between "sheep" and "goats". This is seen most dramatically in cases of expulsion from the Party, where one's degradation is not confined to the political level.

These standards of behaviour extended throughout Yugoslav society, so that dealings between functionaries and the public were frequently characterised by what in Western Europe would be regarded as rudeness and aggression. In the absence of systematic study of these issues anecdotal evidence will have to make the point. Whereas in western Europe clients approaching bureaucratic organisations typically deal with officials over an open counter, or if through a security window at least they confront each other on a level. I have repeatedly observed in Yugoslavia, however, that the client is expected to bow uncomfortably in order to converse with functionaries through a small aperture set at waist height.

If there is a difference of historical tradition between the regions of Yugoslavia, perhaps it is to be found in this area. The bureaucratic culture of Austria-Hungary bequeathed a rigidity to conduct which, unmodified by an infusion of civility has led to constant sense of frustration whenever one is compelled to deal with a functionary. In regions which lie outside of this cultural sphere it is more characteristic to resort to the pulling of strings and deployment of *veze*.[17] Both of these strategies, however, betray equally the absence of a culture of civil manners.

A post-script is provided neatly by the following brief report circulated on the *AIM* network in May 1998.

> Andrea Anieli, IPTF spokesman in Tuzla, informed that (*sic*) "The Course about Human Dignity will start next week in Modrica", adding that "twenty seven policemen will attend this course" (D.PERANIC@SARAJEVO.aim.zerberus.de).

The failure of citizenship and civil society

The death of President Tito in May 1980 can be given an exaggerated significance. He did provide a charismatic focus, embodying the *partizan* myth and all that it stood for in Yugoslav life. Laslo Sekelj habitually and ironically refers to him as "the charismatic individual" (Sekelj 1993). Nevertheless, as I have indicated, the return to the power of that generation and the authority of that rhetoric after 1974, instead of finding new sources of legitimation and a sense of direction, only served to consolidate the old elite as the focus of blame for the country's problems. The really destabilising events therefore had already taken place before Tito's death, laying the groundwork for the discredit of the regime.

It is interesting to note here the relevance of Alvin Magid's work (Magid 1991). Undertaken in 1983-4, his interviews show that at this stage there continued to be a strong sense of residual legitimacy in the *system*, but a deepening sense of disillusionment with the *regime*. The Yugoslav ideal still lived: but there was a loss of faith in those who supposedly embodied it.

Throughout the 1980s successive governments struggled to manoeuvre the country towards at first "stabilisation" (*stabiliziacija*) and then economic restructuring, in the face of the determined resistance of a large section of the Communist political establishment. Their efforts were hampered by the sometimes extreme conflicts of regional interest to which the growing emphasis on the power of the republics gave free rein. Things finally came to a head in December 1988, when the government of Branko Mikulic resigned over its failure to secure acceptance of a reform package.

The rhetoric of Yugoslav politics, however, denied legitimacy to any alternative ways of conceptualising, expressing and hence engaging realistically with conflicts of political or economic interest. The failure of self-management to generate a legitimating rhetoric left a vacuum in the political life of the country, into which nationalism moved. It was able to do so because it was sanctioned by the regime as the only (although semi-legitimate) rhetorical vehicle for the expression of conflict (Allcock 1992c). The political structure of the country, including the six republics and two autonomous provinces, had been created to solve the post-war problem of creating a legitimate alternative to the Serbian hegemony of the Karadjordjevic monarchy. The self-determination of nations had been a vital component of the regime's self-definition. So although the officially-sanctioned account of Yugoslav history opposed "nationalism" and "communism", and there was a constant series of attacks on "chauvinism", "irredentism" and "nationalism", the regime itself elevated the republics and provinces to the status of being the only legitimate bearers of openly competing interests within the system. In this way it prepared for itself a major contradiction within which it became ensnared.

Communism after 1945 did not replace an incipient sense of citizenship and a rudimentary civil society with a more "primitive" collectivism. It merely redirected traditionally collectivist habits of thought and action by restricting the terms in which collective identities could be rendered politically relevant. What the League of Communists did was to privilege national identities politically. In this respect, however, the Communist period in Yugoslavia can not be said to have reversed an earlier growth of either citizenship or civil society. Communism did not stand inter-war politics on its head, but merely took over and adapted some existing forms to its own needs. Citizenship failed in the Yugoslavia: and this was both a precondition and a consequence of the disintegration of the former federation.

The future prospects for achieving a stable configuration involving citizenship, civil society and democratic politics in the entire region are not good. If it were the case that the political culture of the region could be characterised simply as "weak states embodying strong nations", then those prospects might be expected to remain poor indefinitely. It is more accurate to say of the present time, however, that we see "weak states tied to the development of ambiguous identities and incompletely formed nations". Under these circumstances it would be wrong to counsel despair based upon the view that ethnicity will always undermine the process of modernisation. Paradoxically, it is in the weaknesses of political culture in the region which offer the greatest hope for future change.

Notes

1. A Jesuit college had been founded in 1595, but closed following the dissolution of the Jesuit order, in 1773. A seminary was opened in 1791.

2. It is significant that the Academy was entitled the *Jugoslavenska Akademija Znanosti i Umjetnosti* (*JAZU*—Yugoslav Academy of Science and Art), not the *Croatian* Academy.

3. Sarajevo and Travnik were also the seats of important Jewish cultural institutions.

4. A similar to that of Macedonia fate befell the Albanians in Kosovo, whose first clear expression of a national movement has been the formation in 1887 of a "Central Committee for the Defence of the Rights of the Albanian Nationality"--in Istanbul (Pollo 1993:82. Malcolm 1998:220-1 overlooks this point.). The division of the Albanian lands, placing Kosovo under Serbian rule after the Balkan Wars, altered irrecoverably the political designs conceived by the League of Prizren in the wake of the Congress of Berlin.

5. An excellent idea of the nature of Serbian institutions in this period can be obtained from Mallat 1902, esp. Vol. II.

6. On the nature, extent and importance of Serbian state paternalism towards the peasantry during the nineteenth century, see esp. Jovanovic 1930:39-43. These general issues relating to the nature and significance of *traditionalism*, and the need to distinguish it from *tradition*, are discussed more fully in Chapter 11.

7. It is worth noting the several pro-labour measures passed by the government during the inter-war period, including elementary social insurance and a minimum wage measure. See Naval Intelligence Division 1944: Vol. 2, 278. Not unnaturally a rather one-sided view of things has been fostered by historians during the Communist period.

8. The brief survey by Ivo Lapenna is a rare exception to this generalisation (Lapenna 1964). Charles McVicar also gives place to a consideration of changes in the judiciary (McVicar 1957: Chap. XI). For general descriptions of the Yugoslav system of justice see Blagojevic 1977 and Trajkovic 1984.

9. An unusual study of the development of the Yugoslav media under Communism is Robinson 1977.

10. The ambiguity reflected exactly formulations in the constitution and relevant laws of Royal Yugoslavia. See Beard and Radin 1929:251.

11. For the more recent development of mass communication in Yugoslavia a useful survey is provided by Thompson 1994. I have relied heavily also upon the regular coverage of issues relating to freedom of speech in Yugoslavia in the journal *Index*.

12. For coverage of the religious development of post-war Yugoslavia see Alexander 1979, Ramet 1989 and 1992. An official account is provided by Kurtovic 1980. See also the chapter on "tradition" for discussion of other aspects of religion in Yugoslavia.

13. The literature on self-management is immense, and I make no attempt to provide a systematic account of it here. For a relatively recent survey, however, see Eames 1987.

14. It is interesting that before the break-up of Yugoslavia Vesna Pusic (1992) began to explore the possibility that an alternative business elite was in the process of emerging.

15. Pragmatic politics, however, actually undermined to some extent this formal equality, as the Austrians (perhaps with good reason) were never persuaded of the full loyalty of the Serbs, and tended to prefer Muslims as a way of minimising the territorial ambitions of both Serbs and Croats.

16. It is a pity that Elias' study of the "civilising process" was confined to western Europe. There is room for a major study of Islam in this respect.

10

THE FORGING OF NATIONAL IDENTITY

It might seem that it goes without saying that among the most significant of the long-term continuities in Balkan society has been the central part played by nationality in politics. Several types of evidence could be adduced in support of this view: the use of nationalist rhetoric in the ideologies of the various movements for the independence of South Slav states, going back to the early nineteenth century; the antiquity of the historical symbols which are deployed by all groups, which appeal to a sense of national identity; the part played by national conflict in the politics of both the inter-war period and the civil war of 1941-45; and the re-emergence of nationalisms as the typical form in which post-Communist politics has crystallised in the period since 1989.

The current upsurge of nationalist movements is often viewed in this way as a return to the past, in that Communism put into cold storage the underlying spiritual reality of Balkan life, and its passing sees a reversion to more natural forms of expression in the politics of the region. Nationality has now emerged from its state of suspended animation, it is argued, and has played a leading part in the downfall of Communism. The consequences of the end of the Soviet Union also included the releasing of the

Balkans from the sense of a "Soviet threat", which had served to bind the peoples of the region in a negative unity.

This tendency to view nationalism in terms of a *reprise* of long-standing historical themes in south eastern Europe is encouraged by the recirculation after 1989 of the names of political parties from the pre-1941 period--Radicals and Democrats in Serbia; the Slovene People's Party; the Croatian Peasant Party; IMRO in Macedonia. Montenegro once again resounds to discussion of "Greens" *versus* "Whites". It is on the basis of these echoes of history that it has become customary in the press to talk of the "age-old hatreds" by which the Yugoslav war is fuelled, and which are alleged to provide the key to its understanding.[1]

In spite of the undoubted interest of these points, many commentators on the region have taken a diametrically opposed view, insisting that the armed conflict surrounding the break-up of the Yugoslav federation is *not* principally a national conflict. Nationalism is to be understood as a manipulated ideology which serves the interests both of the cynical legatees of the bankrupt League of Communists and those who opportunistically seek to displace them. It flourishes not because it is deeply rooted in the culture of the people, but because under conditions of economic collapse, political disorientation and direct terrorism, there is little else left to individuals by way of material from which to construct an understanding of their world and what has befallen it.[2]

In the first of these views, the existence of nations and the expression of their consciousness in nationalism is the incontrovertible founding datum upon which an understanding of Balkan politics must be built. In the second view nationalism is a reflexive response to the more immediate crisis, and an epiphenomenal and mystificatory miasma given off by some other underlying reality. In this respect discussion of the fall of former Yugoslavia recapitulates a wider debate in social science about the nature of nationality and ethnicity, in which "primordialists" are set off against "instrumentalists" and "modernists".[3]

One of the primary causes of the failure of the Yugoslav state is often said to be the eruption of nationalism. The problem is, however, that the terms "nation" actually covers a wide variety of ways of constituting consciousness of collective identity. "Nationalism" refers to a variety of discourses about such identities. The primary point of this chapter is to question the unitary character of "nations" and of "nationalism", and to develop and illustrate the variety of these ideas with reference to the history of nations and national consciousness in the region.

Different nations within the Yugoslav region have become and are "nations" in different ways; and the consequences of these different types of national communities and forms of national consciousness consequently vary considerably. It is therefore a misleading oversimplification to account for recent developments in Yugoslav politics and society by reference to a blanket explanation in terms of "nationalism".

A comprehensive review of the literature on nationalism would be out of place in this context, and will not be attempted. Similarly, a systematic history of the development of national consciousness in the Balkans is a task well beyond the scope of this volume. Nevertheless, I expect that through selective attention to some aspects of Balkan history it will be possible to use sociological theory in order to illuminate some specific aspects of the development of nationality among the South Slavs. In the attempt to avoid the repetition of a narrative the main lines of which will by now be familiar to the reader, I organise discussion around a number of general themes which will be *illustrated* historically, rather than attempt a continuous and comprehensive historical narrative.

First of all I will consider the *constructed* character of national identity. Next I will examine the *dialectical* form of that process of construction. Then I will turn to the idea that a nation should be considered as an "imagined community", and consider some of the range of symbolic resources which have been brought into play as the basis for such acts of imagination. In each case the purpose of discussion will be to build a sense of the diversity of the phenomena which pass under the common description of "nations" and "national consciousness" in this region, and to suggest in doing so that their political consequences are not always identical.

It has been an important feature of the misunderstanding of Yugoslav affairs that the nations of the region have been represented by outsiders as more or less political and cultural equivalents. The Serbo-Croat conflict has been treated almost at the level of the battle between Tweedle-Dum and Tweedle-Dee, and during the Bosnian war it was a commonplace of press reporting to hear the contending parties referred to as "factions". What we have witnessed in the region, however, is a series of conflicts which have involved different types of community, which have developed different modes of political discourse. The greater part of the difficulty in reaching a negotiated reconciliation of the competing political aspirations of different groups, therefore, is not that they both make claims to the same territory, but that the kinds of claims which are made, and the modes of discourse which frame them, are incommensurable.

The construction of national identity

Nationality is a term which "lives in the house of culture", to paraphrase Max Weber. Consequently nations are not irreducible natural objects upon which society arises and which give form to it: they are *representations* of collective experience. National identities grow out of older strata of group consciousness (whether or not these are described as "primordial", or "perennial"). Even if the symbolic resources from which identity is constructed are very ancient indeed, however, the awareness of this antiquity and the precise form in which it is represented themselves become elements in a process of construction. All groups probably possess a number of *potential* primordial identities; but the question which remains to be addressed is the manner in which these are selected, composed and framed at the expense of others.

This sociological insistence upon the *construction* of identity differs from earlier approaches to national identity which told the story of the "national awakening" of peoples.[4] The implication of this metaphor is that during the nineteenth century peoples began to awake to the *discovery* of national identities which were presumed to have been always implicitly present, but did not live in the consciousness of the "sleepers". So deeply sedimented has this image of awakening become in European thought that we tend to forget that it is no more than a metaphor.

In the case of the most recently crystallised of the Balkan nationalities (Macedonians and Bosnian Muslims, for example) it has often been alleged that these are largely *artificial* creations of the post-war period, and at worst manipulative devices developed by the Communists. There certainly has been a change in the nature of the identificatory processes in which terms such as "Macedonian" or "Muslim" figure and function. It is entirely wrong, however, to see the processes of ethnogenesis in each case as somehow spurious or artificial. It is important is to recognise that whereas the construction process in these cases is quite recent and hence more visible to us, it is not fundamentally different in character from that experienced by other nations, whose nation-building is now to some extent concealed from us by historical distance. *All nations* emerge as the result of a construction process: they do not simply "awaken".

The emphasis on nationality as constructed carries two important implications. In the first place, there was a time when it was not possible for a people to conceptualise their own identity in national terms. The construction process takes place at a specific time, at which *genuinely novel identities are called into being.* Furthermore, *it is possible to identify the constructors*--groups of people who are the primary initiators and executors of the construction process. Both of these claims can be illustrated from the history of the South Slavs.

i) The novelty of "national" identity

Accounts of the Battle of Kosovo commonly conceptualise "Serbs" as they could never have understood themselves in the fourteenth century. The battle is often described in terms of a struggle between "Serbs" and "Turks"; but who actually fought at the Battle of Kosovo? A sociological (as opposed to a national-mythological) account would depict two armies which represented complex feudal political structures. On the "Turkish" side an *Ottoman* nobility led an army composed not only of other Muslims but also contingents from other European groups who were their vassals--including other Slavs, among whom were Serbs. Accounts vary of the force which the Serb ruler *Knez* Lazar Hrebeljanovic led at Kosovo Polje: Serbs, Albanians, Wallachians, Croats, Hungarians, Bosnians, all are mentioned by various commentators as having been among the participants. The most precise version I have traced is that of Georges Castellan.

> What is clear is that Murad's army was reinforced by contingents from his Christian vassals: Prince Constantine of Velbuzd a Bulgarian, Marko Kraljevic a Serbian and enemy of Lazarus but also Muslim vassal Emirs and allies from Asia Minor. Basileus John V was missing as he was no longer able to muster sufficient troops. Against these were drawn the armies of Lazarus and King Tvrtko which were reinforced by Wallachian contingents from the Voevod Mircea and Albanians under George Balsha and Demeter Jonima. (Castellan 1992:54)[5]

"Serb" forces not only comprised a feudal alliance, which united contingents drawn from Lazar's vassals and allies, but also large numbers of mercenaries, for which the Nemanjic armies were renowned. It seems that the event was not a direct confessional clash between armies of Christians and Muslims. However it may have come to be mythologised as an occasion upon which the "Serbs" fell to defeat guarding the gates of Christendom against the Turkish infidel, historical research shows it to have been an encounter between two typical alliances of feudal aristocrats of no clear ethnic or religious loyalty. A fifteenth century chronicler of this period typically refers to the state as the "Serbian or Raskan kingdom", and this state is invariably identified with *the ruling house* rather than the "nation" (Mihailovic 1975). Whatever the "Serbs" are today, it is clear that the term was not used in the same sense at the time of Kosovo. The continuity is, from a sociological point of view, a mythological construction.

The notion of the "thousand year" struggle for Croatian national recognition can be shown to be equally mythological, reflecting the concerns of a feudal nobility to protect their customary rights. Historians acknowledge the rise of a "Croatian" kingdom in the tenth and eleventh centuries. Its character differed from that of the southern Balkan states in that there developed a structure of landholding which resembled more closely that of western Europe. Land rights came to be detached from the *zupe* (clans) and more closely identified with the nobility (Tomasevich 1955:50-54). The *zupan* often became a royal official rather than a tribal chief, rewarded for his allegiance to the king by the grant of substantial lands.

> Thus the feudal organization in the mediaeval Croatian state developed slowly and gradually under the domestic dynasties from the ninth to the beginning of the twelfth century, through the advancing political and economic differentiation between tribal leaders and the common members of the tribes whereby the latter became economically dependent on the former, and through the granting of estates, offices, and privileges by the ruler to individuals and families in his trust and to the Church. (Tomasevich 1955:52)

Following the death of the last Croatian king, Zvonimir, and the union of the crown with that of Hungary (1102) this differentiation of an aristocracy was reinforced. As Tomasevich observes, "the system of donational feudalism (implemented by the Hungarian crown) favoured large feudatories" (1955:57). The Church also emerged as a major landowner. These grandees were separated from their peasants by a huge cultural and economic gulf.

The effect of the Ottoman invasion during the first half of the sixteenth century was catastrophic. As in the south, Ottoman advance came about in large measure as a result of dissention between the Christian princes, in this case particularly the struggle between the Bathory and Zapolyai families. Indeed, in 1526 Zapolyai became a vassal of Sultan Suleiman in alliance against other Christians (Bérenger 1994, esp. Chaps. 8 and 12; Castellan 1992:90-99; Eterovich and Spalatin 1970:6-7). The rout of Christian forces in 1526 (and the physical destruction of a large section of the feudal nobility) resulted in the *de facto* destruction of the Croatian state.

To these processes the Slav peasantry were in large measure indifferent:

.... the peasants had become second class citizens and cared little for the struggle against the Ottomans and thought that there was little to choose between one serfdom and another. Sometimes they fancied that the Ottoman yoke was lighter than that of the Hungarian lords and it was a people totally demoralized that confronted the great conflicts of the sixteenth century. (Bérenger, 1994:111; cf. 157)

As Bérenger points out, the sixteenth century was marked by bitter wars between peasantry and nobility. To set these aside in order to postulate confrontation between a unified "Christian" West and the alien hordes of Islam is to indulge an extremely one-sided account of history.

Although Croatian historians have insisted upon the preservation of a "relic" of independence lying along what is now the Slovene-Croatian border, this seems to rest upon legal niceties rather than socio-political reality. Stavrianos affirms that in this period the Venetian possessions "represented the only significant challenge to Ottoman hegemony in the Balkans" (Stavrianos 1958:65; also Fine 1987: 590-95). Certainly throughout most of the sixteenth century the entire region continued to suffer periodic devastation by Ottoman raiders, whose expeditions regularly ranged as far as Kranj.

More significant than these intermittent depredations was the extent of depopulation. Many of the Slav population fled ahead of the Ottoman raiders, in many cases encouraged and led by the nobility (Sugar 1977:87-8). Unlike in Macedonia and Kosovo, however, the Ottomans were not able to bring in migrants to repopulate the area, and agriculture sank into neglect.

> When they ran away the land rapidly deteriorated; spring floods and unregulated rivers, sand dunes and alkali flats produced a wasteland of marshes. Newly settled nomads working basic small *cifts* could not have survived under these conditions. The original damage caused by Suleyman I's first campaigns could possibly have been repaired had not the civil war between the two kings, Suleyman's numerous interventions, and finally the fact that the Habsburg-Ottoman wars, which lasted almost continuously until 1699, made these lands into a permanent frontier battlefield creating an erosion that can be observed even today. (Sugar, 1977:88)

The claim to the continuity of a state and a people is based upon the sustained claim to titular rights of the nobility *vis-a-vis* the Hungarian crown. These were developed and deployed throughout the nineteenth century by an aristocracy which was "Croatian" in that they occupied a specific juridical relationship to the Hungarian crown, in order to defend their political prerogatives. It is important however, to distinguish "Croatian" identity in this sense from the modern concept of Croat ethnic identity. Many of these aristocrats were, measured by linguistic and other cultural criteria, often not "Croats" in this latter sense. The claim of the continuity of a "Croat nation" is intelligible within, and only within, this context, and is unintelligible if one tries to render it in terms of the continuous link between a state and nation. "Croat", like "Serb", is a construction which only acquires anything like its present form in the late nineteenth century.

Clearly the terms "Serb" and "Croat" were in existence during the later mediaeval period to describe what Smith has called *ethnies* of some kind (Smith 1986). When one examines accounts of the political process relating to this period, however, it is clear that these *ethnies* were significantly different in character in important respects from modern "nations". The historical actors on these occasions were not "nations" but the representatives of particular social elites.

Gellner describes such societies as "stratified horizontally segregated layers of military, administrative, clerical and sometimes commercial" ruling groups, superimposed upon "laterally insulated communities of agricultural producers" (Gellner 1983:9). The most significant features of the organisation of society at that time was the division between nobles and peasantries. Serbian and Croatian historians, in constructing the nation, have read back into the past the existence of unified "nations" which at that time were not there.

The affirmation of a less complicated historical pedigree is a vital part, however, of the process of constructing a nation which took place in the nineteenth century, when new elites working under quite different structural constraints sought to legitimate novel political forms by appeal to the supposed superior antiquity of their own "nations". National history, here as everywhere, is a fabulation, the telling of a story, which helps to make sense of who "we" are by reference to a constructed past which recounts how "we" came to be, and our right to be here.

Armstrong, Connor and Smith have all looked at the ways in which modern national identities can be rooted in much older, pre-modern "ethnic" identities (Armstrong 1982; Smith 1986; Connor 1996). (Writers on the Balkans typically assume that we are dealing with "ethnic" nationalism, and use "ethnicity" and "nationality" as complete synonyms.) I insist that it a fundamental mistake to believe that such identities are somehow exempted from the construction process. The notion of the *ethnie* (as opposed to the "nation") seems to refer to something essential and enduring, almost as if it is rooted in a notion of a genetic stock. *Ethnie* carries echoes of "blood" and nature. I insist, however, that *ethnicity is also constructed; it is not an independent warranty of the authenticity of claims to the continuity of "national" identity.*

In the chapter on population movement I have dwelt at some length on the patterns of migration and assimilation which have characterised the Balkan peoples since the earliest times. The notion that it might be possible to find in that region groups of people who can demonstrate unproblematically continuous descent is, against this background, absurd. What we encounter here is a *rhetoric* of ethnicity, which utilises selectively reference to images of pre-modern peoples in order to validate claims in the contemporary world about the relationship between groups, or the link between groups and territory. The historical continuity even of such pre-national *ethnies* can also be shown to be equally fluid.

The general point can be illustrated by reference to the origins of Albanians and Montenegrins, where in the contemporary world the sense of distinction and even opposition between the two peoples is relatively clear and marked. They will trace these differences back to quite different, pre-modern ethnicities, and the implication is that differences of "ethnicity" *then* provide a secure foundation for the differentiation of "nations" (and consequently of states) *now*. The former will insist that their people are the ancestors of the ancient Illyrians. The latter will claim continuity with the Slavs of early mediaeval Duklea and Zeta. The delineation of Albanians from their neighbours historically is, however, a complex task which is hampered rather than aided by these glib responses.[6]

In her fascinating compendium of historical and anthropological material, *Some Tribal Origins, Laws and Customs of the Balkans*, Edith Durham devotes her first chapter to the tribes of Albania and Montenegro (Durham 1928). It is clear from her account that the boundary between the two peoples, and indeed the ways and degrees to which they may have distinguished between themselves, have changed significantly over time. Key factors here have been the shifting balance between religion and language, as well as the imposition of state borders (quite late in the process). The question at issue here is not so much one of determining spatial as *psychological or cultural* boundaries between the two "peoples". In this respect there is evidence that over time various groups have become "Albanicised" or "Slavicised", and have changed their own self-definition and identity.

Relying principally upon oral tradition, Durham tells us that one "Albanian" tribe (Gruda) was reckoned in 1908 to consist of around five hundred "houses", of which roughly 80 traced their descent from a very old indigenous stock, whereas the remainder "said they were immigrants from Hercegovina, and that the Gruda church was built three hundred and eighty years ago, soon after their arrival" (Durham 1928:18-19). This event is linked to the arrival of the Turks in Hercegovina, and the displacement of Roman Catholic families southwards into a region which was then still free from Ottoman control. At the time of Durham's visit Gruda was still a mixture of Muslims and Catholics. Many Slavs of the region were converted to Christianity by missionaries in the Latin tradition. We appear to have here a case of the assimilation of Slavs to a subsequent "Albanian" identity under the influence of their common religious identity.

The process of "Albanisation" is by no means limited to this case. The "Krasniqi" (an "Albanian" tribe traditionally associated with lake Plav) are without doubt "Krasnici", who as a predominantly Muslim Slav tribe had undergone a similar process of assimilation to an Albanian identity as a result of their having a religious allegiance which linked them to Albanians while differentiating them from "Montengrins".

The process of assimilation was not unidirectional, however, and Durham also cites several cases of tribes which considered themselves to be "Montenegrin", yet which had either demonstrable or probable "Albanian" origins. That most characteristically

"Montenegrin" name, Crnojevic she considers as possibly having an Albanian

etymology, as does Voglic. More significantly: "the Piperi and the Vasojevitchi of

Montenegro and the Hoti and the Krasnitchi of Albania all trace descent from a

common ancestor" (Durham 1928: 40, 44 and 45). She also gives a reasonably

detailed account of the manner in which an important section of the (Albanophone and

Catholic) Triepshi in the course of the nineteenth century became Orthodox in religion

and Serbophone, as a consequence of their decision to fight along with their Slav

neighbours against the Turk. They traced their origins to "the Albanian tribe, Berisha,

the oldest in the Northern mountains" (Durham 1928:52).

A crucial factor reducing the fluidity and ambiguity of identities in the region was

the changing complexion of the early Montenegrin state. After 1516 the headship of

the Montenegrin tribes was vested in the *Vladika*, or prince-bishop. This union of

secular power and ecclesiastical authority at the same time placed the headship of the

state above the warring chieftains, and unambiguously identified the embryonic state

with Orthodox Christianity. Throughout the eighteenth century the ambiguities

surrounding Albanian/Montenegrin identity were gradually resolved in ways shaped

in large measure by the relationship of different tribal groups either to the nascent

Montenegrin state or to the Turkish Empire.[7]

National identity is characteristically constructed in a dialectical relationship

between past and present. Even where the names of peoples of unquestionable

antiquity have survived into our own day the relationship between modern peoples

and their origins needs to be scrutinised carefully and critically. Even if we grant that

there is some kind of historical continuity between people who call themselves

"Albanians" and earlier "Illyrians", or in the identity of "Montenegrins", from a sociological point of view this is to postulate some kind of *symbolic* continuity which is interesting and important. The existence of an *ethnie* is thus constructed retrospectively and selectively in relation to symbolic values which are active in the present. It should not be assumed that the processes of historical construction of identities which I have illustrated here are unusual. They are in fact thoroughly typical of *all* of the peoples of the Balkan region, and probably more widely also.[8]

ii) Identities and their constructors

To speak of the construction process implies that we can also identify constructors-- specific groups who have been the primary focus for the formation of national identity. The groups to which this role has fallen in south eastern Europe have varied considerably, and have shifted over time even for specific nationalities. Some aspects of this have received considerable comment in the literature. In particular the importance of the "network of interlocking diasporas" into which the urban mercantile strata were organised within the Ottoman lands has been described (Stoianovich 1960; and 1994:168-176).[9] The part played by the clergy also in the preservation and development of national identity and consciousness has also been studied (Arnakis 1963; Rogel 1977a; Ramet 1989). Contemporary nationalist parties, therefore, can only be considered as the groups which have most recently taken on this role. I offer here two illustrations which have emerged from my own research, and which are of particular contemporary interest. The point has often been made that nationalisms are the product of specific social groups, such as intellectuals or the creators of newly found mercantile or industrial wealth. Generalisation at this level can serve to conceal sociologically and historically important differences. The specific contexts of cultural or class opposition can act to produce rather diverse nationalisms, as the Balkan experience reveals. The "intelligentsia" is a very different group, and functions in rather different ways in Macedonia, Slovenia and Bosnia. The "bourgeoisie" does not play the same part in Dalmatia and Belgrade.

The emergence of a Macedonian nation has been controversial at the level of scholarship as well as that of politics (Poulton 1995). Little attention has been paid, however, to the composition the groups who have been the principal constructors and bearers of this idea. The central figures in the nineteenth century Macedonian autonomist movement were quite disproportionately *teachers*--Hristo Batandziev; Anton Dimitrov; Dame Gruev; Dimitar Miladinov; Gorce Petrov; and Hristo Tatarcev; (Apostolski ed. 1979:123 and 146; also Vishinski ed. 1973). Although trained in the Military Academy, Goce Delcev also worked for a time as a school teacher. Other groups played their part (especially artisans, but also traders and the clergy), but the significance of the teacher is exceptional.

From 1870 onwards, when the Bulgarian Exarchate was established, and with redoubled intensity after the Congress of Berlin deprived Bulgaria of its San Stefano gains, there was intense competition for the identity of Macedonians between Greek and Bulgarian interests. Anticipating that eventually Macedonia would be wrested from Ottoman control, Greeks and Bulgarians vied with each other for ecclesiastical appointments, and opened schools which it was expected would instil national identity along with literacy.[10] The circumstances of the emergence of a struggle for

Macedonian national identity thus led directly to a focus upon *language and literacy*. The position of the school at the forefront of the competition for identities presumably recruited into education those who were most committed to the national struggle, and placed education at a particularly exposed point where it was necessary to declare one's national identity.

In this area there could be little competition from other social groups. As members of ethnic diasporas (often Greek, Jewish or Vlach-*Cincar*) merchants often had little attachment to the region in which they lived, and hence their national consciousness was directed to distant spaces. Teachers (like craftsmen and soldiers) were more often genuine locals, who travelled to receive an education or training along with which they also became acquainted with the idea of national autonomy, but returned. Few had completed a University course, many only the *gimnazija*, and were closer to their own people.

Teachers in Macedonia shared with their counterparts in Slovenia in particular this prominent position in the nationalist movement of the late nineteenth century. In both cases there seems to be a close connection between the role of the educator as a primary constructor of national identity, and the focus upon language and basic literacy as the primary badge of that identity. In each case this role has continued into the later twentieth century. There is a clear contrast with the situation among Bosnian Muslims, for example, for whom there has been a major shift from a mixture of clerics and landlords in the nineteenth century, to secular intelligentsia and functionaries during the Communist period.[11]

During the nineteenth century, then, the South Slav peoples found themselves located at the margins of two collapsing empires, both of which (for different reasons) were ill-suited to manage the demands of modernity. In the first phase of their development as nations the bearers of national consciousness were often the new social classes associated with an urban way of life or the development of a market economy, who pressed for new forms of the state in opposition to the old imperial orders. The bearers of the national idea were linked to the modernisation process, which brought them into direct contact with the bureaucratic interests of the Empire, and the identification of economic power within the Empire with other groups and cultural milieux.

In this respect, the role of the national idea among Dalmatian merchants, faced with not only the spread of Austrian or Hungarian *culture* but more significantly *capital*, in the last quarter of the nineteenth century, is worth commenting upon (Allcock 1989: esp. 11-13). It is difficult to separate the question of the intrusion of foreign capital along the Adriatic from the rise of nationalism in the area. Commercial competition between the Austrian and Hungarian parts of the Dual Monarchy was reflected in the contest for primacy between Trieste and Fiume (Rijeka). Similarly Austrian investment in the Istrian resorts was countered by Magyar enterprise further south. Within this context indigenous Slav interests began to see the need for specifically commercial resistance to both germanisation and magyarisation.

Crikvenica and Vinodolski were initially developed as tourist resorts during the last quarter of the nineteenth century, with indigenous Slav capital, as ripostes to the resorts of Istria. Croatian entrepreneurs sometimes collaborated with Czechs as suitably neutral and authentically Slav partners in such projects. Tourism was taken

up as an issue by the nationalistic press. The variety of tourist societies, associated

with the development of amenity and the beautification of Adriatic municipalities,

acquired a distinctly patriotic overtone.

Certainly within this region local entrepreneurs can be regarded as among the most

significant constructors of national consciousness. The active part played in the

development of a national movement in Dalmatia, by this mercantile group, meant

that the kind of Croatian nationalism which developed in the region differed quite

noticeably from that which emerged in other Croat regions. In particular, Dalmatian

Croats always had a lively sense of South Slav fraternity, and were little impressed by

the classic aristocratic arguments about state right, which had no relevance to their

region.[12]

The specific circumstances of capitalistic development gave a very different

character to the national consciousness of the stratum of Belgrade "merchants artisans

and speculators" known as the *carsija* (Vucinich, in Jelavich and Jelavich eds.

1963:90). Serbia's urban socio-economic elite in the mid-nineteenth century was

based upon an alliance of livestock traders with rentiers whose fortune was founded

on the sale of expropriated Turkish estates, and above all civil servants. The

"opportunistic and unpatriotic" outlook of this group, in which the interests of class

predominated over those of nation, was reflected in the idea of the Serbian state. Their

view of the world, framed by considerations of trade and external security, was

dominated by the interstitial position of the kingdom between the Ottoman Empire

and Austria-Hungary. It is indicative that the attempts of Vuk Karadzic to develop a sense of Serb identity broadly based upon linguistic criteria met with little sympathy from this group.

Bearing in mind the common equation in the Balkans (as elsewhere) between "folk" and "national" culture, it is interesting to comment on the role of "folk" culture in relation to the development of national consciousness and national movements. The "folk" in the sense of the peasantry in the Balkans have never been the primary agents in the creation of national identity, or independent bearers of the national idea. The *idea* of the peasantry has been enormously important as a resource in the construction of national mythologies throughout the entire region. Folk culture has also provided a rich source of material to be worked over in the "imagination of the community" (to which I will return below). Although the peasantry has been taken as the principal guarantor of the "primordial" character of South Slav national identities, they have served this function passively, providing the symbolic resources out of which urban groups have constructed that vision of the primordial origins and entitlements of the nation--a tradition which continues to this day.

Alexandru Dutu has suggested that:

> the unequal diffusion of print culture isolated the village from the modern circulation of ideas. The national states encouraged this tension by connecting higher education to public service and to the rapid development of a complicated bureaucracy which exploited the "uneducated" i.e. the peasants. For the inhabitants of villages a special type of literature was produced: the "popular books" were printed for peasants and children and they offered them the scattered limbs of the "common culture". (Dutu 1997:199-200)

Although his work has centred principally upon Romania, his comments are no less true of the Yugoslav lands.

There is a risk that this emphasis upon the constructors of national identity might reduce the study of nationality to what the philosopher D.M. Mackay once called "nothing buttery" (Mackay 1974: Chap. 4). It is a risk which has attended the sociological study of ideology ever since Marx, that attempts to identify links between ideas and the specific social groups who are their generators and bearers, might end up as little more than a debunking of them as "nothing but" masks for their sectional interests. My intention is much more positive than this.

Certainly the entire approach to nationality in terms of construction tends towards the conclusion that things could have turned out otherwise than they did. The nation could, under different circumstances, have come to be conceptualised differently. Unless we are to resign ourselves to the idea that these processes are entirely mysterious, however, it is important to attend to the historical mechanisms by which nations come to acquire *specific identities*, at *specific times*, and to express these identities under the leadership *of specific social groups*, in *specific cultural forms*.

The dialectics of national identity

Just as at the personal level self can only be comprehended only in relation to significant others, so nationality refers to the sense of identity which groups possess, and depends upon not only the existence of the group, *but also upon its context of significant collective others*. Identity can neither be defined nor function either at the personal or the collective level without reference to others--those who are not like us and from whom we need to distinguish ourselves. In this respect Armstrong has drawn attention to the important part played by symbols of national identity as "border guards" demarcating groups each from the other. The flow of history forms and reforms groups, and brings these into contact with a shifting range of significant others. The creation and disintegration of nations mirrors this irregular flow of mutual self-definitions (Armstrong 1982, building upon Barth 1969).

This emphasis on the dialectical nature of national self-definition is vital in understanding nationality in the Balkans. One can not attempt to understand what it means to be a Slovene, a Croat or a Macedonian without addressing the question of which *relevant boundary* is defined by these expressions of identity. Each has its relevant antithesis. It is important to realise, however, that far from being defined by a permanent and stable set of positive attributes, national identities are changeable responses to sometimes quite novel contextual, negative features.

Opposition (or even antagonism) is not free-floating, and certainly not a "primoridial" social-psychological tendency. Talk of "age-old hatreds" as the basis for contemporary political conflict in the Balkans is sociological nonsense. Where antagonisms do emerge, they are tied intimately to highly specific political processes which bring groups into certain kinds of contact with each other at particular times. In relation to these processes, the concept of the nation and the content of national identity function in different ways in the course of the modernisation process; and the various forms which this dialectic takes are tied intimately to different aspects or dimensions of modernisation. I will illustrate two aspects of this dialectic here,

447

looking first at some aspects of the development of Serb-Croat relations, and then considering the thorny question of "Muslim" ethnogenesis.

i) Serb versus Croat: eternal enmity?

National identity can be conceptualised in relation to different polar identities as a response to the shifting relationship between state and nation. The most dramatic instance of this must be the terms "Serb" and "Croat". Since the inter-war period it has become customary to see these as perpetually linked in conflictual embrace. If one looks back into the nineteenth century, however, affirmations of Serbian or Croatian identity were not typically intended to mark the hostility of these groups to each other. To claim to be a Serb more typically set one off from Turks or Muslims, and subsequently the primary focus of conflict for the Serbian state was the opposition of Austria to its ambitions.

Although Serbia had achieved a measure of independence by 1830 the fact of political independence to some extent concealed the real extent of its backwardness. The development of capitalism in Serbia can be measured in terms of the gradual extension of market relations rather than industrialisation, which was almost non-existent before the Balkan Wars. "Capitalism entered the remote areas by way of pigs in Serbia" (Castellan 1992:344).

It is important to recall the extreme ethnic homogeneity of Serbia as it was then constituted. The extension if its borders before the Balkan Wars was regularly accompanied by the expulsion of "Turks" (McCarthy 1995). Although under Ottoman rule craft guilds had been dominated by Muslims, under Milos Obrenovic attempts were made to Serbianise handicraft production (Petrovich 1976:182-84). The right of Jews to trade in Serbia was abrogated in 1856, although the Congress of Berlin required the abolition of this rule, which had been given constitutional status in 1869 (Stokes 1990:340). Serbia did not incorporate until 1913 any of the regions of significant ethnic difference which were later to acquire such controversial status-- Kosovo, the Sandzak, the Vojvodina, or Macedonia and the Bulgarian "outlands". For the Serbs of Serbia itself there simply was no "Serb/Croat" problem before the creation of the unified "Kingdom of Serbs, Croats and Slovenes" in 1918.

Nationalist accounts of the growth of the Serbian state depict it as an expression of strength in opposition to the "sick man of Europe": but the early Serbia was actually a very weak state the growth of which depended crucially upon the support of external allies and against powerful external enemies. Particularly after the Austro-Hungarian occupation of Bosnia-Hercegovina was formalised as annexation in 1908, and Serbia launched upon its Macedonian adventures as a means of securing a strategic outlet to the sea, Serbian national identity was imagined primarily in dialectical opposition to *external* enemies--the Austrian and the Turk. This externally focussed image of national identity was intensified by the experience of the Balkan Wars and the Great War, which took the nation through the "Golgotha" of the retreat through Albania, to the triumphant "resurrection" of the recovery of Kosovo.

In Croatia throughout most of the nineteenth century, similarly, to identify oneself as Croat was to take a stance in relation to the claims of Magyars or Austrians, not to emphasise one's distinctive identity in relation to Serbs. A problem for Croatian nationalists was the extreme historical diversity of the "Croat lands", which incorporated not only Croatia proper, but Slavonia, Dalmatia and Istria. All had a common problem as areas of Slav settlement within a multi-ethnic empire dominated by Austrians and Magyars, and by Venice, but the precise political circumstances of these regions differed, and consequently the expression of nationalist aspirations varied.

One of the earliest expressions of Croatian nationalism was the "Illyrian" movement of Ljudevit Gaj, inspired by Napoleon's "Illyrian Provinces". This emphasised a generic Slav identity, and is reflected in Gaj's approach to language. Although this has often been represented as focussed upon the common cultural foundations shared by Serbs and Croats, *the principal object of the unifying "Illyrian" idea was the overcoming of the acute regional differences which separated "Croats" from each other* (Gross 1993).

The politics of nationality in the Croat lands was brought into focus first by the replacement of Latin by Magyar as the official language in 1843-4, as an expression of Magyar nationalism. Far from setting off Serb against Croat at this time, the "national" struggle might be seen as bringing them together, as when "Serb" troops from the Military Frontier played a major role in backing *Ban* Jelacic in the suppression of the Magyar revolt of 1848. From the 1840s there was a constant struggle to resist the constitutional encroachment of Hungary on the privileges of the Croatian *Sabor*, if anything intensified by the *Nagodba* of 1868; but this struggle was one in which Serbs and Croats had a common interest.

It was during the 1850s that Ante Starcevic and Eugen Kvaternik launched the Party of Croatian Rights, as the first expression of modern Croatian nationalism, distancing themselves from the Illyrian tradition, and incidentally introducing the idea of a "millennial" Croatian state. In 1898 the banner of "revolutionary nationalism" was unfurled by Josip Frank, when his Pure Party of Rights ("Frankovci") broke away from Starcevic, and promoted for the first time the brand of extreme and aggressive Croat nationalism which was later to reach its apotheosis in the *Ustasa* movement. While it is necessary to acknowledge the place of this tradition within the Croat national movement it is equally important to note its relatively minor significance. Starcevic was always outdistanced in political support by the "Yugoslav" idea of Bishop Josip Strossmayer and the National Party: Frank was never able to challenge the Radic brothers and their Croatian Peasant Party (Irvine 1993: Chap. 1).

Political alliance between Serbs and Croats (often under the banner of "Yugoslavism") was particularly important in Dalmatia, where the urban middle classes combined forces across the confessional divide.

> In Dalmatia the Serbian minority tended to unite with the Croatian majority in one same brand of South Slav nationalism because the history of the province within the Venetian context had weakened the separate traditions of the Croatian and of the Serbian states, because both Croats and Serbs had to assert in common their Slavism against the continued economic predominance of the Italian urban element, and because ethnic divisions did not entirely coincide with religious divisions. Dalmatia was the only region with a substantial number of Catholic Serbs. (Pavlowitch 1971:46)

A separate Serb party did not appear in Dalmatia until 1879 (Gross 1993).

Following Austrian occupation of Bosnia-Hercegovina in 1878 things took a different turn. The occupation of Bosnia-Hercegovina was carried out largely with Croatian troops (Eterovich and Spalatin 1970:51). Starcevic and the Croatian extreme nationalists saw the occupation in the longer term as a possibility of creating a "Great Croatia", incorporating the province into a future Croatian state. The Austrians played off Serbs against Croats within Bosnia, and also promoted divisions between these Christian groups and local Serbo-Croat speaking Muslims, as a means of bolstering their own authority. Similarly, in Slavonia the movement to change the status of the Military Frontier (eventually abolished in 1881) was the subject of manipulation of this kind, and resulted sometimes in growing mutual hostility. The response, however, was often to increase Serb-Croat co-operation.

It is really only in a united Yugoslavia that Serb and Croat came to be defined as mutually antagonistic groups. This antagonism emerged primarily from the fact that two quite contrasting traditions of the state were brought into conflict with each other within the newly unified state. Although not exhausted by this issue, the range of politics within inter-war Yugoslavia certainly came to be dominated by Serb-Croat relations. Even within this context, however, it was by no means always the case that all Serbs saw eye to eye, as *precani* (Serbs from West of the Drina) brought with them a different experience and cultural tradition from those of the Serbs of the Serbian kingdom, and these differences of outlook were reflected throughout the period of the "First Yugoslavia" in the opposition between Radicals and Democrats in the representation of Serb political opinion (Banac 1984).

The experience of the Second World War, of course, took and intensified these possibilities. Croatian *Ustasa* and Serbian royalists fought against the Yugoslav ideal for their own reasons, and especially in Bosnia-Hercegovina each saw the other as the principal domestic obstacle to the achievement of their goals.[13]

The disintegration of Yugoslavia into national states has not terminated this oppositional framing of ethnicity, although it has refocussed it. Now the focus of opposition has switched in part to *minorities* within Croatia and Serbia, and their dubious presumed loyalty to the national state (especially Serbs within Croatia, and Albanians within Serbia).[14] Curiously, in the case of Serbia, external hostility during the break-up of the Yugoslav federation found its focus as much in Slovenia (an ally throughout the period of the First Yugoslavia) as in Croatia. This is reflected both in the foiled "Meeting of Truth" which Serbs from Serbia proposed to hold in Ljubljana in December 1989, and the subsequent mutual economic boycott of 1990-91.

At each stage of this process the significance of "Serb" and "Croat" identities, the extent and character of their mutual or dialectical relevance, have been conditioned and framed by the framework of state and inter-state structures within which they have been brought together.

ii) Changing "Muslim" identity and the modernisation process

The second way in which identity can be shown to be defined dialectically or oppositionally is *in relation to the modernisation process itself*. These oppositions are of general interest in relation to the study of nationality: indeed, for some commentators the idea of the nation is the quintessential badge of modernity.[15]

Typically certain groups come to be identified either as the bearers of modernity, or as exemplifying backwardness, traditionalism and the retardation of the progress which one wishes for one's own nation. The dialectic of conflicting national identities is shaped by these perceptions. This is been an important aspect of the process of nation formation among the South Slavs. I shall illustrate the issue by reference to the changing definition of "Muslims".

The entrenched "orientalism" of western European and North American observers tends to align their perceptions with the predeliction of many Balkan peoples to identify Islam with backwardness. The Ottoman period is almost invariably construed, in a tradition founded in the emerging nationalist historiographies of the nineteenth century, as "five hundred years of Turkish night". In fact, the axis of opposition "Muslim/non-Muslim" has had an extremely variable significance across Balkan history, sometimes identifying Islam with civilisation, cultural advancement or even modernity rather than with backwardness and traditionalism.

The arrival of the Ottoman armies on the Balkan Peninsula may have begun as a recursion of the old European theme of the invading Asiatic hordes. Nevertheless, the social organisation and culture of those who fell to their conquest (with the exception of Byzantium itself) laid tenuous claim to the term "civilisation". The Empire of Dusan "The Mighty" had already disintegrated by the time of the Battle of Kosovo. The Ottoman state remained one of the great powers of Europe certainly until the end of the seventeenth century (Crete fell under Turkish rule only in 1669). Under the Sultans, Islam represented not only military might, but also wealth, status and civility.[16]

The transition of "Turk" to the mark of degradation and backwardness only begins

during the later eighteenth century.[17] The real process of demonisation gets under way

in the nineteenth century, and coincides with the period of the creation of new national

bourgeoisies, intent upon the building of new national states, and establishing their

own cultural credentials by setting up the "Turk" as the symbol of alterity. In this task,

of course, they were aided and abetted more than willingly by western Europeans,

whose colonial ambitions by this time also brought them into conflict with the Porte.

The association of all that is Turkish with backwardness (the antithesis of modernity)

was intensified during the First Yugoslavia. Ironically, the faults for which the

Karadjordjevic regime have been subsequently castigated in large measure boil down

in the end to its rather botched commitment to modernisation, which rode rough-shod

over a wide range of entrenched traditionalisms including that of the Croatian Peasant

Party.[18]

The major political voice of Muslims throughout this period was the *Jugoslavenska*

muslimanska organizacija (*JMO*), which in spite of its consistent commitment to

Yugoslavism could be seen as confirming the link between traditionalism and Islam.

Its platform declared its support not only for the equality of treatment of the three

principal faiths of the country (and the constitutional integrity of Bosnia-Hercegovina)

but the defence of Muslim educational institutions and the continuing authority of the

sharia courts. The price of its agreement to participation in ruling coalitions was

amelioration of the impact of the Land Reform programme, which threatened in

particular the smaller Muslim landlord. (Purivatra 1974: see esp. pp. 596-599 and

605-609.)

Curiously, it is under the Communists, with their initially very aggressive commitment to secularism, that Islam begins to change its association with backwardness. After 1945 the complexities of the ethnic settlement in Bosnia and Hercegovina gradually compelled the abandonment of the initial attempt to subsume Muslims as "indeterminate Yugoslavs" (*Jugosloveni neopredeljeni*), and eventually resort to the device of declaring the existence of a Muslim "nation" (*Muslimani u smislu narodnosti*).[19]

The policy was ambivalent, and difficult to sustain, as events have shown since the disintegration of the federation. Nevertheless, by divorcing Islam in its more narrowly confessional sense from the idea that it is possible to be the legatee of a diffuse cultural tradition which is neither Serb (Orthodox) nor Croat (Catholic), Muslims were given a special stake in the republic. The political wisdom of this move is that it managed for several decades to remove the Muslim population from Serb/Croat rivalry over their "true" identity. While underplaying "clericalism", therefore, the League of Communists actively promoted a "Muslim" identity. Under its auspices, thousands of people were able to secure privilege as the official embodiment of this order, especially academics, intellectuals and functionaries. To declare oneself a Muslim became not only the key to personal advancement, but also the symbol of the cultural modernisation of Bosnia and Hercegovina. Paradoxically, "Muslim" identity was promoted by an overtly atheist regime, and as a counter to religious traditionalism. Specifically *confessional* identities of all kinds were tarred with the brush of nationalism and traditionalism, but these "Muslims" bore their badge of identity in the *national* sense.[20]

Although the situation has become more controversial since the break-up of Yugoslavia, the same lines of distinction can be traced. Both Serb and Croat party leaderships have attempted to mobilise their own ethnic groups against the Bosnian state by recourse to images of Islam as ultra-traditional--references to *mujaheddin*, the waging of a *jihad* against the Christian West, and so on (Sells 1996; Mojzes 1994). Even within the Muslim camp there have been those who have fought against the secularisation of Islamic identity, and who have called for a return to the theologically grounded understanding of Islam as the *umma* of all the faithful, rejecting secularised notions of a "European Islam". Nevertheless, a strong voice still argues for the acknowledgement of a *Bosnjak* identity, closely entwined with the Muslim inheritance of the region, though not submerged by it. This has advanced the cause of a multi-ethnic Bosnia which could stand as almost the sole representative of the European idea of a state based upon civic rather than ethnic identity. Islam, in this guise, once again, finds itself allied at least in part with the forces of modernisation against ethnic traditionalism.

The nation as an "imagined community"

One of the most influential of recent approaches to nationality is that of Benedict Anderson, who writes of nations as "imagined communities" (Anderson 1991). We need to make sense of the utility of Anderson's idea in relation to Pierre Bourdieu's concept of "symbolic capital" (Bourdieu 1977; Jenkins 1992). Identities are important as symbolic resources which permit the mobilisation and co-ordination of those who are interpellated by them.[22] Print is important as a medium through which the sharing in the imagined community became possible in the late eighteenth and nineteenth centuries. (Today also radio and possibly more importantly TV play the same role.) We need to address the question not only of the medium through which the imagined community is constructed, but also *what is the symbolic stock upon which the imagination does its work*. Here Anderson is rather less instructive, although he does deal *en passant* with maps, museums, demographic statistics, and above all with language.

A study of the Yugoslav area provides us with ample opportunity to look at the diversity of symbolic resources which are available for utilisation in the imagination of the nation. In the case of Croatia one might consider the role of law, or recent attempts to invent a Croatian language. The factor of language would also be important in relation to ethnogenesis in Slovenia and Macedonia. Religion has clearly been generally significant throughout the Balkans. In order to illustrate the diversity of this aspect of the development of national identity, however, I will draw attention to a rather neglected factor, that of *space*, or more particularly of landscape.[23]

Often it is not the community itself which is directly imagined, but it is *indirectly* called to mind by things which could be said to constitute metonymic representations of it. The map as a representation of national territory can function in this way, as a kind of "logo" for the nation (Anderson 1991:174-75). Anderson's work clearly abuts onto that of Edward Said in that his attention rests upon the role of the former imperial powers as the drafters of such maps, bestowing spatial identities upon their former colonies (Said 1978). As with Said's "orient", the role of external powers in constructing identity in the Balkans has often been of central importance. My

concerns differ from those of Said and Anderson, however, in two important respects.

In the first place, the frame which organises their efforts is pre-eminently *political*: it

has to do with the asymmetries of power which in one way or another privilege the

representations of one group over others. It can be read as an extension and

elaboration of the discussion about "hegemony" which goes back to Gramsci, and

which is developed in Pierre Bourdieu's concept of "symbolic violence" (Bourdieu

1977:190-7; J.B. Thompson 1984: Chap. 2; Jenkins 1992:104-10). Put at its simplest,

it has to do with the ways in which the discourses of the powerful (the West, colonial

powers) are effective in determining the discourses, and hence the self-consciousness,

of those who are subjected to their power. As a consequence they tend to marginalise

those cultural materials which are available to "peripheral" peoples which might serve

as resources for their own *self*-construction and *self*-imagination.

In the second place, these studies are insufficiently sensitive to the general point

upon which Giddens insists, that it is necessary to consider the interweaving of time

and space (Giddens 1979:201-206). A central idea which I argue here is that the

symbolic freight of space (that which is actually *signified* by references to space in

their relation to national identity) is intimately interwoven with the consciousness of

history of the people in question. Spaces are *significant* spaces: and the significances

with which they are endowed are to be understood in terms of the historical narratives

which link people to territory or places.[24]

The commonplace link between contemporary nationalisms and the retrospective

identification of national territory with the great mediaeval Empires, where each at its maximum extension symbolised a golden age of greatness, and delineated an ideal national territory. My point is different, in that the various constituent parts of the former Yugoslav federation offer a superb range of *different ways of conceptualising symbolically the spaces within which they see themselves as belonging*, and in relation to which they have come to define themselves over time. The manner in which space functions in relation to the imagination of a national community varies considerably, interacting with variables such as political or cultural experience, and religious or linguistic distinctiveness, in the creation of the nation. It is important to note in this respect that I distinguish here the *symbolic space* in relation to which the nation is imagined from *the territory which is appropriated by the state*, as these may differ considerably.

The crystallisation of Montenegrin identity can be said to have come about in significant measure in relation to *landscape*. The story of the unstinting heroism of this "smallest among peoples", whose resistance beat back "the swarm of Turkish Islam for five hundred years", moved Alfred Lord Tennyson to salute "Great Tzernagora!". This history of resistance against the Turk is partly conceptualised in terms of landscape--its inhospitable character. Two items of folk wisdom are worth recording here which underline this point.

A Montenegrin account of the Creation tells how, when he made the world, God found at the end of his labours that he was left with a bag of unused stones. The place where these were tipped is Montenegro. A common explanation given of the failure of the Ottoman forces to subjugate the mountain tribes of the area is that in such a land "a small army is beaten, a large one dies of starvation".

These folk sayings contain more than a mere commentary on the barrenness of the land. Three important ideas are held together here. The landscape is desperately inhospitable: but its condition on the one hand is linked to the Divine will, and on the other provides the essential condition for the freedom of Montenegro. The importance of this configuration of images emerges clearly from the great literary masterpiece of Montenegrin poetry, the *Mountain Wreath* of Petar Petrovic Njegos, the nineteenth century *vladika* (prince-bishop). Two main subjects run throughout his poetry (according to J.W. Wiles) "the fight for freedom and man's relation to God" (Wiles 1930). These key themes are held in relation to each other by "our Rock"--not only a reference to Mount Lovcen in its context, but coming from an Orthodox bishop must also be intended to bear a theological reading.

Although the territorial core around which the Montenegrin state grew was originally tiny (no more than the Katunska *nahija*) this identification between national character, national destiny and landscape has remained an important component of the self-definition in the imagination of the community. Whereas there remain huge areas of ambiguity surrounding Montenegrin identity, especially concerning the thorny question of the relationship between Montenegrin and Serb, this essentially spatial imagery remains at the heart of any attempt to symbolise their differences. Landscape offers a resource without which it has become impossible to imagine Montenegro.

The enduring association between Montenegro and its landscape contrasts sharply with the shifting focus of spatial identity in Slovenia. The lack of a significant mediaeval state to which Slovenes can trace the primordial ancestry of their state, and the steady contraction of the area over which Slovene speakers have been dispersed, has left no very clear notion of the limits of the space which "naturally" demarcates Slovenia. Nevertheless, images of landscape have provided key metonymic points of reference for the imagination of the Slovene nation. Curiously, however, these have shifted over time.

In the seventeenth and eighteenth centuries the Slovenes were known especially to the outside world through the karst regions of the country's south-west. If the Slovene lands were known to the outside world at all in this period it was for the geomorphic and cultural oddities of Crknicko Jezero, and not for Triglav (Carmichael 1993). The arrival of the railways did little to change this. The first line to be opened, between 1846 and 1850, was the link between Vienna and Austria's major port, Trieste, via Ljubljana, Celje, Maribor and Graz (Naval Intelligence Division 1944: Vol.III, 417). This East-West axis of communication was confirmed a decade later by the construction of the line to Budapest, via Ptuj, and the Zagreb-Ljubljana line in 1862. Economic development, and consequently population, tended to concentrate along these axes. Consequently, the Alpine region was relatively under-populated, poor and aside from the main lines of communication, until the rail link Villach-Kranj-Ljubljana was opened, associated with the development of steel-working at Jesenice after 1891.

Slovenes themselves were relatively indifferent to interest or the significance of their mountains. Even Alpine exploration to a large extent was largely carried on under the auspices of the Austro-German Alpine Association (*DÖAV*). The leading figure in this endeavour, Dr. Julius Kugy (1858-1944) was an Austrian from Trieste (Kugy 1934; see also Collomb 1978; Triglavski narodni park, 1985:129-36).

The discovery of the Julian Alps as a primary symbol of Slovene identity only begins in the twentieth century. A primary impetus for this change of spatial focus has been the experience of Slovenia within Yugoslavia. The Alpine region was a significant focus of conflict during the First World War, although the Isonzo front involved the struggle between Italy and Austria. The end of the war placed the border through the middle of the Julians, following the line of the watershed, leaving the Trenta and Soca valleys in Italy and dividing the major populations of Slovene speakers. This situation was largely rectified after 1945, but left Trieste as a continuing bone of contention. The disputed border with Austria also focussed attention on the Julian region, when the Klagenfurt referendum of October 1920 resulted in the separation of Slovene from Slovene along the Karawanken ridge. (Useful maps covering these issues are to be found in Naval Intelligence Division 1944: Vol. II, 150-1.)

The significance of the Alps was further heightened by the fact that it was in and around the Karawanken that the *partizan* movement was most effectively established after 1941 (Barker 1990). Consequently, in post-1945 Yugoslavia the Julian region came to occupy the foreground in the picture of the struggle for Slovene unity and identity as well as the defence of the borders of Yugoslavia.

As relations soured between Slovenia and the other republics of Yugoslavia, culminating in the declaration of independence in July 1991, the Alps came to serve quite another symbolic purpose. As Yugoslavia's only alpine region, the mountains served to identify Slovenia's difference from the other South Slav peoples, and its community with other (advanced, democratic, and above all European) alpine countries to the north—in spite of the fact that only a fifth of the republic has a truly alpine character. The new slogan of the Slovene tourist industry said it all: "Slovenia: the sunny side of the Alps".

Croatians have an exceptionally problematic and confused imagination with respect to the relationship between space and the nation. A mediaeval kingdom reached its maximum extension under Zvonimir, who died in 1089. His realm is interesting in that it both included territories which were subsequently dissociated from "Croatia", and excluded others to which Croats have subsequently become deeply attached. (See Darby *et al.* 1966:26)[25] Areas of Bosnia and Hercegovina fell under the control of Tvrtko (ruled 1353-91), and were later conquered by the Ottoman Sultans, to be united with a Croatian state again only during the brief and ignominious interval of the *Nezavisna drzava Hrvatska* (1941-45). Zvonimir's kingdom lacked most of Istria, eastern Slavonia and "Syrmia" (Srijem), and Dalmatia south of the Neretva estuary.

With the death of Zvonimir and the subsequent dismemberment of his kingdom began a historical divergence in the experience of its parts. This divergence was even more marked after the Ottoman invasion, which reached its maximum extent after the Magyar defeat at Mohacz in 1526. Although Croatian historians have always insisted upon the continuity of a Croatian political entity, even if only as the *reliquiae reliquiarum* (the relic of the relics), the former "Croatian lands" embarked upon quite different historical trajectories. Istria and Dalmatia were attached primarily to Venice; the Ragusan Republic sustained an independent existence until its destruction by Napoleon; "Syrmia" was simply incorporated into Hungary. The question of the status of Croatia was complicated further from the end of the seventeenth century, during the revival of Habsburg fortunes against the Ottomans, by the creation of the Military

Frontier, which owed direct allegiance to Vienna although "civil Croatia" through its

Ban and *Sabor* was attached to the Hungarian crown.

Spatial claims figure centrally in discourse about Croatian statehood; and it is not by

accident that the publication of two Atlases took place with great *eclat* shortly after

the declaration of independence of the Republic. Both of these imply fairly directly

that the internationally agreed borders of that republic are far more conservatively

drawn than should be the case, aspiring not only to most if not all of Bosnia-

Hercegovina and the Vojvodina (Klemencic 1993; JAZU 1993; also Boban 1992 and

Beljo ed. 1993). The *variety* of these maps is more striking than their agreement.

There is a deep ambiguity surrounding the definition of just what does constitute the

historical "Croatian lands", which does not depend upon the nationalist claims of

Starcevic and his vision of a "Greater Croatia" extending from the Alps to Bulgaria

and from the Danube to Albania.

As there is no clear sense of just what is meant by "Croatia" in a spatial sense,

therefore, discourse about the nation and its embodiment in a state tends to allow

these ambiguities to rest, and appeal has been directed instead to *the law* as providing

a far more secure foundation. This is spelled out with extreme clarity (if in a

historically tendentious manner) in the preamble to the Croatian constitution

(Constitution of the Republic of Croatia 1991:29-31). One of the strongest elements of

the tradition of Croat nationalism has been that of "state right"—the continuity of the

juridical foundations of the state across an apparently discontinuous series of political

entities. This makes it possible to avoid direct encounter with the potentially embarrassing question of just what was the spatial reference of any of these "Croatias".[26]

Possibly the most generally cited but completely misunderstood of the uses of space in relation to the imagination of the South Slav nations has been the idea of "Great Serbia". It has become commonplace to present this is if there has been an agreed, explicit and consistent conception of the ideal territorial extension of a Serbian state. Many commentators on the "Wars of the Yugoslav Succession" have tended to explain these in large measure as the consequence of a wholly self-conscious attempt to implement this grand design (Beljo *et al.* 1993:23-26). Indeed the version of this interpretation of events which is favoured in Croatian circles traces a direct lineal descent between the first adumbration of this scheme by Ilija Garasanin, in 1844, and the 1986 Memorandum of the Serbian Academy, *Polozaj Srbije i srpskog naroda*.[27] This vision of a consistently conceived ideal space which defines "Serbia" constitutes a severe distortion of history.[28]

In 1844 Ilija Garasanin, Minister of the Interior to the restored Karadjordjevic dynasty (the Obrenovices were deposed in 1842) prepared a long memorandum outlining the principles upon which he believed the foreign policy of the state should be based. The document, known as the *Necertanje* ("outline", or "draft") has been widely interpreted as a vision of a "Greater Serbia", and as such as the first manifesto of an aggressive Serb nationalism. The document will not bear this interpretation. Garasanin offers us a piece of unashamed *Realpolitik*, in which he advances his own credentials with his Prince (the allusion to Machiavelli is deliberate) by espousing a

foreign policy which directly contradicts the pro-Austrian stance of the disgraced
Obrenovic regime.

The starting point of the *Nacertanje* is the conviction that the days of the Turkish
Empire are numbered, and that the most important forces making for this end are
Austria and Russia. The primary problem for Serbia is posed by its relationship to
Austria, in that the Habsburgs have a stranglehold on Serbia's trade, at that time
directed predominantly through Zemun. The alternative is to create a new outlet to the
Adriatic, with Serbian control of the Adriatic ports between the Gulf of Kotor and
Durres.

This thrust to the south-west was motivated primarily by economic and political
considerations. While recognising the value of the creation of a Serbian consciousness
in the Orthodox populations in the region as a means towards his end, this document
does not convey a blindly chauvinistic nationalism, but is a clearly enunciated and
hard-headed piece of political-economic analysis, identifying the perceived needs of
the state.

Three features at least separate the conception of Serbia represented here from any
notion of a consistent Serb spatial vision continuous with that which has prevailed in
Serb nationalist circles during the break-up of Yugoslavia. Garasanin was a servant of
the Karadjordjevic dynasty, whose foreign policy orientation was somewhat different
from that of their Obrenovic rivals. It is difficult to trace a consistent policy
throughout the nineteenth century which could be said to simply reflect his argument.
Indeed, historical investigation suggests that Garasanin's document did not become
primarily significant until the inter-war years, in the hands of Croat critics of Serb

hegemony within the unified South Slav state. The link between his plan and Serbian foreign policy has been heavily overdrawn.[29]

Secondly, the direction of his proposed expansion lay through eastern Hercegovina, Montenegro and northern Albania, bounded largely by the Drina and the Drin. This is a radically different line of advance from that which preoccupied Serbian foreign policy between the Congress of Berlin and 1918, during which period Austrian occupancy of Bosnia-Hercegovina compelled a turning to the *South*, through Macedonia towards Salonika—a prospect to which Garasanin was relatively indifferent.

In its third phase the Serbian spatial imagination has been preoccupied with the position of the Serb diaspora in Bosnia and Croatia, particularly under the shadow of the experience of the Second World War. This was reflected during the break-up of Yugoslavia in the attempt to set up the Bosnian and Croatian *krajine* as states associated with Serbia. On this occasion the problem of defining a specifically Serb state was posed by the constitutional history of the Yugoslav federation, and its ideological counter-position of "nations" and "nationalities". Its territorial reference was defined primarily in relation to the dispersion of Serb minorities in other republics, and by the specific circumstances of inter-republican conflict leading to Yugoslavia's disintegration. If a "Serbian" outlet to the sea was envisaged in this phase it appears to have been contemplated principally along the coast between Karlobag and Sibenik—an area which had no significance at all for Garasanin.[30]

There has been no consistent vision of a "Greater Serbia" defined in concrete spatial terms, although it different times there have been different visions of the enlargement of the Serbian state to meet the strategic needs of the Serbian state or to encompass

one part or another of the large Serb diaspora. The "Greater Serbia" which

preoccupies the Serb imagination is, on the whole, a *metaphysical* space defined by

points of symbolic reference such as Kosovo and the monasteries of the Fruska Gora.

It is not for nothing that Serbs designate themselves as *nebeski narod* (a heavenly

people). "Serbia" is imagined primarily *not* as a stable and continuous physical space,

but as a rather abstract metaphysical entity, symbolised and evoked by *places* and by

the idea of shared experiences which these evoke. The affirmation that "wherever

there is a Serbian grave, there is Serbia" (*Gde je sahranjen Srbin, tude je Srbija*)

implies both that Serbia might be anywhere--or nowhere except in Heaven.[31] Because

srpstvo (Serbdom) is an idea, therefore, rather than a concrete space, the actual space

within which a Serbian state is eventually confined has no natural or necessary

boundaries. This does make it possible for populist demagogues to mobilise Serbs in

pursuit of projects of expansion, as in the years 1991-95. It also tends to reduce the

actual definition in practice of "Serbia" to a matter of force of arms--whatever can be

defended--as more common means of defining the national territory (such as

ethnography, language or law) are set aside.

Conclusion: nationhood and the future of the South Slav peoples

At the start of this chapter I indicated that the ideas of "nation" and "national

consciousness" actually cover a diversity of phenomena. It is clear that in some senses

the disintegration of Yugoslavia has been bound up with these, although I do not believe that it can be explained solely by reference to them. An understanding of the diversity of ways in which nations come into being and come to be aware of themselves is very useful in illuminating the fate of Yugoslavia. Reciprocally, however, an understanding of developments in Yugoslavia is of considerable value in giving us a deep appreciation of the differential ways in which nation and national consciousness can figure in general in the processes of political modernisation. I want to bring out the significance of this diversity in relation to Yugoslavia by making three brief points of comparative reference which emerge from the chapter.

Some of Yugoslavia's nations are better placed than others in relation to the process of modernisation. By this I do not have in mind the commonplace notion of the presumed greater *economic advancement* of some regions as opposed to others (discussed in earlier chapters of this book). Regions can also be compared in terms of the degree of congruence between their experiences of nation-formation and the cultural exigencies of the modernisation process.

Slovenia is the most obvious candidate in this respect, although not the only one. The Slovenes are not burdened by the pursuit of a state based upon the illusory boundaries of a past empire which supposedly defines their primordial title to territory or greatness. They do not construct themselves, and neither are they constructed by others, in relation to historical images which stand in a contradictory relationship to their contemporary experience. Slovene national consciousness is rooted in large measure in a language which is sufficiently different from Serb-Croat to remove it from contention on the part of other South Slavs. The structural attributes and geographical range of that language are not (with minor exceptions) a matter of dispute in relation to others. Their isolation by language from the other South Slavs is given symbolic expression in the use of landscape. They have been able to relinquish their former identification with the karst areas. This is a landscape which they not only share with other South Slav peoples, but which is redolent with the imagery of a kind of ethnographic museum. They have sought to replace this with an "alpine" mythology, which projects the Slovene people symbolically into Central Europe rather than the Balkans.

At the other end of the scale are Serbs and Croats, who seem to have the worst of all possible worlds. Lacking clear linguistic identity, and an ambiguous attachment to space, they are equally burdened by historical mythologies in terms of which they define themselves in relation to others. Defining themselves in relation to a past cannot satisfy their inner needs for solidarity. In the case of the Croats, too many of their own people, and too much of their experience, lies outside of those ill-defined spatial parameters. In the case of the Serbs, historical definitions of their "proper" space necessarily bring them permanently into conflict with their neighbours, in one way or another. In each case, the materials out of which they have come to construct identity give them no help in orienting themselves in the modern world.

The alternative is to fall back upon religion. This too has become backward looking. Croatian Catholicism cannot serve as it has in Poland, as the symbolic core of a nation defined in terms of resistance to Communism. In as much as it can be said to have had such a history, it is too compromised with elements of anti-modernity, above all its ambiguous association with fascism during the Second World War. To place Catholicism in the foreground of Croat identity also places Croats in a difficult situation in Bosnia-Hercegovina, where they are acutely divided between the pietistic insularity of rural Hercegovina and the urbane ecumenism of Sarajevo. The one leads them in the direction of a full-blown "Greater Croatian" romanticism, and the other towards an acceptance of a multi-ethnic secular state. The Serbian Orthodox Church has never seriously addressed the issue of coming to terms with modernity. The break-up of Yugoslavia has mired it, possibly irretrievably, in traditionalism.

For both Serbs and Croats, therefore, their attempts to build national communities will continue to constitute a barrier to their accession to modernity, closing them in upon themselves them in a world which increasingly demands openness. In this respect the ambiguities of their identification with space constitute a source of embarrassment rather than a positive resource.

Between these extreme cases can be placed the interesting intermediate cases of the Bosnjaks, Montenegrins ands Macedonians, together with Kosovar Albanians.[32] They are in many respects rather unlike cases. In all of these cases, however, the manner in which national consciousness has developed elicits no direct contradiction with modernity, and the fostering of *certain forms* of national consciousness with the materials at their disposal could actually, under favourable circumstances, be expected to foster it. The obstacles to their incorporation into the modernisation process, however, are found in their common situation, as small countries, heavily dependent by virtue of their situation upon more powerful neighbours who regard the development of their separate identities in a hostile fashion, and indeed question in some respect the legitimacy of their existence as nations.

In conclusion it is interesting to note the arresting observation of Catherine Lutard, that "the present explains the past (rather than its deterministic inverse)" (Lutard 1996:133). This might seem to be an odd view to be articulated in a work of historical sociology. It is essential, nevertheless, to the view which I take of the importance of nationalism in Yugoslavia. The point of the emphasis upon the diversity and fluidity of the forms of national consciousness among the South Slavs is to prepare the ground for the belief that these processes continue in the present. Nations are constantly being constructed and reconstructed. Like Walter Benjamin's Angel of History, the nation also flies into the future, but facing towards the past (   ). The past is constantly being rewritten, but in the light of ever new contexts. It is far from being the case that an irreducible national spirit, ideal or identity emerges progressively in history, resisting attempts to suppress it, asserting itself eventually despite the denials of communist cosmopolitanism. The nation is constantly reinventing itself, with shameful indifference to its own past, spinning an ever-new thread of narrative from the stuff of mythologised history. My view is strongly critical of that of Walker Connor (Connor 1994). I agree with his insistence upon the cultural and psychological nature of the nation, and the folly of overlooking the power of the struggle to make and sustain identities as a factor in politics. This does not mean that we are trapped in a world in which the political script is already written for us, inscribed in blood upon the walls of the past. In politics we make our future: and the remarkable thing about the imagined community of the nation is its aptitude for constant reinvention, as a *bricoleur* working and reworking the myths of its own past.

Notes

1. Steven Burg, for example, refers to Yugoslavia's "descent into atavistic ethnic violence" (Burg 1993:357). See also Mestrovic 1993, 1993a, 1993b and 1994. This view is more characteristic of lay than of academic sources.

2. See for example Sekelj 1993; Denitch 1994; Akhavan and Howse eds. 1995; Woodward 1995;

3. The concept of "primordialism" goes back to Shils (1957), and has been developed in Geertz (1973), Armstrong (1982), Connor (in several articles collected in 1994), and above all by Smith (esp. 1986). The emphasis upon the modernity of the nation, and its "instrumental" link to the ideology of specific classes, dates back in sociology to Deutsch and Folz (1966), although its most influential exponent has been Gellner (1964 Chap. 7 and 1983). See also Hobsbawm and Ranger (1983). In many respects, of course, the roots of these ideas are far older, and can be traced to the Enlightenment and to Romanticism.

4. The "constructivist" approach grows out of the work of Peter Berger and Thomas Luckmann (1967: esp194-200). They argue that knowledge is a constructed element in the social process. identity, within his framework, is that knowledge which we possess about ourselves, and can be regarded as the result of a dialectical process of social construction on a par with any other kind of knowledge. They shift the burden of analysis from the level of epistemology (the nature of knowledge) to that of pragmatics (what *passes for knowledge* in society). By the same token I am interested in what passes for identity in general, and national identity in particular.

5. For a straightforwardly nationalistic account of the battle, which obfuscates entirely the role of Marko, see Petrovitch 1915:58-62. (Also Laffan 1918: 21.) Although the Bosnian king Tvtko was an important participant in the action it is curious how frequently his role is down-played, especially since mentions of Croat and Hungarian contingents on the "Serb" side are probably best accounted for as his

vassals. References to Bulgarian participation are interesting, since *both* sides claim Bulgarian support. This ceases to be mysterious once one realises that feudal leaders who identified themselves as "Bulgarian" may well have fought on each side. I am taken by the humorous observation of Colin Imber. "The incidents surrounding (the Battle of) Kosovo and the succeeding years seem to be, *are*, extremely obscure. Only Serbian historians know *exactly* what happened: nobody else." (Paper delivered to the conference on "The Encounter between Islam and Christianity in South Eastern Europe", Fitzwilliam College, Cambridge, April 1997.) I recommend to the reader the recent treatment of these issues in Malcolm 1998:Chap. 4, although this reached by attention too late to be incorporated systematically into my own discussion.

6. Valuable work has been done demystifying some aspects of this topic by Wilkes 1992.

7. A precisely similar development in all probability can be traced, in which the boundary between Slav and Albanian identities in Kosovo has been similarly fluid (with the added complication of the interposition of the Vlahs). Some aspects of this issue are treated in an excellent review in Malcolm 1998: Chap. 2.

8. Malcolm, Fine and others have recently gone to great pains to demonstrate the antiquity of a distinctive Bosnian identity. Whereas they have offered us some impressive scholarship which is by no means without value, their efforts are in many respects beside the point when it comes to a discussion of the existence of a Bosnian "nation". They certainly do not contribute to a demonstration of the antiquity of the *nation*; but they do contribute a great deal to the contemporary process of its retrospective, symbolic construction at a time when the legitimation of a Bosnian *state* is fundamentally contested. (See Malcolm 1994; Donia and Fine 1994; Pinson 1994.) Recent attempts also by Macedonians to demonstrate the primordiality of a distinctive Macedonian identity also, of course, fall under this criticism.

9. The apt phrase quoted here is from a lecture by Paschalis Kitromilides, "Orthodoxy and collective identity in the 18th. century Balkans", St. Antony's College, Oxford, 31 May 1993.

10. The Serbian intervention in the competition for Macedonia began rather later, and never achieved the scale of either Greek or Bulgarian efforts.

11. The JMO was always a landlords' party. See Banac 1984; Purivatra 1974..

12. It is interesting to note in this respect the composition of the Yugoslav Committee, during the First World War, which contained a disproportionately large number of Dalmatians. Pavlowitch 1915:11-12; Jankovic and Krizman 1964:11.

13. To reduce the 1941-45 struggles to their ethnic dimension, however, would be to distort their character considerably. Above all it is necessary to give adequate place to the fact that Serbs and Croats were themselves divided along political lines. Croats fought both for the *NDH* and for the Communists: Serbs for Nedic, Mihailovic or Tito.

14. There is a curious asymmetry about the nation that Serbs and Croats "hate each other". Whereas it is true that Serbs have in recent times become the negative pole against which Croatian nationalism defines itself, for Serbs this role is much more likely to be played by Muslims or Albanians—reduced indiscriminately once again to "Turks", *balija* or *siptari*.

15. See esp. Kedourie 1960 and Gellner 1983. For reviews of the literature in this respect see Smith 1983 and Hutchinson and Smith 1994.

16. Although the *devsirme* (the infamous "tax on children") has been portrayed as the most burdensome and barbaric of oppressions, it clearly opened the door to the advancement of subject peoples, and parents are known to have sought this avenue for the preferment of their own children.

17. *Opposition* does not necessarily indicate a view of the enemy as *degraded*. There are images of the Turk in early Balkan literature, which counteract in interesting ways the characteristic negativity of "orientalism": Isakovic's *Hasanaginica* is an example.

18. Throughout this period ethnic differences were typically referred to as "tribal" in official discourse. Serbs, Croats and Slovenes were described as "three tribes of one nation".

19. In the census of 1948 they were categorised as "indeterminate Muslims" (*neopredeljeni muslimani*); in 1953 as "indeterminate Yugoslavs" (*neopredeljeni Jugoslaveni*); in 1961 as "Muslims in the ethnic sense" (*Muslimani u etnickom smislu*); in 1971 as "Muslims in the sense of nationality" (*Muslimani u smislu narodnosti*); and in 1981 finally listed as a "nation" (*narod*)--*Muslimani*. For the significance of the distinction between *narod* and *narodnost*, see pp. 000-000.

20. Attempts to revert to an explicitly theological emphasis on Islamic identity met with repression, as in the treatment of Alija Izetbegovic following the circulation of the *Izlamska deklaracija*.

21. This association is by no means easy or uncontroversial. See Allcock and Norris, in Carter and Turnock eds. forthcoming.

22. A development of Bourdieu's approach is that of Anthony Giddens, who engages with the study of the distribution of symbolic *resources*. I take the concept of "interpellation" from Louis Althusser. (Althusser 1984)

23. The symbolic and social significance of space and place has only recently come to receive adequae recognition within sociology. See, however, Lash and Urry 1994; Urry 1995.

24. My argument abuts at many points onto the work of Todorova (1997) and Goldsworthy (1998). These works both came to my attention too late to consider them fully in this chapter.

25. Darby and his colleagues remark that "the extent of medieval Croatia is ... difficult to estimate" (Darby *et al.* 1966:26).

26. Subsequent to the break-up of Yugoslavia attention has switched in some measure to language as providing the core of this process of imagination, partly in response, I suspect, to the weight of international pressure against the redefinition of state boundaries.

27. Account of the sources and problems of identifying a text.

28. Although the notion of "Greater Serbia" has received a good deal of currency in the press it is important to note that it is rarely given house room by serious analysts. Susan Woodward remarks: "Slovene and Serbian leaders are thus accused of following a plan (particularly Milosevic, as regards a "Greater Serbia"). This is unlikely. Responding to specific events politically, they were choosing tactics of consequence, but they were not necessarily thinking out the chain of those consequences or the logic of their daily steps." (Woodward 1995:94)

29. The story of the knowledge and influence of Garasanin's document is complex, partly obscure, and deserves to be the subject of a monograph in its own right. As far as I am able to judge no historians cite it until 1906 (see Novak 1930), and it did not become an object of debate until the inter-war years. Stavrianos (1958:853) cites a source in 1923; but the text was not published until Stojankovic's version appeared in 1939. Banac (1984:82-84) provides a brief discussion of the issue. It

is important in this kind of interpretative exercise to place documents in their context. In that respect I find Banac's comment interesting, that "the *Nacertanije* was prepared at a time when most notables of autonomous Serbia were still mistrustful of outsiders, even when they happened to be Serbs from the Habsburg Monarchy. One of the main purposes of Serbia's new national plan was to break .... the Chinese wall by which Serbia had cut itself off from its neighbours". This is a rather more modest ambition than that attributed to its author by today's critics of Garasanin as the founder of an aggressive policy of creating a "Greater Serbia". At the time of writing I have not been able to explore the matter in further detail.

30. Possibly a fourth line of expansion is emerging, as Macedonia is lost through independence, probably Kosovo may have to be sacrificed in the interests of the stability of the state, and the greater part of the formerly Serb-settled areas of Bosnia-Hercegovina are more or less "cleansed" ethnically of their former inhabitants. It has emerged recently that there has been an aggressive movement of settlement in the Vojvodina, at the expense of the Magyar and Croat minorities there.

31. This point is underscored by the singular reluctance of Serbs to actually live in Kosovo. The province has been the object of colonisation policies since 1921 (down to and including to present) all of which have failed markedly to halt the inexorable urbanisation process. Serbs are willing to live only in the mythical Kosovo; and the stories of Albanian terror have served as a convenient cover for the conspicuous gap between myth and history.

11

THE PASSING OF TRADITIONAL SOCIETY?

"Culture" and the nature of "tradition"

In this chapter on the "passing of traditional society" I want to address the question of

the nature of cultural continuity in relation to the concept of "tradition". The

relationship between "tradition" and "modernity" is one which is frequently

misunderstood; and within the general framework of this book it is important that I try

to clarify the issue.

In setting out with the aim of providing us an account of the cultural dimension of

developments in the Balkans, it is important to keep in sight what we should

understand by "culture". It is a mistake to look at culture as a closed and determinate

inheritance. It should be regarded as a resource out of which it is possible to go on

creating new chains of signification, which become the medium of constantly

unfolding patterns of agency, adapting us to a changing world. It is in this context that

I understand also the concept of "tradition".

Those who act "traditionally" address the questions posed by contemporary living by

reference to the past, using it as a resource for the development of strategies of

signification and action in their lives. To act traditionally is not simply to follow a custom, or to behave habitually. As Max Weber insists, "action" properly speaking is characterised by meaning.[1] To act "traditionally" one has to act in relation to the past. There is an important difference, however, between tradition and traditional*ism*. Both of these involve drawing upon the past as a resource in order to endow with meaning one's own actions and those of others. Traditional action accepts unproblematically that action in the present is modelled upon past action. Traditional*ism*, however, implies a more positive, reflexive affirmation of the past in relation to the possibility that one's present action might not be modelled upon the past.

The distinctive character of traditionalism can be grasped more clearly in relation to modernity. Appeals to modernity also involve drawing upon symbolic resources in order to indicate the significance of one's actions. On this occasion, however, those resources are typically legitimated by reference to a projected future. Giddens has characterised modernity by its capacity to "colonise the future" (Giddens 1991:144-5). What is more, this is usually a future guaranteed by the experience of significant others outside of one's own group.

Where communities resort to accounts of their action by explicit reference to tradition, they are often revealed by that very fact as already embarked upon the modernisation process. The explicit reaffirmation of continuity with the past constitutes a riposte to claims about the desirability, necessity or inevitability of change, and particularly change which is seen as intrusive, threatening or disorienting. Traditionalism in this way exemplifies the greater reflexivity which is held to be characteristic of modernity.

In looking at South Slav culture it is possible to identify action which is both traditional and traditionalist. As I have already indicated, looking at the economic transformation of agriculture and the process of industrialisation, it is undeniably the case that "peasant society" is a thing of the past (except perhaps in small corners of the Balkans). This does not mean, however, that tradition is dead. An important part of the understanding of contemporary South Slav culture, in all regions, must be founded upon an awareness of the way in which tradition still can feature in life. This may not take the form of inert custom or blind habit: but as a more or less reflexive charting of a course through life, using models and standards of reference from the past as ways of making sense of and pragmatically negotiating the demands of the present.

In the remainder of the chapter I consider in turn five areas of life in which custom, tradition, and cultural resources which are rooted in peasant society, continue to provide important resources for living in the present. These are: family life; land ownership; relationships of clientship based upon locality; religion; and politics. These areas differ from each other, however, in the extent to which they provide examples of the ways in which the continuity of customary patterns of action remain available (albeit in modified forms and in new settings) to provide a structure for life. The last two in particular are significantly different, in that they have become the objects of traditionalism--vehicles for a self-conscious symbolisation of the past--and in this manner serve to comment upon the present and to define contemporary identities in relation to images of the past.

Family life and kinship

The centrality of family life has been accepted since the foundation of sociology as the defining feature of pre-modern society; and the modernisation process has often been considered to be virtually synonymous with the differentiation of spheres of action out of the net of kinship.

A dramatic feature of social change during the past century throughout the South Slav lands has been the reduction in family size. The extent and complexity of kin-based households among the Slavs was a feature which attracted the attention of early sociologists and anthropologists.[2] The *zadruga* has been regarded as one of the most distinctive features of the culture of the region as a whole (Mosely, in Byrnes ed. 1976:58-69; Stahl 1986).

> (The *zadruga*) can best be defined as an extended family consisting of two or
> more small biological families (father, mother, minor children), owning land,
> livestock and tools in common and sharing the same livelihood. In a society of
> zadrugal tradition, a family may grow for several generations without
> undergoing division of the household or its property. I had occasion before the
> war to study zadrugas of fifty, sixty-four, seventy-five and eighty-three
> members, although family communities of eight to twenty members were
> encountered far more frequently. One special feature of the zadrugal tradition,
> one which distinguishes it from the patriarchal family, is that each male member
> of it possesses a recognized, if latent, right to a share of the communal property
> and is free, if he chooses, to leave the zadruga, to take its share of the communal

property, as defined by customary or written law, and to found either a small family or, in cooperation with one or more members of the former large household, a new and smaller zadruga. (Moseley, in Byrnes ed. 1976:59)

In former times these families were distributed widely throughout south-eastern Europe, although differing to some extent regionally in their structure. They seem to have been altogether absent only in Slovenia

The more complete inclusion of the South Slav peasantry into the market economy during the nineteenth century was associated with the break-up of these large collective households--a process which was stimulated also by changes in state policy, and the legal entitlement to land, especially as a consequence of land reform. Vera Erlich has documented these changes in a study now regarded as a classic of the ethnography of the region (Erlich 1966).

The structural changes implied by the decline of the *zadruga* should not be confused with other changes with which they coincided; and in particular the reduction in the numbers of children born into any family. In the Balkans changes in the rates of reproduction have followed patterns identical to those documented throughout the rest of Europe (and elsewhere), associated with modernisation. Following a period of the rapid reduction of infant mortality and the soaring rise of population, there has been a period of the equally rapid reduction in fertility. In the late nineteenth century, and even down to the period of unification, the South Slav lands had among the highest birth rates in Europe, comparable with rates in some Asian or Latin American countries.

For Yugoslavia as a whole, birth-rates declined historically from 36.7 per thousand

in 1921 to 15.3 per thousand in 1987. In the same period rates of natural increase fell

from 15.8 per thousand to 6.2 per thousand. These figures are reflected in changing

family size, which in 1921 averaged 5.10 persons/household and in 1981 3.62. In spite

of an increase in the number of households from 2.4 million in 1921 to 6.1 million in

1981, the number of households with 8 or more members fell in the same interval

from 358,953 to 247,031. (Savezni Zavod za Statistiku 1989: 39-43). These aggregate

figures conceal large regional differences. In the post-1945 period rates of population

growth in Slovenia, Croatia and the Vojvodina have fallen from around 12 per

thousand to bare replacement, whilst in Kosovo the fall has been much more modest--

from around 29 to 25 per thousand.

These changes have been bound up in large measure with the changing position of

women. The advance in the social and economic emancipation of women is often

cited as one of the more significant discontinuities, particularly since the Communist

take-over in 1945. A good deal has been made of the importance of the contribution

made by women to the National Liberation Struggle (Jancar 1985; Tomsic 1983.) In

spite of the existence of an "impressive corpus of legislation" (Jancar 1985:201)

directed at securing the greater equality of women in post-1945 Yugoslavia, the

evidence points unambiguously neither to the wartime struggle as a simple break in

the historical story, nor to unqualified progress since then.

There is good evidence to suggest that the process of emancipation for women had

begun during the inter-war years, measured both in terms of the existence of an active

women's movement and in terms of real changes in the socio-economic situation of women (Jancar 1985:210-2, based upon the work of Sklevicky). Furthermore, in spite of the undeniable expansion of the frontiers of women's activity in Yugoslavia during the wartime struggle itself, just as British women found that the return from their men from the front after both the First and Second World Wars signalled pressures to return to domesticity and a restoration of economic opportunities to men, so too there was a period of the re-traditionalisation of women's roles during peace-time, clearly indicated in Jancar's own research. (See also Morokvasic 1986:126-7.)

The expansion of women's economic role is readily indicated. Women made up 29.5% of those employed in the social sector in 1945, and 39.4% in 1988 (Savezni Zavod za Statistiku 1989:58). It is important to bear in mind, however, that these changes are largely measured in urban and industrial employment. The peasant economy has always had a definite place for the productive activity of women, even though this goes along with a strict segregation of gender roles and the subordination of women in other senses. The economic role of women has remained virtually unchanged in agriculture, with women providing 41.0% of the active labour force in agriculture in 1921, 40.3% in 1948, and 41.5% in 1981 (Savezni Zavod za Statistiku 1989:39)

Literacy is widely accepted as a significant broad indicator of cultural equality. Whereas in 1921, 60% of women and 40% of men were illiterate, already these proportions had fallen by 1948 to 34% and 15%. By 1981, illiteracy among women had declined to 15%, and among men to 4% (Savezni Zavod za Statistiku 1989:39). The overall impression of progress is marred, of course, by the relativities here: in

1921 the illiteracy rate for men was two thirds that of women, whereas by 1981 it was only one third!)

At the other end of the educational ladder, opportunities for women have steadily widened in higher education, although it is notable that rates of change have stagnated at the level of the highest qualifications.

Table 11.1: Changes in the opportunities for women in higher education (women as % of total)

Year	Enrolled students	Graduated students	Awarded doctorate
1922	16.5	11.8	2.2
1947	33.9	29.1	5.3
1957	30.0	34.0	16.4
1967	31.3	31.3	26.5
1977	39.3	45.5	20.2
1987	41.6	49.1	21.2

Source: Savezni Zavod za Statistiku 1989:363

The limited achievement of the Communist period can be assessed in part by the way in which women have found acceptance as actors in public life, in that in 1953 there were no women at all among the members of the federal, republican and municipal assemblies (Table 11.2). The changes since then can hardly be considered as spectacular progress.

These figures do highlight a significant feature of the partial nature of the transformation of women's roles in Yugoslavia. They have experienced the *addition* of economic tasks outside the home, while retaining the primary responsibility for the home--the phenomenon referred to by several writers as the woman's "double day" (Morokvasic 1986:127-8; Jancar 1985:204; Tomsic 1983:290). This means that there are serious limitations of time and energy when it comes to their shouldering public responsibilities in addition to those of paid employment and domesticity.

Table 11.2: Representation of women in the membership of federal, republican and local assemblies (%)

	1963	1974	1986
Federal Assembly	19.5	13.6	16.2
Republican Assemblies	20.8	16.8	19.3
Municipal Assemblies	5.1	15.2	11.5

Source: Savezni Zavod za Statistiku 1989:31-2

The limited nature of these advances is also indicated by the continuing differentials between average earnings for men and women. The average monthly pay for women in the social sector in 1986 was 86.9% of the average for men--a limited advance on the situation a decade earlier, when the proportion was 84.4% (Savezni Zavod za Statistiku 1989:79. "(Women) are concentrated in the highly labour-intensive manufacturing industries and in the typically female sectors: textiles, clothing industry, services and administration" (Morokvasic 1986:126). My own research into the tourism industry supports this picture, indicating an over-representation of women in the less-skilled and more poorly paid grades of labour (Allcock 1989).

488

An important feature to watch in the post-communist period is the renewal of pressure towards the re-traditionalisation of the position of women. This has become a particularly sensitive political issue in both Slovenia and Croatia, where since independence there has been a marked growth of the direct influence of the Roman Catholic Church upon politics. In both republics the question of abortion, and other issues which bear particularly upon the position of women, have become the centre of political controversy. These questions became particularly acute during the time when an attempt was being made in Slovenia to sustain a ruling coalition which included with secular parties the Christian Democratic Party. The problem is by no means confined to these areas, however; and Sabrina Ramet has drawn attention to the way in which Serbia and Montenegro have also experienced a "patriarchal backlash", which is expressed particularly in Milosevic's Socialist Party of Serbia, support for which is drawn disproportionately from rural males (Ramet 1992:109-10).

> In tandem with the cult of blood and soil, the new Serbian nationalists also
> summoned to life the symbolic mediaeval figure of mother Yugovitch—the
> long-suffering, brave, stoic mother of nine, offering her children up to death in
> the defence of the fatherland. Maternity is now to be seen as an obligation, not
> as a free optiuon for women; the sexuality of women has to be controlled and
> reduced to procreation. (Zalovic, cited in Hughes, Mladjenovic and Zajovic
> 1995:521)

In this respect the point is illustrated well that tradition comes into its own when it is a self-conscious replication of action rather than an unreflective reproduction of action.

I mentioned above that tradition and modernity should not be looked at as antinomies, but as bound up together in a complementary relationship. Two points serve to underline this inter-dependence of tradition and modernity. There is a real ambivalence in the area of family size, which is signalled by the response to high levels of Albanian fertility. I have been struck by the fact that wherever I have been in conversation with Yugoslavs on the question of ethnic relations, and the problem of the Albanian minority has been raised, discussion invariably turns on the Albanian birth-rate. What is remarkable is the real antagonism here expressed particularly by *women*--usually urban women who themselves have exercised considerable restraint in the limitation of the size of their own families. Having themselves adopted the position that the limitation of family size is important (i.e. regarded positively from a "modern" point of view) they seem to feel betrayed by those who have not broken with this aspect of traditionalism.[3]

Mirjana Morokvasic raises another issue in a highly perceptive discussion (Morokvasic 1986:132-3). The spread of "consumerist" orientations in Yugoslavia can be regarded as highly ambiguous from the point of view of women. On the one hand "consumerism" can be looked at as one component of the wider configuration of changes of values which go along with the modernisation process. In that sense, they can be seen as impinging upon the situation of women in a somewhat emancipatory fashion, strengthening the power of women as controllers of disposable income--as economic agents. On the other hand, the realm over which these decisions is expected to be exercised is very much framed by traditional mentalities, and can be seen as an element of the re-traditionalisation of society, in that "consumerism" actually operates to bind women ever more firmly into the orbit of domesticity.

Land ownership

In spite of half a century of Communism Yugoslavia displays a remarkably wide dispersion of the ownership of agricultural land. (Some of the reasons for this have been discussed in an earlier chapter.) An earlier generation of writers about peasant society dwelt upon the peasants' deep-seated attachment to land. This persisting pattern is not readily reduced to this kind of conservatism, which has often been exaggerated. In a period during which urban and industrial occupations come to replace rural and agricultural employment it is perhaps natural that, failing the actual ejection or displacement of people from the land (as in the Scottish Highland clearances of the nineteenth century) ownership of the land should be retained as an insurance against the potential failure of these new ventures.

The distribution of land holding has been remarkably constant over a long period of time in Yugoslavia. Systematic recent figures are difficult to obtain: but there were still 2,676,341 individual farms in Yugoslavia in 1981 (Savezni Zavod za Statistiku 1987: Table 211-26). Data from Slovenia indicate that the aggregate number of agricultural holdings fell from 194,855 in 1960 to 156,549 in 1991. There was a tendency over the same period for the number of small plots to increase, rising from 20.9% of the total in 1961 to 28.4% in 1991 (Statisticni Urad Republike Slovenije 1995:260).

Following the failure of the collectivisation programme between 1947 and 1953, in spite of the widely discussed process of the "senilisation" of the economically active farm population, and some associated changes in land use, the structure of land holding has remained remarkably constant. One reason for this inertia is that fact that, in simple institutional terms, the under-development of property institutions has been a serious barrier to the exchange of land, and there has been no proper market in this as in other factors of production.

The availability of rural land has also been an important resource, however, which has been used in a variety of ways by an increasingly urbanised population. The shortage of housing in the cities (and the generally small size of urban family apartments) has meant that the *vikendica* (week-end cottage) has been an extremely valuable recreational resource. The continuing contact with rural family has secured a regular supply of fresh produce, including fruit and vegetables, wine and spirits, cheese and honey. These have emerged as vital necessities in periods of economic crisis, inflation and war.[4]

These economic ties have utilised and at the same time strengthened ties of family. Urban members are able to reciprocate with other services. The continuing importance of these links with the land, and with the peasant way of life, should not be considered as traditionalism, however, but more usefully as simply rational economic and social strategies within the context of post-war developments.

Other elements of the rural past, however, do form the basis for traditionalism. Aspects of folklore, especially folk music, continue to be extremely popular throughout the Balkans, featuring regularly as the basis of TV broadcasts and making up a substantial part of the diet of radio. The stock in trade of a number of very popular singers (such as Zvonko Bogdan), while not actually consisting of folk music in the strict sense, communicates a nostalgic sentimentalisation of the rural way of life.[5] Land holding itself, however, is not the object of this traditionalism, and should be distinguished from it.

Relationships of sponsorship and clientship

Institutions which ritually extend kin ties have long been commented upon as distinctive of South Slavs. It is generally acknowledged both that they do not correspond exclusively to any particular ethnic group (although they are far weaker among Slovenes) and that they are probably pre-Christian in origin (Hammel 1968:5).

The most important of these relationships is that of *kumstvo*, usually translated as either "godparenthood" or "sponsorship". There are three ceremonies at which the sponsor may be required by custom: baptism, marriage and the ritual first cutting of a child's hair. Although the first two of these have some place within canon law, "local practice and customary law have vastly elaborated the skeletal provisions of canonical regulation" (Hammel 1968:8).

Often the relationship of *kumstvo* is inherited, usually in the male line. Great importance is attached to it in some areas, both as a privilege and as a responsibility. My impression is that whereas the extension of the kinship network in general has been conspicuously attenuated in the process of urbanisation, *kumstvo* has proved itself to be rather more robust. Shorn of its specifically Christian associations it has continued in some respect even among relatively high status, urban and even actively Communist families.

A desirable, though not indispensible, feature of sponsorship is differential status: one's *kum* is preferably of higher status. The mercenary exploitation of this type of link is generally deprecated; but nevertheless, especially in urban areas, sponsorship merges into a wider and looser patron/client relationship, which can be extremely important.

The history of these practices in the Balkans is probably a long one. Kettering has suggested that they are far more widely prevalent in the Mediterranean region than former Yugoslavia, which might indicate great antiquity.[6] She has also hypothesised that some aspects of political clientilism may be rooted in Ottoman practices (Kettering 1988).

Ties of patronage outside of *kumstvo* are generally grouped together under the heading of *veze* (connections). The English phrase "it's not what you know but who you know" sums up effectively the accepted and normal manner of getting things done throughout the Balkans. There may well be, and typically are, complex official routes through the normal bureaucratic maze which grows up around the hypertrophied Balkan state, and business institutions. Goods and opportunities may well be in short or erratic supply. Characteristically, the intolerable delays and frustrations occasioned by these situations can be short-circuited by the deft resort to networks of interpersonal obligation--*veze*.

In significant measure this system is rooted in the locality, and thus ties in with kinship more narrowly conceived. The village historically has been a vital focus of networks of communication and mutual practical assistance, particularly for the exchange of labour (*moba*) in order to achieve large or complex tasks. These are not customarily confined to kin (Vukosavljevic 1953; Stahl: 1986; Mallat 1902:139-40; Avramovic 1925:44).

The sense of connectedness, or rootedness in a specific locality, may not be surprising in view of the relatively recent urbanisation of most Yugoslavs. Even so, it is by no means unusual to encounter references to "my village", or "my wife's/ husband's village", on the part of people whose urban credentials extend over several generations. Oral tradition supports not only a strong sense of genealogy, but also a clear sense of local attachment.

In spite of the fact that I have encountered no social-scientific study of these networks, anybody who has worked in Yugoslavia for any length of time will have encountered them. Invitations to visit the countryside with Yugoslav friends, at the week-end, turn out to involve not just a commercially acquired *vikendica*, but more usually a cottage which, if it is not actually an old property which has been in the family for some time, is built upon the family's land.

An anecdotal illustration will serve, in the absence of more impersonal and systematic data, to substantiate the importance of informal links based upon *veze* and locality. Several years ago I was working in Macedonia, funded by a scholarship. I was met at the airport in Skopje by a representative of my host organisation, and in my hotel we reviewed the programme which I had requested. Everything was in place with the exception of the contact with representatives of the *sindikat* (trade union), for which I had specifically asked. I was assured that this omission would soon be rectified. As time passed I reminded my mentor that there was still no news of the promised meeting with the *sindikat*, with the same result. At last, as the end of my visit drew near, in desperation I fixed up my own interview. The revelation of what I had done was slightly embarrassing, but instructive. It transpired that all of my interviews had been with people from Berovo: my man hailed from Berovo. Sadly, he had no personal *veze* in the trade unions from his own locality.[7]

In a situation in which the Communist structures to some extent abrogated civil society, and urbanisation has in any case outpaced its potential development, networks of clientship and locality can be said to serve some of its functions. The explanation of the importance of networks of clientship of this kind probably should follow along the lines sometimes advanced for the prevalence of corruption in modernising states. The state is in important respects insufficiently developed to cope with the demands placed upon it. Hence networks of clientship should not be regarded as an element of traditionalism in the sense outlined above, but as an adaptation of customary relationship rooted in peasant society in order to cope with the novel demands of urban life. It is impossible to understand Balkan life without taking such relationships into account. Their theoretical interest is considerable.

One of the characteristics of modernity which has been identified by Giddens is the change in patterns of trust. Trust he defines as "confidence in the reliability of a person or system, regarding a given set of outcomes or events, where that confidence expresses a faith in the probity or love of another, or in the correctness of abstract principles (technical knowledge)" (Giddens 1990:34). This is immediately linked to his more general discussion of processes of "disembedding": modernity requires trust not only in abstract principles but also in individuals not known to us personally, but identified only impersonally by their expertise. The persistence of the reliance upon kinship, clientship and locality in South Slav society is therefore interesting as an indication of the failure to develop these kinds of relations of impersonal trust, and the continuing life of pre-modern attitudes. It is an interesting question as to whether this lack of trust is to be explained specifically by reference to the Communist system, or whether it should be interpreted as a response to a period of very rapid social change.

Religion

Discussion of religion in relation to Yugoslavia has been dominated until very recently by the configuration of issues which might be described as "Church-state relations". This is the primary interest of Alexander's survey (1979), of the work of Kristo (1987) and of Ramet (1989, 1990 and 1992).[8] The selection of this emphasis is understandable within the context of an interest in Communism. During the period of the break-up of Yugoslavia this question has largely been pushed aside by discussion of the importance of ethnicity in the Balkans, and the widely recognised links between ethnic and religious identities (Dunn 1996; Mojzes 1993 and 1993a; Van Dertel 1992; Vrcan 1995).[9] There are other key issues which merit attention, however, especially in relation to my interest in the tradition/modernity axis.

A useful point of departure here is the long-standing conceptual distinction in anthropology which contrasts the "Great Tradition" and the "little community" (Redfield 1956). Redfield's concern is with the development of a framework in which to understand peasant societies. Its relevance here lies in his emphasis upon the importance of distinguishing between the formalised, rationalised and often hierarchical and bureaucratic elaboration of major cultural traditions based in metropolitan centres, and the "partial" dependence upon these of informal, non-rationalised, typically oral traditions, rooted within local contexts and practices, which are characteristic of peasant cultures.

The debate about religion couched principally at the level of church-state relations typically confines its interest in the phenomenon of religion to the "Great Traditions", providing an account which is not only *about* but characteristically provided *by* members of the intellectual and metropolitan elite.[10] The aspects of religious life and experience which might fall under Redfield's rubric of the "little community", and which might be described otherwise by sociologists as "folk religion", receive scant attention. The task of providing a more balanced account of the importance of religion among the South Slavs is hampered by the relative indifference to these problems on the part of indigenous social scientists; and it is primarily from the work of anthropologists that we can gain the greatest illumination.[11] The preoccupation with Church-state relations is not irrelevant to my interests here, although perhaps it does need to be at least partly re-framed.

In common with other parts of the world it is possible to trace a historical process of secularisation in the South Slav lands. As in other countries, however, the concept of secularisation often carries with it a dangerous looseness, covering a variety of changes which are at least logically separable (Lyon 1985). In the case of those states formerly dominated by Communist regimes there is a tendency to allocate to the experience of Communism primacy as an explanatory factor in this process, and also to exaggerate its extent and significance.

Certainly, as elsewhere in eastern Europe, the hegemony of the League of Communists was marked by a hostility to religion (at least in the early post-war years) or at the very best an official indifference to it. The programme of the nationalisation of land in 1945 included church holdings among those which were subject to expropriation, and more than 10% of the land fund was drawn from this source (Savezni Zavod za Statistiku 1989:205).[12]

The variable and ambivalent conduct of religious authorities towards the fascist and occupation regimes between 1941 and 1945 was used by the Communists to discredit them, and the general ideological attack upon religion was driven home by several high profile trials for collaboration of leading clerics--most notably that of Cardinal Stepinac. Understandably the close historical links between religion and nationalism reinforced the habitual antipathy of socialists to religion, and led to a policy of attempting to control ecclesiastical activities. Official associations of priests were set up as a means of their co-optation; religious education was suppressed and restrictions were placed upon the religious press. (Alexander 1979 and Ramet 1992; for an official account of the situation see Kurtovic 1980.) Two problems here deserve attention.

Apologists for religion (aided and abetted by nationalists, who have seen in the attack on religion principally an attack on the *nation*) have tended to exaggerate the importance of religion in popular life before the arrival of Communism. The churches as institutions were powerfully placed, both in the South Slav lands before unification and within the First Yugoslavia. It would be false to assume, however, an uncomplicated relationship between Churches and people, and that ecclesiastical authorities enjoyed the unqualified support of their flocks. The comment of Cedomil Mijatovic before the First World War remains true today.

> The religious sentiment of the Servians is neither deep nor warm. Their churches are generally empty, except on very great Church festivals. The Servians of our day consider the Church as a political institution, in some mysterious manner connected with the existence of the nation. They do not allow anyone to attack her, nor to compromise her, although when she is not attacked, they neglect her. (Quoted in Malcolm 1998:13-14)

There is some evidence not only of distance between religious authorities and their parishioners, but even of anti-clerical sentiment expressed in both nationalist and other popular movements. Although the distance between Church and people was less in Serbia than elsewhere, the political position of the clergy has often been the subject of deep controversy. During the term of office of Metropolitan Mihailo the relationship between the ecclesiastical hierarchy and the crown was particularly difficult. Perhaps it is not surprising that Svetozar Markovic's socialism took a broadly anti-clerical position: nevertheless, there was strong strain of anti-clericalism in the early Radical Party, which was expressed in 1875 in a petition signed by 50 opposition deputies demanding that the monasteries be stripped of their assets and that they be totally reformed. (Mousset 1938: esp. 361-2).[13]

The Croatian Peasant Party of the Radic brothers in Croatia was distinguished from the Frankist approach to nationalism in part by its anti-clericalism. Although clerical influence was strong in the Slovene People's Party, its opponents among the Slovene liberal bourgeoisie, represented by the paper *Slovenski narod* and the National Progressive Party, tended to be critical of the Church (Banac 1984:343; Rogel 1977:40-5). Here, as in Croatia the uneasy relationship between the peasantry and the clergy was rooted in the power of the Church as a landowner.

Macedonia's IMRO, particularly its socialist wing, was also characterised by substantial elements of anti-clericalism, standing out against the manipulative use of ecclesiastical institutions by Bulgarians, Greeks and Serbs for the purposes of promoting the national assimilation of Macedonians.

Although the situation is somewhat different in the case of Islam, where within the dominant Sunni tradition the position of the clergy is quite different from that of either Orthodox or Roman traditions of Christianity, here too it is important to note the complexity of the social and political situation of the formally organised religious communities. Both in Bosnia and in Macedonia the avowedly confessional parties of the pre-Communist period (the *Jugoslavenska Mulsimanska Organizacija*, and the *Çemijet*) were unambiguously landlords' parties. Although the former did secure a wide measure of recognition as the political voice of Islam in Bosnia and Hercegovina, their confessional representativeness was constantly undermined by their economic partisanship. (Purivatra 1974: Chap. XI; Banac 1984:367-78)

As a great landowner, as a collaborator with other oppressive and exploitative elite groups, the ecclesiastical hierarchies were often extremely unpopular with the peasantry and with the poorer urban strata. They also had little in common with the newer, modernising urban middle classes, whose nationalism was often inspired by western European, secular rationalism. It is important, therefore, to distinguish between the forms of popular religious sentiment, and attachment to religious tradition, of the Yugoslav peoples (especially the rural population) and the extent to which religious authorities can be regarded as standing in a position of "leadership" and as enjoying some kind of representative status *vis-a-vis* the nation. In this respect, the gulf between the religious "Great Traditions" and the "little communities" in Yugoslavia was often considerable.

As elsewhere in Europe, a long term reduction in general religiosity can be documented across the Balkans which clearly cannot be reduced to the hostility of Communism. Measures of religiosity (or its converse) are always open to question, but a broad and consistent picture emerges. Open commitment to atheism, measured in a number of sociological studies over the post-1945 period, has remained generally at less than a fifth of the population.[14] The proportion of the population identified as "believers", however, while falling from a high of 87% in 1953, has fluctuated around 45-50% (Ramet 1990:201; 1992:140; cf. Djordjevic 1990:161).

There is some evidence of considerable variation between regions and ethnicities in this respect. Ramet observes that: "the decline has been sharpest among the traditionally Orthodox and least noticeable among the Muslims, while the smaller neo-Protestant sects such as Seventh-Day Adventists and Jehovah's Witnesses have probably grown in membership." (Ramet 1990:200)

A study by Djordjevic in the late 1980s estimated that rates of non-belief varied from a high of 38.4% among Serbs to 12.7% among Albanians (Djordjevic 1990:163) (Not surprisingly, 64.1% of those describing themselves as "Yugoslavs" disclaimed any religious attachment.) A series of investigations in Slovenia (the area about which we have the most complete and regular coverage) report a decline in the number of those claiming some sort of religious attachment from 85.7% in 1953 to 45.3% in 1978 (Roter 1982:29). Although the lack of strict comparability of studies makes judgement difficult, these proportions seem to compare closely, on the whole, with information from other eastern European countries.[15]

Of remarkable interest here is the study by Ibrahim Bakic, in which he documents the surprising variability over a relatively short period in the reported religious identity of respondents in Bosnia-Hercegovina. In surveys conducted in 1988, 1989 and 1990 the proportion of respondents describing themselves as "believers" fluctuated between 32.12%, 13.83% and 27.56%. Although the general pattern held good for adherents of all three of the principal faiths, it was most pronounced among Muslims, 30.87% of whom described themselves as believers in 1988, but only 16.5% the following year (Bakic 1994:50). In a situation of growing insecurity and fluidity, in which the social and political relevance of both national and religious identification was changing, the implications of claims to either will have been under constant pressure to change.

As in other European countries we find among the South Slavs a marked contrast between widespread nominal confessional identification and practical devotional indifference. Those who can be identified as having a marked commitment to religion (however that may be measured) are a small minority. A study conducted in Serbia in the mid-1970s found only 5% of respondents to exhibit a "religious orientation" (Popovic ed. 1977:370). The number of respondents in the Slovene studies reported as *cerkveno dosleden* (consistently religious) declined from 21.7% in 1968 to 11.8% a decade later (Roter 1982:35). As far as one is able to tell, these figures do not indicate that Yugoslavs have been, by European standards, either conspicuously religious or irreligious.[16] It is hard in this context, therefore, to separate the supposed negative impact upon religion of Communist rule from the wider effects of the modernisation process.

Patterns of response and conduct clearly also vary not only regionally but with socio-economic status and by confessional group. Religious involvement is greater in rural areas as opposed to cities; among peasants, the self-employed and the unskilled manual working class as opposed to qualified and especially professional people (Roter 1982: 139-41; Popovic ed. 1977:371-82; Ramet 1990:200-203). A Croatian survey reported in 1985, in a pattern which appears to be typical, that the percentage of those with a "religious orientation" varied from a high of 25% among peasant cultivators to a low of 4% among routine white-collar workers, with an average of 10% (Elakovic and Brangjolica 1985:310).

Among the most important functions of religious identification is its role in the preservation of the identity of the family and the locality: and these associations come across very strongly when one turns to the work undertaken by anthropologists. Popular religion is characterised primarily by the persistence of certain ritual forms, either those which bring the community together to celebrate collectively the major annual religious festivals (such as Christmas, Easter, or Ramadan), or to mark the principal "rites of passage" such as weddings or funerals.[17] Alternatively, it takes the form of mystical, gnostic or ecstatic cults concerned with personal sanctification.

The gap between popular religiosity and ecclesiastical authority of this kind has been illustrated nowhere as well as in the case of Medjugorje. In June 1981 a group six children in a small Hercegovinian village experienced a vision of the Virgin Mary; and for some time afterwards, at the same time every day, the experience was repeated in the village rectory, during which they claimed to have conversation with her (Markle and McCrea 1994). These events were treated consistently with caution by the episcopal authorities, who hesitated to pronounce upon their authenticity. It seems that close to the heart of the events in Medjugorje was a dispute between local Franciscan friars, who were perhaps closer to the spirit of local religion, and the episcopate (Markle and McCrea 1994:201-4; also Ramet 1990 199-200).[18] The situation can be understood as illustrating the frequent gap between locally based folk belief and the authority of ecclesiastical hierarchies. On another and wider plane, however, Markle and McCrea have argued that "in the most general sense, the Medjugorje phenomenon—indeed all such apparitions—may be conceptualized as a revolt against modernity, a revolt against secularization" (1994:200). They go on to note that the Medjugorje visions are not alone in Yugoslavia in marking this kind of confrontation with modernity.

A similar diversity of belief can be documented in relation to Islam. The politicisation of Yugoslav Islam has tended to produce a rather uniform view of it; and a significant part of its actual diversity has been provided by the strength of the mystical (largely sufic) orders. These have always had an important part to play in Balkan Islam (Norris 1993). The officially sponsored Islamic Community has generally taken a hostile view of them, however, and in the post-1945 period of radical atheism an attempt was made to suppress them. Against the "extremely violent reaction" of the Community, however, Popovic reports that by the late 1970s nine of the mystical orders were active in Yugoslavia, with an estimates 160 *tekkes* in 1976 (Popovic 1986:349-51).

Although there is some evidence that basic religious instruction might be quite widespread in Croatia and Slovenia, in spite of Communist attempts to suppress religious education, there is no tradition of popular critical discourse about religion anywhere in Yugoslavia. When we compare religious life among the Czechs or East Germans it is clear that official hostility to religion can not be the only answer. The Reformation passed the region by (or was obliterated by counter-reformation in Slovenia). Consequently the traditions of popular religious learning associated with English Non-Conformity have no counterpart there. Religious associations are largely pietistic, or to a lesser extent charitable, and consequently it is upon *ritual* that the weight of religious observance primarily falls.

The strength of the *slava* (festival of the patron saint) among the Orthodox is notable (see for example Halpern and Halpern 1986[1972]: Chap. 5). Christmas and Easter have also remained significant celebrations more generally. Irene Winner reported that in Zerovnica, in spite of the disapproval of the Communist authorities the majority of marriages included the performance of the religious as well as the civil rite, and the principal religious holidays were still observed (Winner 1971:198-9). Indeed, freed from official disapproval there has been an evident increase in the visibility of both of these Christian festivals, both in Orthodox and Catholic regions.

Religious rituals of this kind have been transmuted subtly in two directions. On the one hand, as in western Europe, they have undergone a process of privatisation, with a heightened emphasis upon the family. (These may also be occasions upon which family ties with the village are reinforced.) On the other hand customary religion has shown signs of persistence and even growth where it has come to be seen as an important badge of identity, and especially *ethnic* identity.

Duskovic accounts for the continuing popularity of infant baptism in Croatia, and even its recent growth in urban areas, in terms of the link between Roman Catholicism and the affirmation of Croatian national identity (Duskovic, in Rihtman-Augustin ed. 1991:177-83).[19] Similar observations have been made about the significance of funerary rites (Zoric, in Rihtman-Augustin ed. 1991:193-204).

Although religious practices encountered by William Lockwood among Muslim villagers in Bosnia clearly fell a long way short of the Koranic ideal, he nevertheless insists upon the role of certain customary observances as badges of communal identity (Lockwood 1975:48-9). Discussing the observance and non-observance of fasting during Ramadan, Bringa sums up the importance of at least outward conformity.

As one of the five pillars and a key event in the Islamic ritual calendar, Ramadan sums up the role of practised Islam in Muslim identity formation in Bosnia. First, it is an individual expression of faith and devoutness; second, it is concerned with earning *sevap* [any action which is considered meritorious because it pleases God] and seeking blessing for oneself and one's household members; third, it serves to display the moral unity of the household; and fourth, as a practice which is uniquely Muslim it serves as a vehicle for the expression of a distinctive Muslim *nacija* identity vis-a-vis other non-Muslim Bosnians.

(Bringa 1995:169)

Active participation in public church rituals may be everywhere perfunctory, and lacking in easy familiarity with liturgy. We should not confuse either this, or the disestablishment of the churches from public life, however, with an uncomplicated "decline of religion". Customary religion has yielded an important cultural resource which has been available in order to frame questions about ethnicity.

Neither should we confuse information about religious toleration with the idea that somehow religious identities do not matter to those who espouse them. Here it is opportune to correct some ill-informed impressions about religious identity.

During the course of the conflict mixed marriages have often been cited as proof of the traditional "tolerance" of Bosnian (*bosniaque*) society. Exactly what does this consist of?

Historically the phenomenon of mixed marriages is foreign to Bosnian society as it emerged from the Ottoman Empire, in which there was strict communal endogamy. It only developed in the twentieth century, and thus represents a sign of the modernisation and transformation of this society.

In the 'eighties the percentage of mixed marriages in Bosnia-Hercegovina (about 12%) was equivalent to that in Yugoslavia as a whole. Given the importance of the mixture of populations in Bosnia such a percentage perhaps indicates rather the permanence of communal barriers. ....In Bosnia-Hercegovina mixed marriages were essentially a feature of the urban elite and manual workers, and were the most frequent between Serbs and Croats. In any case, the growing participation of Muslims in mixed marriages after 1945 attests to the social advancement and modernisation of this community.

Finally, the regions of Yugoslavia in which there was the highest proportion of mixed marriages were the Vojvodina (28%) and Croatia (17%). Sarajevo (with 28%) had fewer mixed marriages than some Croatian towns, such as Pakrac (35%) and Vukovar (34%). (Bougarel 1996:87).[20]

What we see here is the fact that religion may be a significant component of a traditionalist orientation to a way of life more generally (Popovic ed. 1977)[21] We need to divert our attention away from questions about religion as an "institution" to the study of patterns of life style, and to assess realistically its place within these patterns. Here religion emerges as one important available resource for the construction of identities.

Politics as tradition

Elsewhere I have identified "traditionalism/modernism" as a primary axis around which Balkan politics has come to be oriented (Allcock 1991a:307-8). This has primarily been a feature of the post-Yugoslav scene, but also some of the less fruitful conceptualisations of political differences in terms of "hard line" versus "liberal" Communism might yield more profitably to this conceptualisation. Certainly it makes more sense of some features of the diversity of political parties in the region than the historical, western European contrasts between left and right.

At one level there is very little tradition in the political scene of any of the post-Yugoslav republics, if that term is used in the sense of continuity with the past. Across the former federation are to be found parties which seek to buttress their claim to be taken seriously by appropriating the titles of former parties. Hence Serbian politics resounds once more to the competing claims of Radicals and Democrats: IMRO rides again in Macedonia: Slovenia has its Slovene People's Party. Usually there is no detectable continuity with the pre-Communist models whose prestige their aspire to capture. To the best of my knowledge only one party can claim with any seriousness to carry the baton handed on directly by its political forebears, and that is the Croatian Peasant Party, which sustained its existence after 1945 in exile in Canada.[22]

Nevertheless, contemporary politics in the region does seem to be characterised by forms of traditionalism in very important ways, even though often this takes the form of the "invention of tradition". In particular, I have been struck by the appositeness of Dragoljub Micunovic's phrase, "the folklorisation of politics".[23] This extends a long way beyond the resuscitation of pre-war party names and encompasses the rhetorical deployment of a wide range of historical images--positive or negative. The process of "folklorisation" involves the exhibition of images from political folklore going beyond their use as simple badges of group identity, to the extent where they begin to substitute for policy. Political discourse becomes constructed around mythologies rather than programmes or ideologies.

Examples of the positive embrace of such symbols include the revival of the term *cetnik* (by other Serbs) to describe irregular Serb military formations; Vuk Draskovic's adoption of the cult of St. Sava in 1989 and 1990; Slobodan Milosevic's flirtation at

about the same time with the imagery of Kosovo; and Vojislav Seselj's appropriation of the historic military title *vojvoda*. Nor is this process confined to Serbia: it can be matched in Croatia by the deployment of coats of arms; the parading of honour guards outside the Presidential Palace dressed in kitsch mediaeval uniforms; and the repeated public references to the millennial character of the Croatian state. Examples of the negative use of folkloric symbols, typically to demonise other groups, are the revival of the terms *cetnik* and *ustasa* to refer to the military or political activists of the other side; the tendency of non-Muslims to refer to all Muslims as "Turks"; and the rekindling of anti-semitism in Croatia.

Curiously the most obvious candidate for the role of focus of political traditionalism, the monarchy, seems to have made little progress. Michael Karadjordjevic has retained a prudent distance from Belgrade politics, and the ambitions of Tomislav have not been reflected in corresponding popular support. Although the mortal remains of the former Montenegrin king Nikola (deposed in 1918) and members of his family, were returned in state to Cetinje in October 1989, the monarchy has played no part at all in the resurgence of Montenegrin autonomism. Perhaps this suggests that the support for royalty is actually too close to a political *programme* to function effectively as the kind of vague, mythological, folkloristic symbol represented by saints, battles, bandits or fancy uniforms.

How is the concept of "traditionalism" actually cashed out at the level of political culture? It is largely a matter of *style* rather than any specific programme, and no particular platform can be deduced from it. I have defined traditionalism in terms of a reflexive orientation to the past, whereby "our past" comes to be set up as the standard of value, versus the external authority of the modern. The constituents of "our past", however, can take a multiplicity of forms. Curiously, nationalism can be manifested in both traditionalist and modern forms.

Croatian nationalism is generally speaking more backward-looking, appealing constantly for its legitimacy to the presumed past of a Croatian state. Slovene nationalism, while containing elements of real ambivalence, has a powerfully modernist strain, which emphasises the economic and cultural proximity of Slovenia and the Slovenes to western Europe and their distance from all *juznjaci* ("southerners").

Curiously, socialism too can appear in both modernist and traditionalist guises. In this respect Victor Kiernan's characterisation of it in terms of "prophetic memory" is entirely apt (Kiernan 1975).[24] Modernism has always been a key structural component within socialism (exemplified by Lenin's remark to the effect that socialism in the village amounted to "Soviets plus electrification"). The centrality of industrialisation to the general thrust of Communist policy since 1945 is also characteristic. During the break-up of the Yugoslav federation the reconstituted fragments of the League of Communists typically identified themselves as "modern parties of the democratic (sometimes 'European') left", and distanced themselves from nationalist traditionalism (Allcock 1991 and 1994a). On the other hand, socialism has donned traditionalist forms, especially in Serbia, where Milosevic's Socialist Party of Serbia has expropriated nationalism and secured him support in the heartland of small town and rural Serbia. He is outflanked on the left by the League of Communists-Movement for Yugoslavia (Subsequently absorbed into the Yugoslav United Left--

YUL), which bases its appeal in part on an attempt to keep alive the traditions of the Communist movement itself.

The peasantry can also (perhaps paradoxically) provide the basis for both modernising and traditionalist approaches to politics. Although the imagery of peasant society most immediately brings to mind nostalgic reference to a communal, rural past threatened if not destroyed by urban and industrial society, and the firm values of a moral order based in religious faith, this does not exhaust its potential by any means. The peasant can also serve as an image of the continuing vigour of private enterprise, and as the bearer of an ecological sensitivity which is lacking elsewhere. The former is certainly evidenced by such groups as the Party of Cultivators of Macedonia.

Conclusion

It may appear that a major feature of the break-up of the Yugoslav federation has been a retreat from modernity. Certainly if one confines one's attention to politics it seems that the rout of modernity has been almost complete. The matter is not as simple as this.

Dr. H. Lorkovic has put the question pointedly: "With the contest between tradition and modernity the question is not 'which tradition' but 'which modernity'?"[25] The question is a very good one, and apart from anything else points to the need to avoid the assumption that modernity (and in particular its dimension of globalisation) necessarily involves a homogenisation of society and culture. In some respects there has been at a number of levels a "re-embedding" of society and culture in the South

Slav lands in institutional structures and images derived from the past--a return to reliance upon kinship, locality and religion. Tradition does not only operate in this way, however: and in other respects we can see that tradition (in the sense of a reflexive orientation to the past) functions in interesting and important ways to provide also the symbolic resources out of which it is possible to construct an approach to modernity and the future. In adopting the description of Yugoslavia and its successor as wrestling with the trials of modernisation, it is not necessary to subscribe to the belief that this involves the necessary abandonment of tradition. Tradition and modernity, as I have suggested in this chapter, can be seen as bound up together in a dialectical process in which (to borrow expressions from Attila Agh) it is possible to identify both "traditionalising modernity" and "modernising traditionalism".[26]

Notes

1. Weber distinguishes "the merely unreflective formation of habit" and "the conscious acceptance of the maxim that action should be in accordance with a norm". (Weber 1978:I, 327).

2. Emile Durkheim, for example, made repeated reference to the *zadruga* throughout his discussions of the family. Among other writings, he reviewed Alexa Stanischitsch, *Ueber den Ursprung der Zadruga*. Durkheim 1969[1907] 639-42. See also Durkheim 1975: Vol.3. See also Sir Henry Maine's article on "South Slavonians and Rajputs" [complete reference].

3. Note the relatively short time which separates us from equally high birth rates in Croatia and Slovenia. Noel Malcolm has drawn attention to the fact that birth rates are equally high among rural Serbs in Kosovo, emphasising the fact that these rates are characteristic of a social milieu and not determined primarily by ethnicity (Malcolm 1998:330-3).

4. These issues are discussed additionally in Chapter 00, pp. 000-000.

5. Although Ramet has made a great deal of the cultural significance of rock music in Yugoslavia, I wonder if the case is not overdrawn (Ramet 1992: Chap. 5). The other side of popular music to which I refer here, on the other hand, seems to me to be a seriously underestimated cultural manifestation.

6. Hammel (1968) also indicates that these specifically South Slav patterns of association are probably historically continuous in some way with cultural patterns which are more widely distributed in southern Europe. See, for example, Campbell 1964: esp. Chap. IX, for discussion of a Greek example. I find it astonishing that a phenomenon so pervasive and so practically important as a constituent of everyday social life should pass without systematic comment in the *sociological* literature on the region.

7. Some time later I was based in Dubrovnik, and conducting a series of interviews with directors of tourism-related organisations. One of the things which interested me was the way business operated in the absence of a market. I asked one interviewee how he went about obtaining supplies of commodities (perhaps meat) for his large hotel. He began by explaining that he was a lad from the Pile (a small, very old, district just outside the city walls). He knew everybody there, and many of his neighbours had gone into the trade. He would begin his search by contacting an appropriate neighbour or former neighbour. Then at *gimnazija* he had got to know young people from across the city. If the neighbourhood failed him he would resort to this network. The third line of defence was the Konavle (the coastal area between Dubrovnik and the Bay of Kotor). What he produced for me was an account

which bore a startling resemblance to the system of nesting lineages with which Evans-Pritchard

described Nuer society (Evans-Pritchard:1940: Chap.V, and 1940a).

8. See also the survey in Kurtovic 1980. This rather one-sided approach to religion is partly to be

explained in terms of its place within a wider scholarly focus upon the problem of religion in

Communist societies. For a valuable bibliographical survey see Mojzes (ed.) 1987: esp. pp.81-85. The

ground for this preoccupation with church-state relations appears to have been laid before the rise of

Communism in Yugoslavia. See Mousset 1938. A primary cause of the fixation upon this area has been

of course, the controversial role of the churches during the 1941-45 period.

9. I deal with related aspects of this question in Chap. 0, pp. 000-000.

10. Illustrating the elite nature of these concerns is the "ecumenical" discussion which took place

(particularly in Slovenia) concerning Marxism and Christianity. See, for example, Frid ed. 1971.

11. A valuable bibliography listing the principal Yugoslav writers on the sociology of religion is

provided by Bakic 1994. See also Cvitkovic 1995:26-27, who emphasises the marginality of work on

the sociology of religion within Yugoslav sociology. For several examples of the kinds of concern

followed by Yugoslav sociologists, and especially the lack of empirical work in this field, see *Revija za*

sociologiju, XX(1-2) 1989.

12. For the sake of conciseness I use the term "the Churches" to cover all formal religious

organisations. Islamic foundations (*vakuf*) were also affected by these events.

13. See esp. Stokes 1990:217-9. Broadly speaking, it seems, the Orthodox Church had little time for

the Obrenovic dynasty and its supporters--and the antipathy was mutual. Mousset is a fascinating

source of coverage of this generally under-researched topic. Ivo Banac insists that open anticlericalism was, even so, less pronounced in Serbia than in any other part of the Balkans (Banac 1984:68). See also Castellan 1967: Chap. 9.

14. Statistics on religious observance or participation are notoriously difficult to interpret, but doubly so in a country where there have been obvious public disincentives to the honest reporting of religious attitudes and behaviour under the Communists, and perhaps equally obvious incentives to the over-reporting of these within a climate of nationalist politics.

15. A survey for Russia in 1995 reported 4% of respondents claiming that religion was "basic" in their lives, and a further 19% as "significant". Only 14% claimed to be atheists. (*Segodnya*, 2/9/95.) A comparative survey of studies in eight countries of the region between 1991 and 1993 showed low rates of frequent participation, a broad but variable penumbra of loosely defined adherents, and between 11 and 19% of self-rated atheists (*East-West Church and Ministry Report*, 2(3) Summer 1994:6-7). Poland appears to be the significant exception here, with much higher rates of regular participation, and a lower rate of declared atheism. Levels of religious knowledge did not appear to be appreciably better in Poland than elsewhere.

16. Some comparative figures for Britain can be found in Davie 1994, esp. Chap. 4 (see particularly p.50), and for Europe more generally p.78.

17. Bringa discusses this in terms of the relationship between "orthodoxy" and "orthopraxy"-- "the authoritative uniform practice is more important than authoritative uniform interpretation of the texts" (Bringa 1995:160). She recognizes that this might be a problematic distinction, but I find it helpful.

18. Laurentin and Rupcic (1984:14-5) treat Bishop Zanic's letter in *Glas Concila* of 16 Aug. 1981 as a courageous defence of the visionaries in the light of official Communist hostility to the phenomenon. (A slightly different translation appears in Kraljevic 1984. They also reproduce his letter to Sergej

Krager, 15-6.) The Bishop denies that "the Church authorities have preached against the events in Bikekovici": but this falls somewhat short of an affirmation of the validity of the experience of the visionaries, for which local people had hoped. For comment on other aspects of the Medjugorje phenomenon see Sells 1996:98-100.

19. Ivan Grubisic (1991) claims that about 76% of Croatian children attend basic religious instruction in the parish. Even before the fall of the Communist regime I am aware that parish catechistic centres operated in the large housing estates of Zagreb. For additional comment on the link between Croat national identity and Catholicism, see Kristo 1987:85-87.

20. See also the careful statistical analysis of mixed marriages in Yugoslavia in Mrdjan 1996.

21. Flere argues, exceptionally, that there is a weak link between commitment to religion and attitudes to modernity (Flere 1990). I am sceptical, on the basis of the narrow and contentious manner in which "modernity" was defined and measured for the purposes of his study.

22. Shortly after the first contested, multiparty elections in Croatia, in the course of the research which resulted in Allcock 1991, I interviewed senior representatives of the CPP in Zagreb. I asked if it was possible to obtain copies of their statute and manifesto. Apologetically, I was told that a proper manifesto was not yet available-- and handed in its place a copy of the collected speeches of Stjepan Radic!

23. In a personal conversation. I have no idea whether Micunovic is also responsible for the title of the paper by Colovic (in Morokvasic ed. 1992:165-170, "Le folklore et la politique: une affaire moderne"). I say more about this area in the chapter on violence.

24. In this context it is perhaps appropriate also to recall Bauman's image of socialism as an "active utopia" (Bauman 1976).

25. In a personal communication.

26. Undated paper: "Tradition and modernity in the development of non-European national cultures".

12

VIOLENCE IN SOUTH SLAV SOCIETY

One aspect of the encounter between tradition and modernity I believe should be singled out for particular attention in this context. Popular and press images of the Balkans (which are to a large extent reflected in more academic discussion of the region) frequently draw upon the theme of violence. Along with the themes of fragmentation and confusion, violence has become a component of the definition of the term "Balkan". Not surprisingly this emphasis has come to the fore particularly during the "Wars of the Yugoslav Succession".

The interpretation of the nature and role of violence in the culture of the region takes two quite contradictory directions. The first of these accepts the normality of Balkan violence: this is what one should expect of the Balkans. "How could things be otherwise in this part of the world?" This seems to be implied by Alvin Magid, for example, when he writes of the "bitter atavism" of the common past of the South Slavs, or by Stjepan Mestrovic' reference to the inevitable recurrence of the aggressive personality of "Dinaric Man" (Magid 1991:6; Mestrovic 1993). The other interpretation, which is perhaps more typically focussed upon recent events, and especially upon the reports of atrocity which have emerged in the course of the civil war, sees violence as something which is exceptional, and which requires explanation. "How can these things possibly come to pass in modern Europe?"

Although in many respects the question of violence has fallen outside the purview of mainstream sociology, it is so salient a feature of recent Yugoslav history, and in many respects appears to offer such a huge obstacle to the understanding of the region by outsiders, that I feel obliged to address it directly. My aim is to provide some sociological insight into *the specific cultural forms taken by collective violence in the Balkan context*. I am keenly aware in embarking upon this discussion that I might be rushing into the examination of an area of problems where angels fear to tread. Before beginning the task properly, therefore, it seems important to take note of some of the serious dangers which await the fool who ventures there.

Knowing the "Other": the practice of knowledge

The problems which attend the construction of peoples of other parts of the world have been effectively enunciated already by writers such as Edward Said (1985) and Stuart Hall (1992). (With specific reference to the Balkans see Allcock, in Allcock and Young eds. 1991 and Todorova 1996.) It is not necessary in this context to reproduce that discussion; but before moving to a consideration of the longer term importance of violence in Yugoslav society it will be useful to offer two illustrations which underline the nature of the difficulties in this area. Let us look for a moment at the stories of atrocities which have circulated freely in the press since the start of the Yugoslav war, two examples of which have engaged my attention recently.

In the first of these it is reported that a small boat was intercepted floating down the River Sava, laden with corpses. To it was fastened a board on which was written: "Meat for Belgrade Market". The story is not inherently improbable. It merits closer inspection, however, because several similar versions of the same story are in circulation, which differ in significant details. In one, the boat is filled with heads, not corpses. In another, the specific market in question is named. In yet another, the river becomes the Drina, not the Sava. The corpses are identified in one version as those of a mother and her children. Most remarkable of all is the fact that versions of the same story circulated before 1945, in another war. There is no way in which any of these can be accredited, and their importance does not lie in their having had any factual basis. What we are confronting here has all the attributes of myth. They are powerful symbolic compilations, whose importance has long since ceased to depend in any way upon their veracity. A significant difficulty which attends work in this area of questions is the disentanglement of myth from reality.

A propaganda leaflet from the Serbian Information Centre in London featured a photograph in which "a Muslim soldier displays the head of ... a Serb".[1] The soldier was identified specifically as a Saudi Arabian volunteer, and his victim was named. It would seem that here at least we have a verifiable configuration of historical facts recorded on film. My attention was not drawn to the historical status of the event, however, but to its significance. The 12 June 1993 edition of *The Independent Magazine* carried an article in which it disclosed that the American Office of Wartime Information had in its possession a huge archive of photographic and other material from the Second World War the circulation of which, for a variety of reasons, had been suppressed.[2] One of the items reproduced by *The Independent* was a photograph of the severed head of a Japanese soldier hanging from a tree.

The situation which any inquirer faces with respect to the facts of violence in Balkan societies is on all fours with that of journalists, historians and social scientists on innumerable other occasions. The truth is hard to establish, and to separate from various forms of deliberate or incidental fiction. It is worth noting in this context, however, the importance of an additional dimension to the problem. Because of our tendency to approach Balkan societies through the screen of images which has been erected over the centuries, which emphasises their otherness, we embrace facts about them which we hide from ourselves when these apply also to our own society. Perhaps it is true that Balkan societies are more violent that "western" societies: perhaps not.[3] Nevertheless, we should not overlook the possibility that our perception of difference rests in part upon the existence within "western" societies of mechanisms which systematically suppress the open portrayal of certain kinds of violence when they occur "at home".

Legitimacy, violence and social order

In making any comparative sociological investigation it is important to be on one's guard against those things which are so taken-for-granted in one's own cultural context that the need to question their general applicability is not recognised. This problem arises in the case of the comparative study of violence, in that in western Europe it can almost be regarded as a cultural axiom that violence is illegitimate.

It is essential to point out, however, that an essential step towards the understanding of violence in the Balkans is the recognition of its structured character. Violence is not necessarily random, arbitrary, meaningless, pathological or anti-social. It may be patterned, directed, significant, normal and constitutive of the social. This claim is also true of our own society, of course, only we find it more difficult to recognise its truth. In general keeping with the modernisation process, legitimate violence has come to be regarded as one among many fields of special expertise--the police and the professional military. The public outcry in Britain following the shooting incidents at Hounslow and Dunblane, and the stabbing of a London head teacher, and the massive popular movement at the time of writing in favour of further legal restriction on the availability of hand guns and knives, makes the point that we are intolerant of illegitimate violence, rather than that violence is becoming more prevalent in contemporary Britain. It is not violence *per se* that is illegitimate, but *unofficial* violence. In coming to understand the character of violence in our region, then, it is useful to begin by examining the diverse forms in which legitimate violence has been structured historically.

My review treats two broad dimensions which might be said to make for the positive sanctioning of violence, both of which find their place within the general interpretative framework in terms of processes of modernisation. The first of these is a study of *the forms of legitimate violence*, which I consider in terms of the general level of the militarisation of society, in relation to the feud, and in terms of other violent role-models. I then turn to the level of *the symbolic interpretation of violence*, and discuss the ritualised character of atrocity, as a prelude to the examination of the important links between violence and religion in Balkan societies. Finally, I offer a coda on those types of violence which from the point of view of Balkan cultures might be considered aberrant.

The forms of legitimate violence

i) The militarisation of Balkan society

By "militarisation" I refer to the incompleteness of the process of "disembedding" which Giddens has depicted as characteristic of modernisation (Giddens 1990:21-9). "By disembedding I mean the 'lifting out' of social relations from local contexts of interaction and their restructuring across indefinite spans of time-space" (p.21). He identifies "two types of disembedding mechanisms intrinsically involved in the development of modern social institutions": "symbolic tokens" (such as money) and "expert systems" (p.22).

This process is already to some extent familiar in sociology through the work of Max Weber, who characterised the modern state partly in terms of its monopolisation of the means of legitimate violence. Detached from the clan or aristocratic patronage these means were at the disposal of the state across the entire territory over which it claimed jurisdiction, or indeed wherever its interests were to be pursued. The legitimate deployment of violence in this process came to be the sole prerogative of military experts in the service of the state. A degree of demilitarisation can therefore be said to constitute an expected dimension of modernity.

The retardation of this aspect of modernisation in the Balkans is understandable in relation to the history of the region. Its character as an "imperial borderland" ensured that for long periods the Balkan Peninsula was subjected to intermittent warfare. Even in times of "peace" its frontier status promoted a high degree of insecurity, and predisposed its population to militarisation. This state of affairs was completely institutionalised, of course, in the Habsburg Military Frontier and in the Ottoman institution of the *kapetan*. The continued defence of Montenegrin autonomy can be said to have been premised upon the almost complete militarisation of society.

During the long period of decline of Ottoman authority the indiscipline of the Jannissaries constituted a strong incentive for the local *reaya* to seek to defend their own lives and property. In spite of the formal prohibition against the bearing of arms by Christians the regularity and seriousness of peasant rebellions testifies to the extent to which this was never effectively enforced. Indeed, on occasions the Porte was forced to rely upon the support of loyal *knezovi* (local Slav magnates), organising local resistance, in order to assert its authority over its own dissident troops. The Serbian revolts which created the independent principality emerged from this kind of configuration.

Even within the independent Serb kingdom the tradition of defence based upon a general *levée* of the peasant militia resisted strongly attempts to replace it with a more formalised and rationalised force under the more immediate command of the state, as the Timok rebellion bears witness (Stokes 1990: Chap. 8). Such was the fragility of the Serbian state in the late nineteenth century that it could be said with some justification that the military should be regarded less as an arm of the state distinguished by its professional expertise and more as a species of parallel government.

In the Habsburg lands the continuing militarisation of society (with the exception of the Military Frontier, already mentioned) took a different form. Here military institutions were incompletely disembedded from aristocratic hierarchy, which in turn was patterned upon the ethnic divisions of the Empire. Perhaps it is more appropriate to speak here of a militarised *estate within society*.

The era of peasant revolts was to some extent replaced by an age in which armed rebellion was used to challenge the hegemony of the state, especially with respect to the conflict over the relationship between state and nation. The Kvaternik uprising in Croatia in 1871 offered such a challenge, as did the several outbreaks of armed violence in which Croat units of the former Habsburg armies joined with discontented peasants to form *zeleni kadrovi* in 1918 (Banac 1984:88; 127-9). Between 1918 and 1924 the newly installed government of the unified South Slav state faced a series of attempts by Albanians to resist their incorporation into an alien regime and to force the redrawing of the international boundary (Malcolm 1998: Chap. 14; Banac 1984:296 9 and 302-6). The incorporation of Montenegro into the unified South Slav state in 1918 was only achieved by the suppression of a brief civil war (Banac 1984:284-8).

Throughout the inter-war period, high levels both of internal ethnic tension and external threat tended to entrench military institutions within the state, to reinforce the links between militarism and specific ethnic groups, undermining in both directions the creation of an independent professional military. Conscription remained the basis of the armed forces, ensuring a broad diffusion of military skills.

The militarisation of society could be said to have been carried to an extreme point in the 1941-45 period. In many respects that state of affairs was merely institutionalised at a lower level in the post-1945 period, with the development of the doctrine of total people's defence and the reliance upon territorial militias in order to supplement the somewhat more professionalised officer corps of the Yugoslav Peoples' Army. The link between party and army remained very close, and as James Gow has argued, "regime legitimacy" and "military legitimacy" remained intimately interdependent. (Gow 1992. See also his essay in Milivojevic, Allcock and Maurer eds. 1988.)

The direct representation of the military in organs of the League of Communists remained broadly constant and significant, even through the supposed liberalisation of the 1960s. Following the conflict with the leadership of the Croatian LC in 1971-2, and the constitutional restructuring of 1974, the position of the military within the League was strengthened.

In 1974 the proportion of military officers in the Central Committee doubled to form 10.8 percent of the total membership. Moreover, the "new" military contingent (16 of the 18 officers) was made up almost entirely of members of the prewar and wartime political generation ... The increase of military representation in the Central Committee, and particularly the older more conservative military personnel, was clearly related to the support that Tito and the "party center" received from the armed forces during the political risis of 1971-1972. The re-emergence of what has been described as the "virtually symbiotic" relationship of the party and the military during the Partisan

resistance, reflected conservative disenchantment with the constellation of

reformist political forces that had achieved elite office during the 1960s. (Cohen

1989:159)

That active engagement of the military elite in the wider political struggle continued

to be apparent during the period leading to the eventual break-up of the Socialist

Federation (Cohen 1993:85-88 and 181-192).[5]

Yugoslav society can therefore be said to have remained highly militarised over a

long period of time, at the level of the organic ties between the military and other elite

groups; at the level of the dispersion of military skills, technology and experience

throughout the population; and at the level of the significance of values relating to the

use of violence which remained embedded within general culture. The three following

points all illustrate and explore in one way or another aspects of that residual

militarisation of South Slav cultures.

ii) Obligatory violence: the feud

Before the Yugoslav federation began to break up in war it is likely that if asked to

free associate about the idea of violence in the Balkans a large number of people

would have talked about the blood feud. In modern western Europe the idea of killing

for revenge is seen as unquestionably primitive, signifying either the failure of "law

and order" and an ineffective state or a criminality which defies the state, courts and

the orderly settlement of disputes. The exaction of vengeance is perceived as individualistic, anarchic and to do with the satisfaction of a personal emotional drive where there ought to be impersonally and rationally administered justice.

The perception of the blood feud in terms of "revenge" is largely to misunderstand it. The taking of blood in south eastern Europe has been typically a highly structured phenomenon. One did not seek revenge because of an uncivilised disregard for convention. One sought to take blood as a duty. The occasion upon which blood vengeance had to be sought, the agent who was required to enact it, and the means by which the debt of blood had to be assuaged were all codified in terms known to all. The events which may precipitate a feud and the conditions under which it may be extinguished were equally the subject of public definition.

These claims are illustrated most clearly in the traditional Albanian "Law of Lek", a thorough account of which has been provided by Margaret Hasluck (1954).[6] Although this tradition has survived into the contemporary period in its most explicit, codified and developed form among Albanians, it is known to have played a significant part in the traditions of other Balkan peoples on a far wider scale (Simic 1967). Its waning has been brought about by the extension of effective state power: the monopolisation of the use of legitimate force by the state. It is likely that it both anticipated the establishment of viable states and underwent a resurgence in those periods when the state failed to act as the sole source of the effective dispensation of justice. The tradition of vengeance has been largely associated with those parts of the Balkans which were formerly under Turkish rule, and in which the state was for long periods both ineffective and illegitimate.

Edith Durham identifies the specific characteristics of blood-taking as follows:

The blood-feud is misunderstood when it is spoken of as "vengeance" and regarded only as a punishment for crime. It has almost a religious quality; ... in the minds of the people there was a vast difference between killing a man as a result of a quarrel, or when robbing him, and "taking blood." The first is murder; the second is a duty, painful, dangerous, fatal perhaps--but a duty that must be done. (Durham 1928:162)

Durham reports that, in conversation with those who had "taken blood" in this way, they insisted that they had done so because they were obliged to do so.[7]

Far from representing the breakdown of order, the feud is the expression or implementation of order: *not the decay of structure but the process of structuration itself*. Violence is order in operation, enjoined upon actors in the fulfilment of their roles, not *prima facie* evidence of the failure of their socialisation.

This observation throws into sharp relief the question which so frequently accompanies reports of "ethnic cleansing" in the British press: "How could they possibly do this to their neighbours?" The point which this question fails to grasp is that traditional codes of morality in the past would have required that people be ready to kill their neighbours, as these were precisely the people with whom it was most likely that one might be "in blood".

iii) Heroic role-models of violence

Extending the notion of the institutionalised character of violence in south eastern Europe, it is important to acknowledge the occasions on which the perpetrators of violent acts have come to be presented as positive role models. In this respect a more or less continuous lineage can be traced which unites the period before the creation of modern states on the Balkan Peninsula and the present day.

Our genealogy begins with the *hajduk*. Stories of the activities of the *hajduci* (bandits) make up a large part of the stock of folk literature, giving to such individuals the proverbial character of the English Robin Hood.[8] In much the same way the *hajduk* was honoured as the symbol of continuing resistance against the Turk, although as Eric Hobsbawm insists: "Haiduk banditry was .... in every respect a more serious, permanent and institutionalized challenge to official authority than the scattering of Robin Hoods or other robber rebels which emerged from any normal peasant society" (Hobsbawm 1969:66).

The legitimate violence of the Balkan bandit stands in an interesting and revealing contrast to the widely-noted tradition of hospitality in the region. Travellers throughout the region over the centuries have remarked upon the open-handed hospitality with which they were received; and this is a cultural asset which has been made much of by the tourist industries of the Balkan countries. Tradition clearly distinguishes between two statuses and the behaviours which are expected towards them: the guest and the alien. Coming into the local community the former is attached to specific members of it, and in a sense sponsored by them. Typically, the travellers of the nineteenth and early twentieth century, whose accounts of their journeys make such fascinating reading today, were accompanied on their journeys by local guides. To the "outsider" whose status was guaranteed through association with an identifiable "insider" were extended the privileges of hospitality.

This definition of the situation did not hold where "outsiders" were not guaranteed in this way, or whose identity was established as that of alien/enemy groups. These then became fair game for plunder or ransom. The Turk, the foreign merchant, the stranger, all travelled in fear of their purses if not of their lives; and over large areas of the Balkan Peninsula even into the twentieth century they were typically accompanied by armed guards.

Looking at accounts of *hajducija*, then, it is clear that the bandit can not be regarded as "deviant" in Balkan society in any simple sense. To be an "outlaw" was to live in a situation which was by no means without rules or clear definition, even if it placed the person outside the law. The term suggests to us somebody who is outside, not only the law, but outside of *society*. The study of banditry in the Balkans shows clearly that this is not the case; it has to be understood as a feature of these societies.

The famous Uskoks of Senj provide a case which stands in some respects mid-way between banditry and more formalised military traditions (Bracewell 1992). In this case an entire community made its living largely from raiding. The *Uskoci* emerged in the early sixteenth century as communities of independent warriors along the northern coast of Dalmatia. Loosely attached to the Venetian and Habsburg states as irregular troops providing garrisons along this part of the frontier against the Ottoman Empire, they by no means confined their depradations to the Turk. Acquiring the reputation of pirates, their presence in the Adriatic was regarded as a mixed blessing. When the Ottoman menace began to abate in the seventeenth century they were finally suppressed by the co-operative action of Venetian and Habsburg forces.

Like the *hajduci* the *uskoci* were for a long time regarded as mere "outlaws"
symptomatic of political disorder.

> .... the warfare that developed along these borders is sometimes described as
> anarchic, a *bellum omnium contra omnes*, in which frontiersmen raided
> indiscriminately, constrained by little but their own immediate interests.
> Nonetheless, these frontiers did operate according to their own laws, although
> not necessarily those of the states that claimed to rule them. In the frontier no-
> man's land where the authority of the state did not reach, the inhabitants worked
> out their own codes of behaviour. They also developed new forms of
> community and identity. (Bracewell 1992 :13)

One feature unites both the *hajduci* and the *uskoci* to the present day, even though in
the case of the latter more than two centuries have elapsed since their extinction. Both
have acquired a significant place in the folk literature of the region, and are looked
back to by contemporary locals with some pride rather than with shame.[9] They
provide role-models of heroic conduct which are partly defined in terms of a capacity
for violent challenge to the state.

The importance of violent groups and individuals as positive role-models in South
Slav culture is underlined by the long history of peasant rebellion. Sporadic outbursts
of armed resistance by the peasantry against their overlords were endemic throughout
the Balkan Peninsula, particularly during the eighteenth and nineteenth centuries. The
frequency of these is underestimated in most western European historical treatments
of the region, which find a place only for those which grew to such a degree of
seriousness that they began to impinge upon international relations. Such was the

Bosnian revolt of 1874, which eventually led to the Austro-Hungarian protectorate over the province. After 1870 the steady disintegration of the Ottoman state was further accelerated by the activities of armed irregulars, proselytising the national identity of their fellow Slavs with the aid of the bomb and the bayonet.

The tradition of peasant revolt has been given much greater significance by domestic commentators. These uprisings have been read by nationalist historians as the early stirrings of national movements of liberation from foreign oppression, and by socialist historians as the forerunners of proletarian revolution, along the lines of Engels' analysis of *The Peasant War in Germany*. The two most celebrated examples of these rebellions are the uprising led by Matija Gubec in 1573, which affected northern Croatia and parts of Slovenia, and the Serbian *Kocina krajina* of 1788.

Gubec called for the restoration of the peasant's "ancient rights", and the establishment of a peasant government in Zagreb which would owe direct fealty to the Emperor without the mediation of an oppressive nobility (*Enciklopedija Jugoslavije* 1958:Vol.3, 633). Although Gubec himself was tortured to death, folk legend tells the Croat version of an extremely widely-known European fable, which describes Gubec as drinking red wine with his associates inside a mountain, awaiting the time when he will rise again and play his part in the freeing of the people.

In 1788 a merchant named Koca Andjelkovic, with covert Austrian backing, raised an army which for some time drove the Turks from a swathe of northern Serbia (*Kocina krajina*). The rug was pulled from under the Serbs by Austria's signature of the Treaty of Sistova in 1791 but nevertheless the episode remained celebrated in folk memory (*Enciklopedija Jugoslavije* 1958:Vol.5, 286).

The stories of such peasant revolts deepen and extend the images of nations founded in violent struggle, exemplified by Montenegrin self-definitions as those who never ceased to fight the Turk; by the importance placed by Serbs upon the uprisings led by Karadjordje Petrovic (in 1804) and Milos Obrenovic (in 1813); and by the Macedonian portrayal of the Ilinden uprising as the moment when the nation found its soul.

These armed uprisings have left in the folk memory a deep and lasting precipitate of *komitadzi*, *cetnici* and other heroic irregulars, who are available as exemplars of justified violent resistance against alien rule or class exploitation. All of these images are brought together in the *partizan* tradition of 1941-45, when they take on the function of providing historic-mythological sanction both for social revolution and a "war of national liberation". *In this respect Communism enshrined violence rather than ended it.* Far from providing a revolutionary break with the past, at this level at least it merely provided a transposition of old themes into a new key.

The same point holds good about the forms in which violence has been cast in the period following the collapse of the federation. The former Serbian Democratic Party leader Dragoljub Micunovic has coined the apt phrase the "folklorisation of politics" in order to describe the ideological recasting of Yugoslav politics during and since the period of disintegration.[10] This process can be taken as running from the sentimentalisation of all things alpine on the part of the Slovenes; through the phase in which the head of the Serbian Party of Renewal, Vuk Draskovic, sought to infuse Serbian nationalism with the cult of St. Sava; to the plagiarism of the title "IMRO" (the Internal Macedonian Revolutionary Organisation) by contemporary Macedonian nationalists. One of its most blatant aspects, however, has been the adoption by the leaders of various irregular formations of military titles which hark back explicitly to these earlier role-models: *Vojvoda* or *cetnik*, for example.

At a more popular and personal level, the concept of *junastvo* (heroism) continues to provide a central component of an ideal masculinity throughout the Balkans, which is constantly urged upon male children.

The symbolic interpretation of violence

i) Ritualised atrocity[11]

Acts described as "atrocities" have provided the focus for a great deal of the press coverage of the Yugoslav war outside the region, and have constituted an important part of the propaganda effort of all sides, seeking to discredit their opponents. More than anything else, atrocity stories have served to buttress the image of the fundamental alterity of the South Slavs.

It is no doubt the case that in any armed conflict injury will be inflicted upon a defeated enemy which the majority of members of that society would find abhorrent. By suggesting that we might examine critically the boundaries of the concept of atrocity I have no intention of implying that by treating as contextually "normal" some acts which we would regard as atrocious there is no limit on those actions which might pass as acceptable in war. Many of the actions in question appear to me to be deeds of the type which Peter Berger has identified as demanding:

... not only condemnation, but damnation in the full religious meaning of the word--that is, the doer not only puts himself outside the community of men; he also separates himself in a final way from a moral order that transcends the human community, and thus evokes a retribution that is more than human.

(Berger 1971)

Nevertheless, these things do yield to historical and sociological analysis. Perhaps there can be (and indeed ought to be) a "sociology of damnation": and the next section of this chapter can be read as a tentative and reluctant contribution to that sub-discipline.[12] When we begin to examine those acts which we would damn as atrocious in the Yugoslav civil war we do find that there are historical echoes, regularities, rationality, and indeed what might be described as a "rhetoric of atrocity".

The more or less systematic mutilation of the enemy has a long pedigree in the history of the region. The shadow of the eleventh century Emperor Basil II (the "Bulgar-slayer") lies across the entire peninsula. The Turks brought with them a reputation for appalling punishments inflicted upon enemies and criminals. Following the defeat of a revolt against Turkish rule in 1809 the Turkish commandant of the garrison at Nis ordered that the heads of defeated Serbs should be used to build a tower, as a permanent discouragement to any who were tempted to disobedience in the future.[13] A standard form of execution employed during the years of Ottoman domination was the impaling, graphically described by Ivo Andric in his *Bridge on the Drina* (Andric 1959:42-52).

Any belief that this kind of judicial atrocity was the sole prerogative of the Turk is challenged by the manner of death of Matija Gubec--subjected to a mock coronation

538

with a crown of red-hot iron. Although judicial tortures at least as horrific as these were commonplace in western Europe (burnings at the stake; the drawing and quartering of the bodies of hanged criminals, preferably while they retained consciousness) these practices were largely eliminated by the end of the eighteenth century. In the Ottoman Empire, however, they evidently persisted into the late nineteenth century.

Actions which we might regard as atrocious appear to have roots among the South Slavs themselves, however, and can not be dismissed as the actions of external oppressors. Edith Durham records the practice of "nose-taking" among the tribes on Montenegro, a case of which she finds as late as 1912.

> Kovatchevitch, the lame schoolmaster at Podgoritza, "Professor of Modern Languages", and proud of having been in British employ in Egypt, said to me gleefully: "Now you will see plenty of noses! Even baskets full." I told him sternly that such conduct would disgust all Europe. He flew into a rage and declared nose-cutting was a national custom and Turks not human beings. ....
> The desire to take a nose was so great that a man whose hands were not free would seize his enemy's nose in his teeth and try to bite it off. (Durham 1928:177-8)

The practice of cutting off the noses of slain enemies (or even of those who were merely wounded) and hanging these from the belt by means of the accompanying moustache, bears resemblance to the native American custom of scalping. That we are dealing here with something more than mere individual derangement as an explanation for such acts is evident from their standardised, customary, and even ritualised, aspects.

It is the ritual character of atrocity which perhaps gives us the strongest clue as to its significance. Many of the actions which we would so designate are clearly associated in the mythical and the historical record with religion. One of the most dramatic illustrations of this is the occasion known to historians as "The Montenegrin Vespers". Its significance is such that it is recalled in two of the greatest contributions to Montenegrin literature, the folk epic *Sve-Oslobod* ("Wholly Free") and the *Gorski Vjenac* ("Mountain Wreath") of Petar Petrovic Njegos.

The story is told that so incensed were the tribesmen by the capture and torture by the Turks of their *Vladika* Danilo, that on Christmas Eve 1703, after taking a solemn oath and consecrating themselves, the Montenegrin chiefs offered all who had converted to Islam the choice of baptism or death.[14] It is no exaggeration to speak of this legendary act in terms of "atrocity as sacrament", for it is through slaughter that its perpetrators claim to have earned the title "wholly free".

It is only within this framework, I believe, that it is possible to make any sense of the appalling horrors committed by the Croat *Ustasa* movement during the Second World War. The openly espoused policy of the indigenous fascist *Nezavisna Drzava Hrvatske* (NDH: Independent State of Croatia) was the elimination of ethnic minorities regarded as hostile to it--especially the large Serb minority, and gypsies. This was to be accomplished partly through the export of "undesirables" as forced labour. Additionally, however, the notorious camp at Jasenovac was set up, modelled in part upon those designed to accomplish Hitler's "final solution" to the Jewish problem. Less bureaucratic methods were generally adopted by the *Ustasa*, however, bands of whom descended upon Serb villages, compelling "conversions" to Roman Catholicism and torturing and murdering those who refused to comply (Bulajic 1989; Steinberg 1992).

Although no good purpose can be served by dwelling upon the details of the grotesque virtuosity demonstrated by the *Ustasa* in this work, something of the peculiar character of atrocity among the South Slavs can perhaps be illuminated by reference to the language which is used in giving account of it. Here two words will provide us with the key which might unlock the special character in particular of *Ustasa* atrocity, but which are possibly of more general relevance.

The key concept is that of *klanje*, or "slaughter". The import of this word is unavoidable. It is normally used of cattle; but it was also used both by the *Ustasa* and their prospective victims to describe terrorist killing. The stereotypical method of killing on these occasions was the knife. In describing to me these events Yugoslavs have spontaneously talked of people being "put to the knife" as a synonym for the general process of ethnic extermination.[15]

As in all structuralist analysis one needs to look for the contrast of marked and unmarked signs; and here the intended comparison is with death by shooting. In war one shoots one's opponents: but in doing so they are not denied recognition of their humanity. The cutting of throats, however, places the victim quite explicitly on a par with animals, both in the method of meeting out death and in the verbal description of it. The cutting of throats (or beheading, also used by the *Ustasa*) is not a randomly vicious act: it communicates within a rhetoric of atrocity in a very precise manner.

The point is driven home by an examination of a second key word here: *zrtva*, which is the word typically used to refer to the victim of atrocity. In the dictionary the first meaning of this term is a "sacrifice". The conjunction of *klanje* and *zrtvovanje* is too striking to pass over. Killing of this kind is more than mere killing: it is the offering of the slain as if they are sacrificial animals. It is atrocity raised to the level of sacrament.

Probably one of the most arresting facts about the material which I have presented is the manner in which the commitment of atrocity is embraced by its perpetrators as having symbolic value. The celebration of *victims* is not at all unusual by religious or national communities. The crucifixion of Jesus and the Jewish holocaust are no doubt only the most well-known illustrations of what Glenn Bowman has described as "constitutive violence" (Bowman 1994).[16] Nevertheless, it is the *Montenegrins* and not the Turks who "constitute" themselves in relation to the "Montenegrin Vespers", finding in it the defining moment of their nation. It is the post-independence Croatian government which has, in the face of vigorous regional criticism and the expressed unease of other European governments, emphasised the historical continuity between the new Croatia and the *NDH* regime of 1941-5.[17] Although there is a substantial component of denial that anything untoward has ever happened, an equally powerful and totally contradictory component of Serb public response to the atrocities against Muslims in Bosnia actively embraces these events as a part of the eternal mission of the Serb people (Cigar 1995:Chap. 6).

I believe that the case developed by Michael Sells, to the effect that both Serbs and Croats have been motivated over a long period of time by a "Christoslavic" ideology, which endows their intolerance and acts of persecution with religious significance, is overdrawn (Sells 1996; reviewed Allcock 1997). Nevertheless, I acknowledge the importance of exploring the connection between atrocity and religion in the Balkans, in the sense that it directs our attention towards the examination of the *symbolic* character of such violence.

A valuable *aperçu* is offered to us by Michel Foucault's analysis of torture in *his Discipline and Punish* (Foucault 1979). Foucault documents the movement in penal practice from a punitive regime of physical penalties which were effected directly upon the body of the accused, to one in which the individual is deprived of liberty.

> ... the punishment-body relation is not the same as it was in the torture during public executions. The body now serves as an instrument or intermediary: if one intervenes upon it to imprison it, or make it work, it is in order to deprive the individual of a liberty that is regarded both as a right and as property. ....
> Physical pain, the pain of the body itself, is no longer the constituent element of the penalty. From being an art of unbearable sensations punishment has become an economy of suspended rights. (Foucault 1979:11)

The punishment formerly visited upon the body of the accused spoke eloquently of the nature of the crime, culminating in the monstrous tortures described in Foucault's first chapter, reserved for the regicide. I suggest that in atrocity we might find a harking back to actions which through their direct impact upon the body speak eloquently of the symbolic significance of the victim. Atrocity is intended above all to communicate. If we find ourselves in the realm of symbols here it is worth attending more precisely to the nature of that symbolism.

ii) Atrocity as "implicit religion"

I have already commented in an earlier chapter upon some aspects of the importance

of religion in Balkan societies. There is an additional sense, however, in which the

sociological analysis of religion can help to provide an interpretation of the symbolic

significance of violence, although in a sense different from that suggested by Michael

Sells. It will be useful to begin this section with Emile Durkheim's definition of

religion.

> A religion is a unified system of beliefs and practices relative to sacred things,
>
> that is to say, things set apart and forbidden--beliefs and practices which unite
>
> into one single moral community called a Church, all those who adhere to them.
>
> (Durkheim 1915 [1912]:47)

Coming as it does near the start of his *Elementary Forms*, this passage prepares the

way for his discussion of the importance of the sense of heightened sociability which

attends the participation of believers in religious ritual--which he terms

"effervescence". Another dimension of Durkheim's definition, however, is his

attention to the symbols which lie at the heart of these collective celebrations.

Durkheim's concept of the "sacred" is worth noting in this context, which he

characterises in terms of "things set apart and forbidden" (Durkheim 1915:47). What

he is telling us here is that we need to pay attention to that sense of the exceptional

vividness of symbols which might make them adequate to the task of generating and

sustaining "effervescence".

The contemporary sociological notion of "implicit religion" emerges from

Durkheim's observation that in secularised societies there is perhaps a continuing need for objects or practices which, while outwardly secular, nevertheless provide the same symbolic focus for solidarity which is offered by more conventionally sacred things (Durkheim 1983 [1955]:91).[18] The ordinary, banal or everyday event is not apt for sacralisation: in this context I suggest that perhaps atrocity is.

One of the features of culture which has excited the interest of anthropologists over a long period of time has been the effectiveness of the ritual inversions of the normal everyday order of things is providing symbolic foci for ritual, whether explicitly or implicitly religious. Phenomena of this kind have figured in such contrasting theoretical traditions as Max Gluckman's *Custom and Conflict in Africa* (1965) and Claude Levi-Strauss' *The Savage Mind* (1962).[19]

The kind of grotesque and deliberate inversion of the normal seems to me to be characteristic of the ritualised atrocity which has marked the "Wars of the Yugoslav Succession". In this respect, Bruce Lincoln has provided us with an analysis of the discourse implied by the exhumations of the bodies of religious, and their public display, by republican forces during the Spanish civil war, with which it is instructive to compare recent atrocities in the Balkans (Lincoln 1989).

"Rituals of collective obscenity" are used by Lincoln as the symbolic key to underlying social processes.

> ... if it is true, ... that in some measure society is constructed (and continually reconstructed) through the exercise of symbolic discourse, then the deconstruction of widely recognized and even revered symbols may be seen as an attempt to undo their effects, that is, to deconstruct the social forms that others have constructed and maintain through them. (p.117)

.... For just as the thin layer of preserved skin spread across the mummified corpses served only to accentuate the death and decay beneath, so also the veil of sanctity in which the Church cloaked itself served only to accentuate its underlying corruption. (p.126)

Lincoln insists that such acts can not be dismissed as merely "aberrant and impious acts of violence".

Such a simplistic analysis is untenable .... they were a ritual in which the traditionally subordinate segment of Spanish society sought by means of a highly charged discourse of gestures and deeds to deconstruct the old social order.(p.127)

This idea that the conduct of violence is endowed with meaning naturally points towards a more detailed analysis of the codes which govern communication in this area. Although I have formed unsystematic ideas of the forms of violence and the selection of its victims, some of which emerge in these pages, the task of providing anything which matches the accepted rigours of semiotic analysis will not be attempted here. Several collections of material are in circulation which document in intimate and horrific detail the kinds of injuries to which victims or war have been subjected during the disintegration of Yugoslavia. (The following are representative of the *genre: Croatian Medical Journal* 1992; Lajtman ed. 1991; Isakovic ed. 1992.)[20] The selection and display of such material tells me at least as much about those who deploy it as it does about those who are alleged to be the original perpetrators of the act portrayed. In this respect it is important to distinguish between the "semiotics of atrocity" (the investment of violent *acts* with meaning) and the "semiotics of the representation of atrocity" (the investment of *depictions* of atrocity with meaning).

Similar issues arise, although in a more concentrated form, in relation to the controversy about the character and incidence of rape during the Yugoslav wars.[21] It has often been alleged that a particular feature of the recent Balkan conflicts has been the frequency of rape, and indeed there have been widely reported claims that this has taken an organised form, and even that rape on a massive scale has been adopted as a part of a deliberate policy of intimidation. The conflict in Bosnia-Hercegovina has been singled out as "the rapists' pinnacle" (Meznaric 1993:126). Whereas rape is a regrettably regular feature of human communities throughout the world and across history, particularly during times of war, these allegations of scale, organisation and policy have marked out the recent experience of Yugoslavia as highly unusual if not unique. Consequently it might appear that discussion of the matter ought to be deferred to my section on "aberrant" violence.

It is hard to assess the arguments in this area, for a variety of reasons. Statistics of the incidence of rape are notoriously unreliable, if for no other reason than the fact that as a crime there are powerful disincentives to the reporting of it by its victims. These may be presumed to be particularly strong in societies such as those which occupy the Balkan peninsula, which are characterised by high value placed upon the "honour" of women, and the shame attached to their violation (Drakulic 1993). As measured by official criminal statistics, rape has been a relatively uncommon crime in former Yugoslavia.[22] Nevertheless, there have been repeated claims about the very high frequency of this crime during war: Silvana Meznaric cites a variety of estimates ranging from 16-50,000.[23] It is particularly hard to assess arguments in this area not only because of the inherent difficulty of obtaining reliable information, but also because of the tendency of press coverage to sensationalise the issue, which in sections of the British press has created a kind of legitimated pornography. The problem is compounded the obvious propaganda value which attaches to such stories, as components of a campaign of the demonisation of the enemy.

For these reasons, stories of "rape camps" are to be distrusted. A briefing document from the UNHCR cites a claim (originating with the government of Bosnia-Hercegovina) that 35,000 women were held in so-called "rape camps" (Women Living under Muslim Laws 1994:595). The report's authors add, however, that "no human rights organisation or NGO has been able to corroborate the existence of special camps .... we suggest that numerical estimates of any aspect of the issue be treated with caution". There have been well-substantiated reports of the creation of *ad hoc* bordellos on a relatively small scale. The sexual abuse of women held in various forms of detention has been widespread: but to designate these as "rape camps" carries an additional symbolic freight, with its obvious rhetorical echoes of concentration camps, which might account for the use of the phrase in spite of its evident liability to distort the truth. Although there is clearly an important phenomenon to be explained here, any discussion should bear in mind Meznaric's caution: "data and resources are not reliable" (Meznaric 1993:127).

Three points should be made in approaching the interpretation of the incidence of rape during the Yugoslav conflict. In the first place, it does not appear to be true that the frequency of this crime has been uniquely high during the course of the Yugoslav

conflict. A French study notes that:

> Earlier, in Japan, in 1937 after the sack of Nankin, where thousands of women
>
> were violated, the Japanese government decided to provide "girls" for the
>
> soldiers in order to avoid the worsening of anti-Japanese feeling. Consequently
>
> around 200,000 Asian women (mainly from Korea) were enclosed in military
>
> brothels. It was South Korean feminists who lifted the veil over this in 1980.
>
> (Visser 1993:45)

Thousands of German women were raped by the Russians in 1944, in Viet Nam by

American forces, and during the Algerian civil war (Visser 1993:45; Women Living

under Muslim Laws 1994:565; Seifert, in Stiglmayer ed. 1994:54). Yugoslav

historians Dedijer and Miletic have observed that "in the Balkans, rape was always a

part of military campaigns" (cited in Meznaric 1993:126). For these reasons,

therefore, claims about the uniqueness of recent Yugoslav experience have to be

regarded with suspicion.[24]

A third point to note in this context is the characteristic "normal" pattern of sexual

violence in Yugoslavia. Although I have remarked upon low rates of reported rape,

this contrasts with relatively high rates of domestic violence. The seriousness of this

problem is also reported to have increased during the course of the war (Sander, in

Morokvasic ed. 1992). There are few reliable data concerning the ethnicity of either

rapists or their victims in Yugoslavia. Nevertheless, an interesting study

commissioned by the Forum for Human Rights in 1990, following a period of the

growth of particular concern about allegations of rape in Kosovo between 1986-88, actually concluded that *inter*-ethnic rape was relatively rare, and that the incidence of intra-ethnic rape was heavily over-represented (cited in Meznaric 1993:122-25).[25]

Bearing in mind these observations, it does not seem unreasonable to suggest that in the circumstances of the war perhaps the phenomenon of rape in Yugoslavia has not been particularly unusual. There is doubt as to whether it can be considered as "aberrant" (sociologically speaking at least: its moral status is another matter!) What is remarkable, however, is the prominent part played by the *discourse of rape* during the period of the disintegration of the federation. From this point of view, the approach which I have outlined above in terms of the importance of attending to the *symbolic role of atrocity* emerges as potentially valuable as a framework in which to interpret rape. Although there are differences between the way in which this idea is used by different authors, this general idea has been put forward by several Yugoslav feminist writers.

Two points emerge from the literature in this connection. Firstly, there is widespread agreement that rape can not be understood as a phenomenon in isolation. It has to be considered in relation to other aspects of gender relations in society, and to other forms of the expression of aggression (esp. Visser 1993:45; several of the contributions in Stiglmayer ed, 1994: esp. Seifert, xix-xx). Secondly, there is a wide range of differing theoretical approaches available which seek to conceptualise the nature of the symbolic processes which are at work here. There is no room within this context to review this extensive and multi-disciplinary discussion.[26] There is a recurring theme to many of these, however, which can be summed up in the words of Ruth Seifert. "The rape of women ....communicates from man to man" (Seifert, in

Stiglmayer ed. 1994:59). The act of rape has to be separated from its overtly sexual character: "one can say that the rapist's sexuality is not at the centre of his act; it is placed instrumentally at the service of the violent act" (p.56). She insists that "rapes are part of the 'rules' of war". They have to do with the manner in which war engages masculinity in a variety of projects, including the diminution of the masculinity of other males, the denigration of their culture, and even the living out of the "culturally rooted contempt for women" which characterises their own culture. It is this communicative aspect of rape which identifies it, therefore, not as a *prima facie* case of "aberrant" violence, but as a supreme exemplar of the kinds of "sacramental" or "implicitly religious" representations which I have discussed above.

The interpretation of violence which I have offered here is admittedly speculative, but necessarily so. Tentative as it is, however, I suggest that the advantage of my approach is that it does enable us to grapple sociologically with materials which we might otherwise be tempted to dismiss as beyond understanding.

Coda on "aberrant" violence[27]

It is not always possible to trace the forms and rhetoric of violence to the continuing importance of historical and cultural models within South Slav society, in the manner which I have outlined here. Some features of violence in the Yugoslav civil war can be regarded as more or less aberrant--at least with respect to their immediate cultural context. It pays in such cases to look for exogenous models.

In this search it is interesting to examine the role of the western entertainment media. Films such as the "Rambo" and "Mad Max" series have provided a range of models, if not of conduct then certainly of the presentation of self which are visibly significant. The popularity in Croatia of the Brazilian TV series based upon the bandit Lampiao is also worth recalling. The creation of the Serb militias in the *krajina* was accompanied by "hype" about the *knindje*, which drew quite obviously upon the current craze for the American cartoon series featuring "teenage mutant Ninja turtles".

Rambo sweatbands or bandoliers, bizarre haircuts or idiosyncratic "uniforms", or the use of black balaclavas, by paramilitaries have been assimilated as components of a *style* of warfare, the sources of which must be found outside the Balkans. I suggest that a more detailed examination of the iconography of war in the Balkans would reveal some significant patterns in this respect. These supposedly "aberrant" features of contemporary violence among the South Slavs nevertheless have one thing in common. They underline the cultural *integration* of the region with the rest of Europe and "The West", rather than its essentially alien character.

Another of the features of the "Wars of the Yugoslav Succession" which might be regarded as "aberrant" has been the technology of war. In an earlier discussion of war in Yugoslavia I argued that any future war in Yugoslavia would almost certainly not be a re-run of the 1941-45 *partizan* struggle, simply because this kind of warfare depended upon the availability of a certain kind of social structure to support it which is no longer there (Allcock in Milivojevic, Maurer and Allcock eds. 1988). This claim has turned out to be remarkably prescient. One of the most characteristic features of the recent war has, in fact, been the siege conducted primarily by means of artillery.

This was an important characteristic of the war in both Croatia and Slovenia, conducted against *JNA* installations, as well as the more highly publicised urban sieges, such as Vukovar, Dubrovnik and Sarajevo.

The siege is a relatively efficient way of containing forces with a relatively small counter-force, especially if (as in the case of the urban sieges mentioned) these forces are equipped with an abundance of destructive technology. This was precisely the situation, in particular, of the army of the *Republika Srpska*, hampered by a shortage of manpower, and the extreme parochialism of that which was available, limiting their mobility. As a manipulated, "top down" conflict characterised by massive rates of desertion, manpower has generally been short, especially on the Serb side. Serb resistance crumbled, both in the *krajina* and the *Republika Srpska*, when they were confronted by highly mobile and committed units which included effectively trained and deployed infantry.

The technology with which siege actions were conducted can not be considered to be specifically indigenous, but belong within a *global* military culture. Yugoslavia has become since 1945 a very important player within the international arms market (Milivojevic 1990). If we are horrified by what we see in the Balkans it is not enough to remain comfortably within the stockade of an argument which explains what we see in terms of long-term indigenous cultural continuities. The implication of the region within processes of globalisation is indicated just as vividly by the facts of our providing them with "cultural munitions" as it is by our participation with them in an international arms trade. In this respect as in so many others, perhaps when we look more closely we might begin to discern our own image in the mirror which they hold up to us.

There has been a lively debate in recent years about the changing nature of modern warfare, which counterposes to an emphasis upon professionalism and high technology a model of "post-modern war" conducted by "paramilitaries, guerrillas, militias and warlords" (Ignatieff 1998:5). The time-scale in relation to which these hypotheses have been framed is too short to see clearly patterns of either kind; and it is a moot point as to which was the determining characteristic of the Yugoslav conflict, the low-level barbarities of "Arkan's" militia, or the massive NATO aerial bombardment which forced the Bosnian Serbs to Dayton.[28] However history gives an account of the conflict of 1991-1995, it will be necessary to place the process of explanation within a context which makes sense of the global changes which might be remodelling warfare.

In a highly polemical essay Stjepan Mestrovic has been moved by what he regards as the tardy and ineffective response of the West to the Yugoslav wars, to suggested that what we have witnessed since 1991 is a process of "the balkanization of the West" (Mestrovic 1995). No longer sustained by the core moral values of its historical culture, the West is collapsing into "decivilisation" under the impact of events in the region. The problem with Mestrovic's formulation of the problem is that it is ambiguous. It is unclear as to whether he intends this to be seen as a process of *cultural diffusion* (like rot spreading in the barrel from the bad apple), or whether we confront in Yugoslavia the general consequences of the plight of "postmodernity". I believe that the thesis of "balkanization" is misplaced, however, for the following reason.

We seem to apply curiously double standards in our expressions of horror about what has happened in the Balkans, and the irruption of violence there, in two respects. Whether or not the "Western" response to the Yugoslav crisis can indeed be characterised as belated, ineffective, or exhibiting a "triumph of the lack of will", there was a general presupposition that we were engaged, and that "something must be done" (Gow 1997). This response stands in dramatic contrast to the response to some other current conflicts. Perhaps it is a reflection of Said's "orientalism" that we are indifferent to the death toll in Algeria since the declaration of the state of emergency in 1992, which according to some accounts has exceeded that in Yugoslavia.

We appear to have been able to contemplate unflinchingly the death of many thousands of Iraqi soldiers in the Gulf War. The real horror which is suggested by this fact is that the kinds of destruction which we witnessed on that occasion might be part of the "civilizing process" itself, where the annihilation of thousands is conducted as an act of policy, in a disciplined manner, by means of high technology, and by legitimated experts in violence. Addressing our own indignant responses to the Yugoslav war, perhaps we ought to be asking ourselves which way does the process of cultural diffusion run? Or is it simply the case that we all inhabit the same, modernising global space?

Notes

1. The Serbian Information Centre London, *Bulletin*, No.6, May 1993.

2. Phillip Knightly, 'Chamber of Horrors', *The Independent Magazine*, 12 June 1993: 51-53.

3. United Nations 1992: Table 28 'Weakening Social Fabric', gives the following figures for intentional homicides (1987-88: per 100,000 people): Yugoslavia, 1.8; average for the industrial developed world, 4.2; OECD countries, 3.8; southern European countries, 1.4; eastern Europe and the USSR, 4.9; North America, 8.3.

4. I believe there to be close links between this aspect of Giddens' model of the modernisation process and that of pacification described by Norbert Elias, as a component of his "civilizing process". I am aware that the definition of "militarisation" adopted here is not uniformly used in sociology and political science. It should certainly be distinguished from "militarism", as an ideology which privileges military personnel and elevates military values. An interesting discussion from a point of view different from my own is found in Huntington 1962:65-8.

5. The extent to which this situation has been sustained in the several states which have replaced the Socialist Federation is intimated in Danopoulos and Zirker (eds.) 1996.

6. See also Gjecov 1989 [1933]:154-86 and esp. 162-84. Customary law of this kind is explicitly distinguished from "judicial law". Cf. Book 11. My choice of the past tense in describing the blood feud is deliberate. The use of the "ethnographic present" is justifiably reputed to be misleading. Although there is ample evidence that the blood feud is still a very active factor in the culture, for example, of Kosovar Albanians, it does seem important to recognise that there has been a secular

decline in its general significance throughout the region. The documentary film *Forging the Blood*

(details) treats the contemporary phenomenon of feuding in Kosovo, and attempts to promote the

reconciliation of the parties. A moving account of the operation of the blood feud, which makes much

of its obligatory character, is given in Kadare 1991. See also on the orderliness of the feud, Gellner

1981:37.

7. The taking of blood repays comparative study alongside the duel in western European aristocratic

society: they were suppressed for the same reasons, and were justified by reference to the same

essentially moral concept--honour. Also (as Margaret Hasluck insists (1954:220): "vengeance could

not be taken indiscriminately, but was governed by a multiplicity of rules". Both were governed by

meticulous prescriptions of proper procedure.

9. A slight but revealing instance of this is the fact that the soccer team of the Dalmatian city of Split

is called "Hajduk".

10. In a personal interview with the author.

11. The following section formed the core of a paper presented to the XIX Denton Consultation on

Implicit Religion, 10-12 May 1996, under the title "Atrocity as sacrament: notes towards a sociology of

damnation". I am grateful to colleagues who were present for their helpful comment.

12. Perhaps the closest I have come to a contribution to this area is Carlton 1994. This takes a

"phenomenological" approach to massacre, exploring in detail the variety of social and historical

settings in which large scale slaughter has occurred. The book is almost without any kind of theoretical

direction: but it does convey rather well the idea that violence (even on the scale which we would

normally find appalling) is typically intelligible in that it occupies a distinctive political niche, is

directed at specific victims, is normatively justified, and is conducted in a more or less systematic way.

13. The Cele Kula, believed to have 952 skulls built into its walls, is now found in the grounds of the military hospital in Nis.

14. The capacity to embrace atrocity appears to have afflicted at least partially those outsiders who have sought to interpret the Montenegrins to the rest of the world. Accounting for these events, Devine (1918:24) writes that: "It must not be supposed that the Montenegrins are in ordinary circumstances a cruel race." Stevenson (1912:125) observes, in the midst of his apologia, that: "No one would attempt to excuse the massacre ... unless he were making it his aim to defend a paradox". A somewhat different account of the process of "Motivating the Perpetrator" is given in Cigar 1995.

15. It is not without significance that the novel by Vuk Draskovic which as much as anything else projected him as a potential leader of Serb nationalism was his *Noz* (The Knife) (Draskovic 1982).

16. See also the chapter on "The heritage of atrocity", in Tunbridge and Ashworth 1996.

17. This involves not only the restoration of state symbols which were used under the NDH but also the naming of streets after prominent fascist politicians and, perhaps most controversially, the renaming of Zagreb's Trg Zrtava Fasizma (Square of the Victims of Fascism) as the Trg Hrvatskih Velikana (Square of the Great Croatians). Maps are widely circulated with semi-official status indicating the "historical" borders of Croatia as those adopted by the *NDH*, which include all of the adjacent republic of Bosnia and Hercegovina, and a substantial tract of the Vojvodina.

18. For a systematic exposition of the concept of "implicit religion", see Bailey 1997.

19. Levi-Strauss' discussion of eagle hunting has provided a model for a long tradition of structuralist analysis. Levi-Strauss 1966:46-51. Probably the best-known example of this genre is Mary Douglas' celebration of dirt in Douglas 1966.

20. Those who wish to pursue the study of this area in greater depth could do worse than begin with Staub 1989, although his approach is that of the psychologist rather than the sociologist or anthropologist. I am at a loss as to what to make of the Croatian politician whom I interviewed who had made a journey to Borovo Selo sepcifically in order to acquaint himself directly with the nature of the mutilations alleged to have been afflicted on the Croat victims of the ambush there.

21. I acknowledge gratefully here the bibliographical assistance of the Centre for Research at Leeds Metropolitan University.

22. United Nations (1992) gives the following figures for reported rates of rape for various countries and groups of countries, per 100,000 women aged 15-19, for 1984-85: Yugoslavia, 27; average for the industrial developed world, 48; OECD countries, 51; southern Europe, 12; North America, 106. It is important to recognise in citing these figures that for a variety of reasons statistics of this kind should be treated with caution.

23. See also several estimates reported by Ruth Seifert, in Stiglmayer ed. 1994:55; also Visser 1993:51. Note the wide variation in the dates of these, and it is always necessary to be aware of differences in geographical scope. The methodological difficulties are highlighted by Meznaric's footnote 5, p. 127.

24. It is perhaps worth noting in this context that the recent Yugoslav conflict took place largely among the civilian population, and not (as in the Gulf War) in a "battle field" where only combatants confronted each other. Sander, in Stiglmayer ed. 1994:xx.

25. In spite of the widespread moral panic about alleged rapes of Serb women by Albanians, "the proportion of Albanians who perpetrate rape is less than their proportion in the total Yugoslav population". There are, of course, good reasons for being cautious about the ready generalisability to the whole of Yugoslavia of the results of a study which related to the highly specific conditions of Kosovo. See Meznaric 1993.

26. See, however, Meznaric 1993:123-24; Stiglmayer ed. 1994.

27. I have not included genocide in my discussion of "aberrant violence", which may seem perverse to some. The omission is deliberate. The UN Convention on the Prevention and Punishment of the Crime of Genocide, of 1951, defines it in Article II as acts committed "with intent to destroy, in whole or in part, a national, ethnical, racial or religious group as such". We tend to think of such acts as *prima facie* incomprehensible, and by virtue of that fact as aberrant. It follows from the above discussion, however, that I believe that genocide in the Balkans *is* comprehensible. This observation should be taken not as a reflection of my lack of capacity to make moral discriminations, but as a sad reflection on the state of the human condition. I hope that it is evident from my discussion that I do not endorse it.

28. The issues are set out and discussed in Bellamy 1997. This is not the place in which to engage with these problems, but I am highly sceptical about the historical validity of the thesis of a distinctive kind of "postmodern" warfare.

13

QUO VADIS, JUGOSLAVIJO?

In recent years a variety of ideas have been in circulation which suggest that in one

way or another the end of the twentieth century is bringing with it important

qualitative changes in the nature of the world order. One might mention here

Zbigniew Brzezinski's *Out of Control* (1993) and the similarly apocalyptic

Pandaemonium (1993) by Daniel Moynihan. Among the most influential of these

rather visionary statements has been Samuel P. Huntington's attempt to redefine the

future of interstate relations in terms of a global pattern of the "clash of civilizations"

(Huntington 1997). Following the fall of the Berlin Wall in 1989, and the

disintegration of Soviet hegemony in eastern Europe, these authors all address in their

own terms the problem of how to characterise a "post-communist" age. (See also

Brzezinski 1989; Mestrovic 1994).[1]

These works can be seen as addressing from a different standpoint the issues treated

by Francis Fukuyama, whose prognosis of an "end of history" hinges upon the idea

that having attained a social state in which freedom and democracy are without

serious contenders in the field, that development has reached its natural conclusion

(Fukuyama 1992). Whatever it is that lies ahead of the human race, it will be

fundamentally different in character from the past.

In relation to the post-communist states of eastern Europe, the analysis of Fukuyama is often echoed in the phrase "transition to democracy". In their "transitional" state, presumably, the countries of the region have not quite reached the "end of history", but are at least entering the home straight.[2] The niggling question remains, however, as to whether the story has indeed been told. Casting an eye over the state of contemporary eastern Europe it is hard to be certain that Communism is indeed dead. In November 1995 in Poland, a Communist defeated in a free electoral contest the great harbinger of the new Europe, the anti-Communist, devout Catholic leader of *Solidarnosc*, Lech Walesa. In the Russian political crisis which is developing at the time of writing, it seems that the succession to Boris Yeltsin will, in one form or another, depend upon the continuing strength of the Communist Party. Slobodan Milosevic's Socialist Party of Serbia appears to have an unshakeable grip on Serbian politics. Across the Balkans Socialist parties continue to play an active part in the political process of almost all of the states of the region.[3]

It is possible to reply to this type of objection that what we observe is merely the terminal twitching of Communism—the uncoordinated residue of motor habits rooted in the spinal column of the beast, which continue to operate briefly after the head has been severed. In this region at least, however, it appears to be fundamentally questionable to state that any of the processes which characterised the political and social development of the twentieth century have reached an end. What is more, it is also difficult to speak with any coherence about a "transition" to anything in particular. Even if Communism is as good as dead, there is no firm assurance that we can expect to replace it with western European liberal democracy.

It is not possible to tackle here these very general questions, other than to express a degree of scepticism about our ability to discern any such global patterns while we are still not only *in media res*, but at the threshold of the process. I address here a much more limited task, namely, that of attempting on the basis of the forgoing discussion to see if it feasible to form any coherent expectations about the future of the Yugoslav region.

Quo Vadis, Jugoslavijo? is the title given to a book edited by Marijan Korosic in 1989, on the eve of the break-up of Yugoslavia. It seems appropriate to attempt an answer to his question in the wake of Yugoslavia's disintegration. In addressing that task, however, I want to begin by qualifying Herbert Butterfield's "Whig interpretation of history" (Butterfield 1931). History is not only written from the standpoint of the present, as the story of how we came to be where we are. It involves also a dialectical process which includes where we think we are going in the future. If we cannot think about the past without at least implicit reference to the future, it is equally true that engagement with the future cannot be undertaken without reference to the past. The peoples of the South Slav region carry with them their history, not only as an objective past which conditions action in the present, but also as a subjective past. This shapes their consciousness and provides the material out of which they weave accounts both of the past and the future.

It has been said that the Balkan region suffers from a surfeit of the past: and certainly attempts to elucidate what has happened to the South Slav lands since 1989, and projections of the region's future, tend to draw heavily upon history. A claim which I have argued throughout this book is that typically the uses to which history is put (both by outsiders and locals) are often misplaced and misleading. Consequently, in approaching the question, "*Quo vadis*?" I have tried to build upon the critical reading of history which I have advocated. I have also attempted to go beyond vague sub-theoretical generalities about a "post-communist" order, or quasi-delphic projections about the future, and to apply the concepts of modernisation and globalisation as a means of framing my discussion in a somewhat more theoretically disciplined manner.

The place of the past: prison or patrimony?

In approaching the task of delineating the likely historical trajectories of the newly-emerging South Slav states, too frequently the relationship between past and future is seen either in terms of the entrapment of the present in the past, or as the rediscovery of the past in the present. History is either a prison or a patrimony. Both of these models constitute analytical blind alleys.

The historical inevitability of cultural division in the Balkans, and consequently the permanent incompatibility of the peoples of the region, is often justified by reference to the division between Rome and Byzantium. Convincing as explanations of the inevitability of cultural difference based on this foundation might appear, the case is far from being "open and shut". Those who appeal to it typically fail to specify which historical division they have in mind. The line of division between the eastern and western Roman Empires on the death Theodosius I in 395 was not identical with the subsequent division between the ecclesiastical jurisdictions of Rome and

Constantinople in 1054. Neither of these juridical divisions was reflected in the actual patterns of confessional allegiance which had developed on the ground by the thirteenth century (Darby *et al.* 1966:24). If any of these lines identifying supposedly indelible cultural divisions is taken seriously, then the greater part of Montenegro should be ineradicably Roman Catholic! (Furthermore, Ottoman invasion resulted in further redistribution, and the overlaying of earlier cultural patterns by others.) Argument of this kind, in short, simply fails Max Weber's test of "adequate causation" (Weber 1949:164-188). As I have indicated at several points during the foregoing discussion, these historical cultural divisions might be considered as relevant contributory factors in our attempt to understand subsequent development; but if the problem which we set out to explain is the trajectory of modernisation, then they can by no means be included among the primary determining factors.

If the peoples of the region are not imprisoned within cultural dungeons from which they are fated never to escape, however, neither are they handed by the past a patrimony which they are committed to conserve.

Across the region nationalist movements depict the end of Communist hegemony as an opportunity to rediscover in the present the essential character of the nation which has for so long remained hidden from view. "Nationalism", however, in itself is contentless: it is an empty vessel waiting to be filled by the imagination. Even if we accept a Durkheimian view of the nation as a community towards which, by virtue of our solidarity with it, we experience a sense of moral obligation, the content of the representations which carry that binding force remain to be determined.

Traian Stoianovich has given a superb illustration of this. We might ask ourselves why the militaristic virtues summed up in concepts such as *junastvo* (heroism) should have come to be regarded as essential to the Serb national patrimony. He quotes the following passage from the pre-war Serb Agrarian Socialist leader, Dragoljub Jovanovic.

> The most vivid picture left by the [First World] War in the memory of the Serbs is not of a cemetery or a blood-stained battlefield, although Serbia had given a formidable number of victims and had been the scene of the fiercest fighting. The most clear-cut impression of the Serbian campaign is the motley, pitiful spectacle of the *bezanija*, that endless, disorderly flight of fugitives muffled to the eyes, old women, children, on foot or in wooden carts patiently drawn by emaciated and exhausted oxen, driving in front of them some cattle and carrying on their backs or under their arms some chattels, the number and importance of which grew less with every stage of this removal which was always beginning again and never coming to an end. In short, the outstanding event of the Serbian war is not a great battle, such as at Verdun, but the Great Retreat, that retreat which led the Serbs into exile through Albania—the last after so many others following on each advance of the enemy. (Quoted in Stoianovich 1994:65-6)

When I read this passage I could not help but frame it between two other great images from Serb history—the myths of the great migration to the Vojvodina of the 1690s and the collapse of the *krajina* in 1995. Surely the self-same images would have applied equally to these events also? Surely in that greatest source of Serb national iconography, the Kosovo legends, it is possible to find metaphysical validation for the image of a nation perpetually in defeat and diaspora?

My point is not to argue that Serbia is "really" encapsulated symbolically either by heroic exaltation in glorious but bloody victory, or by the image of the stoical and patient bearing of wretched defeat. The point is that choices are made. What people take to be their symbolic patrimony, their heritage which they are obliged to recover and conserve, is open-ended. When human communities (nations, states, classes, confessions) draw upon their history in order to enable them to interpret and face their future, the past is neither a prison nor a patrimony. It is simply a resource, which is available to be exploited.

What, within that context, are we to make of "post-communism"? The first step to be taken in this endeavour is to recognise that any sociologist looking at south eastern Europe will be sceptical of any tendency to lump together all "Communist" states. Their experience of "Communism" has not been identical. In the case of the different eastern European countries it is clear that their incorporation under Soviet hegemony involved a reworking of quite different historical legacies.

> The term "postcommunist" is widely but somewhat misleadingly used to describe the period emerging after the decline of communist regimes. The postcommunist world, however, continues to be divided, not only economically or socially, but also politically. (Puhovski, in Akhavan and Howse 1995:121)

This observation is important also in relation to the peoples of Yugoslavia, for whom the experience of Communism has been relatively diverse. Nevertheless, that experience has bound these post-Yugoslav states and peoples together in a common past, so that for all their current protestations about their necessary and inevitable separateness, the various components of former Yugoslavia will inescapably carry with them into their futures (whether common or separated) the mark of that experience. It is not only intellectual laziness or a failure of verbal inventiveness which will cause them to be known as "former Yugoslavia" for some time to come. Drawing upon that common past, however, the peoples of the region will create a variety of subjective (partly mythologised) Communist and Yugoslav pasts, which will orient them in very different ways towards the "postcommunist" future.

Those continuities, and the processes within which the region is embedded, are also much wider than the region itself. An essential part of my claims in this book has been the idea that the Balkans are not other than Europe, but always have been a part of Europe, and indeed, increasingly a part of global processes of development. The "postcommunist" future for these countries will, therefore, also involve the melding of significant features of an entirely local character with those which are proper to their continental and indeed their global context.

Why did Yugoslavia fall apart?

Since the outbreak of the Yugoslav wars in 1992 there has been an "unprecedented outpouring" of both scholarly and journalistic writing on the causes of the break-up of Yugoslavia (Stokes *et al.* 1996:136). Gale Stokes and his colleagues reviewing this literature discuss more than forty items which in one way or another address this issue, drawing on the literature in English alone.[4] As they point out, the task of producing an account of the collapse of the Yugoslav state is an immensely difficult one, however, not because of the wealth of information which is now available, but more significantly because of its poverty.

> Few archival sources of the sort that historians are now using to inform their understanding of the collapse of the First Yugoslavia in World War II and the creation of the Second Yugoslavia in that war's aftermath are yet available to scholars. (Stokes et al. 1996:136) [5]

Consequently a good deal of the writing of "instant history" which has so far been undertaken in this field rests upon a significant degree of speculation and conjecture, and upon evidence which is often fragmentary and anecdotal. Even the more solidly-based of these accounts can be treated as no more than prolegomena to a history of the period. Acknowledging the caution with which this task should be undertaken, therefore, I believe that it will be useful to provide a brief summary of the factors which have emerged from my own discussion of the longer-term trajectory of historical change in the South Slav lands, which can be taken as relevant to this explanatory project. This stands as an essential prelude to the framing of expectations about the likely future of the emerging states of the region.

Popular and journalistic discussion of the reasons for the collapse of the Yugoslav state have often taken it for granted that its primary cause was the rise of nationalism—that the country was destroyed by inner forces welling up from below, having their origins in popular sentiment. This is conveyed most vividly in the often-used metaphor that President Tito "kept the lid on the boiling pot" of national antagonism. The majority of academic commentators, however, believe that the roots of the problem lay in the Communist system and in particular in a crisis proper to its elite. Disintegration was a process driven from the top, not the bottom. This idea merits further explanation and exploration.

The principal themes of this book have been the insertion of the Yugoslav region into the wider processes of modernisation and globalisation. This approach, I believe, gives coherence to the mass of separate explanatory factors which have been variously adduced in relation to the end of the Second Yugoslavia. It also enables us to focus on the issues which are likely to remain significant in shaping the future of the post-Yugoslav states of the region. I want to attend to the importance of the failure of the modernisation process in Yugoslavia, and in particular to the contradictions engendered by the relationship of the Yugoslav state and society to their global context.

At the outset it is important to separate two questions which are often confused. "Why did the Yugoslav system fall apart?", and "Why did the failure of that system take such a violent form?" Approaching the first of these questions, we must recognise that Yugoslavia's collapse was not an isolated event: it was one element only in the general crisis of "real socialism" in this period, which still continues to be unresolved. This is still a question which is not only under-theorised but under-addressed, inhibited by the theoretical blind alley created by the imagery of "transition". The root problem is that the "real socialist" systems did not offer an alternative to the route to modernity presented by capitalism. This fact is concealed by the Marxist rhetoric of history, which in its schema of historical stages places socialism beyond capitalism in the modernisation process. In fact, in many respects, socialism can be regarded as an *anti-modern* force, at least in its effects if not in its

ideological vision. Socialism is essentially "utopian" (Bauman 1976). Like so many

utopias, however, it conceals within its vision of the future a rejection of the present

and a celebration of idealised elements of a lost past. The specific form which this

took was the belief that the state could assume the burden of communitarian solidarity

which characterised (or was believed to have characterised) the pre-industrial world.

This aspiration was unrealisable, and flew in the face of the realities of modernisation

in two respects.

1. Modernisation entails the creation of *impersonal* and general or abstract

   mechanisms of organisation, modelled upon the market, which control not only the

   conventional "factors of production" but increasingly the distribution of other kinds

   of services and values. These replace the localised and ascriptive mechanisms

   characteristic of community. The state in the modern world cannot become a

   substitute for community.

2. The diversification of institutional orders, and in particular the elaboration of civil

   society, gives greater flexibility and adaptability to social structure. The attempt of

   the state to assume direct responsibility for the day-to-day management of these

   functions inhibits this capacity for structural adaptation..

The establishment of a Communist regime in 1945 interrupted the progress of these

developments in the Balkans, generally retarded throughout the region as a

consequence of its marginality to the major centres of European capitalism.

Communism replaced the mechanism of the market with the mechanism of choice

centrally controlled by functionaries as the standard mechanism for the distribution of goods and services. It actually inhibited or even sought to reverse, the process of structural diversification by submitting all areas of activity to the supervision of the state.

The particular forms which Yugoslav socialism took can be seen as superimposing upon the general pattern of "real socialism" an intensified form of the mythology of the utopian community, driving politics and society ever more firmly into the pre-modern straight-jacket of the imagery of the solidary community of "working people" organised along self-managing principles.

It is certainly the case that in some respects Yugoslavia can be seen as steering a middle way between western capitalism and Soviet communism. The extent to which this was so, however, has been seriously over-estimated. There has been insufficient recognition of those ways in which Yugoslavia had actually become committed institutionally and ideologically to a more thoroughly radical and utopian version of socialism, which lay beyond rather than short of the prevailing East European practice. In that respect Yugoslavia was less rather then more advantageously positioned to make an adaptive "transition" out of the socialist blind alley.

At one level gestures were made in the direction of economic modernisation, especially in terms of technical change and commercial exchange with the capitalist world. These were everywhere contradicted, however, by the network of particularisms which constituted the system of workers' self-management. At the same time, by forcing everything into the pattern of state-sponsored self-management, the possibilities of generating any effective and genuinely autonomous institutions within civil society were subverted.

A consequence of the real-socialist dependence upon the state as the primary mechanism of social activity is that it becomes particularly vulnerable to the need for legitimation. All political systems require regular replenishment of their legitimacy. Jürgen Habermas has expanded in particular upon this idea in his discussion of the nature of the "legitimation crises" within capitalism which have resulted from the "spending" of the heritage of legitimation derived from the religiously based economic moralities which provided the foundation for its expansion in the eighteenth and nineteenth centuries (Habermas 1976). The crucial failure of "real socialism" was that by attaching the notion of "scientific socialism" to its analysis it shackled itself to a set of ideological images which were in principle fixed, and hence incapable of revision. For this reason at least sociologists might have expected that any crisis of legitimacy would have been likely to be experienced in a more acute form in socialist than in capitalist systems.

The Yugoslav system experienced this crisis in an especially severe form, because to the general principles of the legitimation of its socialist elite it added the specific experience of the "National Liberation Struggle". At first this gave a powerful and genuinely popular basis for the legitimation of the regime. There was never adequate attention paid, however, to the risks which attended reliance upon this experience. Unlike legitimacy which depends upon the claims to the superior adequacy of the understanding of history, which are not in principle the property to any one generation of leaders of socialist states, legitimacy which derives from the possession of highly specific experiences can not be passed to their successors, who are condemned necessarily to epigonism. "Scientific socialism" points (at least in principle) to the possibility that the mantle of "science" can be passed to a new generation. The "partizan generation" could have no successors.

In this respect Yugoslavia epitomised Max Weber's observations about the necessary crisis which attends succession to charismatic authority. The problem arises not simply because of the need to replace Tito, but because the transition from charismatic to legal-rational authority was required of the elite stratum, which was unable to grasp let alone to address this problem.

Far from constituting a kind of half-way house between "the West" and the "Soviet bloc", and hence presumably *better* placed than others to manage the general crisis of socialism, Yugoslavia represented a case of *greater exposure* to the hazards of relegitimation.

In these remarks I have attempted to convey the idea that at a theoretical level there is nothing particularly surprising about the vulnerability of the Yugoslav state to radical crisis. There is certainly a heavy irony in the fact that throughout the post-1945 period both the Yugoslavs themselves and many external commentators should make such a point of the uniqueness of the Yugoslav system (Allcock 1989a). The point is, however, that in the event the unique features of that system turned out to constitute elements of particular vulnerability rather than of its peculiar strength.

Why, however, should the failure of the Yugoslav experiment have been attended by such violence and disorder? Here it is necessary to turn away from broad considerations of theory to particular features of the Yugoslav situation. It is at this point that the factor of nationality becomes relevant.

The shock with which most ordinary Europeans greeted the outbreak of war in Yugoslavia is a relevant starting point. These lay perceptions have a direct bearing upon the task of explanation. In the 1970s Yugoslavia was among the more prosperous of the real-socialist states of Europe. It GDP/capita in 1989 of US$ 2,679, exceeded that of Albania, Romania, Hungary and Poland, and the economically more-developed regions of Slovenia, the Vojvodina and the Dalmatian coast outranked Bulgaria, and compared well in these terms with Czechoslovakia and Greece.

In spite of various restrictions upon freedom of political expression, Yugoslavia was the most open of the states of the region, not only receiving large numbers of foreign tourists with little control or even formality, but permitting its citizens to travel freely also. It was taken as commonplace that the better-off Yugoslavs from Zagreb or Ljubljana would make shopping trips to Trieste, or those from Skopje would patronise the boutiques of Salonika. Western European and other foreign news and entertainment media were readily available. In 1986 there were 5.99 Yugoslavs to every telephone (in Hungary 6.90; Czechoslovakia 4.18), and 5.27 to every TV set— more widely available than in Greece (5.76). Apart from members of the League of Communists religion was practised more openly than in most other Communist states.

In very large measure these characteristics did not reflect the superior virtue of the leadership of the LC, but the distinctive situation of Yugoslavia in relation to the Cold War. Western governments welcomed the existence of a state which was avowedly socialist, but which stressed the differences which divided the "Yugoslav road to socialism" from the Soviet line. By holding out to the other countries of the region the model of a relatively successful socialist state determinedly outside the Soviet bloc they kept in being the possibility of creating divisions within the socialist camp.

Reciprocally, the Yugoslav LC needed western support in order to maintain its stance of independence with confidence. The possibility of Soviet armed intervention at some future point, in order to restore the recalcitrant Yugoslavs to the fold, was never far from their minds; and the events of East Germany in 1953, Hungary in 1956, Czechoslovakia in 1968 and the militarisation of Poland under Jaruzelski (in order to forestall direct intervention) in 1981, provided obliging regular reminders of the reality of that threat.[6]

An important medium through which this mutually satisfactory relationship was constructed was credit. For reasons which need to be more closely researched, the flow of credit was poorly managed, with insufficient control both by the lenders and by the Yugoslav state—money was raised abroad not only at the Federal level but by republics, enterprises and municipalities. It was also used unwisely, funding not only prestigious public projects but providing a constant element of subsidy for the standard of living of the entire population. "There was no country like Yugoslavia, in which one could live so well while working so little" (Puhovski, in Akhavan and Howse 1995:128)

> At the domestic level, for the great majority of people, Yugoslavia offered a
> predictable life, with a sense of protection and security provided by the
> "system". Generation after generation followed the same pattern of protected
> careers and well-planned futures. Tuition from nursery school to university was
> free. Jobs were easily available (before the 1980s), housing was provided by the

state, health service was free, and pensions were guaranteed. The system

encouraged mediocrity as a way of life, but this "stable stagnation" was a very

comfortable environment for ordinary people, happy with the average and

protected from changes and challenges. This philosophy was illustrated by the

popular wisdom: "We pretend to work, and the state pretends to pay us." (Pajic,

in Akhavan and Howse 1995:153)

The first real challenge to this situation came in the seventies, with the shock of the

raising of oil prices. Yugoslavia had developed an industrial structure which depended

heavily upon its reworking of imported raw materials, using also imported energy.

Whereas economically more developed countries were able to respond to the energy

crisis by shifting to the more efficient uses of energy resources, it was a general

feature of the less developed states that they failed to make this adaptive move.

Between 1979 and 1987, therefore, Czechoslovakia reduced its consumption of

energy, measured in terms of tons of coal-equivalent/capita, from 6.49 to 6.31, and

Austria from 4.28 to 4.02. States such as Yugoslavia continued to increase their per

capita energy consumption—Yugoslavia from 2.08 to 2.42, Greece from 2.09 to 2.45,

Hungary from 3.80 to 3.82.[7]

Probably the single most important blow to the integrity of Yugoslavia came in

1983, when in the context of world-wide concern about debt the IMF finally

demanded a reckoning. The context was mounting growing general anxiety about the

indebtedness of "Third World" states, some others of which were at more serious risk

than was Yugoslavia. The onset of world depression in the later 1980s steadily

deepened the problems.

The development of Yugoslavia's economic problems can therefore be seen to be essentially conditioned in part by its insertion into wider, global, economic processes. This point is underlined by reference to other events. It was at the very time when Yugoslavia was struggling with the need to reorient itself economically that the Berlin Wall fell in 1989. This cut two ways for Yugoslavia: it reduced the external threat which concentrated minds previously, making for enhanced internal solidarity, and reduced considerably Yugoslavia's significance for the West in strategic, economic and propaganda terms. If Yugoslavia needed the West more than ever, the West needed Yugoslavia less than ever.

The magnitude and relatively unexpected character of these global developments arrested the attention of the leaders of western states, and in particular confronted them with a need to redefine the terms of reference of the principal instruments of interstate co-operation which had evolved in the post-1945 world—such as the European Union and NATO. The collapse of Soviet hegemony gave an urgency to the development of alternative conceptions of security, and led to tentative experiments with new institutions for managing European inter-state processes, in the CSCE mechanisms. International trade arrangements were simultaneously under review, and at this time extremely protracted and contentious negotiations which had repeatedly threatened to stall entirely, came to a conclusion.

Following the signature of the Single European Act in 1986, the EU embarked upon a process of internal re-evaluation and reorientation, in which the aspirations of its members began to move beyond the level of the creation of a common market, and to entertain the possibility that new forms of political collaboration might be developed.

The resolution of long-standing budgetary problems at the Brussels Summit in 1988, the Delors Plan for Economic and Monetary Union, and the adoption of the European Social Charter of the following year, might be taken as markers along the way to the Maastricht Treaty of 1991.

Foreign political leaders responded to the Yugoslav situation with a mixture of inattention in relation to what were perceived to be larger issues, and the definition of the specific situation in terms of perceived generalities of the emerging "postcommunist" order. In particular, European leaders fell on the problem almost as a welcome opportunity to demonstrate the need for (or even the reality of) a new phase of European co-operation, extending into an emergent common foreign policy. When they did react practically to the inescapable severity of the situation in 1991, they were under-informed, and firmly fixed within an inferential structure which led to a serious misperception of the state of affairs. At the level of inter-state political relations as well as that of economic relations, therefore, Yugoslavia can be seen to have been locked into a configuration of external events which either made for or exacerbated the country's internal problems.

An important part of my argument throughout the book has been that internal problems in post-1945 Yugoslavia were met characteristically with constitutional rather than economic reform, which merely shifted the burden of meeting the problems without addressing them. Although a relatively realistic move had been made towards the development of a market economy under the 1963 constitution, which had paved the way for the reforms launched in 1965, these developments were scuppered rapidly by the conservatives--a process already begun by the "Amendment" process in the late 1960s. It was not only nationalism, but perhaps more significantly realistic economic reform which was suppressed in 1972.

The internal constitutional processes of Yugoslavia constantly made for greater complexity (resulting indirectly in rigidity) rather than in flexible adaptation to real-world issues. The 1974 constitution and *ZUR* (the Law on Associated Labour) constituted an appreciable and significant re-Stalinisation of politics, and a confirmation of the structural and ideological rigidities of the system, rather than a significant move towards participatory democracy (as they have often been represented).

In 1980 President Tito died. The importance of this event has often been both over-stated and misunderstood. The disintegration of Yugoslavia is frequently seen as a consequence of the loss of his firm hand and charismatic presence. The system which had to face these mounting problems, however, was his creation, at least in part. He was indeed important as a symbolic focus, and a valuable component of the legitimation process. He had also been, through the personalisation of the regime, one of the chief sources of inflexibility. His legacy consisted not of an openness to movement towards institutions which might permit greater flexibility, but à permanent tendency towards stasis and indecision, while deflecting political attention to other problems. If his death was a direct contributing factor its significance lay more in the fact that it marked symbolically the end of the legitimating power of *partizan* mythology, and exposed his successors to the imperative demand for re-legitimation, which they were largely unable to meet.

To the extent that the loss of Tito was a contributory factor in the "death of Yugoslavia", however, it is interesting that the effects took ten years to work through the system! It seems unquestionably to be the case that there must have been other factors making for integration which continued to operate in his absence, and in spite of rather than because of his legacy.

The discovery in 1983 of the actual scale of Yugoslavia's indebtedness produced the most tremendous political shock. This discovery only intensified the growing regional discord, and intra-party discord about the need for, and the necessary course of, economic and political reform/modernisation.[8] The combination of the disappearance of the taken-for-granted international framework within which Yugoslavia had operated, the unremitting erosion of standards of living and basic economic security, and the progressive collapse of its internal political system, threw Yugoslavs into an unprecedented state of anxiety. While it left ordinary Yugoslavs in a condition of bewilderment, it brought to the surface deep differences between sections of the elite, who fell into increasingly mutually destructive competition in the attempt to rescue their own positions and authority. In this situation people were prone to political mobilisation in a variety of directions, should movements and leaders arise offering the prospect of a way forward. Nationalism was seized upon to this end.

Since so much popular and press treatment of the "death of Yugoslavia" has focussed upon Serbia and the Serbs, it is appropriate in turning to the topic of nationalism to begin there. The emergence of the Milosevic strategy in Serbia is partly comprehensible without using Serb nationalism as the foundation for explanation. The growing challenge to the integrity of Yugoslavia posed by its economic and political crises threatened Serbia with particular severity. The possibility of the loss of both Kosovo and the Vojvodina in any post-Yugoslav carve-up would have robbed the republic of a substantial part of its mineral reserves, its energy generation capacity, and its most productive and profitable agriculture. "Inner Serbia" would have been left with an industrial structure which was obsolescent in its base (such as steel-making) which in turn undermined the competitiveness of its manufacturing sector.

Economic and political elites in Slovenia and Croatia could contemplate the disaggregation of the federation with a measure of equanimity. Slovene manufacturing and food processing, and Croatian tourism, constituted relatively strong sectors of their economies around which it was possible to contemplate the building of autonomous states. The prospect of political and economic reconstruction struck the Serbian leadership as holding out to the republic only the prospect of disaster.

Located at the "hinge" between the economically developed and the under-developed areas of the federation, the break-up of the federation implied for Serbia the tearing-apart of the republic itself along lines of conflicting economic interest. It is not unsurprising, therefore, that the promulgation of the Markovic strategy for economic reconstruction should have been met by the forthright advocacy of an alternative approach by Serbia (viewed sympathetically by Bosnia-Hercegovina, Macedonia and Montenegro).

The general crisis of legitimacy in Yugoslavia presented elites with a choice of bases upon which any attempt at relegitimation might be founded. That choice can be conceptualised in terms of the opposition between *ethnos* and *demos*--or between an "imagined community", upon whose will and assent government could be based, defined either in terms of shared ethnic identity or common citizenship. My analysis

throughout this book has shown that across the history of the entire Yugoslav region

the nature of political development has made for the subversion of any possibility of

building political community upon a generic sense of citizenship. The lines of

political division shaping the definition of identities have always worked to undercut

the creation of a more complex civil society, and to reinforce the ethnic principle.

Consequently, the contradiction between *ethnos* and *demos* as the bases of legitimacy

of any new political order was built into the system as a whole, and can not be laid at

the door of any one ethnic group or region. Nevertheless, there are particular reasons

why the position of Serbs and of Serbia emerged as a central difficulty for Yugoslavia

as a whole. The problem manifested itself at two levels--the position of ethnic Serbs

outside the Republic of Serbia, and the situation of non-Serbs within that republic.

The consistently applied principle of ethnicity, as a means of defining political

identities within the successor states of Yugoslavia would have left large numbers of

Serbs as ethnic minorities within other republics, in which their status and rights could

have been in dispute. The adoption of ethnicity as the founding principle of new states

also threatened the integrity of the Serbian republic, as the presence within Serbia of

large ethnic minorities (and especially their historical association with quasi-republics

in the two autonomous provinces) held out the prospect of the division of Serbia

itself--and the further reduction of Serb populations in these new republics to the

status of minorities.

With hindsight it can be seen as in the interests of Serb political leaders to have

espoused vigorously the principle of *demos* rather than *ethnos* in the struggle over the principle of legitimation within the Yugoslav state. The fatal error made by Milosevic and others, however, was to opt for the ethnic principle.

Slobodan Milosevic has often been depicted both within Yugoslavia and the West as the natural voice of Serb nationalism, and as a supremely cunning politician in pursuit of the "Great Serbian" vision. Both of these interpretations of the Milosevic phenomenon are fundamentally questionable.

Although the rise of Milosevic has come to be interpreted principally as a consequence of nationalism, it should not be forgotten that his initial platform was that of "anti-bureaucratic revolution"—a rather poorly-focussed populism which exploited the anxieties and insecurity of ordinary people against the stratum of functionaries of the LC. Nationalism was subsequently grasped (and at first hesitantly) as an effective political vehicle for his ambitions. His seizure of the Kosovo issue in 1989 has been represented almost universally as a supremely agile piece of political opportunism, which enabled him to ride to power (not only in Serbia but possibly elsewhere also) on the tiger of nationalism. It is probably more accurate to see his stumbling into the nationalist position (and especially his entrapment by the Kosovo Serbs) as his greatest political mistake. It condemned him definitively and permanently to identification with *ethnos* rather than with *demos* as the fundamental ideological plank of his platform. This resulted in his emergence as the architect of the downfall of Yugoslavia through ethnic conflict, and probably the ultimate catastrophic break-up also of Serbia as a state. Milosevic is best understood as a nationalist by miscalculation, who through the narrowness and lack of imagination of his political vision (rather than the manifest greatness of his native political talent) pushed the

Socialist Party of Serbia, Serbia itself, and consequently Yugoslavia, away from the only track which might have saved them all.

The movement from the early populism of Milosevic's "anti-bureaucratic revolution" to the politics of *ethnos* led him into a bizarre political misalliance with the traditionalist Serbs of the *krajina*, Bosnia and Kosovo and created exactly the kind of diabolical "Other" which was needed to provide elites in Slovenia and Croatia with the excuse to pursue their own separate roads. The significance of the Kosovo problem for the disintegration of Yugoslavia can scarcely be overestimated. The configuration of issues of economic equity and political oppression placed the most enormous strains upon the legitimacy of the federal government. The Slovene and Croat leaderships were prepared to redefine the problem as a question of republican rather than federal responsibility, and to permit the Serbs to act as they wished in Kosovo. This condemned the problem to treatment at the level of conflict between Serb and Albanian, and foreclosed any possibility of its being addressed as an issue of citizenship, potentially affecting all ethnic groups in Yugoslavia, of which federal government might present itself as the principal defender.

Post-Communism in Yugoslavia: six theses

In setting out my own agenda for the analysis of "post-Communist" and "post-Yugoslav" developments in the region I draw attention to six important problems which will remain generic to the former Yugoslav states for the foreseeable future. Predictions about the future of individual states would be foolhardy in view of the complexity of the processes of change in which the entire Balkan Peninsula is involved. For this reason I concentrate upon the way in which these issues will continue to figure as problems, rather than upon any anticipated solutions to them.

These are: (i) the impact of demographic factors; (ii) the continuing importance of the paternalist state; (iii) the rootedness of populist democracy in a fundamentally collectivist political culture; (iv) the long-term significance of patterns of ethnic diversity; (v) the uneasy balance between tradition and modernity; and (vi) the tension between the local and the global. These factors cut across the conventional lines of regional comparison in Yugoslavia. Each of them is of considerable significance in shaping the future trajectories of change in all of the South Slav states.

i) The importance of demographic change

States have no future at all without populations, and concern about population has been high throughout the region. Population in Slovenia, for example, has been at best static for a decade, and declining since 1991 *(Statisticni letopis* 1995:79). More than half of Croatia's communes recorded a net natural decrease in the intercensal period between 1981 and 1991, and 40 had increases of fewer than 5 per thousand (Klemencic ed. 1993:60-61. For a more detailed analysis, see Nejasmic 1991.) At the other end of the scale, the rapid rates of natural increase on the part of the Albanian population have been frequently noted.[9] Overall there has been an opening up of regional differentials within and between states, and these patterns must affect the shifting balance of regional politics.

Of the pre-war Serb population in Croatia of more than half a million perhaps only 100,000 remain. Of Bosnia-Hercegovina's 4 million inhabitants at the 1991 census perhaps half have been forced to relocate in some way, many outside the republic and even as refugees in other non-Balkan states. Neither should the indirect impact of war be overlooked, in terms of its longer term effects on longevity and birth rates, and the "brain drain" of qualified personnel. Although international relief agencies and domestic governments talk of the return of refugees, the degree to which this can be achieved should be regarded with considerable scepticism. As the demographic structure of regions change, so will their political and economic complexion, although in the absence of any systematic information about the social profile of those affected by war detailed comment is difficult.

My impression is that on the whole refugee movement has consisted disproportionately of a process of urbanisation, which has to be counterbalanced in some particular areas by a return to agriculture under the compulsion of unemployment and poverty. There is much speculation about the local importance for politics of the long-term existence of large refugee diasporas (based on the Palestinian experience), and claims have been advanced about the radicalisation of young men through military experience.

The proper assessment of these and other changes will be of considerable importance in shaping the economic and political future of the region, but must await the availability of systematic data. Nevertheless, theory warns us that most of these indicators point in the direction of the instability of political behaviour. Looking at the future of the region in the light of its changing demographic profile, therefore, we should perhaps be sceptical about the possibilities of any general and untroubled transition to democracy.

ii) The continuing importance of the paternalist state

One of the key theoretical and practical issues which has provided a central point of reference in relation to the notion of "post-Communism" has been the attempt to create capitalist economic institutions which facilitate the operation of a free market in the factors of production. The process was begun in Yugoslavia by a series of measures introduced under the Markovic reform programme in 1989-90. All of the states emerging from the Yugoslav federation have since then made moves towards the further institutionalisation of private property, and the dismantling of the former social sector, although the rate at which this has been achieved varies from the significant to the nominal. In every case, however, there are continuing signs of the strength of a paternalistic culture of the state, and the incomplete differentiation of economic from political life.

It is not sufficient to account for this in terms of the shortness of the time scale, although clearly the economic impact of war in modern societies always works in the direction of augmenting the role of the state. The historical origins of this pattern antedate Communism by a considerable period. The prevailing idea of the proper role of the state in this region is quite different from that embodied in western European social-democratic notions of the "welfare state". The latter focus upon the presumed importance of the state in creating a moral community of its citizens, by minimising the more damaging impacts of economic change, whereas eastern European traditions tend to centre upon an assumption that the proper function of the state is to exercise a generalised control over the conditions of their activity. Regardless of whether they have emerged from an "Ottoman" or a "Habsburg" legacy, the legal culture inherited from the past has tended to presuppose that activities are not permitted until they are allowed expressly by the law.

Here we encounter a paradox which is common to all of the former "real socialist" countries, in that the state has taken upon itself the responsibility of managing the task of dismantling the apparatus of state economic control, and determining its own proper future. The struggle to determine what this role should be in the modernisation process will continue to figure as one of the central issues of politics across the entire Yugoslav region. It is not unreasonable to suggest that one of the most problematic of the legacies of the war will be the fact that the states of the region do not trust their own citizens in any major field of activity, and his bodes ill for the development of the free market.

Even in Slovenia there have been concerns that key elements of the economy should remain under "national" control, which have inhibited the privatisation process. Slovene concerns about the possible consequences of a free market in land, and the prospect of the extensive ownership of real estate by foreign nationals, delayed the conclusion of the Articles of Association with the EU, and have worked against the creation of conditions which could stimulate the inflow of foreign investment. The problem has manifested itself in spite of the energetic commitment of successive Slovene governments to the reconstruction and modernisation of the economy.

iii) Collectivism in political culture

To a large extent this over-reliance upon the state is linked to long-standing forms of

collectivism in the political culture of the region. Significantly, there has been a

general failure to develop a sense in practice (and often also in law) of *individual*

rights, and an institutionalised tendency to think in terms of *collective* rights, which

subsume the person.

As I have already observed in discussing democracy, there have been two major

traditions of discourse in talking about democratisation. "Representative" democracy

tends to focus attention upon the interplay of contending groups, and the process by

which a diversity of interests, all recognised as legitimate, come to insert themselves

into the political process. "Participatory" democracy tends to presume the existence of

mechanisms for the expression of the "will of the people", so that those who challenge

that will are *ipso facto* beyond the pale of legitimacy. Across all of the states emerging

from Yugoslavia there is a tendency to treat democracy in this latter sense.

This presupposition is enshrined in constitutions across the region, which almost

uniformly contain in their preambles statements to the effect that the republic is

identified with a *people,* rather than simply with the citizens who dwell therein.[10] The

notion that democracy means the unchallenged rule of the majority has only shifted

from the organised working class (the "working people of Yugoslavia", under the

leadership of the League of Communists) to the dominant ethnic group. The new states emerging in the post-Yugoslav space have, for this reason, often been referred to as "ethnocracies" rather than "democracies".

If Slovenia appears to be different from other states in the region in this respect it is for the simple reason that as an ethnically largely homogenous state, virtually all parties which emerged post-1989 were in some sense "Slovene nationalists". Taking this background assumption for granted, it has been possible to form the beginnings of a structure in which parties articulate issues and compete for support on a more complex basis, as "representative" democracy. The casualties of Slovene independence, represented strongly at the time of the first elections by a multiplicity of parties and pressure groups, have been precisely those "alternative" groups which sought to advance and defend personal rights. This version of "civil society" (as it came to be defined in Slovenia) consisting of a fringe of dissident groups advancing these individualistic concerns, evaporated with independence.[11]

This kind of collectivism rooted in the populist traditions of the region, in which the state speaks authoritatively in the name of "the people", has probably been expressed most forcefully in Croatia. Here the ruling CDU refused to hand over civic government in Zagreb to opposition parties, following defeat in an election in October 1995, on the grounds that it was impossible that the capital city should be out of step with the government of the country.

The impact of these collectivist habits of thought can be seen in particular in the way in which ethnic diversity has been conceptualised. The problem has been defined invariably in terms of the rights of *minority groups*, rather than the rights of *citizens* regardless of their ethnicity. (This can be traced back as much to the struggle over the position of Slavs within the Austro-Hungarian state as to the legacy of the Ottoman *millet* system.)

Ethnicity is not the only historical source of collectivism in the region. Probably the most enduring legacy of self-management, in spite of the disappearance of its organisational forms and rhetoric, will be the reinforcement which the system gave to habits of collectivist thought already rooted in the culture of the Balkans, giving to collective rights and responsibilities priority over those of the individual.

It is often in the persistence of aspects of traditionalism, however, that the rudiments of civil society can be seen to have been best preserved (especially in religious institutions), and it is partly through the dialogue between tradition and modernity that the future of civil society in the region will be resolved. These traditionalist institutions, however, are also strongly committed to the affirmation of collective identities and obligations. Although expressed in diverse forms in different areas, therefore, the variety of collectivisms rooted in Balkan political culture will continue to shape the long-term development of the region. For this reason, given the theoretical link between modernity and individualism, the region will remain of special continuing interest for sociology.

iv) *The future of ethnic politics*

It might seem that the centrality of national identity to South Slav politics is so obvious that it hardly requires comment. In one sense it is perhaps even true to say that *all* politics in the post Yugoslav states can be said to be nationalistic. Appeals to national identity and solidarity differ profoundly across the former federation, however, and no particular form of politics can be read off automatically from nationalism itself. Consequently, although ethnicity will certainly continue to shape the politics of all states in the post-Yugoslav Balkans, the form and direction of that political process will vary considerably.

In particular, it is important to note the difference between those states which are broadly speaking ethnically homogeneous (Slovenia, and perhaps Croatia after the collapse of the *krajina*) and those in which ethnic diversity remains a primary factor. The affirmation of national sovereignty and national identity *vis-a-vis an outside state* results in a political discourse and political relationships which are fundamentally different from the conflict of nationalities *within the state*. The general pattern of the political relationship of an ethnic majority to its co-resident minorities will take on a special character where these internal issues have a direct bearing upon relations with neighbouring states.

This difference is exemplified most vividly by the position of the Albanian population. Scattered across three states bordering Albania itself (Montenegro, Serbia and Macedonia) their futures can not be considered independently. Developments in one area will stimulate or inhibit developments in all the others, so that in each case attempts to understand the position of Albanians simply as a minority in any of them will be far from adequate to the task. A similar problem arises with the dispersion of Serbs (located in Croatia, Bosnia-Hercegovina, Montenegro as well as Serbia) and Muslims (strongly present not only in Bosnia-Hercegovina but also in Macedonia, Serbia and Montenegro).

The fact that the disintegration of Yugoslavia appears, on the whole, to have entrenched notions of ethnic self-determination as the basis for state-formation will only intensify the difficulties of those states in which this principle can not be applied consistently, and in which their stability would be enhanced by the preferement of *demos* over *ethnos*.

As a consequence, the issue of ethnicity in politics will continue to be important not only for the countries of the region, but also for social theory. The pattern to which I refer here, in presenting a challenge to attempts to conceptualise the issues in terms of "minorities", points strongly towards the importance of developing models of diaspora. Beyond this, it underlines the importance for sociology of moving away from the old habits of thinking in terms of discrete, quasi-organic "societies" and to address social processes within a framework of globalisation.

v) The uneasy balance between tradition and modernity

The recasting of political culture in the post-Yugoslav period offers two possible new orientations--the search for new legitimacy and models for social life may be grounded either in the past, or in a commitment to the future. In this respect, as I suggested earlier, we should anticipate that a continuing major axis of party differentiation across the region will lie between traditionalists and modernisers.

The significance of this categorisation often escapes western European commentators accustomed to conventional Left/Right oppositions in politics, or who have fallen into the trap of explaining Yugoslav politics (and eastern European politics more generally) either as a contest between Communist "hard-liners" and "liberal" reformers, or more recently in terms of the rise of nationalism. It is important, however, to differentiate the various nationalist parties along this axis.

In the change to multi-party systems of politics, the reformed Leagues of Communists typically presented themselves as modernisers, in opposition to nationalistic traditionalists. (Exceptions here are the Socialist Party of Serbia, and left minor parties, which take a traditionalist stance towards a lost socialist golden age.) Alternatively, modernism appears as centre-right liberalism, as in Slovenia and Macedonia. Political traditionalism can be represented by the ideal of the nation (as in the CDU or IMRO), by religion (such as Slovene Christian Democrats or increasingly the Party of Democratic Action in Bosnia-Hercegovina), or class utopians (the Croatian Peasant Party, or various "Craftmen's" Parties). The interest of the struggle in Serbia is that the Socialist Party of Serbia is in many respects traditionalist, although nationalistic. It is opposed by an Albanian party which, while also nationalistic (the Democratic League of Kosova), is on the whole a modernising force.

In many respects parties which are superficially opposed to each other in ideological terms along other dimensions can provide working coalition partnerships because they share similar locations along the modernist/traditionalist axis. In Macedonia, for example, a modernising coalition between former Communists in the Social-Democratic Alliance of Macedonia and the Albanian Party of Democratic Prosperity, has cut across national lines. Similar co-operation might be possible in Montenegro.

Regardless of the shifting terms in which these divisions are expressed, I expect that this will continue to be one of the primary axes of the differentiation of Balkan politics. This contrast will be important not only in determining the shape of the internal politics of the states of the region, but it will also influence their relations with each other, and with the European community more generally. In all areas except Serbia it is possible to see ways in which modernising coalitions might be put together which could manage the processes of restructuring and reorientation. A precondition of this is often the splitting or displacement of dominant, traditionalist, nationalist parties (especially the CDU in Croatia and the PDA in Bosnia-Hercegovina). Only in Serbia does the configuration of parties not hold out such a possibility, even in the event of the displacement of Milosevic from the leadership of the SPS. The bleakness of the future for Serbian politics, therefore, can not be attributed only to "nationalism", but substantially also to the failure of any alternative, modernising vision.

vi) *The tension between the local and the global*

It is one of the great ironies of the history of the region that the South Slav peoples are creating national states at a moment when it has become abundantly evident, even in very large and well-established states, that the extent to which it is possible to contain as objects of national policy processes which are global in character and scale, is increasingly in doubt. Secession from the Yugoslav federation has been rationalised in terms of the desire of small nations to take greater control over their destiny without the interference of others, at a time when the realities of globalisation have been emerging ever more clearly and dramatically at every level. Sadly, in the contemporary world, nobody controls their own destiny in this way! The reconstruction of politics and society in the former Yugoslav states has been a matter of the triumph of localism in the face of these global developments.

While acknowledging the importance of the processes of globalisation, it is necessary to get away from the romanticism which has hitherto attended the vision of an increasingly universal state, which would accompany the steady expansion of our moral horizons to encompass the human race. Perhaps there is evidence of the extension of universalism at some levels: but it has come to be increasingly accepted that the building of both global identities and global structures can only go hand in hand with the consolidation of local identities and structures. The global and the local do not necessarily negate each other, although the balance between them is, and will remain, a difficult one.

In the past in the West we have become accustomed to thinking of the state as the institutional embodiment of more universal values, and as the guarantor of these in the face of the potential encroachment of local particularisms. It is a radically new characteristic of the globalisation process, however, that the role of the state is being reworked, so that the state is coming to be the guarantor and defender of *local* identities and interests. This does not imply that supra-national entities such as the EU or the UN will simply become larger states, which is a frequent misunderstanding of their role and character. Their future form and function are still far from clear. They will, nevertheless, come increasingly to be important as the arbiters and enforcers of more universal values and codes of conduct, and perhaps in this respect as an important defence of the individual citizen against the local collectivisms embodied in the state. The International War Crimes Tribunal for Yugoslavia, at the Hague, is perhaps an important illustration of these developments.

The states emerging from the former Yugoslav federation are coming to birth at a time when, although this process and its importance are discernible, there can still be no clear vision of how these contradictory models of the state are to be defined, given institutional form, and legitimated. In a period when the expectations of their peoples are particularly high, in the wake of independence, these issues will continue to pose acute problems for states across the region.

Conclusion

I remarked at the outset that I hoped to improve understanding of Yugoslav society by demonstrating its involvement in our common European history—a history which can be plotted theoretically between the axes of modernity and globalisation.

The disintegration of the Yugoslav federal state after 1990 can not be reduced to the result of some arcane psychological principles inherent in the Balkan personality. It has come about because the country found itself to be particularly exposed to a conjunction of factors and developmental processes which have characterised our continent as a whole, and especially those parts of it which participated in the experiment of "real socialism".

I see the future in these terms too: and if this closing chapter has suggested that the coming decades hold out little hope for an untroubled "transition to democracy" for the post-Yugoslav states, then this is only because they will continue to face those choices which confront all European citizens in the late modern age.

Notes

1. Fukuyama prefers (following Vaclav Havel) "post-totalitarian" to "post-communist" (Fukuyama 1992:33).

2. The intellectual foundations upon which the study of the transformation of "post-communist" states is built are older than the phenomenon itself. The Whig interpretation of history, as defined by Herbert Butterfield, is that approach to the past which sees it as the story of the development of liberty of the individual and democratic institutions (Butterfield 1931).

3. Proponents of the thesis of "post-communism" in a strong sense, of course, have to turn a blind eye to the uncomfortable fact of China. (Hobsbawm 1994:)

4. To their coverage might be added Samary 1995; Ullman ed. 1996; Bokovoy, Irvine and Lilly eds. 1997.

5. A substantial and so far under-utilised resource is the material collected in the library of King's College, London, following the production of the BBC documentary series *The Death of Yugoslavia*.

6. Crampton 1994 provides a valuable coverage of the broad picture here.

7. *Statisticki Godisnjak SFRJ*. Not all of the imported energy had to do with value-added. The ownership of private cars in Yugoslavia was at the same level as in Greece—7.3 inhabitants per vehicle.

8. In the light of the recent demonisation of Serbia and its conflict with Bosnia, it is worth noting that these two republics co-operated as conservative forces at this time, largely because of the centrality of the conflict over development/underdevelopment which lay at the heart of Yugoslavia's economic difficulties.

9. The most systematic coverage of this issue is contained in Roux 1992:143-58. See also Malcolm 1998:330-3.

10. The *Constitution of the Republic of Slovenia* (1992) begins its "Basic Constitutional Charter", while announcing itself in the name of the Slovenian people and the citizens of the Republic of Slovenia", subsequently compromises this sense of equal participation in the state: "we Slovenians created our own national identity and attained our nationhood ...". The *Constitution of the Republic of Macedonia* (1991) describes the republic as "a national state of the Macedonian people". The *Constitution of the Republic of Croatia* similarly states that "the Croatian nation reaffirmed .... by its freely expressed will its millennial statehood ...". Bosnia-Hercegovina and Serbia avoid this explicit identification of the state with the collective identity of a specific ethnic group. An interesting exception here is Article 3 of the Serbian Constitution.

11. It is interesting that one of the major forms of cultural and political dissent which emerged in Slovenia during the last years of the Yugoslav federation was the movement known as *Neue Slowenische Kunst*, which was distinguished partly by its insistence upon *collective* responsibility for the work of art. The musical group *Laibach* persistently refused interviews with its individual

performers, and the group of painters associated with the movement always signed their work with the collective name "Irwin".

BIBLIOGRAPHY

Ahmed, Akbar S. and Donnan, Hastings (eds.) (1994), *Islam, Globalisation and Postmodernity*.

London: Routledge.

Akhavan, Payam and Howse, Robert eds. (1995), *Yugoslavia, the former and future: reflections by*

scholars from the region. Washington: The Brookings Institution, and Geneva: United

Nations Research Institute for Social Development.

Albrow, Martin (1996), *The Global Age: state and society beyond modernity*. Cambridge: Polity Press.

Alexander, Stella (1979), *Church and State in Yugoslavia since 1945*. Cambridge University Press.

Allcock, John B. (1975), "Sociology and history: the Yugoslav experience and its implications",

British Journal of Sociology, XXVI(4):486-500.

Allcock, John B. (1977), "Aspects of the development of capitalism in Yugoslavia: the role of the state

in the formation of a 'Satellite' economy", in, F.W. Carter ed., *An Historical Geography of*

the Balkans. London: Academic Press.

Allcock, John B. (1980), "'The socialist transformation of the village': Yugoslav agricultural policy

since 1945", in, R.A. Francisco, B.A. Laird and R.D. Laird eds., *Agricultural Policies in the*

USSR and Eastern Europe. Boulder CO: Westview Press, 199-216.

Allcock, John B. (1981*), The Collectivisation of Yugoslav Agriculture and the Myth of Peasant*

Resistance. University of Bradford: Bradford Studies on Yugoslavia, No.4.

Allcock, John B. (1983), "The development of tourism in Yugoslavia: some conceptual and empirical

lessons", I. Dobozi and P. Mandi (eds.), *Emerging Development Patterns: European*

Contributions. Budapest: EADI/Institute for World Economy of the Hungarian Academy of

Sciences.

Allcock, John B. (1983a), "Tourism and social change in Dalmatia", *Journal of Development Studies*, 20(1):34-55.

Allcock, John B. (1986), "Yugoslavia's tourist trade: pot of gold or pig in a poke?", *Annals of Tourism Research*, 13(4):565-88.

Allcock, John B. (1989), "The historical development of tourism in Yugoslavia to 1945", in John B. Allcock and Joan Counihan, *Two Studies in the History of Tourism in Yugoslavia*. University of Bradford: Bradford Studies on Yugoslavia, No. 14.

Allcock, John B. (1989a), "From eccentricity to the mainstream: theorising Yugoslav society in English language sociology". Paper presented to the Annual Conference of the Yugoslav Sociological Association, Belgrade.

Allcock, John B. (1991), 'Constructing "the Balkans"', in John B. Allcock and Antonia Young eds., *Black Lambs and Grey Falcons: Women travellers in the Balkans*. Bradford University Press.

Allcock, John B. (1991a), "Yugoslavia", in Bogdan Szajkowski ed., *New Political Parties of Eastern Europe and the Soviet Union*. London: Longmans, 293-368.

Allcock, John B. (1992), "Economic development and institutional underdevelopment: tourism and the private sector in Yugoslavia", in Allcock, Horton and Milivojevic eds. pp. 387-413.

Allcock, John B. (1992) "Rhetorics of nationalism in Yugoslav politics", in, John B. Allcock, Marko Milivojevic and John J. Horton eds., pp. 276-296.

Allcock, John B. (1992a), "Nationalism and politics in Yugoslavia", *Eastern Europe and the Commonwealth of Independent States: 1992*. London: Europa Publications Ltd., 290-7.

Allcock, John B. (1995), "'Civil society' in Slovenia: a Durkheimian critique", in, Kenneth Thompson ed. *Durkheim, Europe and Democracy*. Oxford: British Centre for Durkheimian Studies, Occasional Papers No. 3, pp. 62-86.

Allcock, John B. (forthcoming), "Yugoslavia in the wake of World War II", in Luciuk and Kenzer eds. *Under Threat: an atlas of refugees and forced displacement*. University of Toronto Press.

Allcock, John B., Horton, John J. and Milivojevic, Marko, eds., (1992), *Yugoslavia in Transition:* choices and constraints. Oxford: Berg.

Allen, W.E.D. (1920), *The Turks in Europe: a sketch study*. New York: Charles Scribner.

Almond, Mark (1994), *Europe's Backward War: the war in the Balkans*. London: Heinemann.

Althusser, Louis (1984), *Essays on Ideology*. London: Verso.

Anderson, Benedict (1991*), Imagined Communities: reflections on the origin and spread of* *Nationalism*. London and New York: Verso, 2nd. ed.

Anderson, Perry (1974), *Lineages of the Absolutist State*. London: Verso.

Andric, Ivo (1959), *The Bridge on the Drina*. London, George Allen & Unwin.

Apostolski Mihaylo *et al*. eds., 1979, *A History of the Macedonian People*. Skopje: Macedonian Review Editions.

Archer, Margaret S. (1988), *Culture and Agency: the place of culture in social theory*. Cambridge University Press.

Armstrong, Hamilton Fish (1951), *Tito and Goliath*. London: Victor Gollancz.

Armstrong, John (1982), *Nations before Nationalism*. Chapel Hill: University of North Carolina Press.

Arnakis, George G. (1963), "The role of religion in the development of Balkan nationalism", in, Charles and Barbara Jelavich eds.

Arnez, John A. (1983), *Slovenian Lands and their Economies, 1848-1873*. New York and Washington: Studia Slovenica.

Avramovic, M. (1924), *Trideset godina zadruznog rada: 1894-1924*. Belgrade.

Axford, Barrie (1995), *The Global System: economics, politics and culture*. New York: St. Martin's Press.

Baerlein, Henry (1922), *The Birth of Yugoslavia*. London: Parsons.

Bailey, Edward (1998), *Implicit Religion: an introduction*. London: Middlesex University Press.

Bakaric, Vladimir (1960), *O poljoprivredi I problemima sela*. Belgrade: Kultura.

Bakic, Ibrahim (1994), *Nacija i religija*. Sarajevo: Biblioteka Znanstvena Misao.

Balazs, Eva H. (1997), *Hungary and the Habsburgs, 1765-1800*. Budapest: Central European

University Press.

Balch, Emily Greene (1910), *Our Slavic Fellow Citizens*. New York: Charities Publication Committee.

Banac, Ivo (1984), *The National Question in Yugoslavia: origins, history, politics*. Ithaca NY and

London: Cornell University Press, rev. ed.

Banac, Ivo (1988), *With Stalin against Tito: Cominformist splits in Yugoslav communism*. Ithaca and

London: Cornell University Press.

Barker, Thomas M. (1990), *Social Revolutionaries and Secret Agents: the Carinthian Slovene*

partisans and Britain's Special operations Executive. Boulder CO: East European

Monographs, and New York: Columbia University Press.

Barraclough, Geoffrey ed. (1978), *"The Times" Atlas of World History*. London: Times Books.

Barth, Frederick (1969), *Ethnic Groups and Boundaries*. Boston: Little & Brown.

Barton, Allen H., Denitch, Bogdan and Kadushin, Charles, (1973), *Opinion-Making Elites in*

Yugoslavia. New York: Praeger.

Bateman, Milford J.B. (1993), *Local economic strategies and new small firm entry in a labour-*

managed economy: a case study of Yugoslavia between 1950-1990. University of Bradford:

Unpublished Ph.D. thesis.

Batou, Jean (ed.) (1991), *Between Development and Underdevelopment: 1800-1870*. Geneva: Droz.

Baucic, Ivo (1972), *The Effects of Migration from Yugoslavia and the Problems of Returning Emigrant*

Workers. The Hague: Martinus Nijhoff.

Baucic, Ivo (1973), *Radnici u inozemstvu prema Popisu Stanovnistva Jugoslavije 1971*. Zagreb:

Radovi Instituta za Geografiju Sveucilista u Zagrebu.

Baudrillard, Jean (1988), *Selected Writings*, (edited by Mark Poster). Stanford University Press.

Bauman, Zygmunt (1973), *Culture as Praxis*. London: Routledge & Kegan Paul.

Bauman, Zygmunt (1974), "Officialdom and class: bases of inequality in socialist society", in, Frank

Parkin ed., *The Social Analysis of Class Structure*. London: Tavistock.

Bauman, Zygmunt (1976), *Socialism: the active utopia*. London: George Allen and Unwin.

Beard, Charles A. and Radin, George (1929), *The Balkan Pivot: Yugoslavia. A study in government*

and administration. New York: Macmillan.

Bejlo, Ante (ed.) (1993), *Historical Maps of Croatia from the Penguin Atlas of World History*. Zagreb:

Hrvatski Informativni Centar.

Bellah, R.N., Madsen, R., Sullivan, W.M., Swidler, A., and Tipton, S.M. (1985*), Habits of the Heart*,

Berkeley: University of California Press.

Bellamy, Christopher (1997), *Knights in White Armour: the new art of war and peace*. London:

Pimlico.

Benson, Leslie (1972), "Market socialism and class structure: manual workers and managerial power in

the Yugoslav enterprise", in Frank Parkin ed.

Berend, Ivan T. and Ranki, Gyorgy (1977), *East Central Europe in the 19th. and 20th. Centuries*.

Budapest: Akademiai Kiado.

Berend, Ivan T. and Ranki, Gyorgy (1980), *The European Periphery and Industrialization: 1780-1914*.

Cambridge University Press.

Bérenger, Jean (1994), *A History of the Habsburg Empire: 1273-1700*. London: Longman.

Berger, Peter and Luckmann, Thomas (1967), *The Social Construction of Reality*. London: Allen Lane.

Berger, Peter (1971*), A Rumour of Angels: modern society and the rediscovery of the supernatural*.

London, Penguin Books.

Bicanic, R. (1936), *Kako zivi narod: zivot u pasivnim krajevima*. Zagreb: Tipografija.

Bicanic, R. (1938), *Ekonomska podloga hrvatskog pitanja*, Split. (2nd. ed.).

Bicanic, Rudolf (1951), *Doba manufakture u Hrvatskoj i Slavoniji: 1750-1860*.Zagreb: JAZU.

Bicanic, Rudolf (1973), *Economic Policy in Socialist Yugoslavia*.Cambridge University Press.

Bicanic, R. (1981), *How the People Live*, (edited Joel Halpern and Elinor Murray Despalatovic),

    Research Report No. 21, Dept. of Anthropology, University of Massachusetts at Amherst.

Bicanic, R. and Macan, Z. (1939), *Kako zivi narod*, Vol. II, Zagreb.

Bicanic, R., Mihletic, A. and Stefek, D. (1939), *Najnuznije narodne potrebe*. Zagreb.

Blagojevic, Boris T. ed. (1977), *Guide to the Yugoslav Legal System*. Belgrade: Institute of

    Comparative Law.

Bloch, Marc (1962), *Feudal Society*. London:Routledge & Kegan Paul, 2 vols.

Boban, Ljubo (1992), *Hrvatske granice: 1918-1992*. Zagreb: Skolska Knjiga.

Bogdanovic, Marija (1988), "Drustvene Nejednakosti", in Popovic ed. pp. 17-77, and, "Drustvene

    nejednakosti i vertikalna drustvena pokretljivpost", pp. 315-346.

Bojanovski, D., Djonov, K. and Pemovska, A. (1955*), Razvitokot na zemjodelstvo vo Makedonija*.

    Skopje.

Bokovoy, Melissa K., Irvine, Jill A., and Lilly, Carol S. eds. (1997), *State-Society Relations in*

    Yugoslavia, 1945-1992. London: Macmillan.

Bombelles, Joseph T. (1968), *Economic Development of Communist Yugoslavia: 1947-1964*. Stanford

    CA: The Hoover Institution.

Boskovic, Blagoje and Dasic, David (1980), *Socialist Self-Management in Yugoslavia, 1950-1980:*

    Documents. Belgrade: Socialist Thought and Practice.

Bougarel, Xavier (1996), *Bosnie: anatomie d'un conflit*. Paris, Editions La Decouverte.

Bourdieu, Peirre (1977), *Outline of a Theory of Practice*. Cambridge University Press.

Bourdieu, Pierre (1990), *Logic of Practice*. Cambridge: Polity Press.

Bowman, Glenn (1994), 'Constitutive violence and rhetorics of identity: a comparative study of

    nationalist movements in the Israeli-occupied territories and former Yugoslavia', in Bruce

Kapferer ed., *Nationalism and Violence*. Oxford University Press.

Bracewell, Catherine Wendy (1992*), The Uskoks of Senj: Piracy, banditry and holy war in the sixteenth century Adriatic*. Ithaca NY: Cornell University Press.

Brandt, Karl ed. (1953), *Management of Agriculture and food in the German-occupied and other areas of fortress Europe: a study in military government*. Stanford CA: Stanford University Press.

Brashich, Ranko (1954), *Land Reform and Ownership in Yugoslavia: 1919-1953*. New York: Mid European Studies Centre.

Braudel, Fernand (1972), *The Mediterranean and the Mediterranean World in the Age of Philip II*, London: Collins, 2 vols., rev. ed..

Bringa, Tone (1995*), Being Muslim the Bosnian Way: identity and community in a central Bosnian Village*. Princeton University Press.

Brown, L. Carl ed. (1996*), Imperial Legacy: The Ottoman imprint on the Balkans and the Middle East*. New York, Columbia University Press.

Brzezinski, Zbigniew (1989),

Bzezinski, Zbigniew (1993), *Out of Control: Global Trurmoil on the Eve of the Twenty-First Century*. New York: Scribner.

Bulajic, Milan (1989), *Ustaski zlocini genocida*. Belgrade: Rad, (4 vols.).

Budin, Tomislav (1992), "Agrarna struktura kao cinitelj razvitka hrvatske poljoprivrede", *Sociologija Sela*, 30(1/2):45-52.

Butterfield, Herbert (1931), *The Whig Interpretation of History*. London: G. Bell & Sons.

Burg, Steven L. (1993), "Why Yugoslavia fell apart", *Current History*, November, pp. 357-363.

Byrnes, Robert F. (ed.) (1976), *Communal Families in the Balkans: The Zadruga. Essays by Philip Mosely and in his honour*. Notre Dame IN: University of Notre Dame Press.

Caldarovic, Ognjen (1987), *Suvremeno drustvo i urbanizacija*. Zagreb: Skolska knjiga.

Carlton, Eric (1994), *Massacres: an Historical Perspective*. Aldershot: Scolar Press.

Carmichael, Catherine (1993), *Ecology and Social Change: Crknica, a village in the Slovene karst,* University of Bradford, unpublished Ph.D. thesis.

Carter, April (1982), *Democratic Reform in Yugoslavia: the changing role of the party, 1964-1972,* London:Frances Pinter.

Carter, Frank W. ed. (1977), *An Historical Geography of the Balkans*. London, Academic Press

Carter, Frank W. (1977a), "Urban development in the western Balkans", in Frank W. Carter ed. (1977).

Carter, Frank and Turnock, David (eds.) (forthcoming), *The States of Eastern Europe*. Aldershot: Ashgate.

Castellan, Georges (1967), *Le Vie Quotidienne en Serbie au seuil de l'independence, 1815-1839*. Paris: Hachette.

Castellan, Georges (1992), *History of the Balkans from Mohammed the Conqueror to Stalin*. Boulder (CO): East European monographs, and New York: Columbia University Press.

Cavoski, Kosta (1989), *O neprijatelju*. Belgrade: Prosveta.

Cigar, Norman (1995), *Genocide in Bosnia: the policy of "ethnic cleansing"*. College Station TX: Texas A&M University Press.

Clissold, Stephen ed.. (1975), *Yugoslavia and the Soviet Union: 1939-1973*. Oxford University Press and the Royal Institute of International Affairs.

Cohen, Lenard J. (1989), *The Socialist Pyramid: elites and power in Yugoslavia*. London, Tri-Service Press.

Cohen, Lenard J. (1993), *Broken Bonds: the disintegration of Yugoslavia*. Boulder CO, Westview Press.

Cohen, Philip J. (1996), *Serbia's Secret War: propaganda and the deceit of history*. College Station TX: Texas A&M University Press.

Collomb, Robin G. (1978), *Julian Alps*. Reading: West Col Productions.

Comrie, Bernard, and Corbett, Greville G. eds. (1993), *The Slavonic Languages*. London: Routledge.

Connor, Walker (1994), *Ethnonationalism: the quest for understanding*. New Jersey: Princeton

    University Press.

Constitution of the Republic of Croatia, Zagreb, 1991.

Cornell, Stephen and Hartmann, Douglas (1998), *Ethnicity and Race: making identities in a changing

    world*. Thousand Oaks CA and London: Pine Forge Press.

Crampton, Richard (1994), *Eastern Europe in the Twentieth Century*. London: Routledge.

Crampton, Richard and Crampton Ben (1996), *Atlas of Eastern Europe in the Twentieth Century*.

    London: Routledge.

Croatian Medical Journal (1992), Vol.33, War Supplement 1, Zagreb, Medicinski Fakultet.

Cukanovic, S. (1971), *Zemljoradnicko zadrugarstvo u agrarnoj politici Jugoslasvije*. Belgrade.

Culinovic, F. (1961), *Jugoslavija izmedju dva rata*. Zagreb, JAZU.

Cunliffe, Barry ed., (1994), *The Oxford Illustrated Prehistory of Europe*. Oxford University Press.

Cvjeticanin ed. (1974) [to be supplied]

Cvitkovic, Ivan (1995), *Sociologija religije*. Sarajevo: Biblioteka Znanstvena Misao.

Cvijic, Jovan (1965), *Iz drustvenih nauka*. Belgrade, Vuk Karadzic.

Dahrendorf, Ralf (1968), *Society and Democracy in Germany*. London: Weidenfeld and Nicolson.

Daniel, Norman (1982), "Edward Said and the orientalists", *Mélanges de l'Institut Dominicain

    d'Études Orientales de Caire*, 15:211-222.

Danopoulos, Constantine P. and Zirker, Daniel eds. (1996*, Civil-Military Relations in the Soviet and

    Yugoslav Successor States*. Boulder CO, Westview Press.

Darby, H.C., Seton-Watson, R.W., Auty, P., Laffan, R.G.D., and Clissold S. (1966), *A Short History of

    Yugoslavia from early times to 1966*. Cambridge University Press.

Davie, Grace (1994), *Religion in Britain since 1945*. Oxford: Blackwell.

Davies, Norman (1996), *Europe: A History*. Oxford University Press.

Dawisha, Karen, and Parrott, Bruce eds. (1997), *Politics, power and the Struggle for Democracy in South-East Europe*. Cambridge University Press.

Dedijer, Vladimir (1967), *The Road to Sarajevo*. London: McGibbon & Kee.

Dedijer, Vladimir, Bozic, Ivan, Cirkovic, Sima and Ekmecic, Milorad. (1974), *History of Yugoslavia*. New York: McGraw Hill.

Denitch, Bogdan (1976), *The Legitimation of a Revolution*. New Haven: Yale University Press.

Denitch, Bogdan (1996), *Ethnic Nationalism: the tragic death of Yugoslavia*. Minneapolis and London: Minnesota University Press.

Deutsch, Karl W. and Foltz, W.J. (1966), *Nation-Building*. New York: Atherton Press.

Devine, Alex (1918), *Montenegro in History, Politics and War*. London: T. Fisher Unwin.

Dimitrijevic, S. (1962), *Privredni razvitak Jugoslavije od 1918-1941g.*. Belgrade: Visoka skola politickih nauka.

Dirlam, Joel and Plummer, James (1973), *An Introduction to the Yugoslav Economy*. Columbus OH: Charles E. Merrill.

Djilas, Aleksa (1991), *The Contested Country: Yugoslav unity and communist revolution, 1919-1953*. Cambridge MA and London: Harvard University Press.

Djilas, Milovan (1957), *The New Class: an analysis of the Communist system*. London: George Allen and Unwin.

Djilas, Milovan (1959), *Anatomy of a Moral: the political essays of Milovan Djilas*. London: Thames and Hudson.

Djordjevic, Dragoljub (1990), "Konfesionalni mentalitet kao faktor (dez)integracije", *Revija za sociologiju*, XXI(1):159-63.

Donia, Robert J. and Fine, John V.A. (eds.) (1994), *Bosnia and Hercegovina: a tradition betrayed*,

London: Hurst & Co.

Douglas, Mary (1966), *Purity and Danger: an analysis of concepts of pollution and taboo*. London,

Routledge & Kegan Paul.

Douglas, Mary (1980), *Evans-Pritchard*. London: Fontana.

Draganov (1906), *La Macedoine et les Reformes*. Paris: Librarie Plon.

Dragnic, in Kerner ed. (1949). "Yugoslavia" [to be completed]

Drakulic, Slavenka, (1993), "Women hide behind a wall of silence", in Rabia Ali and Lawrence

Lifschultz eds., *Why Bosnia? Writings on the Balkan war*. Stony Creek (CT): The

Pamphleteer's Press, 116-121.

Draskovic, Vuk (1982), *Noz*. Belgrade.

Drulovic, Milojko (1978), *Self-Management on Trial*. Nottingham: Spokesman Books.

Dunn, Larry A. (1996), "The role of religion in conflicts in former Yugoslavia", *Religion in Eastern

Europe*, XVI (1):13-25.

Durham, M. Edith (1928), *Some Tribal Origins, Laws and Customs of the Balkans*. London: George

Allen & Unwin.

Durkheim, Emile (1964 [1893]), *The Division of Labour in Society*. London, Collier-Macmillan.

Durkheim, Emile (1969[1907]), *Journal sociologique*. Paris: Presses Universitaires de France.

Durkheim, Emile (1915) [1912], *Elementary Forms of the Religious Life*. London: George Allen &

Unwin.

Durkheim, Emile (1975), *Textes*. ed. Victor Karady, Vol. 3, "Fonctions sociales et institutions", Paris:

Les Editions de Minuit.

Durkheim, Emile (1983) [1955], *Pragmatism and Sociology*. Cambridge University Press.

Dyker, David (1990), *Yugoslavia: socialism, development and debt*. London, Routledge.

612

Eames, Alan (1987), *Self-management in Yugoslav Enterprises 1949-1980. Industrial and institutional development with worker participation: towards a participation society.* Brussels: AJ Associates.

Elakovic, Simo and Brangjolica Vlaho (1985), *Socijalne promene pod utjecajem turizma na Jadranskom podrucju.* Dubrovnik: Centar za Ekonomskih Znanosti, Split and Institut za Ekonomska istrazivanja, Dubrovnik.

Elias, Norbert (1978), *What is Sociology?.* London: Hutchinson.

Elias, Norbert (1994 [1939]), *The civilizing process.* Oxford: Blackwell.

Enciklopedija Jugoslavije (1958), Zagreb, Leksikografski Zavod FNRJ.

Eric, Milivoje (1958), *Agrarna reforma u Jugoslaviji: 1918-1941g..* Sarajevo, Veselin Maslesa.

Erlich, Vera (1966), *Family in Transition: a study of 300 Yugoslav villages.* Princeton University Press.

Eterovich, Francis H. and Spalatin, Christopher (1970), *Croatia: land, people and culture*, Vol. I. University of Toronto Press.

Evans-Pritchard, E.E. (1940), *The Nuer: a description of the modes of livelihood and political institutions of a Nilotic people.* Oxford: Clarendon Press.

Evans-Pritchard, E.E. (1940a), "The Nuer of the Southern Sudan", in, M. Fiske, John (1987), Television Culture, London, Methuen.

Featherstone, Mike, Hepworth, Mike and Turner, Bryan (1991), *The Body: Social Process and Cultural Theory.* London, Sage, 1991.

Fiamengo, (1971), *Osnove opce sociologije.* Zagreb: Narodne Novine.

Fine, John V.A. (1983), *The Early Mediaeval Balkans: a critical survey from the sixth to the late twelfth century.* Ann Arbor: University of Michigan Press.

Fine, John V.A. (1987), *The Late Medieval Balkans: a critical survey from the late XII century to the Ottoman conquest.* Ann Arbor: Michigan University Press.

Fiske, John (1987), *Television Culture*. London, Methuen.

Flere, Sergej (1990), "Raspad moderniteta i religija", *Revija za sociologiju*, XXI(1):147-58.

Flere, Sergej (1994), "Le développement de la sociologie de la religion en Yougoslavia après la

    deuxième guerre mondiale (jusqu'à son démembrement), *Social Compass*, Vol.41(3):367-77.

Fortes and E.E. Evans-Pritchard (eds.), *African Political Systems*. Oxford University Press.

Foster, George M. (1965), "Peasant society and the image of the limited good", *American*

    Anthropologist, 67(2):293-314.

Foucault, Michel (1979), *Discipline and Punish: the birth of the prison*. London, Penguin books.

Franges, Otto von (1934), "The agrarian reform in Yugoslavia", *Monthly Bulletin of Agricultural*

    Economics and Sociology, Rome, International Institute of Agriculture, E89-100, 125-36,

    174-98, 209-30, 269-87, 311-27.

Frank, André Gunder (1969), *Capitalism and Underdevelopment in Latin America*. New York:

    Monthly Review Press.

Frank, Andre Gunder (1971), *The Sociology of Development and the Underdevelopment of Sociology*,

    London: Pluto Press.

Freeman, E.A. (1903), *Historical Geography of Europe*. London, 3rd. ed.

Frid, Zlatko (ed.) (1971), *Religions in Yugoslavia*. Zagreb: Binoza.

Fukuyama, Francis (1992), *The End of History and the Last Man*. London: Penguin Books.

Galeski, Boguslav (1972), *Basic Concepts in Rural Sociology*. Manchester University Press.

Gams, Andrija (1987), *Svojina*. Belgrade: Centar za filozofiju I drustvenu teoriju.

Gazi, Stephen (1973), *A History of Croatia*. New York, Barnes and Noble.

Geertz, Clifford (1973), *The Interpretation of Culture*. New York: Basic Books.

Gellner, Ernest (1981), *Muslim Society*. Cambridge University Press.

Gellner, Ernest (1983), *Nations and Nationalism*. Oxford: Basil Blackwell.

Gerschenkron, (1968), *Continuity in History and Other Essays*. Harvard University Press and Oxford

    University Press.

Gibb, Sir Hamilton, and Bowen, Harold (1950), *Islamic Society and the West*. Oxford University Press.

    Vol. I Islamic Society in the Eighteenth Century.

Giddens, Anthony (1979), *Central Problems in Social Theory: action, structure and contradiction*.

    London: Macmillan.

Giddens, Anthony (1987), *Social Theory and Modern Sociology*. Cambridge: Polity Press.

Giddens, Anthony (1990), *The Consequences of Modernity*. Cambridge, Polity Press.

Giddens, Anthony (1991), *Modernity and Self-Indentity: self and society in the later moden age*.

    Cambridge: Polity Press.

Giner, Salvador (1976), *Mass Society*. London: Martin Robertson.

Gjecov, Shtjefen (1989 [1933]), *The Code of Lek Dukagjini/Kanun I Leke Dukagjinit*, trans. Leonard

    Fox, New York: Gjonlekaj Pub. Co.

Gluckman, Max (1965), *Custom and Conflict in Africa*, Oxford, Basil Blackwell.

Goldsworthy, Vesna (1998), *Inventing Ruritania: the imperialism of the imagination*. New York and

    London: Yale University Press.

Gordon, Jan (1916), *A Balkan Freebooter*. London,

Good, David F. (1984), *The Economic Rise of the Habsburg Empire: 1750-1914*. Berkeley: University

    of California Press.

Goricar (1970), *Sociologija: osnove marksisticke opste teorije o drustvu*. Beograd: Rad.

Govorchin, G.G. (1961), *Americans from Yugoslavia*. University of Florida Press.

Gow, James (1992), *Legitimacy and the Military: the Yugoslav Crisis*. London, Pinter

Gow, James (1997), *The Triumph of the Lack of Will: international diplomacy and the Yugoslav War*.

    London: Hurst & Co.

Grbic, Cedo (1984), *Socijalizam I rad privatnim sredstvima*. Zagreb: Biblioteka Socijalisticko

    Samoupravljanje I Suvremeni Svijet.

Grmek, Mirko, Gjidara, Marc and Simac, Neven (1993), *Etnicko ciscenje: povjesni dokumenti o jednoj*

    srpskoj ideologiji. Zagreb: Globus.

Gross, Mirjana (1993), "The union of Dalmatia with northern Croatia: a crucial question of the

    Croatian national integration in the nineteenth century", in, Mikulás Teich and Roy Porter

    eds., *The National Question in Europe in Historical Context*. Cambridge University Press, pp.

    270-92.

Gross, Nachum T. (1976), "The industrial revolution in the Habsburg Monarchy, 1750-1914", in,

    Carlo M. Cipolla ed., *The Emergence of Industrial Societies*. Hassocks: Harvester Press,

    228-278.

Grubisic, Ivan (1991), "Zupski vjeronauk - prosirenost i utjecaj na religiozno ponasanje", *Crkva u*

    sviejetu, XXVI(2-3):199-206.

Guzina, Ruzica (1959), [to be supplied]

Guzina, Ruzica (1960), "Klasni odnosi u Srbiji, 1903-1914", *Arhiv pravnog fakulteta, Univerzitet*

    Beograda, 1-2:121-34.

Habal ed. (1979) [to be supplied]

Habermas, Jurgen (1987), *The Philosophical Discourse of Modernity*. Cambridge: Polity Press.

Hall, Stuart (1992), 'The West and the Rest: discourse and power', in Stuart Hall and Bram Gieben

    (eds.) *Formations of Modernity*. Cambridge: Polity Press.

Halpern, Joel M. (1958), *A Serbian Village*. New York: Columbia University Press.

Halpern Joel M. and Halpern, Barbara K. (1972), *A Serbian Village in Historical Perspective*. New

    York: Holt Rinehart & Winston.

Hammel, Eugene A. (1968), *Alternative Social Structures and Ritual Relations in the Balkans*.

Englewood Cliffs NJ: Prentice Hall.

Hammel, Eugene A. (1969), *The Pink Yo-Yo: occupational mobility in Belgrade*. Berkeley: University

of California, Institute of International Studies.

Hammond, Nicholas G.I. (1976), *Migrations and Invasions in Greece and Adjacent Areas*. Park Ridge

NJ: Noyes Press.

Hanak, H. (1962), *Great Britain and Austria-Hungary during the First World War*. Oxford University

Press.

Harrison, David (1988), *The Sociology of Modernisation and Development*. London: Unwin Hyman.

Hasluck, Margaret (1954), *The Unwritten Law in Albania*, ed. J.H. Hutton. Cambridge University

Press.

Hegyi, Klara and Zimanyi, Vera (1986), *The Ottoman Empire in Europe*. Budapest: Corvina.

Held, Joseph ed. (1996), *Populism in Eastern Europe: racism, nationalism and society*. Boulder

CO.:East European Monographs, and New York: Columbia University Press.

Hersak, Emil (1993), 'Panoptikum migracija - Hrvati, hrvatski prostor i Evropa', *Migracijske teme*, Vol.

9, 3-4, 227-301.

Heywood, Colin (1993), "Bosnia under Ottoman rule, 1463-1800)", in Mark Pinson ed

pp. 22-53.

Hindess, Barry, and Hirst, Paul (1975), *Pre-Capitalist Modes of Production*. London: Routledge and

Kegan Paul.

Hindess, Barry, and Hirst, Paul, (1977), *Mode of Production and Social Formation*. London:

Macmillan.

Hobhouse, J.C. (1813*), A Journey through Albania and other Provinces of Turkey in Europe and Asia*.

London.

Hobsbawm,Eric (1969), *Bandits*. London: Weidenfeld & Nicolson.

Hobsbawm, Eric (1994), *Age of Extremes: the short XX century, 1914-1991*. London: Michael Joseph.

Hobsbawm, Eric and Ranger, Terence (1983), *The Invention of Tradition*. Cambridge University Press.

Hocevar, Toussaint (1965), *The Structure of the Slovenian Economy: 1848-1963*. New York: Studia

    Slovenica.

Hoffman, George W. (1972), *Regional development strategy in Southeast Europe*. New York, Praeger.

Hoffman, George W. and Hatchett, Ronald LK. (1977), "The impact of regional development policy

    on population distribution in Yugoslavia and Bulgaria", in Kostanick ed.

Hoffman, George W. and Neal, Fred W. (1962), *Yugoslavia and the New Communism*. New York:

    Twentieth Century Fund.

Hoptner, Jacob B. (1962), *Yugoslavia in Crisis, 1934-1941*. New York: Columbia University Press.

Horton, John J. (1990), *Yugoslavia*. Oxford and Denver: Clio Press, World Bibliographical Series

    rev. ed.

Horvat, Branko (1969), *An Essay on Yugoslav Society*. White Plains, NY: International Arts &

    Sciences Press. pp. 99-124.

House of Commons (1992), Foreign Affairs Committee, *Soviet Union/Developments in*

    Central Europe, "Minutes of Evidence" for 6 Nov. 27 Nov. 4 Dec. 11 Dec.

    1991, and 14 and 15 Jan. 1992;.

House of Commons, (1992a), *Central and Eastern Europe: Problems of the Post-*

    Communist Era, 6 Feb. 1992. London, HMSO.

Huntington, Samuel P. ed. (1962), *Changing Patterns of Military Politics*. New York:Free Press.

Huntington, Samuel P. (1996), *The Clash of Civilizations? The debate*. New York: Council for Foreign

    Relations.

Huntington, Samuel P. (1997), *The Clash of Civilizations and the Remaking of World Order*. London:

    Touchstone.

Hutchinson, John and Smith, Anthony D. (eds.) (1994), *Nationalism*. Oxford University Press.

Ignatieff, Michael (1998), *The Warrior's Honour: ethnic war and the modern conscience*, London: Chatto & Windus.

Ilic, Milos (1963), *Socijalna struktura i pokretljivost radnicke klase Jugoslavije*. Belgrade: Institut drustvenih nauka.

Inalçik, Halil (1985), *Studies in Ottoman Social and Economic History*. London: Varorium Reprints.

Inalçik, Halil (1996), "The meaning of legacy", in L. Carl Brown ed., *Imperial Legacy: the Ottoman imprint on the Balkans and the Middle East*. New York: Columbia University Press.

Inalçik, Halil, and Quataert, Donald eds. (1994*), An Economic and Social History of the Ottoman Empire: 1300-1914*. Cambridge University Press.

Irvine, Jill A. (1993*), The Croat Question: Partisan politics in the formation of the Yugoslav socialist State*. Boulder CO: Westview Press.

Isakovic, Svetlana (ed.) (1992), *Genocide against the Serbs: 1941-1945 - 1991/92*. Belgrade, Museum of Applied Arts, 2 vols.

Issawi, Charles (ed.) (1966), The Economic History of the Middle East, 1800-1914: a book of Readings. University of Chicago Press.

Issawi, Charles (1980), The Economic History of Turkey, 1800-1914, Chicago: Centre for Middle Eastern Studies

Issawi, Charles (1996), "The economic legacy", in L. Carl Brown (ed.*), Imperial Legacy: the Ottoman imprint on the Balkans and the Middle East,* New York: Columbia University Press.

Ivsic, Milan (1926), *Les problemes agraires en Yougoslavie*. Paris: Rousseau.

Jambrek, Peter (1975), *Development and Social Change in Yugoslavia: crises and perspectives of building a nation*. Lexington KY: Saxon House.

Jancar, Barbara (1985), "The new feminism in Yugoaslavia", in Pedro Ramet ed., *Yugoslavia in the*

1980s. Boulder CO: Westview Press, 201-23.

Jankovic and Krizman (1964) [to be supplied]

JAZU Atlas of historical maps [to be supplied.

Jelavich, Barbara (1954), "Some aspects of Serbian religious development in the eighteenth century",

    Church History: 144-52.

Jelavich, Barbara (1983), *History of the Balkans*. Vol. 2, Twentieth Century, Cambridge University

    Press.

Jelavich, Barbara (1991), *Russia's Balkan Entanglements, 1806-1914*. Indiana University Press.

Jelavich, Charles and Barbara eds. (1963), *The Balkans in Transition: essays on the development of*

    Balkan life and politics since the 18th. Century. Berkeley and Los Angeles: University of

    California Press.

Jelavich, Barbara and Jelavich, Charles (1977), *The Establishment of the Balkan National States, 1804-*

    1920. Seattle and London: Washington University Press.

Jenkins, Richard (1992), *Pierre Bourdieu*. London: Routledge.

Johnson, Terry Dandeker, Christopher and Ashworth, Clive (1984), *The Structure of Social Theory:*

    dilemmas and strategies. London: Macmillan.

Jovanov, Neca (1979), *Radnicki strajkovi u Socijalistickoj Federativnoj Republici Jugoslaviji od 1958.*

    do 1969. g. Belgrade: Zapis.

Jovanovic, Dragoljub (1930), *Agrarna politika*. Beograd

Jukic, Ilija (1974), *The Fall of Yugoslavia*. New York: Harcourt Brace Jovanovich.

Kadare, Ismael (1991), *Broken April*. London: Harvill.

Karaman Igor *(1991), Industrijalizacija gradjanske Hrvastske (1800-1941)*. Zagreb: Naprijed

Kardelj, Edvard (1959), *Problemi socialisticke politike na sela*. Belgrade: Kultura.

Kardelj, Edvard (19..), "Zemljoradnicko zadrugarstvo u planskoj privredi", *Komunist*, II(3).

Kaser, Michael ed. (1986), *The Economic History of Eastern Europe, 1919-1975*. Vol. III, Institutional

    Change within a planned economy. Oxford University Press.

Kaser, Michael C. and Radice, E.A. eds. (1985*), The Economic History of Eastern Europe,*

    1919-1975. Vol. I, Economic Structure and Performance between the Two Wars. Oxford

    University Press.

Kaser, Michael C. and Radice, E.A. eds. (1986*), The Economic History of Eastern Europe,*

    1919-1975. Vol. II, Interwar Policy, the War and Reconstruction. Oxford University Press.

Kedourie, Elie (1966), *Nationalism*. London: Hutchinson, 3rd. ed.

Kende, Pierre and Strmiska, Zdenek (1987), *Equality and Inequality in Eastern Europe*. Leamington

    Spa: Berg.

Kennan, George F. (ed.) (1993*), The Other Balkan Wars: A 1913 Carnegie Endowment Inquiry in*

    retrospect with a new introduction and reflections on the present conflict. Washington,

    Carnegie Endowment.

Kettering, Sharon (1988), "The historical development of political clientelism", *Journal of*

    Interdisciplinary History, XVIII (3):419-47.

Keyder, Caglar (1991), "Creation and destruction of forms of manufacturing: the Ottoman example",

    in Jean Batou ed , *Between Development and Underdevelopment: 1800-1870*. Geneva:

    Librairie Droz, 157-179.

Kiernan, Victor (1975), "Socialism: the prophetic memory", in Bhikhu Parekh ed., *The Concept of*

    Socialism. London: Croom Helm, 14-37.

Kirk, D. (1946), *Europe's Population in the Interwar Years*. Geneva: League of Nations.

Klanac, Luka (1992), *Demografske promjene obrovackog kraja: 1857-1991*. Zagreb, privately

    published.

Klemencic, Mladen (ed.), (1993), *A Concise Atlas of the Republic of Croatia*. Zagreb: Miroslav Krleza

Lexicographical Institute.

Koledarov, Peter S. (1977), 'Ethnical and political preconditions for regional names in the central and

eastern parts of the Balkan Peninsula', in, Frank W. Carter ed. (1977) pp. 293-317.

Komadinic, M. (1934), *Problem seljackih dugova*. Belgrade.

Komlos, John (ed.) (1983), *Economic Development in the Habsburg Monarchy in the Nineteenth*

Century: Essays. Boulder CO: East European Monographs, and New York: Columbia

University Press.

Kornhauser, William (1954), *The Politics of Mass Society*. London: Routledge and Kegan Paul.

Korosic, Marijan (ed.) (1989), *Quo Vadis, Jugoslavijo?*. Zagreb: Naprijed.

Kosovac, Mladen, Grahovac, Blagoje and Radosavljevic, Ljiljana eds. (1989), *Zakon o preduzecima,*

sa komentarom, obrascima I primerima akata za prakticnu primenu zakona. Belgrade,

Narodna Knjiga.

Kostanick, Harry L. ed. (1977), *Population and Migration Trends in Eastern Europe*. Boulder CO.

Westview.

Kostic, Cvetko (1955), *Seljaci-industrijski radnici*. Belgrade: Rad.

Kostic, Cvetko (1955-57), "Postanak I razvitak 'carsije': (primer 'carsije' Bajine Baste)", *Glasnik*

etnografskog instituta SAN-a, IV-VI:123-149.

Kraljevic, Svetozar (1984), *The Apparitions of Our Lady at Medjugorje*, ed. Michael Scanlon,

Chicago: Fransican Herald Press.

Kremensek, Slavko (nd.), *Zelena Jama: The evolution of a Yugoslav Working Class Community*, (trans.

Tousasaint Hocevar), unpublished TS.

Kristo, Jure (1987), "Catholicism among Croats and its critique by Marxists", in, Dennis J. Dunn ed.,

Religion and Nationalism in Eastern Europe and the Soviet Union. Boulder CO and London:

Lynne Riener, pp. 77-95.

Kugy, Julius (1934), *Alpine Pilgrimage*. London: John Murray.

Kukoleca, Stefan M. (1941), *Industrija Jugoslavije, 1918-1938*. Belgrade: Balkanska Stampa.

Kukoleca, Stefan M. (1956), *Analiza privrede Jugoslavije pred Drgi Svetski Rat*. Belgrade.

Kulischer, Eugene M. (1943), *The Dispacement of Population in Europe*. Montreal, International

   Labour Office.

Kurtovic, Todo (1980), *Church and Religion in the Socialist self-managing Society*. Belgrade: Socialist

   Thought and Practice.

Kuzmanovic, Bora (1995), "Social distance towards individual nations", in Mladen Lazic ed.

   1995:239-260.

Laffan, R.G.D. (1918), *The Guardians of the Gate: historical lectures on the Serbs*. Oxford: Clarendon

   Press.

Lajtman, Ivo (ed.), 1991), *War Crimes against Croatia*. Zagreb, Vecernji list.

Lampe, John R. and Jackson, Marvin R. (1982), *Balkan Economic History: 1550-1950*. Bloomington:

   Indiana University Press.

Lampe, John R. (1989), "Imperial borderlands or capitalist periphery? Redefining Balkan

   backwardness, 1520-1914", in Daniel Chirot ed., *The Origins of Backwardness in Eastern*

   Europe. Berkeley: University of California Press, 177-209.

Lampe, John R., Prickett, Russell O. and Adamovic, Ljubisa S. (1990), *Yugoslav-American Relations*

   since World War II. Durham and London: Duke University Press.

Lane, David (1971), *The End of Inequality? Stratification under state socialism*. London: Penguin

   Books.

Lanfant, Marie-Françoise, Allcock, John B. and Bruner, Edward M. (eds.) (1995), *International*

   Tourism: identity and change. London: Sage.

Lapenna, Ivo (1964), *State and Law: Soviet and Yugoslav Theory*. London: Athlone Press.

Lash, Scott and Urry, John (1994), *Economies off Signs and Space*. London: Sage.

Laurentin, Rene and Rupcic, Ljudevit (1984), *Is the Virgin Mary Appearing at Medjugorje?,*

Washington DC: The Word Among Us Press.

Lavigne, (1992). [to be supplied]

Lazic, Mladen (1983) [to be supplied]

Lazic, Mladen ed. (1995), *Society in Crisis: Yugoslavia in the early 1990s*. Belgrade: Filip Visnjic.

Leake, William M. (1814), *Researches in Greece*. London.

League of Communists (1959), *The Programme of the League of Communists*. London: International

Society for Socialist Studies.

Lederer, Ivo J. (1963), *Yugoslavia at the Paris Peace Conference: a study in frontier-making*. New

Haven CT: Yale University Press.

Lentini, Orlando (1998), "Portrait: Immanuel Wallerstein", *International Sociology*, 13(1):135-139.

Levi-Strauss, Claude (1966), *The Savage Mind*. London, Weidenfeld and Nicolson.

Levy, Marion J. (1966), *Modernization and the Structure of Societies a setting for international affairs*.

New Jersey: Princeton University Press.

Lewis, Bernard (1970), "Some reflections on the decline of the Ottoman Empire", in, Carlo M. Cipolla

ed., *The Economic Decline of Empires*. London, Methuen, 215-34.

Lincoln, Bruce (1989), *Discourse and the Construction of Society. Comparative studies of myth, ritual*

and classification. Oxford, The University Press.

Livingstone, R.G. (1959), *Stjepan Radic and the Croatian Peasant Party, 1904-1929*. Harvard

University: Unpublished Ph.D. thesis.

Lockwood, William G. (1975), *European Muslims: economy and ethnicity in western Bosnia*, New

York: Academic Press.

Lodge, Olive (1941), *Peasant Life in Yugoslavia*. London: Seeley, Service & Co.

Lord, Albert (1963), "Nationalism and the muses in Balkan Slavic literature in the modern period", in

Jelavich and Jelavich eds. 1963: 258-296.

Lukic, Radomir (1970), *Osnovi sociologije*. Belgrade: Naucna knjiga.

Lybyer, A.H. (1966), *The Government of the Ottoman Empire in the Time of Suleiman the Magnificent*,

New York: Russell and Russell.

Lydall, Harold (1984), *Yugoslav Socialism in Theory and Practice*. Oxford, Clarendon Press.

Lydall, Harold (1989), *Yugoslavia in Crisis*. Oxford: The Clarendon Prrss.

Lyon, David (1985), *The Steeple's Shadow*. London: SPCK.

McCarthy, Justin (1994), "Ottoman Bosnia, 1800-1878", in, Pinson ed., pp. 54-83.

Macartney, C.A. (1968), *The Habsburg Empire, 1790-1918*. London: Weidenfeld and Nicolson.

McFarlane, Bruce (1988), *Yugoslavia: politics, economics and society*. London and New York: Pinter.

McGowan, D. Beatrice (1949), "Agriculture", in, Robert Kerner ed., *Yugoslavia*. University of

California Press.

McGowan, Bruce (1981*)*, *Economic Life in Ottoman Europe: taxation,˙trade and the struggle for land*,

1600-1800, Cambridge University Press and Paris: Maison des Sciences de l'Homme.

McGrew, Anthony G. and Lewis, Paul, G. (eds.) (1992), *Global Politics. Globalization and the nation-*

state, Cambridge: Polity Press.

Mackay, D.M. (1974), *The Clockwork Image: a Christian perspective in science*. London: Inter-

Varsity Press.

Maclean, Fitzroy (1949), *Eastern Approaches*. London: Jonathan Cape.

McLellan, Woodford D. (1964), *Svetozar Markovic and the Origins of Balkan Socialism*. Princeton

University Press.

Madzar, Ljubomir (1992), "The economy of Yugoslavia: structure, growth record and institutional

Framework", in Allcock, Horton and Milivojevic eds. 1992, pp. 65-96.

Magas, Branka (1993), *The Destruction of Yugoslavia: tracking the break-up, 1980-92*. London and

New York: Verso.

Magid, Alvin (1991), *Private Lives/Public Surfaces: Grassroots perspectives and the legitimacy question in Yugoslav socialism*. Boulder CO, East European Monographs.

Magosci, Paul R. (1993), *Historical Atlas of East Central Europe*. Seattle & London, University of Washington Press.

Malcolm, Noel (1994), *Bosnia: a short history*. London: Macmillan.

Malcolm, Noel (1998), *Kosovo: a short history*. London: Macmillan.

Mallat, (1902), *La Serbie contemporaine:Etudes, enquêtes, statistiques* , Paris: J. Maisonneuve. Two Vols.

Mamatey, V.S. (1957), *The United Sates and East Central Europe, 1914-18*. Princeton University Press.

Markler, Gerald E., and McRea, Frances B. (1994), "Medjugorje and the crisis in Yugoslavia", in, William H. Swatos ed. *Politics and Religion in Central and Eastern Europe: Traditions and Transitions*. Westport CT and london: Praeger.

Markovic, P.J. (1963), *Strukturne promene na selu kao rezultat ekonomskog razvitka: period 1900-1960*. Belgrade, Zadruzna knjiga.

Matejko (1974), *Social Change and Stratification in Eastern Europe: an interpretative analysis of Poland and her neighbours*. London: Praeger.

Matis, Herbert ed. (1994), *The Economic Development of Austria since 1870*. Aldershot: Edward Elgar.

Maurer, Pierre (1991), *La reconciliation sovieto-yougoslave, 1954-1958*. Cousset (Fribourg): De Val.

Mendras, Henri (1976), *Societes paysannes*. Paris: Arman Colin.

Meneghello-Dincic, Kruno (1970*), Les Experiences yougoslaves d'industrialisation et de planification*, Paris: Editions Cujas.

Mesic, Milan (1992), "External migration in the context of the post-war development of Yugoslavia", in Allcock, Horton and Milivojevic eds. 1992, pp. 171-198.

Mestrovic, Stjepan (with Goreta, Miroslav and Letica, Slaven) (1993), *Habits of the Balkan Heart: social character and the fall of Communism*. College Station TX: Texas A&M University Press.

Mestrovic, Stjepan (with Goreta, Miroslav, and Letica, Slaven) (1993a), *The Road from Paradise: prospects for democracy in Eastern Europe*. Lexington KY: The University Press of Kentucky.

Mestrovic, Stjepan G. (1993b), *The Road from Paradise: prospects for democracy in Eastern Europe*. (with Miroslav Goreta and Slaven Letica), Lexington: University of Kentucky Press.

Mestrovic, Stjepan (1994), *Balkanization of the West: the confluence of post-modernism and post-Communism*. London and New York: Routledge.

Mestrovic, Stjepan (1996), *Genocide without Emotion....*

Meznaric, Silva (1993), "Uspon silovatelja: etnicitet, rod I nasilje", *Revija za sociologiju*, XXIV (3-4)119-129.

Mihailovic, Konstantin (1975), *Memoirs of a Jannissary*. Ann Arbor: University of Michigan.

Mihailovic, Kosta (1980), "Unutrasnje diferencijacije u republikama i pokrajinama", in, Ksente Bogoev, Kiril Miljovski and Nikola Uzunov eds. (1980), *Simpozium: Neravnomerni regionalni razvoj u ekonomskoj teoriji i praksi*. Skopke: Makedonska Akademija na Naukite a umetnostite, pp. 121-138.

Milenkovitch, Deborah (1971), *Plan and Market in Yugoslav Economic Thought*. Yale University Press.

Milivojevic, Marko (1985), *The Debt Rescheduling Process*. London: Frances Pinter.

Milivojevic, Marko (1988), "The Yugoslav People's Army: another Jaruzelski on the way?", *South Slav Journal*, 11(2-3):1-17.

Milivojevic, Marko (1988), "The political role of the Yugoslav People's Army in contemporary

Yugoslavia", in Milivojevic, Allcock and Maurer eds., pp. 15-59.

Milivojevic, Marko, Allcock, John B. and Maurer, Pierre eds. (1988), *Yugoslavia's Security Dilemmas:*

armed forces, national defence and foreign policy. Oxford, Berg.

Miljovski, Kiril ed. (1980), *Simpozium neravnomerni regionalni razvoj u ekonomskoj teoriji i praksi.*

2 vols., Skopje, Makedonska Akademija na Naukite i Umetnostite.

Milosevic, Micha (1980), *Les vicissitudes des cooperatives agricoles dans le developpement socio-*

politique Yougoslave. Geneva, Institut Universitaire d'Etudes du Developpement.

Milward, Alan and Saul, S.B. (1977), *The Development of the Economies of Continental Europe:*

1850-1914. London: Allen & Unwin.

Mirkovitch, Borivoie (1933), *La Yougoslavie: politique et economique.* Paris: Pierre Bossuet.

Mirkovic, M. (1952), *Ekonomska struktura Jugoslavije, 1918-1941.* Zagreb: Skolska knjiga.

Mitrany, David (1961 [1951]), *Marx against the Peasant: a study in social dogmatism.* NY: Collier

Books.

Mojzes, Paul ed. (1987*), Church and State in Postwar Eastern Europe: a bibliographical survey.*

New York: Greenwood Press.

Mojzes, Paul (1993), "The role of the religious communities in the war in former Yugoslavia",

Religion in Eastern Europe, XIII (3):13-31.

Mojzes, Paul (1993a), "The Roman Catholic Church in Croatia and its contribution to nationalist

sentiment", *Religion, State and Society*, 21(3-4):391-3.

Mojzes, Paul (1994), *Yugoslavian Inferno: ethnoreligious war in the Balkans.* New York:
Continuum.

Moore, Barrington (1967), *Social Origins of Dictatorship and Democracy: lord and peasant in the*

making of the modern world. London: Allen Lane.

Moore, W.E. (1945), *Economic Demography of Eastern Europe.* Geneva: League of Nations.

Morokvasic, Mirjana ed. (1992), Yougoslavie: logiques de l'exclusion, *Peuples Mediterraneens*, 61,

628

Oct.-dec.

Mousnier, Roland (1971), *Peasant Uprisings in Seventeenth Century France, Russia and China.* London: George Allen & Unwin.

Mousset, Jean (1938), *La Serbie et son Eglise (1830-1904).* Paris: Librairie Droz.

Mouzelis, Nicos P. (1986), *Politics in the Semi-Periphery: early parliamentarism and late industrialisation in the Balkans and Latin America.* London: Macmillan.

Moynihan, Daniel P. (1993), *Pandaemonium: Ethnicity in International Politics.* Oxford University Press.

Mrdjen, Snezana (1996), "La mixite en ex-Yougoslavie. Integration ou segregation des nationalites?" *Revue d'etudes comparatives Est-Ouest,* 3 (septembre): 103-145.

Mrksic, Danilo (1995), "The dual economy and social stratification", in Mladen Lazic ed. pp. 23-83.

Myrdal, Gunnar (1968), *Asian Drama: an enquiry into the poverty of nations.* London: Allan Lane (3 Vols.)

Naval Intelligence Division (1945), *Jugoslavia,* Geographical Handbook Series, 3 vols.. London, Great Britain, Admiralty.

Nejasmic, Ivica (1991), *Depopulizacija u Hrvatskoj: korijeni stanje, izgledi.* Zagreb, Globus/Institut za migracije i narodnosti Sveucilista u Zagrebu.

Nesovic, Slobodan (1964), *Privredna politika i ekonomske mere u toku oslobodilacke borbe naroda Jugoslavije.* Belgrade: Privredni pregled.

Newman, Bermard (1952), *Tito's Yugoslavia.* London: Robert Hale.

Norris, Harry T. (1993), *Islam in the Balkans: religion and society between Europe and the Arab world.* London: Hurst & Co.

Novak, Mojca (1991), *Zamudniski zvorci industrializacije: Slovenija na obrobju Evrope.* Ljubljana: Znanstveno in publicisticno sredisce.

Olivier, Louis (1901), *La Bosnie et Herzegovine.* Paris: Armand Colin.

Palairet, Micharel (1997), *The Balkan Economies c. 1800-1914: evolution without development*.

Cambridge University Press.

Parkin, Frank (1971), "Yugoslavia", in Margaret Scotford Archer and Salvador Giner eds.

Contemporary Europe: class status and power. London. Weidenfeld and Nicolson,

pp. 297-317.

Parkin, Frank (1971a), *Class Inequality and Political Order*. London: MacGibbon and Kee.

Frank Parkin ed. (1974), *The Social Analysis of Class Structure*. London: Tavistock, pp. 257-273.

Pavlowitch, Stevan K. (1971), *Yugoslavia*, London: Ernest Benn.

Pecjak, Vid (1994), "War cruelty in the former Yugoslavia and its psychological correlates", *Politics*

and the Individual, Vol.4,(1):75-84.

Peculjic (1979) [to be supplied]

Peric, Ivo (1983), *Razvitak turizma u Dubrovniku i okolici*, Dubrovnik: Zavod za povjesne znanosti

istrazivackog centra JAZU.

Pesic, Vesna (1988), *Kratki kurs o jednakosti: koncepcija jednakosti u zvanicnoj ideologiji*

Jugoslovenskog drustva. Belgrade: Biblioteka socioloskog pregleda.

Petrovich, Michael B. (1976), *A History of Modern Serbia: 1804-1918*, 2 vols.. New York and

London: Harcourt, Brace Jovanovich.

Petrovitch, Woislav M. (1915), *Serbia: her people, history and aspirations*. London: George Harrap.

Pinson, Mark (ed.) (1994), *The Muslims of Bosnia-Herzegovina: their historic development from the*

middle ages to the dissolution of Yugoslavia. Cambridge, MA: Centre for Middle Eastern

Studies of Harvard University, Harvard University Press.

Plestina, Dijana (1992*), Regional Development in Communist Yugoslavia: success, failure and*

Consequences. Boulder CO: Westview Press.

Pojatina, Stipe (ed.), (1986), *Klasna borba i socijalna diferencijacija*. Zagreb: Delo/Globus

Popovic, Alexandre (1986), *L'Islam Balkanique. Les Musulmans du sud-est europeen dans la periode post-ottomane*. Berlin: Osteuropa Institut an der Freien Universitat Berlin, and Wiesbaden: Otto Harrassowitz.

Popovic, D.J. (1937), *O cincarima: prilozi pitanju postanka naseg gradjanskog drustva*. Belgrade, 2nd. ed.

Popovic, Mihailo ed (1977), *Drustveni slojevi i drustvena svest*. Belgrade: Institut drustvenih nauka.

Popovic, Mihailo ed. (1988)

Popper, Sir Karl (1960), *The Poverty of Historicism*, London: Routledge & Kegan Paul, rev. ed.

Porter, John (1965), *The Vertical Mosaic: an analysis of class and power in Canada*, University of Toronto Press.

Poulsen, Thomas M. (1977), "Migration on the Adriatic coast: some processes associated with the development of tourism", in H.L. Kostanick ed., *Population and Migration Trends in Eastern Europe*. Boulder CO: Westview Press.

Poulsen, Thomas M. (1992), "Yugoslavia in geographical perspective", in Allcock, Horton and Milivojevic eds. 1992. pp. 33-63.

Poulton, Hugh (1995), *Who are the Macedonians?*. London: C. Hurst.

Pribichevich, Stoyan (1982), *Macedonia: its people and history*. University Park and London, Pennsylvania University Press.

Prout, Christopher (1985), *Market Socialism in Yugoslavia*. Oxford University Press.

Puljiz, Vlado et al. eds. 1972, *The Yugoslav Village*. Zagreb, Sociologija Sela and Department of Rural Sociology. University of Zagreb.

Purivatra, Atif (1974), *Jugoslavenska Muslimanska Organizacija u politickom zivotu Kraljevine Srba, Hrvata i Slovenaca*, Sarajevo: Svjetlost.

Pusic, Vesna (1992), *Vladaoci I upravljaci,*. Zagreb: Novi Liber.

Ramet, Pedro ed. (1989), *Religion and Nationalism in Soviet and East European Politics*.

and London: Duke University Press, rev. ed.

Ramet, Pedro (1990), *Catholicism and Politics in Communist societies*. Durham and London: Duke

University Press.

Ramet, Sabrina P. (1992), *Balkan Babel: politics, culture and religion in Yugoslavia*. Boulder CO:

Westview Press.

Ramet, Sabrina P. (1992a), *Nationalism and Federalism in Yugoslavia, 1962-1991*. Bloomington and

Indianapolis: Indiana University Press, 2nd. ed.

Redfield, Robert (1956), *The Little Community and Peasant Society and Culture*. University of

Chicago Press.

Rihtman-Augustin, Dunja (ed.) (1991), *Simboli identiteta (studije, eseji, gradja.*, Zagreb: Hrvatsko

etnolosko drustvo.

Robertson, Roland (1993), "Globalization and sociological theory", in Herminio Martins ed.,

Knowledge and Passion: essays in honour of John Rex. London and New York: I.B. Tauris,

pp. 174-196.

Robertson, Roland and Khondker, Habib Haque (1998), "Discourses of globalization: preliminary

considerations", *International Sociology*, 13(1):25-40.

Robinson, Gertrude J. (1977), *Tito's maverick media: the politics of mass communications in*

Yugoslavia. Urbana and London: University of Illinois Press.

Rogel, Carole (1977), *The Slovenes and Yugoslavism, 1890-1914*, Boulder CO: Westview Press, and

New York: Columbia University Press.

Rogel, Carole (1977a), "The wandering monk and the Balkan national awakening", in, William W.

Haddad and William L. Ochsenwald (eds.), *Nationalism in a Non-national State: the*

dissolution of the Ottoman Empire. Columbus: Ohio State University Press.

Rosier, Bernard ed., (1968), *Agriculture moderne et socialisme: Une experience yougoslave*. Paris:

Presses Universitaires de France.

Rostow, W,.W. (1964), *The Stages of Economic Growth: a non-communist manifesto*. Cambridge
University Press.

Roter, Zdenko (1982), *Vera in nevera v Sloveniji, 1968-1978*. Maribor: Zalozba obzora.

Rothenberg, G. (1960), *The Austrian Military Border in Croatia, 1522-1747*. Urbana, Illinois Studies

in the Social Sciences, No. 48.

Rothenberg, G. (1960), *The Military Border in Croatia, 1740-1881*. Chicago.

Rusinow, Dennison (1977), *The Yugoslav Experiment, 1948-1974*. London: C. Hurst and the Royal

Institute for International Affairs.

Sahin, Ilhan (19..), "Urbanization and the social structure of the Ottoman Empire in the sixteenth

century", in, T. Devron (?) (ed.), *The Ottoman Empire in the Reign of Suleyman the*

Magnificent, ...[to be checked]

Said, Edward (1978), *Orientalism*, London: Routledge.

Said, Edward (1985), "Orientalism reconsidered", *Race and Class*, XXVII(2):1-15.

Saksida, Caserman and Petrovic (1974) [to be supplied]

Samary, Catherine (1988), *Le marche contre l'autogestion*. La Breche: Publisud.

Samary, Catherine (1995), *Yugoslavia Dismembered*. New York: Monthly Review Press.

Samic, Midhat (1960), *Les Voyaguers français en Bosnie a la fin du XVIIIe siècle et au debut du XIXe,*
et le pays tel qu'ils l'ont vu. Paris: Didier.

Sander, Helke, (1994), "Prologue", in Alexandra Stiglmayer ed.

Savezni Zavod za Statistiku (1987), *Statisticki godisnjak SFRJ*, Belgrade: SZS.

Savezni Zavod za Statistiku (1989), *Jugoslavija 1918-1988: statisticki godisnjak*, Belgrade: SZS.

Seda, Anton (1992), "Gubici i stete uslijed ratnih razaranja, kao podloga za vodjenje qgrarne politike",
Sociologija sela, 30(1/2):19-28.

Sekelj, Laslo (1993), *Yugoslavia: the process of disintegration*. Boulder CO and New York: Social

Science Monographs and Columbia University Press.

Seifert, Ruth (1994), "War and rape: a preliminary analysis", in Alexandra Stiglmayer (ed.).

Sells, Michael A. (1996), *The Bridge Betrayed: religion and genocide in Bosnia*. Berkeley: University

of California Press.

Sepic (1970) [to be supplied]

Seton-Watson, Hugh (1962), *Eastern Europe between the Wars, 1918-1941*. New York and London:

Harper & Row, 3rd. ed.

Seton-Watson, Robert W. (1926), *Sarajevo: a study in the origins of the Great War*. London:

Hutchinson.

Shanin, Teodor (1966), "The peasantry as a political factor", *Sociological Review*, 14(1):5-27.

Shanin, Teodor (1972), *The Awkward Class: political sociology of peasantry in a developing society,*

Russia 1910-1925. Oxford: The Clarendon Press.

Shannon, Thomas R. (1989*), An Introduction to the World-System Perspective*. Boulder (CO):

Westview Press.

Shilling, Chris (1993), *The Body and Social Theory*. London, Sage.

Shils, Edward (1957), "Primordial, personal, sacred and civil ties", *British Journal of Sociology* ....

Siber, Ivan (1974), *Socialna struktura i politicki stavovi,*

Simic, Andrei (1967), "The blood feud in Montenegro", in William E. Lockwood (ed.), *Essays in*

Balkan Ethnography. University of California, Kroeber Anthropological Society, Special

Papers No.1.

Simic, Andrei (1973), *The Peasant Urbanites: a study of rural-urban mobility in Serbia*. New York

and London: Seminar Press.

Singleton, Fred (1976), *Twentieth Century Yugoslavia*. London: Macmillan.

Singleton, Fred and Carter, Bernard (1982), *The Economy of Yugoslavia*. London: Croom Helm, and

New York: St. Martins.

Singleton, Fred (1985), *A Short History of the Yugoslav Peoples*. Cambridge University Press.

Sirc, Ljubo (1979), *The Yugoslav Economy under Self-Management*. London: Macmillan.

Skene, J.H. ("A British Resident of Twenty Years in the East") (1854), *The Danubian Principalities,*

    the Frontier Lands, of the Christian and the Turk. London: Richard Bentley, 2 Vols.

Sklair, Leslie (1991), *Sociology of the Global System*. London and New York: Harvester-Wheatsheaf.

Smith, Anthony D. (1983), *Theories of Nationalism*. London: Duckworth, 2nd. ed.

Smith, Anthony D. (1986), *The Ethnic Origins of Nations*. Oxford: Basil Blackwell

Spulber, Nicholas (1963), "Changes in the economic structures of the Balkans, 1860-1960", in, Charles

    and Barabara Jelavich (eds.), *The Balkans in Transition: essays on the development of Balkan*

    life and politics since the eighteenth century. Berkeley and Los Angeles: University of

    California Press.

Srsan, Stjepan (1993), *Baranja*. Matica Hrvatska, Osijek.

Stahl, Henri (1986), *Household, Village and Village Confederation in Southeastern Europe*. Boulder

    CO: East European Monographs, and New York: Columbia University Press.

Stambuk, Maja (1991), "Agricultural depopulation in Croatia", *Sociologia Ruralis*, XXXI(4)281-289.

Staub, Erwin (1989), *The Roots of Evil: the origins of genocide and other group violence*. Cambridge

    University Press.

Stavrianos, L.S. (1958), *The Balkans since 1453*. New York: Holt, Rinhart and Winston.

Steinberg, Jonathan (1992), "The Roman Catholic Church and Genocide in Croatia during the Second

    World War", Trinity College, Cambridge, unpublished TS.

Stevenson, Francis S. (1912), *A History of Montengro*. London: Jarrold & Sons. (Facsimile edition,

    1971, New York, Arno Press.)

Stiglmayer, Alexandra ed., (1994), *Mass Rape: the war against women in Bosnia-Hecegovina*.

    Lincoln (NA): University of Nebraska Press.

Stipetic, Vladimir (1982), "The development of the peasant economy in socialist Yugoslavia", in,

    Radmila Stojanovic (ed.), *The Functioning of the Yugoslav Economy*. New York: M.E.

Sharpe/Spokesman.

Stipetic, Vladimir, Vajic, Ivo and Novak, Ivan (1992), "Obnova i razvitak hrvatske poljoprivrede, sela i poljoprivrednij gospodarstva", *Sociologija sela*, 30(1/2):7-17.

Stoianovich, Traian (1960), "The conquering Balkan Orthodox merchant", *Journal of Economic History*, 20:234-313.

Stoianovich, Traian (1963), "The Social foundations of Balkan politics", in, Charles and Barbara Jelavich (eds.), *The Balkans in Transition: essays on the development of Balkan life and politics since the eighteenth century*, Berkeley: Univeristy of California Press.

Stoianovich, Traian (1994), *Balkan Worlds: the first and last Europe*. New York and London: M.E. Sharpe.

Stojsavljevic, Bogdan (1952), *Seljastvo Jugoslavije: 1918-1941*. Zagreb: Zadruzna Stampa.

Stojsavljevic, Bogdan (1962), "Istorijski razvitak agrarno-ekonomskih odnosa u selu Jalzabet (1839)1939)", *Sociologija*, (4)1-2.

Stojsavljevic, Bogdan (1965), *Prodiranje kapitalizma u selo: 1919-1929*. Zagreb: Institut za historiju radnickog pokreta.

Stokes, Gale (1990*), Politics as Development: the emergence of political parties in nineteenth century Serbia*. Durham and London: Duke University Press.

Stokes, Gale, Lampe, John, Rusinow, Dennison and Mostov, Julie (1996), "Instant history: understanding the Wars of Yugoslav Succession". *Slavic Review*, Vol.55 (1):136-160.

Strupp, Karl (1929), *La situation juridique des Macedoniens en Yougoslavie*. Paris: Les Presses Universitaires de France.

Sugar, Peter F. (1963), *The Industrialization of Bosnia-Hercegovina: 1878-1918*. Seattle: University of Washington Press.

Sugar, Peter (1977), *Southeastern Europe under Ottoman Rule, 1351-1804*. Seattle and London:

University of Washington Press.

Supek, Rudi and Pusic, Eugen (eds.) (1975-77), *Covjek I sistem: prilozi izucavanju drustvenog*

sistema, Zagreb: Filozofski fakultet. 5 vols.

Suvar, Stipe (1970), *Socioloski presjek Jugoslavenskog drustva*, Zagreb: Skolska knjiga.

Suvar, Stipe (1973), *Izmedju zaseoka i megalopolisa*. Zagreb: Centar za sociologiju sela Instituta za

drustvena istrazivanja Sveucilista.

Suvar nd Puljiz eds. (1972)

Tasic, Nikola and Stosic, Dusica (eds.) (1989), *Migrations in Balkan History*. Belgrade, Srpska

akademija nauka i umetnosti.

Thompson, John B. (1984), *Studies in the Theory of Ideology*. Cambridge: Polity Press.

Thompson, John B. (1995), *The Media and Modernity: a social theory of the media*. Cambridge:

Polity Press.

Thompson, Mark (1994), *Forging War: the media in Serbia, Croatia and Bosnia-Hercegovina*.

London: Article 19, International Centre against Censorship.

Thompson, Paul (1988), *The Voice of the Past: Oral History*. Oxford: The University Press, 2nd. ed..

Tilly, Charles, *Coercion, Capital and European states, AD 900-1990*. Oxford, Blackwel.

Tiltman, H. Hessell (1936), *Peasant Europe*. London: Jarrolds.

Todorov, Nikolai (1983), *The Balkan City, 1400-1900*. Seattle and London: University of Washington

Press.

Todorov, Nikolai (1991), "Les tentatives d'industrialisation precoces dans les provinces balkaniques de

l'Empire Ottoman", in Batou ed. 1991:381-394.

Todorova, Maria (1996), "The Ottoman legacy in the Balkans", in Brown ed. 1996.

Todorova, Maria (1997), *Imagining the Balkans*. Oxford University Press.

Tomasevich, Joze (1949), "Foreign economic relations: 1918-1941", in, Robert Kerner (ed.),

Yugoslavia. University of California Press.

Tomasevich (1953),

Tomasevich, Jozo (1955), *Peasants, Politics and Economic Change in Yugoslavia*, Stanford University

Press.

Tomasevich, Joze (1958), "The collectivization of agriculture in Yugoslavia", in, Irwin T. Sanders

(ed.), *The Collectivization of Agriculture in Eastern Europe*. University of Kentucky Press.

Tomasevich, Jozo (1975), *The Chetniks: war and revolution in Yugoslavia, 1941-1945*. Stanford

University Press.

Tomasic, Dinko (1948), *Personality and Culture in Eastern European Politics*. New York: George W.

Stewart.

Tomsic, Vida (1983), "Emancipation of women - the struggle for human emancipation", in Jovan

Djordjevic, Savin Jogan, Mitija Ribicic and Anton Vratusa eds., *Self-management: the*

Yugoslav Road to Socialism. Belgrade: Jugoslovenski pregled.

Trajkovic, Josif (1984), The Judicial System of Yugoslavia. Belgrade: Jugosolvenski Pregled.

Trifunoski, Jovan (1988), *Albansko stanovnistvo u S.R. Makedoniji*. Belgrade Knjizevne Novine.

Triglavski narodni park (1985), *Vodnik*. Bled: Prirodoslovno drustvo Slovenije.

Trouton, Ruth (1952), *Peasant Renaissance in Yugoslavia, 1900-1950. A study of the development of*

Yugoslav peasant society as affected by education. London: Routledge & Kegan Paul.

Tunbridge, J.E. and Ashworth, G.J. (1996), *Dissonant Heritage: the management of the past as a*

resource in conflict. Chichester: John Wiley.

Turner, Bryan (1984), *The Body and Society*. Oxford: Blackwell

Turner, Bryan S. (1992), *Max Weber: from history to modernity*. London: Routledge.

Turnock, David (1989), Eastern Europe: an historical geography, 1815-194., London: Routledge.

Ullman, Richard H. ed. (1996), *The World and Yugoslavia's Wars*. New York: Council on Foreign

Relations.

United Nations (1992), *Human Development Report: 1992*, Oxford: The University Press.

United Nations High Commission for Refugees (UNHCR) (quarterly) *Information notes*.

Urry, John (1995), *Consuming Places*. London: Routledge.

Van Dertel, Geert (1992), "The nations and churches in Yugoslavia*"*, *Religion, State and Society*,

20(3-4):275-88.

Vanek (1970) [to be supplied]

Vinski, Ivo (1959), "Investicija na podrucju Jugoslavije u razdoblju izmedju dva stetska rata",

Ekonomski Pregled, 10, 601-16.

Vishinski, Boris (ed.) 1973, *The Epic of Ilinden*. Skopje: Macedonian Review Editions.

Visser, Willemien, (1993), "Viols contre les femmes de l'"ex-Yougoslavie"", *L'Europe Feministe*

14(1):43-75.

Vojnic, Dragomar (1995), "Disparity and disintegration: the economic dimension of Yugoslavia's

demise", in, Payam Akhavan and Robert Howse eds., *Yugoslavia, the former and future:*

reflections by scholars from the region. Washington DC: Brookings Institution, and Geneva:

United Nations Research Institute for Social Development.

Vosnjak, Bogumil (1917), *A Bulwark against Germany*. London: George Allen & Unwin.

Vrcan, Srdjan (1995), "The war in former Yugoslavia and religion", *Religion in Eastern Europe*,

XV(2):19-33.

Vucinich, Wayne (1963), "Some aspects of the Ottoman legacy", in Charles ands Barbara Jelevich

eds., *The Balkans in Transition*.

Vucinich, Wayne S. (1968), *Serbia between East and West: the events of 1903-1908*. New York: AMS.

(Originally published by Stanford University Press in 1954.)

Vuckovic, Mihailo (1966), *Istorija zadruznog pokreta un Jugoslaviji, 1918-1941*. Beograd: Institut

    Drustvenih Nauka.

Vuco, Nikola (1968), *Agrarna kriza u Jugoslaviji: 1930-1934*. Belgrade: Srpska Akademija Nauka.

Vukotic-Cotic, Gordana (1991), *Social Transfers and Income Inequality in the Ante-Bellum*

    Yugoslavia, 1988. Washington DC: World Bank, Research Paper Series, Research Project on

    Social Expenditures and their Distributional Impact in Eastern Europe, Paper 3.

Vuskovic, Boris (1976), "Social inequality in Yugoslavia", *New Left Review*, 95, Jan-Feb.:24-44.

Wachtel (1973) [to be supplied]

Ward (1958) [to be supplied]

Wallerstein, Immanuel (1974), *The Modern World-System*, Vol. I: Capitalist agriculture and the origins

    of the European world-economy in the sixteenth century. New York and London: Academic

    Press.

Wallerstein, Immanuel (1980), *The Modern World-System*, Vol. II: Mercantilism and the consolidation

    of the European word-economy, 1600-1750. New York and London: Academic Press.

Warner, Lloyd (19), *Social Class in America*, [to be supplied]

Warriner, Doreen (1959), "Urban thinkers and peasant policy in Yugoslavia, 1918-1959", *Slavonic &*

    East European Review, December 1959:59-81.

Warriner, Doreen (1964), *Economics of Peasant Farming*. London: Frank Cass, (2nd. ed.).

Warriner, Doreen ed. (1965), *Contrasts in Emerging Societies: readings in the social and economic*

    history of South-Eastern Europe in the nineteenth century. London: Athlone Press.

Waterston, Albert (1962), *Planning in Yugoslavia*. Baltimore: The Johns Hopkins Press.

Weber, Max (1963) [1922], *The Sociology of Religion*. Boston MA: Beacon Press.

Weber, Max (1968), *Economy and Society*. New York: Bedminster Press.

Weber, Max (1978), *Economy and Society*. Berkeley: University of California Press, 2 vols.

Waterman, Peter (1993), *Globalisation, Civil society, Solidarity. The politics and ethics of a world both real and universal*. The Hague: Institute fof Social Studies, Working Papers No. 147.

Waterstone, Philip (1962), *Planning in Yugoslavia*. Baltimore: Johns Hopkins Press.

Weber, Max (1930), *The Protestant Ethic and the Spirit of Capitalism*. London: Unwin University Books.

Weber, Max (1978), *Economy and Society*. Berkeley: University of California Press, 2 vols.

West, Rebecca (1942*), Black Lamb and Grey Falcon: the record of a journey through Yugoslavia in 1937*. London: Macmillan. (Reissued 1967.)

Wiles (1930), [to be supplied]

Wilkes, John (1992), *The Illyrians*. Oxford: Blackwell.

Willcox, W.F. ed. (1931), *International Migrations*, Vol. I, "Statistics", Vol. II, "Interpretations". New York: National Bureau of Economic Research.

Williams, Robin M. (1960), *American Society: a sociological interpretation*. New York: Alfred A. Knopf, (2nd. ed.)

Winner, Irene (1971), *Zerovnica: A Slovenian Village*. Providence RI: Brown University Press.

Winnifrith, T.J. (1987), *The Vlahs: the History of a Balkan People*. London, Duckworth.

Wolf, Eric R. (1971), *Peasant Wars of the Twentieth Century*. London: Faber and Faber

Wolff, Larry (1994*), Inventing Eastern Europe: the map of civilization in the mind of the Enlightenment*. Stanford University Press.

Women Living under Muslim Laws (1994), *Compilation of informations on crimes of war against women in ex-Yugoslavia--actions and initiatives in their defence*, Update No.3.

Woodward, Susan L. (1995), *Balkan Tragedy: chaos and dissolution after the Cold War*. Washington DC: Brookings Institution

Wright, Philip (1986*), The State and the Peasantry in Yugoslavia during the First Five-Year Plan,*

Zidaric, V.V. (1939), *Zadrugarstvo*. Novi Sad.

Zukin, Sharon (1980), [to be supplied]

Zukin, Sharon (1975), *Beyond Marx and Tito: theory and practice in Yugoslav socialism*. Cambridge University Press.

Zupancic, Milan (1992), "Posleratna obnova kao mogucnost revitalizacije seoskih podrucja", *Sociologija Sela* 30(1/2):37-43.

Zupanov, Josip, (1983), *Marginalije o drustvenoj krizi*. Zagreb: Globus.